AF890446

Maritime &
Coastguard
Agency

The Ship Captain's Medical Guide

24th Edition

Dr Spike Briggs

Dr Katharine Hartington

London: TSO

williams lea | tso
An RRD Company

Published by TSO (The Stationery Office), part of Williams Lea,
and available from:

Online
www.tsoshop.co.uk

Mail, telephone & email
TSO
PO Box 29, Norwich, NR3 1GN
Telephone orders/General enquiries: 0333 202 5070
Email: customer.services@tso.co.uk
Textphone: 0333 202 5077

Content taken from the Skipper's Medical Emergency Handbook is reproduced with the permission of Marshall Editions, an imprint of Quarto Publishing Plc.

Published with the permission of the Maritime and Coastguard Agency on behalf of the Controller of His Majesty's Stationery Office.

© Crown Copyright 2024

All rights reserved.

Copyright in the typographical arrangement and design is vested in the Crown. Applications for reproduction should be made in writing to Information Policy Team, The National Archives, Kew, Richmond, Surrey TW9 4DU, or email: psi@nationalarchives.gsi.gov.uk.

Dr Spike Briggs and Dr Katharine Hartington have asserted their moral rights under the Copyright, Designs and Patents Act 1988, to be identified as the authors of this work.

Where we have identified any third-party copyright information you will need to obtain permission from the copyright holders concerned.

Whilst all reasonable care has been taken in the publication of this book, the publisher accepts no liability or responsibility for the use of the methods or products described in this book.

Twenty-fourth edition published 2024

ISBN 978 0 11 554149 0
Fifth impression 2024

Printed in the United Kingdom for The Stationery Office.
SD000408

Contents

Introduction

It is over 156 years since the publication of the 1st edition of the *Ship Captain's Medical Guide*, authored by Harry Leach. Some of his introductory comments in that 1st edition have stood the test of time, and are equally apposite to the practice of remote medicine in the 21st century:

> *It is now a duty to tell the reader that the following pages are written with the object of showing not only what to do in cases of accident and sickness, but what to avoid. Doctors have lately learnt much on this head, and will tell you that in the practice of their own profession much harm may be done to the body by meddling and muddling. It is very important that this fact should be widely known, and so, acting thereupon, let the reader remember and apply the following rules:*
>
> *(1) Follow out strictly all the recommendations enjoined in this book.*
>
> *(2) Do not take with you or use any medicines other than those inserted in the official scale.*
>
> *(3) When in doubt as to the nature of a disease, wait and watch.*
>
> *Struggle hard and actively to prevent disease, but when you are called upon to cure, adopt the directions given here, meagre as they may appear, and believe (as you may most assuredly do) that your own humble efforts to restore health and prolong life will receive safe and splendid backing from the wonderful hand of nature.*

The practice of medicine continually advances, and there was a significant change in the practice of 'remote medicine' from that described in the 22nd edition of the *Ship Captain's Medical Guide* (published in 1999) to that in the 23rd edition, published in 2019.

It is now five years since the publication of the 23rd edition, so this, the 24th edition, represents an evolution from the previous edition, rather than a complete revision.

The three areas of transformation in remote medicine over the past 25 years are:

- **Global communications** Transmission of medical advice and data to advising clinicians ashore
- **Medical technology** Point-of-care testing providing objective medical assessment of patients at sea
- **Treatment algorithms** Providing a non-medical professional with a framework within which to think and to effectively treat both medical illness and trauma at sea.

All these areas continue to advance, and pertinent developments have been incorporated into this latest guide.

The guide continues to be a valuable resource for delivering training to those ship's officers who are tasked with delivering medical care at sea. It also reflects the medical stores list detailed in MSN 1905.

Ultimately, integration of medical training, medical stores, and advice from both the *Ship Captain's Medical Guide* and shore-based doctors, will benefit all those who work at sea, improving both health and well-being.

Acknowledgements

From the authors

It has been an honour to be asked to follow the writing of the 23rd edition of the *Ship Captain's Medical Guide* with being the authors of the 24th edition.

We'd like to extend our thanks to all at the MCA and TSO for their advice and guidance during the writing and editing process.

Once again, we hope that this, the latest version of the *Ship Captain's Medical Guide*, improves the health and well-being of all seafarers on the high seas.

I would like to acknowledge the continuing contribution of Dr Campbell Mackenzie who was my co-author for the *Skipper's Medical Emergency Handbook*, upon which much of the previous and present editions of the SCMG are based.

Dr Spike Briggs and Dr Katharine Hartington

From MCA

The MCA would like to thank Dr Sally Bell and Dr James Ferguson for their time, effort and expertise in reviewing the 24th edition of this publication.

Thanks are also due to the user review group who supported and contributed to the development of the 23rd edition:

David Appleton – Nautilus International

Fena Boyle – UK Chamber of Shipping

Mark Carden – National Union of Rail, Maritime and Transport Workers

Derek Cardno – Scottish Fishermen's Federation

Allan Graveson – Nautilus International

Robert Greenwood – National Federation of Fishermen's Organisations

Nigel Lehmann-Taylor – UK Chamber of Shipping (Maersk)

Kathryn Ramsdale – Carnival UK

Mark Ranson – National Workboat Association

Kathryn Westley – Carnival UK

Images

Sliding mat image courtesy of Med Sled at www.medsled.com

Semi-flexible evacuation stretcher image courtesy of SAR products at www.sar-products.com

Neil Robertson stretcher image courtesy of Ferno at www.ferno.com

Scoop stretcher image courtesy of MediKit at https://medikit.co.uk/

How to use this book

This book is divided into six parts:

- Part 1: Emergency care
- Part 2: Trauma
- Part 3: Medical disorders
- Part 4: Medical procedures
- Part 5: Reference material
- Part 6: Appendices.

Always consider calling TMAS early when faced with a casualty. Use the ATMIST AMPLE form to structure the referral. See Appendix III.

Coloured boxes emphasise emergency actions

Red arrows indicate severe risks and emergency responses

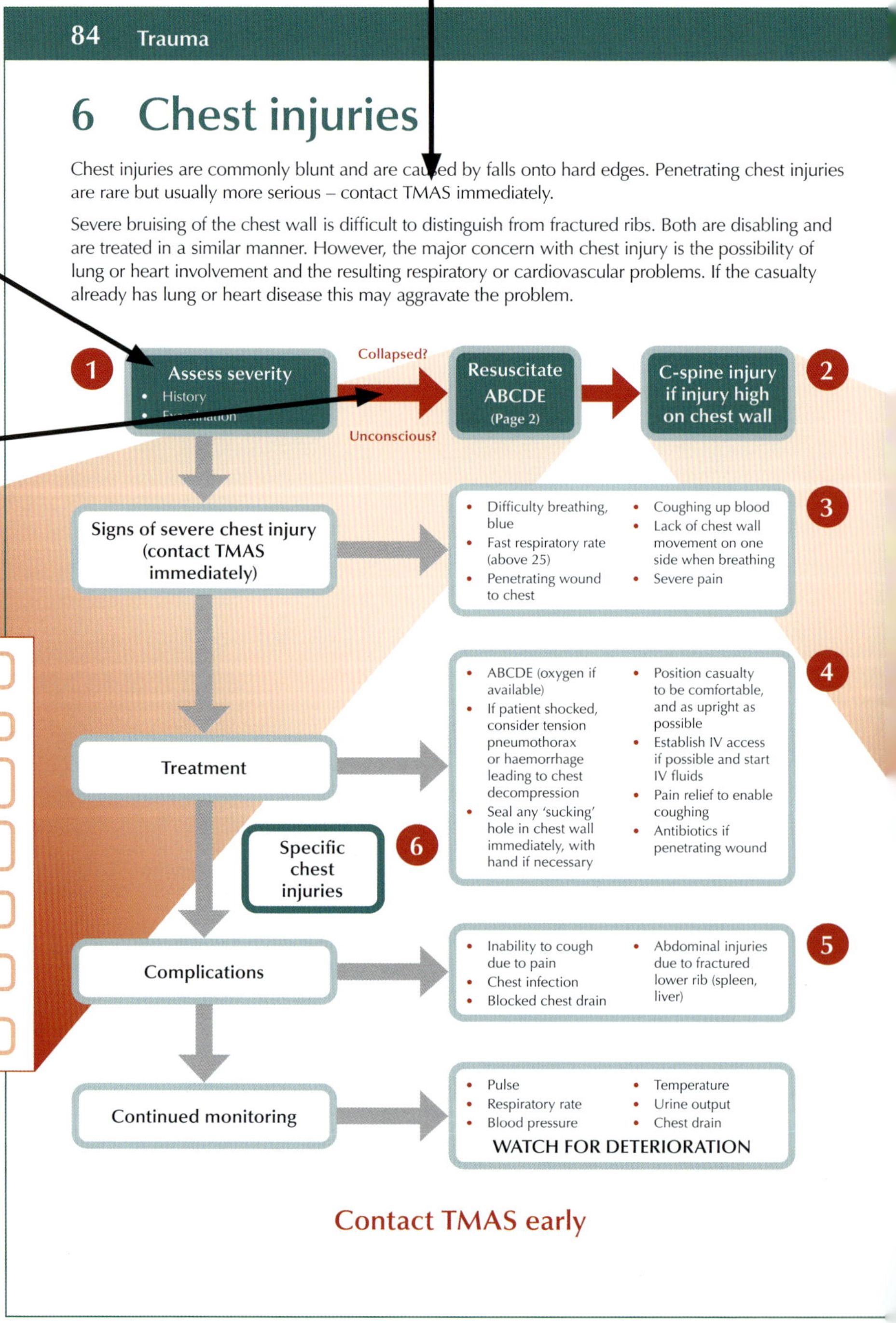

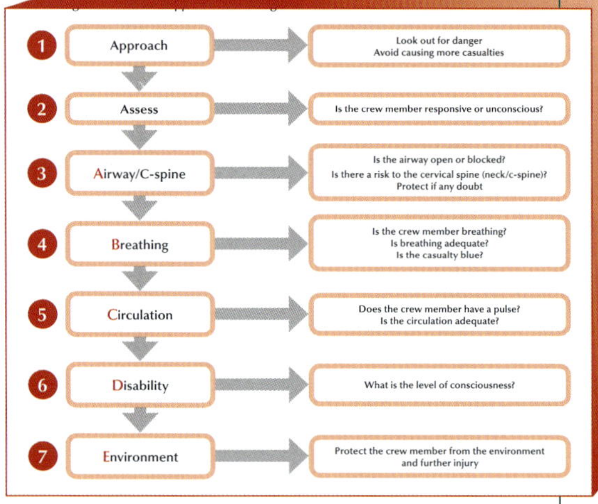

Follow cross-references to further detail or to systematic instructions

The chapters in Parts 1, 2, 3 and 4 all use a similar format. Within the appropriate chapter, consult the flow chart for a condensed summary of evaluation and treatment. The remainder of the chapter will expand on this outline, further explaining what to look for in your examination, giving hints on prevention, and describing the features of specific injuries and treatments.

Part 5 provides useful reference material such as the structure and function of the body, record keeping and continuing care.

Finally Part 6, Appendices contains essentials such as evacuation by helicopter or boat, transporting a casualty and a medicines guide.

The TMAS medical report form is provided on the front flyleaf. The Antibiotics and Pain relief guides are on the back flyleaves.

Chest injuries 85

History and examination

1

- ABCDE takes priority.
- **Take particular care of the neck if there is an injury high on the chest wall.**
- A blue patient is a very bad sign – contact TMAS immediately.
- Anticipate problems with breathing, pulse and blood pressure.
- Get as much information as possible from other crew members about what happened.

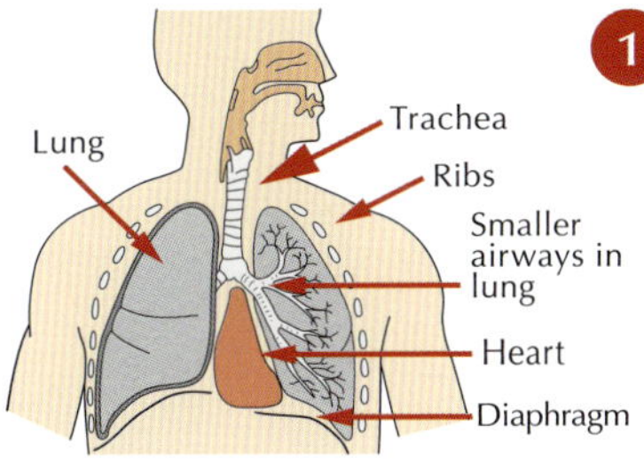

Part 2

Anatomical illustrations provide a guide to major parts of the body, to help you when reporting to on-shore medical support

Important points in the history

- How did the accident happen (mechanism of injury)?
- Shortness of breath
- Pain in the chest
  - location?
  - what makes it worse or better?
- Coughing up blood, sputum?
- Previous lung disease (asthma or bronchitis)?
- Other injuries?

Important points in the examination

- **Look**
  - appearance of casualty (blue/white)
  - obvious injuries to chest
  - look for difference in chest wall movement between each side
- **Feel**
  - tenderness over chest wall
  - position of trachea (windpipe)
- **Listen**
  - harsh or gurgling breath sounds
  - breath sounds in the chest (with a stethoscope)
- **Document** Respiratory rate and other vital signs

Quick-reference lists explain what you need to find out from the casualty and what to look for during an examination

Cervical spine (neck) injury

2

Injuries high on the chest wall may be associated with injuries to the cervical spine (c-spine).

The bones of the neck may be broken and unstable, but the spinal cord may still be intact.

If in doubt immobilise the cervical spine with three-point immobilisation (see page 208).

Signs of severe chest injury

3

- The casualty may be obviously struggling with their breathing and have a high respiratory rate. They will be very distressed by this.
- Low blood pressure may be caused by loss of blood in to the chest cavity (haemothorax) or by air in the chest cavity under pressure, compressing the lungs, heart and blood vessels (tension pneumothorax; see below).
- Any penetrating wound to the chest is serious. It may have damaged lung, heart and blood vessels and even abdominal organs.
- Coughing up blood indicates damage to both the lung and blood vessels.

A numbering system helps you quickly locate more detail on such subjects as complications, specific injuries or disorders, and signs of severe conditions

Part 1
Emergency care

1 Resuscitation

If a crew member collapses on the vessel, or is recovered unconscious from the water, rapid resuscitation is vital and every second counts. The basic and advanced life support algorithms should be known and rehearsed by the medical officer, master and crew on a regular basis so they become second-nature. It may be the most important thing you ever do.

The basic life support (BLS) algorithm is very simple and gives a framework within which to make decisions when the unthinkable happens.

Stabilise the neck (c-spine) if there is any chance of injury (see page 63).

Basic life support (BLS)

Is the crew member responsive?

- Make sure it is safe to approach
- Gently shake or squeeze the shoulder
- Talk or shout loudly in casualty's ear
- If responsive, do not move them; get more help

No

Shout for help

- Get the attention of other crew on deck or below
- Make sure the master and medical officer know there is an emergency

Control c-spine if injured
Check and open the airway
Remove any obstruction from mouth carefully

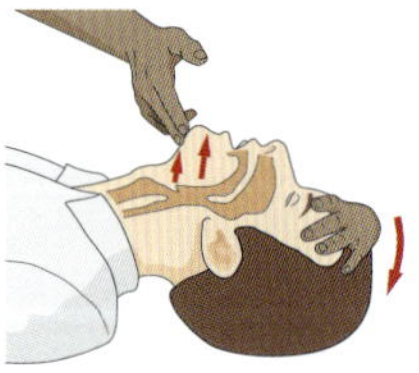

Head tilt and chin lift (page 199)

Is casualty breathing normally?

Yes

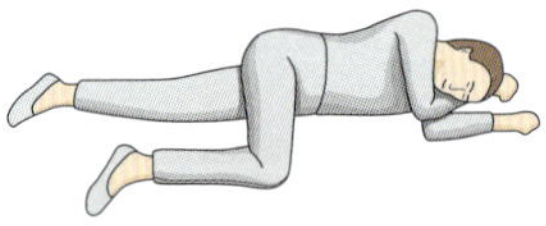

Recovery position (page 204)

No

Give 30 chest compressions

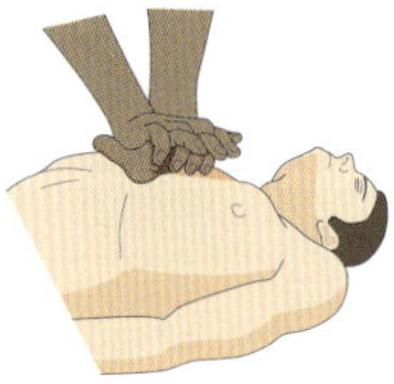

Chest compressions (page 201)

Give 2 rescue breaths and 30 chest compressions

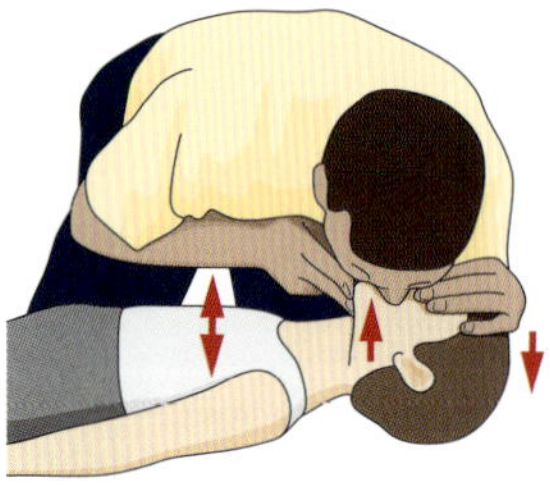

Rescue breaths (page 200)

ADVANCED LIFE SUPPORT (if defibrillator available)

Continue BLS until the crew member is breathing or you start advanced life support (ALS) or you have obtained medical advice from TMAS, or you are exhausted and cannot continue.

Advanced life support

The ALS algorithm (see below) is more complex, requires more skills, and assumes that there is an automated external defibrillator (AED) on board, together with adrenaline and other drugs used in resuscitation.

Advanced life support

Unresponsive crew member?
Call for help

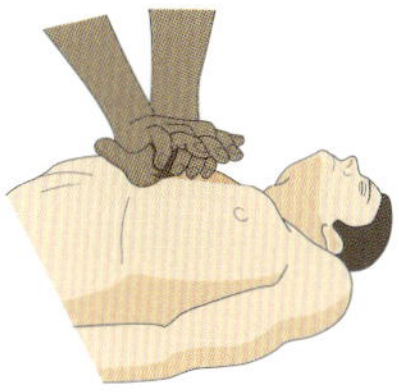

30

+

Basic life support
Give 30 chest compressions
Give 2 rescue breaths
until AED is attached

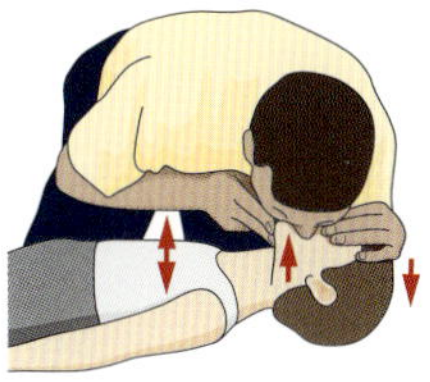

2

Attach AED to crew member and turn on

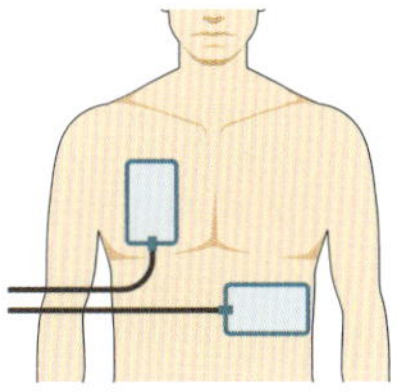

See page 201

Wait for the AED to assess the heart rhythm

FOLLOW INSTRUCTIONS FROM THE AED

No shock advised

Try
- to give oxygen by mask if available
- to establish IV access if possible (page 236)

Give
- adrenaline 1 mg IV every 3–5 minutes

IMMEDIATELY RESTART
Give 2 rescue breaths
Give 30 chest compressions
For 2 minutes
DO NOT DELAY

Shock advised
(Defibrillation)

Deliver one shock
SAFELY
Dry!
Remove oxygen
Warn everyone
Stand clear
(page 201)

IMMEDIATELY RESTART
Give 2 rescue breaths
Give 30 chest compressions
For 2 minutes
DO NOT DELAY

Continue until the crew member is breathing or you have obtained medical advice from TMAS or you are exhausted and cannot continue

2 Assessment of a sick or injured crew member

A severely injured or acutely sick crew member may have multiple problems. Sorting out which task to deal with first may seem complicated initially. However, if the situation is approached in a systematic way, actions will be prioritised correctly. This will ensure that you take correct action rapidly and instinctively when every second counts.

Undertaking a primary survey **first**, followed by a secondary survey, is a very effective way of organising your actions. It is a framework within which to think and work methodically. As with the resuscitation guidelines (see page 198), this framework should be known and rehearsed on a regular basis, both during training and on board the vessel. The sequence of actions should become second-nature so they can be performed promptly and without reference to the medical guide.

The primary survey

The framework shown prioritises the immediate life-threatening problems. It is essential to sort out each stage adequately before moving on. For instance, the unconscious crew member will not survive for very long without an adequate **A**irway, which must be secured before moving on to **B**reathing. The same rule applies to each stage.

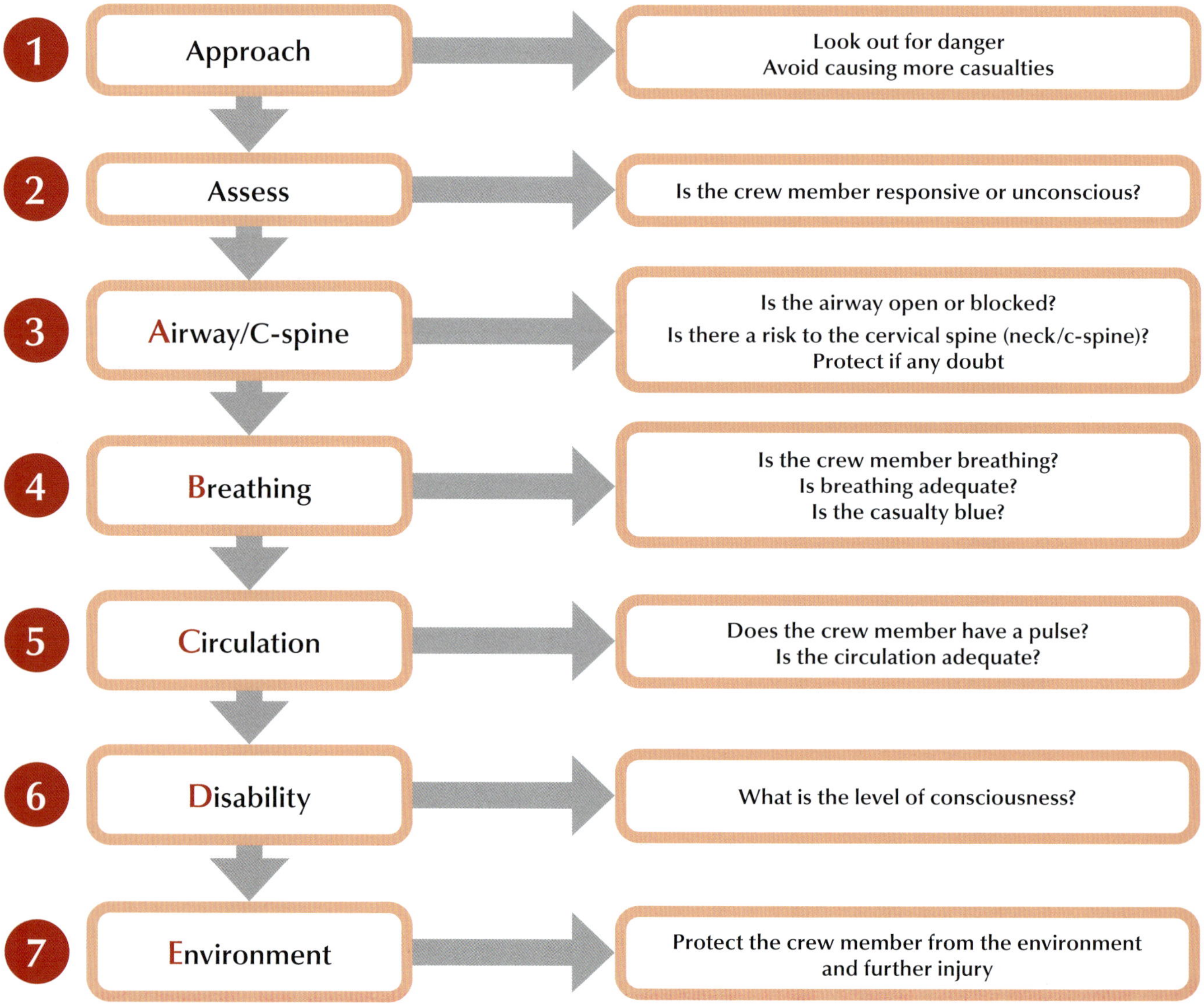

Approaching the sick or injured crew member

1

Don't become a casualty yourself:

- Clear obstacles (e.g. swinging deck gear, wreckage).
- Avoid electrical cables, gas, enclosed spaces etc.
- Wear protective equipment.
- Level the vessel.

Assessing the crew member

2

Find out whether they are responsive or unconscious.

Assess
- Speak loudly in their ear
- Shake gently by the shoulder

→

Action
- If they respond normally, they
  - have an airway
  - are breathing
  - have enough circulation to perfuse their brain
- Keep comfortable, safe and go to 'Secondary survey' (page 6)

Airway and c-spine protection

3

Assess
- Unconscious?
- Level of distress
- 'Seesaw' chest
- Noisy breathing
- Obvious effort on inspiration
- Injury to mouth/face/neck

→

Action
- **Stabilise the c-spine** if any history of injury to head or neck (page 208)
- Open airway using 'head tilt'/'chin lift' (page 199)
- Look in the mouth for obvious objects that may be causing the obstruction
- Use an adjunct airway if available (page 199)

Breathing

4

Assess
- Crew member blue or pale?
- Chest moving up and down?
- Breathing rapid and shallow?
- Obvious injury to the chest that requires immediate attention?
- Measure rate of breathing: fast or slow?

→

Action
- Start basic life support if not breathing
- Give oxygen if breathing (page 202)
- Keep the airway open
- Put in the recovery position or sit up if this helps
- Treat as a pneumothorax if required (page 86)
- Keep warm

Circulation and control of bleeding

5

Assess
- Confused or anxious?
- Cold, sweaty face, hands, feet?
- Obvious bleeding?
- Measure pulse rate and blood pressure

→

Action
- Start basic life support if no pulse
- Place crew member horizontal, raise legs
- Control bleeding (page 30)
- Establish IV access if possible (page 224)
- Give IV fluids if required (page 224)
- Keep warm

Disability

6

Assess
- Level of consciousness? (page 196)
  - A – Alert
  - V – responds to Voice
  - P – responds to Pain
  - U – Unresponsive
- Are the pupils equal and responding to light?

Action
- If reduced conscious level and breathing: place in recovery position (page 204)
- Continue to treat other problems
- Reassess frequently
- Keep warm

Environment

7

Protect the crew member while exposed for examination

Assess
- Increasingly cool and mottled skin?
- Shivering?
- Low temperature?

Action
- Keep exposure time to a minimum while still examining thoroughly
- Remove the crew member from the exposed deck as soon as possible
- When stable, take the crew member below deck and get them warm and dry (page 282)

The secondary survey

The secondary survey is a thorough head-to-toe evaluation of the sick or injured crew member, comprising a complete history and examination. Its purpose is to go through everything methodically to make sure no significant medical problems or injuries have been missed. A significant 'distracting injury' such as an open fracture of the femur may mean that injuries such as broken ribs are missed until days later, unless all parts of the body are examined carefully.

The history includes all the previous medical history of the crew member, and the most accurate account of the events that led to the incident. The history can come from a wide range of sources, especially if the crew member is unconscious.

The secondary survey can only start once the life-threatening problems have been stabilised during the primary survey, which may be a long process.

The history

AMPLE is a simple memory aid for gathering all the essential elements of the history that are vital in managing the sick or injured crew member.

Allergies These are common, especially to some antibiotics, and can be life-threatening, making a bad situation worse.

Medication What does the crew member normally take? Some medications may confuse the situation, causing symptoms in their own right.

Past illnesses Ongoing medical complaints such as diabetes may have a considerable impact on the current problem. The list of medications being taken often gives a clue to past illnesses.

Last meal Time of the last meal gives an indication of whether the stomach may be full, which increases the chance of vomiting, especially if the crew member is unconscious.

Events Finding out exactly what happened, and when it happened, gives a good idea about any possible injuries that may be expected. A fall of more than 2 metres will probably lead to more serious injuries than a fall down just one stair. Try to establish:

- **What** happened?
- **Where** did it happen?
- **When** did it happen?
- **How** did it happen?
- **Why** did it happen (for future prevention)?

The examination

This must be as thorough as possible, given the circumstances. It is not possible to complete a comprehensive examination in the middle of the night, during a storm or a catastrophe but the important things to remember in those situations are that it hasn't been done, and it needs to be done.

There is no need to undress the casualty and examine all parts after an accident involving, for example, a stubbed toe, but it is essential to do so if the crew member has been washed over the side and recovered unconscious, or has fallen from height onto a steel deck. Tailor the examination using common sense, but if in any doubt, be more thorough.

Remember that a body has a front, a back and two sides; therefore the examination is not complete until the crew member has been log-rolled (see page 204) onto their side to allow the back and spine to be examined.

The basis for any examination is: **Look, Listen, Feel, Move**

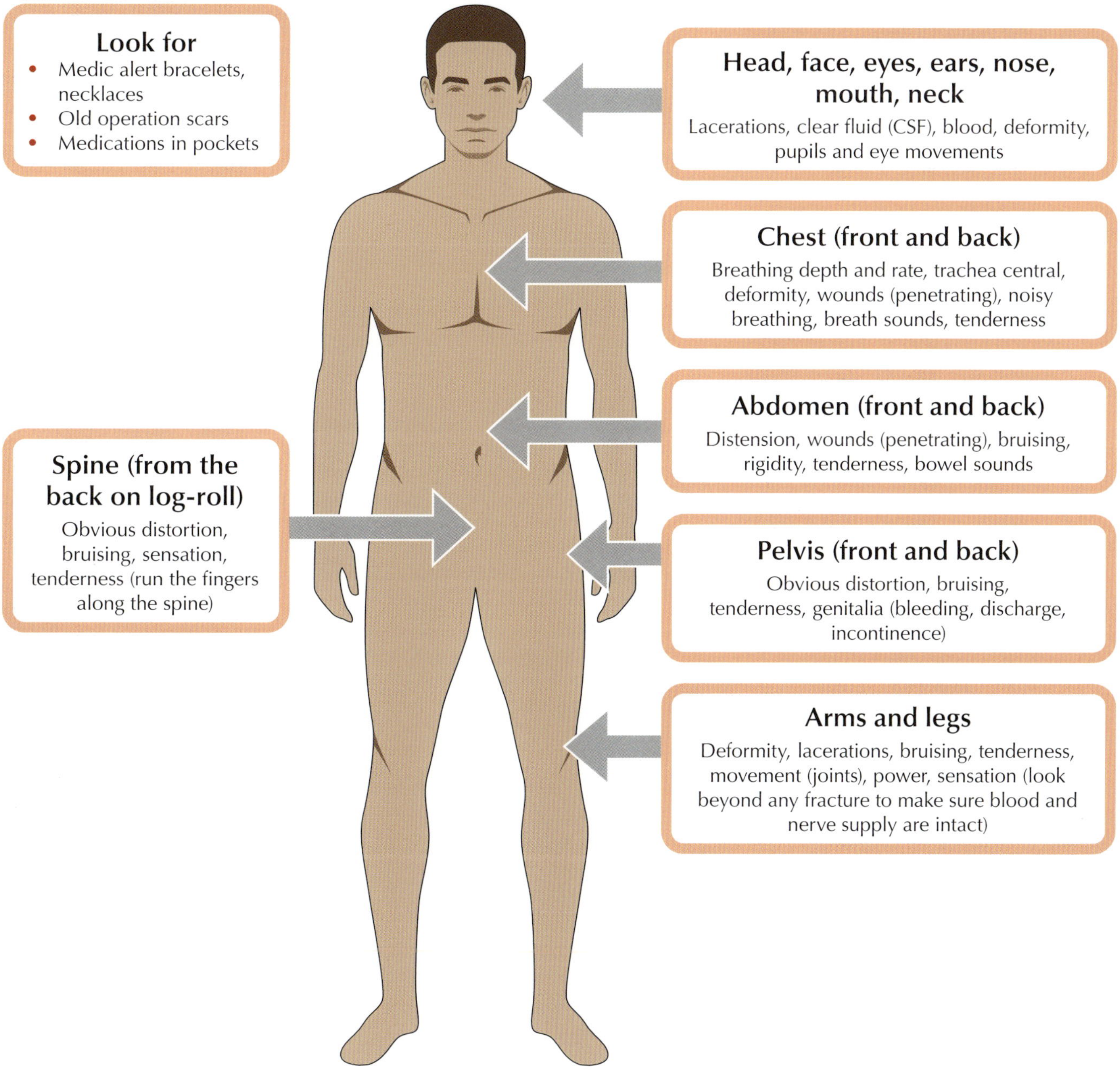

Remember – continue to monitor for deterioration

3 Loss of consciousness

A reduction in a casualty's level of consciousness, to the point of being unresponsive, is a dramatic event and has a variety of causes; sometimes obvious, sometimes not.

There is an immediate risk to airway, breathing and circulation, and these, as always, are the treatment priorities. Once the casualty has been resuscitated and stabilised, finding the cause will significantly help in treating them and reduce the risk of the situation getting worse.

Quite often the casualty will not be completely unconscious but somewhat responsive. AVPU (see page 196) is an emergency method for rapidly defining conscious state. The Glasgow Coma Scale (GCS) (see page 196) is a more detailed method for defining level of consciousness. Responding only to a painful stimulus indicates a serious condition.

Assess patient/casualty
- History
- Examination

Collapsed? Unconscious? → **Resuscitate ABCDE** (Page 2) → **C-spine injury** If head/neck trauma **1**

Reduced consciousness
Not opening eyes
Not obeying commands
No recognisable words

Assess consciousness (page 196)

AVPU
- Alert
- Responds to Voice
- Responds to Pain
- Unresponsive

Glasgow Coma Score	
Eyes	1–4
Verbal	1–5
Motor	1–6
Total	**3–15**

Possible causes
- Faint
- Fit (seizure)
- Alcohol
- Poisoning/drugs
- Carbon monoxide
- Head injury
- Low/high blood sugar
- Hypo/hyperthermia
- Low blood pressure
- Lack of oxygen (hypoxia)
- Stroke
- Infection/Sepsis
- Post-diving
- Low blood salt

Immediate treatment **2**
- Lay down carefully, and put into recovery position
- Give oxygen if available (page 202)
- If fitting for longer than 5 minutes, give medication to stop fit (page 17)
- Check vital signs
- Call TMAS

Continued monitoring
- Pulse
- Blood pressure
- Capillary refill time
- Respiratory rate
- Temperature
- Blood sugar
- Breath odour
- Pupil size

Recovery time
Time taken to become normally responsive
(see page 12 for managing the unconscious casualty)

3
- **Within a few minutes** Likely to be a simple faint
- **Up to 30–60 minutes (following fitting)** Likely to be secondary to fits
- **Longer than 60–90 minutes** More serious with a variety of possible causes

Contact TMAS early

Assessing the casualty

1

A quick examination of the casualty will reveal details that may enable diagnosis.

Most importantly, place the casualty in the recovery position after initial assessment, as this directs any blood, saliva or vomit to drain out of the mouth and not to be inhaled into the lungs.

Look for:

- vital signs (pulse, blood pressure; see page 191)
- obvious fitting
- pupil size and response to light
- smell of alcohol or ketones (like acetone)
- paralysis of one side of the face or body
- head injury
- any other injury and bleeding
- rolling eye movements
- tongue biting
- incontinence of urine or stool.

When determining the level of consciousness, use a gradual increase in stimulation to get the casualty to respond. Start by asking for a verbal response (e.g. 'Are you OK?') in a loud voice. If no response, try gripping their shoulder and gently shaking it (watch the c-spine). If there is still no response, try a painful stimulus:

- Rub the edge of the eye socket under the eyebrow.
- Rub the centre of the chest firmly.
- Squeeze a pen onto the base of a finger nail.

Try the painful stimulus on yourself first, to make sure it is reasonable and will not cause lasting discomfort or injury.

Treatment of prolonged fitting

2

See page 17 on fitting (convulsions).

Recovery of consciousness

3

The time taken for the casualty to recover consciousness gives a guide to possible, or even probable, diagnosis. However, the guides in terms of time are only approximate and should not definitely exclude another diagnosis.

Causes of loss of consciousness (LOC; commonest first)

Fainting

Simple fainting is common and is usually due to a temporary drop in blood pressure causing a 'blackout'. Precipitating factors include severe pain, panic attacks, emotional or physical shock (such as the sight of blood) and excessive heat. Sometimes the patient may twitch while unconscious, but this does not necessarily mean they have epilepsy. The patient should be put in the recovery position, which helps to restore blood flow to the brain. Once this is done, they should recover within a couple of minutes. Check for injuries if the casualty has collapsed.

Low blood pressure

A systolic blood pressure lower than 60 mmHg is likely to cause a reduction in level of consciousness. Some crew members may be more susceptible to low blood pressures than others, particularly those with a history of high blood pressure or diabetes. Restoring blood flow to the head by laying the casualty down and raising the legs is the quickest treatment. The reason for the low blood pressure (such as blood loss) should be treated immediately, and IV access and fluid replacement commenced. A heart attack may cause a cardiac arrest in the extreme, but may also cause low blood pressure. Contact TMAS urgently, as the casualty may deteriorate rapidly.

Head injury

Head injury sufficient to cause a period of LOC may well be associated with injuries to the spine, including the neck. Bear this in mind, and protect the c-spine at all times. A GCS of 13 or more indicates mild injury, while a GCS of 8 or less indicates severe injury. The longer the period of LOC, the more severe the injury, and a period of LOC longer than 5 minutes should be taken very seriously.

Treatment comprises resuscitation and management of the unconscious casualty (see page 12). Any casualty that has suffered LOC due to head injury should be monitored closely for at least 24 hours following the event because deterioration is a real possibility. See page 62 for further treatment

Drug overdose

A drug overdose may be accidental or deliberate, and any overdose that leads to LOC is life-threatening. Prescription drugs such as antidepressants, sedatives and heart treatment drugs may cause LOC, and possibly also fitting (page 178). Illicit drugs used recreationally, especially opioids, can also lead to LOC and because of their illegal status it may be difficult to obtain clear indications that they have been used.

Alcohol

Alcohol is a common reason for a casualty to be unrousable, but hopefully not on a vessel. Fitting may occur after exceptional alcohol consumption, or in heavy drinkers who are then on an alcohol-free vessel. Withdrawal effects such as fitting tend to occur after 2–3 days without alcohol. A history of heavy drinking in the immediate past, or the breath smelling heavily of alcohol, are guides to diagnosis.

These casualties are at risk of vomiting and aspiration of vomit into the lungs when they are unconscious. They should be placed in the recovery position and any prolonged fitting treated, then they should be carefully monitored. See page 180.

Fits

See page 16.

Stroke (cerebrovascular accident)

A stroke (CVA) means a lack of blood flow to part of the brain, either because of a blood clot, or because of a bleed in the brain itself. LOC would be caused by a very large stroke, or a smaller stroke in a critical area of the brain. Fitting may occur, as well as paralysis or abnormal movements down one side of the body. Immediate resuscitation is important, to restore blood and oxygen supply to the brain to limit further damage (see page 125 for further treatment).

Infection and sepsis (including meningitis and encephalitis)

LOC with, possibly, fitting may occur due to infection of the membrane covering the brain (meningitis) or the brain itself (encephalitis). A history of feeling increasingly unwell for several hours to days beforehand, together with a high temperature, and possibly a non-blanching rash (page 124), raises the possibility of infection.

Generalised sepsis ('blood poisoning') may also cause a reduction in conscious level, confusion, and even complete loss of consciousness.

Any fitting should be treated, and high-dose antibiotics should be given IV as soon as possible. See pages 40 and 124 for further treatment.

Low or high blood sugar

This may occur in known diabetics, but there are other causes as well (see page 36). Fitting may well occur, as well as LOC, particularly with low blood sugar levels. It is imperative to check the blood sugar as soon as possible, particularly with known diabetics. See page 37 for further treatment.

Carbon monoxide

Carbon monoxide (CO) poisoning may arise from incomplete combustion (e.g. by a defective or inadequately ventilated gas cooker or generator), or from certain cargoes such as wood pellets. CO blocks the transport of oxygen from the lungs to the brain and other parts of the body. Symptoms tend to be vague: nausea, vomiting, confusion, chest pain, and eventually unconsciousness in severe cases. The casualty may appear very red-faced ('cherry red'). If several crew members have the same symptoms CO poisoning should be considered. The casualty should be removed from the source and given as much oxygen as possible if it is available. See page 181 for further treatment.

Poisoning

Poisoning may occur from inhalation of gases emitted by certain cargoes, from exposure to flue gases, or exposure to toxic substances used on board in working or in living areas, especially in confined spaces. Be aware of the risk of being overcome when entering a cabin or enclosed space to rescue a casualty. See page 178 for information on common exposures and their specific treatments.

Lack of oxygen (hypoxia)

The main reasons for lack of oxygen delivery to the brain of the casualty are loss of airway and lack of effective breathing (and lack of adequate circulation, as above).

It may also arise in enclosed spaces when oxidation and rust formation have removed the available oxygen, or in tanks that have been blanketed with inert gases to reduce the risk of fire and explosion, and where organic cargoes have absorbed oxygen from the air.

LOC and, possibly, fitting due to lack of oxygen is extremely serious, and is very likely to cause permanent damage. Immediate resuscitation (see page 2) is imperative, and oxygen by mask should be given if possible. Fitting should be treated if it persists for more than 5 minutes.

Post-diving

A casualty who becomes unconscious soon after returning from diving is very likely to have suffered an air embolism (decompression illness). Immediate resuscitation is imperative, and the patient should be placed in the recovery position if they are breathing and have a pulse. Oxygen should be given if available, and IV fluids administered if possible. Contact TMAS urgently, and prepare for immediate evacuation, ideally to a decompression facility.

Low blood salt

This is known as hyponatraemia (reduced level of sodium in the blood). The most likely reason is that the casualty has been rehydrated with just water instead of rehydration salts, in warm, humid conditions, when the work rate may be high. Prevention is essential, by ensuring an adequate, appropriate fluid intake. Making a firm diagnosis of hyponatraemia on board a vessel is impossible, and would be based on suspicion only. The only treatment possible on board (after appropriate resuscitation) would be to give IV rehydration fluid (see page 220).

Hypothermia or hyperthermia

Hypothermia is likely to cause LOC at body core temperatures below 32 °C, whereas fitting and LOC are more likely with hyperthermia at temperatures of 40 °C and above. Treatment comprises treating any fit initially, then reversing the hypothermia (see page 44) or hyperthermia (see page 50).

4 Managing the unconscious crew member

Once resuscitation and the primary and secondary surveys have been completed, you may be left with a casualty who remains unconscious. The cause may be obvious from preceding events (e.g. head injury), or it may remain unclear, requiring further examination and testing that is not possible on board. However, there is still much to be done by the medical officer, master and crew.

The unconscious casualty is completely dependent on those around them. The objective of the entire crew is to maintain the casualty and deliver them to shore in the shortest possible time, in the best possible condition.

There are various tasks that must be undertaken to ensure the casualty does not deteriorate and has the best chance of recovery.

Maintenance of the airway

- An unconscious casualty cannot maintain their airway when on their back.
- Place them in the recovery position as soon as possible.
- Use airway adjuncts if necessary (see page 199).
- Monitor at all times:
  - change in normal skin colour
  - noisy breathing
  - chest movement
  - rate of breathing.

Recovery position

- The unconscious casualty must be placed in the recovery position for two good reasons:
  - maintenance of the airway
  - drainage of vomit, saliva etc. out of the mouth and not down the airway into the lungs.
- The method of getting the casualty into the recovery position must be modified if there is a chance of spinal injury (especially the c-spine; see page 208).
- Arms and legs may need to be kept straight if injured or fractured.
- Use a safe and secure position on the vessel where the casualty will not fall forwards or backwards as the vessel rolls.

Injuries

- All fractures must be splinted or immobilised as soon as possible.
- All wounds must be cleaned, washed out if necessary, and dressed with a sterile dressing.
- All injuries should be reviewed every few hours if there is a delay in evacuating the casualty.

Warmth

- Make sure the casualty is warm and dry.
- Monitor the temperature with a thermometer under the armpit.

Pain relief

- Paradoxically the casualty, although unconscious, may still be affected by pain, which may be extremely severe, especially on being moved.
- Look for signs of pain (see page 116).
- Use pain relief carefully: do not give opiates (morphine) or tramadol to head-injured casualties.
- Use non-sedating painkillers (e.g. paracetamol) if the casualty is able to take oral medications.
- Immobilise fractures and attempt to reduce the broken ends (see page 244).

Pressure areas and sores

- An immobile casualty will start to develop pressure sores on the skin on which they are lying if they are left in one position for several hours. Pressure sores may also develop underneath padded or inflatable splints applied to fracture sites.
- Pressure areas will develop more quickly if the casualty:
  - is injured
  - is cold
  - is incontinent
  - is poorly hydrated
  - has low blood pressure.
- It may be necessary to log-roll the casualty from side to side every few hours, depending on other injuries.
- The casualty may have been secured on a makeshift hard, rigid 'spinal board' such as any rigid board, to move them down below, or extracted safely from an inaccessible space such as the engine room. They should be carefully taken off this as soon as is practicable (page 208).

Urinary catheter and nasogastric tube

- If the unconscious casualty is going to stay on board for more than a few hours, it is essential to put in a urinary catheter (see page 217). A full bladder is painful.
- If there is blood at the end of the penis or coming out of the vagina contact TMAS before inserting any catheter.
- A nasogastric tube (NGT) is also very useful (see page 216):
  - to empty the stomach of food, to avoid vomiting
  - as a route to keep the casualty hydrated.
- Always consult TMAS before inserting an NGT, as it is not easy to make sure it enters the stomach rather than the airway; it should only be inserted with their direct advice.
- Do not insert an NGT if the casualty may have a head injury. Use the mouth instead if accessible (see page 65).

Hydration

- It is imperative to make sure the casualty receives adequate fluid while unconscious.
- It is very difficult to assess how much fluid should be given.
- Generally 3 litres per day would be sufficient for a 70 kg person.

- However, this may alter depending on:
  - blood loss due to injuries – this may be to the outside (with open wounds) or to the inside (with fractures or abdominal injuries)
  - if the climate is very hot; sweating increases fluid loss
  - burn injuries (see page 52)
  - blood pressure – a low blood pressure may be increased by giving additional IV fluid in 250 ml amounts.
- There are various ways of giving fluid and judging adequacy of hydration (see page 222).
- If contemplating administering IV fluids, it is essential to contact TMAS prior to and during administration.

Easy tests on board

- Some tests are very easy to perform on board the vessel, and may give very useful information:
  - blood sugar with testing sticks (essential in diabetics)
  - urine for blood, sugar, signs of kidney or bladder damage, with testing sticks
  - pregnancy testing kit
  - malaria testing kit (if available; see page 191 for details on interpretation)
  - pulse oximeter (see page 202).

Monitoring of vital signs

- Monitoring of vital signs is an essential task to spot deterioration at an early stage, and correct it.
- Use a record chart (see Appendix VI, page 294).
- Record every hour as a minimum:
  - pulse
  - respiratory rate
  - temperature
  - pupil reactions
  - blood pressure
  - urine output (if possible)
  - conscious state AVPU/GCS (see page 196)
  - pulse oximeter reading.

Communication and evacuation

- Contact TMAS early.
- Prepare to evacuate at the first opportunity.
- Communicate effectively – prioritise information.
- Know who you are talking to.
- Do not minimise the seriousness of the situation to shore.
- Make sure you know how to evacuate a casualty (see Appendices I and II, pages 278, 280).
- Make sure comprehensive documentation goes with the casualty.

5 Fitting (convulsions)

The sight of a crew member having a generalised fit or convulsion is very disturbing, but it is essential to take swift action to prevent injury and to minimise the after-effects of the fit. The immediate actions are quite straightforward, but need to be performed quickly and correctly.

The priority in all cases is resuscitation, followed by treatment to stop the fitting if it continues beyond five minutes.

There are many causes of fitting; finding out the cause will usually lead to effective treatment to stop the fit and to stabilise the casualty. Checking vital signs, particularly blood sugar, is crucial and may guide immediate treatment.

People known to be suffering from epilepsy and who require medication may be able to work at sea, in near-coastal waters. Seasickness (reducing absorption of oral tablets), work stress, poor nutrition and dehydration may all cause fits in known epilepsy sufferers whose symptoms were previously well-controlled. A person with epilepsy may sometimes get an 'aura' (a feeling that they are going to fit) before they actually fit, and if so it is important to get them to a safe place as soon as possible.

Assess severity
- History
- Examination

Collapsed? Unconscious? → **Resuscitate ABCDE** (Page 2)

Types of fit or seizure (1)
- Generalised (grand mal) – whole body shaking
- Partial – shaking only in part of body or face
- Absence – unresponsive, unaware
- Other types – myoclonic, tonic, atonic

Possible causes
- Known epileptic – not taking usual medications, or vomiting/ diarrhoea, infection, dehydration
- Withdrawal of alcohol or other recreational drugs
- Low blood sugars (hypoglycaemia)
- Head injury
- Drug overdose
- Infections – meningitis, encephalitis, malaria
- Hyperthermia – febrile convulsions in children
- Low or high blood sodium
- Post-diving (decompression sickness)

Immediate treatment (2)
- ABCDE (oxygen if available; page 202)
- If patient is unconscious place them in recovery position in a safe place – be alert for vomiting
- Establish IV access and test blood glucose
- Terminate fitting if drugs available: lorazepam IV, diazepam IV or PR or midazolam (buccal)
- Monitor airway and breathing closely after giving lorazepam or diazepam
- If vomiting, give anti-sickness medications, followed by anti-epileptic medications
- If known epileptic give normal anti-epileptic drugs
- If fits continue beyond 30 minutes, contact TMAS

Continued monitoring
- Pulse
- Blood pressure
- Temperature
- Conscious level
- Respiratory rate
- Blood sugar
- Oximetry if available
- Further fits

WATCH FOR DETERIORATION

Time taken to recovery of consciousness (Page 9) (3)

Contact TMAS early

Types of fit, convulsion and seizure

1

Fits, convulsions and seizures fall into several categories:

Generalised fit (tonic–clonic/grand mal) A fitting episode that involves all muscles in the body. The muscle tremors are random, so there is no coordinated movement. If the casualty was standing, they will fall down, possibly injuring themselves. They will not turn over as that requires coordinated muscle action. The casualty will lose consciousness.

Partial fit Tremors that involve only one muscle or muscle group, even just part of the face or the eyes. It can be hard to recognise them as fits, and the casualty may stay conscious.

Absence seizure The casualty becomes completely unaware of their surroundings, and are not responsive. Their muscles tend to continue to work, so they may stay standing up.

Other types These include:

- Tonic The arms, legs or body becomes stiff and rigid, and the casualty will lose consciousness and fall over; this is normally the precursor to a typical tonic–clonic fit.
- Atonic A sudden loss of muscle tone in the body, or perhaps just the head. The casualty normally falls over. It is of brief duration, normally of up to 20 seconds.
- Myoclonic Twitching of a muscle or group of muscles. It occurs commonly, and can have other causes as well as a fit.

Termination of fitting

2

A fit or series of fits without regaining consciousness, that lasts longer than 5–10 minutes, should be treated to avoid the risk of permanent brain damage. An episode of fitting that lasts longer than 30 minutes is known as *status epilepticus* and is a serious emergency that could well result in permanent brain damage, or even death.

First-line treatment

- Diazepam 10 mg PR:
  - Repeat at 15-minute intervals up to 40 mg

or

- Lorazepam 2–4 mg IV:
  - Repeat once after 20 minutes
  - Lasts for up to 12 hours

or

- Midazolam 5–10 mg buccal:
  - Insert half-dose into cheek on each side
  - Repeat after 10 minutes.

Important Diazepam, lorazepam and midazolam have similar actions, and should not be used together except under medical direction. They will sedate the casualty, reduce their conscious level, and may even stop them breathing; use these drugs carefully.

If fitting continues or recurs contact TMAS immediately.

Time to recovery of consciousness

3

The 'post-ictal' period is the phase after the casualty has stopped fitting, but has not yet regained consciousness. It is usually less than 30 minutes, but it can be several hours. The post-ictal period tends to be longer with more prolonged, generalised seizures, and when more medication has been used to terminate the fit.

It is mandatory to contact TMAS for advice if the casualty remains unconscious after 30 minutes, if it has not been sought previously.

6 Headache

Headaches are very common on land, and even more so at sea. The list of possible causes is long.

They may involve pain affecting the head or shoulders, and may be occasional, or frequent and prolonged. They can be disabling, particularly if migrainous, which, if very severe, can involve neurological problems such as paralysis of parts of the body or visual problems.

Frequent, severe headaches will affect how a crew member functions in their position on a vessel, so headaches can be a serious problem, and need to be diagnosed accurately and treated quickly.

The other problem with headaches is that, very occasionally, they are a manifestation of an underlying serious medical illness. There are various 'red flag' symptoms associated with headaches that should warn of possible impending critical illness.

Assess severity
- History
- Examination

Collapsed? Unconscious? → **Resuscitate ABCDE** (Page 2)

Signs of severe illness
- Persistent headache not responding to normal pain relief
- Headache similar to 'being hit with a baseball bat'
- Bright light causes severe pain (photophobia)
- Neck stiffness (worse with straight leg raise)
- Any sign of weakness, paralysis, slurred speech
- Appearance of non-blanching rash on body
- Confused, reduced conscious level
- Dilated or unequal pupil sizes
- Persistent vomiting

Possible causes
- Tension headache
- Sleep deprivation
- Migraine (particularly if previous sufferer)
- Dehydration
- Sunstroke
- Ear infections
- Dental and sinus infections
- Carbon monoxide poisoning
- Meningitis or encephalitis
- Intracranial bleed
- Head injury
- Dive injury (the 'bends')
- Stroke
- Systemic infection (malaria, dengue fever, etc.)
- Medications and recreational drugs

Immediate treatment
- ABCDE (oxygen if available)
- Regular pain relief if conscious
- Encourage rest and oral fluids if conscious
- If severe, may require IV access for fluids or medications
- Antibiotics if fever and/or rash

Continued monitoring
- Pulse
- Blood pressure
- Temperature
- Conscious state
- Respiratory rate
- Severity of pain
- Pupil size and reactivity
- Blood sugar

WATCH FOR DETERIORATION

Contact TMAS early

Signs of severe illness ('red flags')

Headache not responding to normal painkillers

Paracetamol and ibuprofen are commonly used to treat simple headaches, and if these medications do not provide the usual pain relief, this should arouse suspicion.

Severe, sudden onset, 'thunderclap' headache

This is sometimes described as like being hit around the back of the head by a baseball bat. This is especially concerning if such headaches are recurrent and rapidly getting worse.

Photophobia

The casualty will not be able to look at any light source, keeping their eyes closed. Such a response is frequently associated with a bacterial infection causing meningitis, which is inflammation of the membranes covering the brain (page 124).

Neck stiffness and inability to raise straight legs

The casualty will not be able to make their chin touch their chest, when ordinarily they can do so. When lying on their back, they will experience severe pain in their back and neck, when one or both legs are raised, keeping them straight while doing so.

Weakness, paralysis or slurred speech

Weakness or paralysis may affect one or more limbs, or one side of the face. Speech may be slurred, difficult to understand, in the absence of another cause such as drugs or alcohol.

Rash (blanching or non-blanching)

When concurrent with a severe headache, a non-blanching rash is an ominous sign of meningitis, with systemic sepsis (page 122).

Confused, reduced conscious level

The casualty may be disorientated in time and place or even worse, not properly responsive (page 196 for assessment of conscious level).

Dilated or uneven pupils

Pupils may be abnormally dilated, or uneven when comparing one side with the other. They may also not constrict when a bright light is shone into them.

Persistent vomiting

Continued vomiting with no clear alternative cause.

Causes

Common non-critical headaches

Sleep deprivation, shift work, tension, sunstroke, stress, flu-like illnesses and dehydration are all common problems at sea, and cause the majority of uncomplicated headaches. They should respond to simple pain relief, reasonable hydration, cool shade and good rest.

Headaches caused by problems around the head and shoulders

Dental problems such as infections, abscesses and broken teeth, sinus infections and infected ears are all potent causes of headaches, which can be disabling. The underlying problem must be identified and treated to prevent continuation of the headaches (page 132).

Intracranial problems

Anything that increases the pressure within the skull will cause severe headaches. Causes include blood accumulating after head injury or ruptured aneurysm, growing tumours, and infection. Blood clots causing a stroke (cerebrovascular accident) may also cause severe headaches.

Infections

Infection may affect the membranes covering the brain (meningitis) or the brain itself (encephalitis), both resulting in severe headache. Other systemic infections such as malaria and dengue fever may also cause severe headache (page 162).

Drugs

Overuse of simple painkillers may paradoxically cause headaches, and also many prescription medications may cause headaches as a side-effect. Recreational drugs such as cocaine and amphetamines commonly cause headaches.

Activities/environment

Headaches after diving may be caused by sinus or ear problems. However, severe headaches may be a manifestation of unrecognised decompression sickness (the 'bends').

Carbon monoxide or other toxic gases may accumulate in confined and poorly ventilated areas and headaches may be the only sign of an impending critical illness at sea.

7 Confusion and delirium

There are many causes of confusion and delirium. All are serious and potentially life-threatening if not addressed and treated promptly.

However, it may be difficult to recognise confusion due to its often gradual and insidious onset. Recognition can be even more challenging in fellow crew members or passengers who are new to the vessel, and whose individual personalities are not well known.

Confusion can range from mild disorientation in time and place to complete lack of awareness of one's surroundings.

Delirium is a wider range of symptoms, all part of a general deterioration in a casualty's normal mental state. The symptoms can include an acute onset of confusion, attention deficit, disordered behaviour, detachment from reality (delusions) and hallucinations.

Treating confusion and delirium

Assess patient/casualty
- History
- Examination

Collapsed? Unconscious? → **Resuscitate ABCDE** (Page 2)

Confusion
Deficit in orientation, thinking, reduced awareness

Delirium
Acute onset of confusion ± hallucinations

→ **Assess consciousness** (page 8)

AVPU
- Alert
- Responds to Voice
- Responds to Pain
- Unresponsive

Glasgow Coma Score

Eyes	1–4
Verbal	1–5
Motor	1–6
Total:	**3–15**

Possible causes
- Hypoxia
- Alcohol
- Poisoning/drugs
- Drug toxicity
- Head injury
- Chemicals/solvents
- Sepsis/infection
- Low/high blood sugar
- Low blood pressure
- Carbon monoxide
- Post-diving
- Stroke (CVA)
- Hypo/ hyperthermia
- High altitude
- Post-fitting
- Low blood salt

Further assessment
- Pupil size and response
- Breath odour
- Skin rashes
- Signs of head injury
- Neck stiffness
- Blood sugar
- Increased limb tone
- Facial asymmetry
- Temperature (oral/rectal)
- Needle injection marks
- Awareness of time and place
- Urine dipstick

Immediate treatment
- Remove from danger and ensure ongoing safety
- Give oxygen by mask if available and tolerated
- May require cautious sedation – diazepam 5 mg oral or haloperidol 5 mg oral
- Check vital signs
- Keep warm and hydrated
- Call TMAS

Continued monitoring
- Pulse and blood pressure
- Awareness level
- Respiratory rate
- Capillary refill time
- Urine dipstick
- Temperature
- Blood sugar
- Breath odour
- Pupil size
- Urine output

Contact TMAS early

Confusion

A casualty may become confused gradually (over days) or more quickly (over hours or even minutes).

A confused casualty is often disorientated in:

- Time They will not know what day of the week it is, or what year it is.
- Place They will not know where they are, or be convinced they are somewhere other than where they actually are.

Further symptoms of confusion include the following. The casualty may:

- Have no proper understanding of who they are, losing recognition of their own identity. Sometimes they may think they are someone else entirely.
- Not be able to remember recent events or to take in new information.
- Have difficulty in making decisions or paying accurate attention to their surroundings.
- Have a change in their conscious level, becoming drowsy or agitated.
- Have unusually slow or even slurred speech.

They may even recognise and understand themselves that they cannot think clearly.

Delirium

The symptoms of delirium are more severe, and with some or all of the following:

- Hyperactivity or the opposite (hypoactivity) with a deficit in level of attention, where normal interaction and reasoning with the casualty is not possible.
- A disturbed sleep cycle, so the casualty will tend to be awake during the night and asleep during the day.
- Disordered behaviour, including rapid changes in mood, with slow or muddled thinking.
- Psychotic symptoms such as hallucinations and delusions:
  - Hallucination An experience of thinking that something external to one's self, such as a visual image, smell or sound, is a real thing, when in fact there is no such actual physical stimulus. The casualty is fully awake, and usually believes the perception is completely real.
  - Delusion A falsely held belief (such as that a fellow crew member is intent on injuring them) that is not amenable to logical reasoning.

Possible causes

See pages 120, 182.

8 Choking

Choking is an emergency, and must be treated as such. A casualty who has difficulty with breathing caused by choking may rapidly collapse if the cause is not promptly recognised and effective treatment started.

The cause is commonly a piece of food lodged in the throat, larynx (voice box) or further down, in the wind pipe (trachea). Objects stuck further down may cause spasm of the muscles of the airway or the vocal cords, which can cause blockage of the airway as well.

The blockage may be total or partial, allowing some breathing. The treatment is different in each case. The first things to do are to recognise that someone is choking and then assess the severity. Quite often the casualty will indicate strongly the cause of the problem.

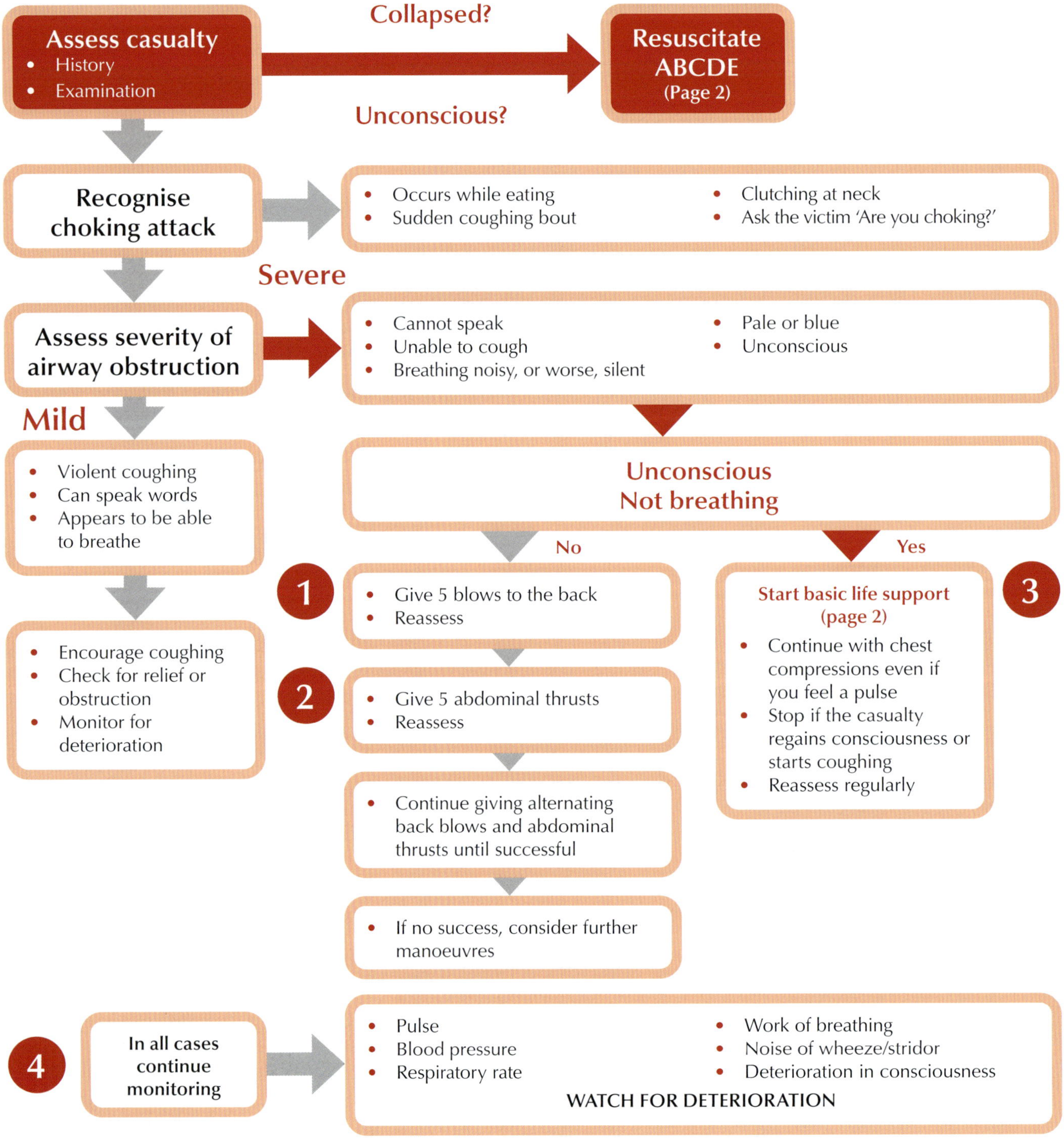

Contact TMAS early

Giving back blows

1

- The casualty must be conscious and able to stand up to do this.
- Briefly explain what you are going to do – it may hurt them.
- Stand to their side, and lean them well forward over your left arm, supporting their chest, as shown in the figure. This will help to ensure that any dislodged object is more likely to come out of their mouth.
- Give 5 sharp very firm blows between their shoulder blades with the heel of your right hand.
- Reassess briefly between each blow. If the object is dislodged or comes out, stop giving the back blows.

Giving abdominal thrusts (Heimlich manoeuvre)

2

- The casualty must be conscious and able to stand up to do this.
- Briefly explain what you are going to do – it may hurt more than back blows.
- Stand behind them and lean them forward. Place one clenched fist in the upper abdomen, just below the ribs in the centre line, as shown in the figure. Cover with your other hand and hold firmly.
- Give up to 5 sharp thrusts to the abdomen.
- Reassess briefly between the thrusts, and stop if the object is dislodged or comes out.

Basic life support continuing chest compressions

3

If the casualty becomes unconscious, basic life support is then required. It is probably worthwhile continuing chest compressions, even if a pulse is felt, because the chest compressions may raise the pressure in the lungs and force the object out of the airway.

Continue with chest compressions until:

- the object is dislodged
- there is a pulse
- you have been given medical advice to stop
- you are exhausted and cannot continue.

Further treatment

4

Even after the object has been dislodged the casualty may remain wheezy and still have difficulty breathing. See page 144 for further supportive treatment.

9 Chest pain and heart attack (myocardial infarction)

The heart is a muscle and it depends on its blood supply to keep going. If the blood supply is reduced this may cause pain (angina). If the blood supply reduces even further this may cause a heart attack, which involves damage to the heart muscle; this is known as myocardial infarction. This is usually very painful and is often described as a crushing central chest pain. Sometimes a heart attack may stop the heart from beating properly in a regular rhythm, which may then cause the blood pressure to fall, or it may cause a cardiac arrest.

Heart attacks are very rare in the young and fit but more common in older crew, especially those with a history of angina or previous heart attacks. Some of those with such a history will still be able to work at sea, while others may be considered unfit.

There are many reasons for chest pain, and a careful history and examination is essential in finding out the cause.

Assess patient/casualty
- History
- Examination

Collapsed? Unconscious? → **Resuscitate ABCDE (Page 2)**

Signs of heart attack (myocardial infarction)
- Recent onset of central crushing chest pain
- Pain down left or right arms, up to neck or jaw
- Paleness and sweating
- Shortness of breath, faintness
- Similar pain to previous heart attack or angina
- Feeling of impending doom

Immediate treatment
- ABCDE and oxygen if available
- Morphine 10 mg IV or IM injection or tramadol 50–100 mg if no morphine on board
- Glyceryl trinitrate (GTN) spray under tongue
- Aspirin 300 mg by mouth (or clopidogrel)
- Contact TMAS immediately
- Prepare for emergency evacuation

Continued monitoring
- Pulse
- Blood pressure
- Respiratory rate
- Conscious level
- Oxygen saturation if a pulse oximeter available
- Temperature
- Severity of pain

WATCH FOR DETERIORATION

Other possible causes of chest pain

Indigestion (page 151)
- History of reflux
- History of indigestion
- Pain responds to antacids

Chest wall bruising (page 88)
- History of trauma
- Tenderness over chest wall to firm palpation

Chest infection (page 144)
- Fever and/or cough
- Green sputum
- Feels unwell

Pneumothorax (page 234)
- Pain on breathing in/out
- Shortness of breath
- Trauma or spontaneous

Contact TMAS early

Treatment of heart attacks

If the casualty collapses it is imperative to give rapid resuscitation and advanced life support (see page 2 on resuscitation). The cause of collapse may be an irregular heart rhythm (ventricular fibrillation or tachycardia) which stops the heart pumping blood properly. Rapid defibrillation with a defibrillator, if available, may return the heart to its normal rhythm.

In less serious heart attacks there are a few simple treatments to give that may reduce the chance of the heart attack getting worse, or happening again: morphine, oxygen, glyceryl trinitrate (GTN), aspirin.

Morphine 10 mg IM

Give a morphine injection in the shoulder, firmly (see page 229). Give an injection of anti-sickness medicine (cyclizine) as well. This will reduce the pain and anxiety of the casualty, reducing strain on the heart.

Oxygen by face mask (if available)

The face mask should be placed on the casualty's face as soon as possible, with a flow rate of 5 litres per minute. This will increase the supply of oxygen to the heart, reducing further damage to the heart muscle.

Glyceryl trinitrate spray under the tongue

A GTN spray twice under the tongue should be given as soon as possible. If the chest pain does not go away, or comes back, it can be repeated. It may lower the blood pressure or give the casualty a headache if used too much. The GTN will dilate the coronary arteries, increasing the blood supply to the heart muscle.

Aspirin 300 mg by mouth

Give this in the dispersible form if possible; absorption from the stomach will be quicker. Aspirin will reduce the chance of clot forming in the coronary arteries, which probably caused the heart attack.

Clopidogrel 300 mg by mouth

If the casualty is known to be intolerant of aspirin (for example, if it causes indigestion) you can give clopidogrel 300 mg by mouth instead. This also reduces the chance of a clot forming in the coronary arteries, making further heart attacks less likely. Do not give clopidogrel with aspirin as both together may cause spontaneous bleeding.

Ongoing treatment

This depends on the physical state of the casualty. **It is essential to contact TMAS immediately.** If advice is not available, it will be worth continuing treatment as follows (until the advice is available):

- aspirin 75 mg per day (as long as there is no stomach upset or bleeding)
- GTN spray if the chest pain returns
- morphine 5 mg or tramadol 50 mg IM injections if the chest pain returns (depending on the conscious state of the casualty).

10 Shortness of breath

Everyone will experience shortness of breath when undertaking strenuous physical exercise. However, shortness of breath when undertaking minimal exertion such as walking slowly upstairs, or even when at rest, is a serious problem and must be promptly recognised and treated.

The feeling of being abnormally short of breath is extremely unpleasant for the casualty, and they may well become very distressed, which can make the problem worse.

The underlying problem causing the shortness of breath may come on acutely, or may have a more gradual onset. With a gradual onset a normally sedentary casualty may only notice something is wrong when they become short of breath doing everyday activities such as getting out of bed or getting dressed.

The cause of the shortness of breath may be a problem with the heart, lungs, circulation, or a systemic problem affecting the whole body, such as a severe infection, allergic reactions, anaemia, or diseases affecting muscle function.

Assess severity

- History
- Examination

Collapsed? Unconscious? → **Resuscitate ABCDE** (Page 2)

Signs of severe illness

- Pale, clammy, agitated, reduced consciousness
- Unable to talk in full sentences or count 1–10 in a single breath
- Respiratory rate above 25 breaths per minute
- Chest pain, low blood pressure
- Blue lips, under tongue and nail beds
- High or low heart rate (above 120 bpm or below 50 bpm)
- High or low temperature (above 38° C or below 36 °C)

Causes of shortness of breath

Acute heart problems

- Heart attack
- Angina
- Arrhythmias
- Pulmonary embolus
- Pericarditis

Respiratory problems

- Asthma
- Chest infection
- Pulmonary oedema
- Inhaled foreign body
- Pneumothorax

Systemic problems

- Allergic reactions
- Sepsis
- Panic/anxiety
- Narrowing of the upper airway, secondary to allergic reaction, infection, trauma
- Diabetes, poisoning

Chronic reasons (see page 27)

Immediate treatment

- ABCDE (oxygen if available)
- Keep sitting up if that improves symptoms
- Remove from polluted air (e.g. exhaust fumes)
- Consider antibiotics if fever and green sputum
- Consider bronchodilators and steroids if wheezy/known asthmatic/chronic chest disease
- Pain relief if in pain
- If severe, insert IV access for fluids/medications

Continued monitoring

- Respiratory rate
- Pulse
- Blood pressure
- Oximetry if available
- Temperature
- Able to talk in full or partial sentences?
- Colour of lips/under tongue
- Blood sugars

WATCH FOR DETERIORATION

Contact TMAS early

Causes of shortness of breath

There are many causes of shortness of breath, and the list below includes the commonest.

The commonest causes are related to lung or heart problems. Acute problems of the lung include asthma, chest infections, and pulmonary embolism. Acute problems of the heart include myocardial infarction, angina and arrhythmias. More chronic problems can also present with worsening shortness of breath, such as chronic obstructive pulmonary disease (commonly related to smoking), lung tissue diseases and congestive cardiac failure. Anxiety-related problems can also produce very similar symptoms.

The speed of onset may give an idea as to the cause and therefore the treatment, but certainly severe shortness of breath can be life-threatening, so prompt assessment and an immediate call to TMAS is mandatory.

Acute onset

Heart problems (pages 24, 140)

- Myocardial infarction (heart attack)
- Angina (heart muscle pain without permanent damage, usually on exertion)
- Arrhythmias (irregular or other abnormal patterns of heartbeat)
- Pulmonary embolus (large blood clot in lung arteries)
- Pericarditis (inflammation in space around heart with fluid build-up).

Respiratory problems (page 140)

- Asthma (including allergic triggers)
- Chest infection
- Pulmonary oedema
- Inhaled foreign body
- Pneumothorax (secondary to chest trauma or spontaneous).

Systemic problems

- Allergic reactions (anaphylaxis) (page 42)
- Sepsis (page 40)
- Panic/anxiety (page 182)
- Narrowing of the upper airway, secondary to allergic reaction, infection, trauma
- Diabetes, poisoning (metabolic acidosis).

Chronic, long-term onset

Heart problems (pages 24, 140)

- Congestive heart failure
- Valvular heart disease.

Respiratory problems (page 140)

- Chronic obstructive pulmonary disease
- Interstitial lung disease.

Systemic problems

- Anaemia
- Muscle weakness (diseases of nervous and muscular systems)
- Narrowing of the upper airway, such as tracheal stenosis.

11 Shock and haemorrhage

Shock is a condition where not enough blood circulates around the body. This may be for a variety of reasons. The net result is that not enough oxygen gets to the body's organs, such as the brain, heart, kidneys and liver, and eventually these organs will fail to function properly.

The main causes of shock are:

- Reduced blood volume

Blood loss – haemorrhage (internal or external), diarrhoea and vomiting, burns, severe dehydration and diabetic problems

- Failure of heart to pump sufficient flow of blood

Myocardial infarction (heart attack), arrhythmia (abnormal heart rhythm), chronic heart failure, cardiomyopathy and valvular disease

- Blockage (obstruction) of circulation

Fluid build-up around heart (cardiac tamponade), pulmonary embolus (blood clot in the lungs) and tension pneumothorax

- Failure of correct blood volume distribution (fluid loss from circulation into body tissues)

Anaphylaxis, sepsis and failure of nerve supply to blood vessels.

Assess severity
- History
- Examination

Collapsed? Unconscious? → **Resuscitate ABCDE** (Page 2)

Signs of shock
- Pale, clammy, cool peripheries, mottled skin
- Fast heart rate (above 120 bpm)
- Low blood pressure (systolic below 90 mmHg)
- High respiratory rate (above 25 breaths per minute)
- Low urine output
- Lethargic, reduced conscious level

Immediate treatment
- ABCDE
- Oxygen (if available)
- Lay casualty down and raise legs – 'shock position'
- Control any external bleeding
- Establish IV access if available
- If unable to feel radial pulse give 250 ml IV fluids if available
- Try to establish cause

Specific treatments
- External haemorrhage – see below
- If diarrhoea and vomiting/ dehydration give oral fluids (if casualty is conscious) (page 220)
- Sepsis – IV antibiotics with IV fluids if available (page 40)
- Tension pneumothorax – decompress chest (page 234)
- Anaphylaxis – treat with IM adrenaline (page 42)
- Myocardial infarction, arrhythmia (page 24)

Continued monitoring
- Pulse
- Blood pressure
- Temperature
- Blood sugar
- Conscious state
- Respiratory rate
- Peripheral perfusion
- Urine output
- Oximetry if available

WATCH FOR DETERIORATION

Contact TMAS early

Blood loss (haemorrhage)

A casualty who is bleeding is one of the most alarming and dramatic emergencies on board a vessel. Even a small amount of spilt blood looks appalling.

If the bleeding (haemorrhage) is not stopped rapidly, shock may develop and on a vessel in the middle of the ocean this will be life-threatening.

Immediate action is crucial; there is absolutely no time for delay.

Bleeding may be external – in which case it is obvious there is a problem and that action is needed to stop it – or internal. This is more difficult to recognise, assess and stop.

Major causes of internal bleeding are:

- blunt trauma to the chest or abdomen (pages 84, 90)
- penetrating injury to the chest or abdomen (pages 84, 90)
- arm and leg bone fractures, particularly the femur (page 102)
- pelvic fractures (page 94)
- other causes – from stomach, intestines or uterus.

Symptoms	Estimated blood loss	Treatment
• Some bleeding • Minimal symptoms: more in the old, less in the young	Blood loss up to 750 ml	May need no treatment
• Heart rate above 100 beats per minute • Breathing rate up above 20 per minute • Anxious, unsettled	Blood loss 750–1500 ml	Will need fluids, preferably IV or IO
• Heart rate above 120 beats per minute • Reduced blood pressure • Breathing rate up above 25 per minute • Cool skin and very pale • Confused	Blood loss 1500–2000 ml	Needs urgent fluids to stop deterioration
• Heart rate above 140 beats per minute • Very low or unrecordable blood pressure • Cold and white skin • Markedly confused, barely conscious	Blood loss more than 2000 ml	Immediately life-threatening Any delay in giving fluids will be fatal

Normal blood volume for a 70 kg person is 5000 ml

Immediate treatment

- Resuscitate ABCDE
- Lay casualty down
- Raise legs
- Gain venous access if possible (see page 224)
- If you are unable to feel the radial pulse, give 250 ml IV fluid (page 221).

How to stop external bleeding

- Direct pressure
  - This is the best way of stopping external bleeding.
  - Use gloves.
  - Apply very firm pressure to the point from where the blood is coming.
  - Press on either side if there are bones sticking out.
  - Continue for as long as possible until the bleeding stops.
  - Use compression dressings (field dressings) to apply more pressure.

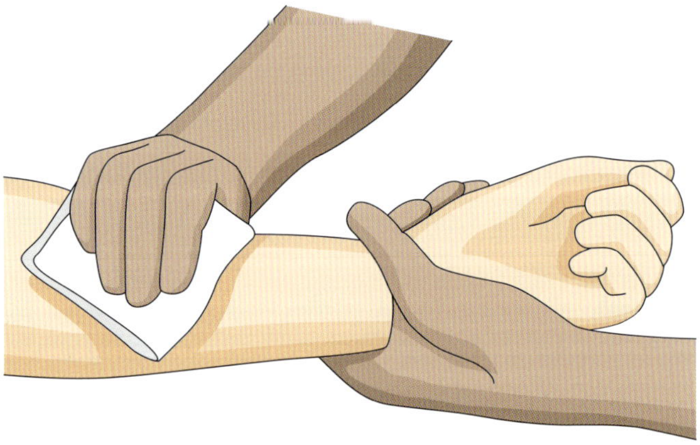

- Pro-clotting agents
  - Haemostatic dressings and pro-clotting granules – these agents stimulate blood to clot and can be used to limit major haemorrhage, particularly for penetrating wounds.
  - Tranexamic acid injection can be used in cases of major haemorrhage. Usual dose is 1 g IM, IV or IO over ten minutes. A further 1 g may be given over the next 8 hours, but get medical advice from TMAS.

- Tourniquet (page 225)
  - This can be used in extreme circumstances when other methods have not been effective.
  - It will significantly reduce blood flow to distal arm or leg, but it may be required for a time, until control can be established.
  - Once a tourniquet is in place, discuss releasing or removing it with TMAS.

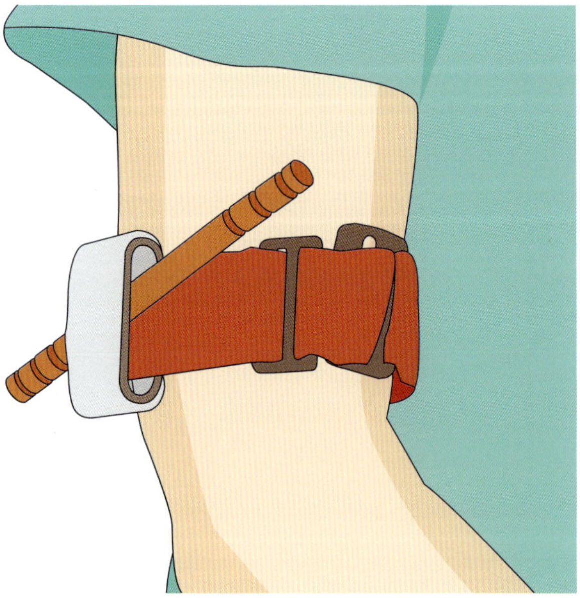

- Splinting (pages 240–3)
  - A splint will put the broken ends of the bones back as close as possible to the normal position.
  - Splint firmly (not too tightly) in that position.
  - If the pelvis is fractured, hold together with a strap or sling around the pelvis.

- Immobilisation
  - Keeping the casualty still, in their bunk, gives any clot that forms the best chance of staying in place by sealing up the bleeding point.
- Elevation
  - Elevating the part of the body, usually the leg or arm, will reduce bleeding from veins and skin.
  - It is unlikely to be effective with arterial bleeding.
- Stitching (pages 230–3)
  - Putting the wound edges back together and stitching or stapling them in place is a good way of stopping bleeding.

Young and old casualties

- Older people compensate less well for blood loss and should be treated sooner.
- Younger adults compensate for blood loss to a much greater extent than older people.
- Conversely, when young people start to show symptoms of blood loss, they are in serious trouble and need urgent treatment.

Blood loss in fractures

• Fractured upper arm (humerus)	Up to 500 ml
• Fractured thigh (femur)	Over 1000 ml per leg
• Fractured pelvis	2000 ml or more

If the fracture is 'open' (i.e. the bones stick through the skin), blood loss may be much greater.

Medications that may complicate blood loss

- Drugs such as aspirin, warfarin, clopidogrel, rivaroxaban and apixaban thin the blood and are commonly used in people with heart conditions. They make bleeding much worse and should be stopped in the bleeding casualty.
- Vitamin K (phytomenadione) can be used to reverse the effects of warfarin if the casualty is taking this. Discuss this with TMAS prior to taking potential treatment.
- Betablockers (metoprolol, atenolol etc.) slow the heart rate and may hide or suppress the rapid pulse response to significant blood loss.
- Anti-seasickness tablets may sometimes make users sleepy, reducing their conscious state significantly in the event of blood loss.

12 Gastrointestinal bleeding

Loss of blood may occur anywhere along the gastrointestinal (GI) tract, from mouth to anus. Bleeds may range from long-term loss of small amounts of blood in normal-looking stool to vomits of large amounts of fresh or black blood, or passage of large amounts of fresh or black blood from the anus. Such events are very disturbing to both casualty and observer. Major bleeds are immediately life-threatening.

Appropriate and urgent action is required, both to restore circulatory stability and to minimise the risk of further bleeds. The definitive hospital treatment for large bleeds is to inspect the inside of the GI tract with an endoscope, to make a diagnosis and to treat accordingly, but this is not possible at sea. However, there are other simple yet effective actions that can be taken in a timely manner.

Assess severity
- History
- Examination

Collapsed? Unconscious? → **Resuscitate ABCDE** (Page 2)

Signs of GI bleed

- Blood in vomit
  - fresh red
  - black 'coffee grounds'
- Blood in stool
  - black stool (melaena)
  - fresh red mixed in stool
  - fresh red on stool surface
- Obviously shocked casualty with no external bleeding
- Obviously anaemic casualty with no obvious signs of blood loss – may be chronic GI bleed

Possible causes

Upper GI bleed (vomiting blood or melaena)
- Gastroduodenal ulceration
- Severe vomiting
- Use of NSAIDS and steroids
- Oesophageal varices
- Use of anticoagulants
- GI malignancy (cancer)

Lower GI bleed (fresh blood on or in stool)
- Inflammatory bowel disease
- Diverticular disease
- GI malignancy (cancer)
- Haemorrhoids

Immediate treatment

- ABCDE (oxygen if available)
- If casualty is shocked, lay down and raise leg
- Establish IV access, if possible, for fluid resuscitation
- Give 500 ml IV fluid and measure response: aim for systolic BP ~ 90 mmHg
- Give antacid and stomach acid production inhibitor (lansoprazole or famotidine)
- Stop NSAIDs, steroids, spicy foods, anticoagulants
- Monitor urine output
- If shocked, will require emergency evacuation

Continued monitoring

- Pulse
- Blood pressure
- Temperature
- Blood sugar
- Able to talk in full or partial sentences?
- Respiratory rate
- Peripheral perfusion
- Urine output
- Oximetry if available

WATCH FOR DETERIORATION

Contact TMAS early

Signs of gastrointestinal bleed

Blood in the vomit

Blood in the stomach is a very potent stimulus for vomiting, so generally blood will not stay in the stomach for long. The blood may be from the oesophagus, the stomach itself or the initial part of the duodenum (see page 91 for anatomy diagram).

Fresh blood This is bright red and a sign of a large bleed that may be ongoing. The blood will have been vomited up immediately.

Black blood This is commonly known as 'coffee grounds' due to its appearance. It will have been in the stomach for long enough to clot, and for its appearance to change due to its exposure to gastric acid. It may be followed soon after by fresh blood.

Blood in the stool

Blood may appear in the stool having originated anywhere in the GI tract from the stomach down. The exact appearance of the blood, and its relationship to the stool, may give guidance to diagnosis, even at sea. The stool will require close inspection, which will not be pleasant for even the most seasoned crew member.

Black, tarry stool Known as melaena; an extremely offensive, noxious stool. It is usually a sign of a large bleed in the duodenum or stomach. It may continue after the bleeding ceases as the GI tract (small and large bowel) will be full of blood.

Bright red blood This usually comes from the lower GI tract, and can be mixed in with the stool, or on the surface of the stool. If it is mixed in it usually comes from the wall of the large bowel. If it is on the surface it is usually from haemorrhoids (piles) which are located at the anus.

Chronic blood loss

This may show as a crew member becoming very pale from blood loss (anaemic), although this is hard to check at sea. If there is no obvious sign of bleeding from anywhere, there is the possibility of gradual blood loss from somewhere in the GI tract, which may have been ongoing for months or even years.

Causes (see pages 146–51 for further details)

Peptic ulceration

Ulceration of the stomach or duodenal lining may occur because of acid secreted in the stomach. The presence of a certain type of bacterium may make this more likely. Ulcers usually cause pain, but they may sometimes erode into a blood vessel and cause severe bleeding, or they may perforate the wall of the gut leading to severe pain and peritonitis.

Oesphageal varices

Liver disease can cause a rise in the pressure in veins at the lower oesophagus, just above the stomach. These veins then become dilated and are prone to severe, sudden bleeds.

Non-steroidal anti-inflammatory (NSAID) use (ibuprofen, naproxen, diclofenac etc.) and steroids (prednisolone etc.)

These classes of drugs are freely available worldwide and some are used on a long-term basis by many crew members. They can often cause ulceration and bleeding from the lining of the stomach and duodenum, similar to peptic ulceration.

Severe vomiting

Repeated strenuous retching can cause tears of the wall of the oesophagus and stomach, causing bleeding, with blood in vomit and/or stool. This is usually self-limiting and will stop after 24 hours or so.

GI malignancy (cancer)

Malignant tumours can occur anywhere along the GI tract, more commonly in the large bowel.

Inflammatory bowel disease (Crohn's disease and ulcerative colitis)

Inflammation of the bowel lining occurs mostly in the large bowel, but it can occur further up as well. It is often a long-term condition and the casualty may have a history of previous episodes. If the bowel is inflamed so severely as to cause bleeding the casualty will normally be very unwell and require emergency evacuation.

Haemorrhoids (page 151)

Known as piles, these are very common, often painful, and may cause minor bleeding, usually on the surface of the stool. They can become infected as well, adding to the discomfort.

Anticoagulants (blood-thinning medicines)

Medicines may be used to thin the blood for the treatment of disorders such as blood clots, which can cause heart attacks (myocardial infarctions) and strokes (cerebrovascular accidents). These medicines include warfarin, aspirin, clopidogrel, rivaroxaban, apixaban and others. These medicines may cause bleeding by thinning the blood too much (over-anticoagulating), and causing spontaneous bleeds. In addition, they may make bleeding, caused by NSAIDS, for instance, much worse. See pages 30–31 for specific management if the crew member is taking warfarin.

13 Diabetic emergencies

Diabetes is becoming increasingly common. The fundamental problem is not enough insulin in the blood. Insulin drives sugar from the blood into cells where it is needed. A diabetes sufferer has poor control over the sugar levels in their blood as the body produces little or no insulin, causing the body's cells to be starved of energy. Insulin injections or anti-diabetes tablets repair this deficiency, so that sugar can enter cells in the normal way.

Assess severity
- History
- Examination

Collapsed? Unconscious? → **Resuscitate ABCDE** (Page 2)

Normal blood sugar 4–6 mmol/l

1 Test blood sugars

	Very low Below 2.5 mmol/l	Very high Above 20 mmol/l
Signs of severe illness	• Sweating, feeling hungry • Confused, agitated • Slurred speech • Aggressive, seems drunk • Fitting • Reduced awareness or loss of consciousness (low GCS)	• Lethargic, sleepy • Continually thirsty • Breathing rapidly • Passing large amounts of urine • Reduced awareness or loss of consciousness (low GCS)
Immediate treatment	**2** • Give oxygen, gain IV access if possible • If conscious: Give a sugary drink or dextrose 40% gel orally • If unconscious: Give 100 ml 10% glucose IV or IO if possible (or equivalent) and glucagon 1 mg IM inj if available	**3** • Give oxygen • Give insulin 20 units IM injection • If conscious: Encourage oral fluids – electrolyte solutions • If unconscious: Gain IV access if possible • Give Ringer's lactate IV fluid 1000 ml
Continued treatment	• Check observation including blood sugars • If initially low GCS, this should improve within 10 minutes if due to low sugars • Continue IV dextrose until sugars in normal range • Check for cause (drugs, infection, other disease)	• Check observations including blood sugars • Give insulin 10 units IM/hr until sugars are below 15 mmol/l • Continue IV fluid 500 ml/hr for 4–6 hrs • Consider changing fluids to IV dextrose when sugars are below 15 mmol/l

Continued management

- GCS, P, BP, RR, temperature
- Test urine for ketones
- Start fluid balance chart – urine output/fluid intake
- Blood sugars hourly
- Consider antibiotics
- Look for cause – drugs, infection, other disease

WATCH FOR DETERIORATION

Contact TMAS and prepare for evacuation

Normal blood sugar	4–6 mmol/l
Dangerously low blood sugar	Below 2.5 mmol/l
Dangerously high blood sugar	Above 20 mmol/l

Control of blood sugar in diabetes

Diabetes may be controlled in three main ways:

- injection of insulin one or more times a day
- oral anti-diabetic tablets
- a diet with restricted carbohydrate (sugar) intake.

Treatment often progresses from diet to tablets and then to insulin. Crew members on insulin may be restricted to near-coastal waters and should not work alone.

Diabetes may be a known condition suffered by the crew member before getting on board, or it may arise for the first time while they are at sea. This can pose an immediate danger to life as it is unexpected and may not be diagnosed promptly. The casualty may be extremely sick and need urgent help.

In those with known diabetes the blood sugar may be too high (too little insulin or too few tablets) or too low (too much insulin or too many tablets). Both can be acute medical emergencies. Test the amount of sugar in the blood if you have a blood glucose testing meter and sticks; otherwise urine dipsticks can be used to detect high, but not low, levels of blood sugar.

Testing the blood sugar 1

To test the blood sugar, jab the end of a fingertip, squeeze out a drop of blood onto the testing stick and wait for the required period (check the instructions), then read the meter.

Treating low blood sugars 2

With a known diabetes sufferer, this may be the result of too much insulin or too many tablets, together with too little food. Strenuous work or exercise may also cause the blood sugar level to drop. Some people with diabetes will know if they are having a 'hypo'; others may just collapse. If there is a diabetes sufferer on the vessel it is worth finding out whether they know if they are having a 'hypo'. Very low blood sugars in people without diabetes are unusual and may be due to drugs, alcohol, malaria or possibly a mistake where they have taken insulin or tablets.

Giving sugar

This can be in the form of a biscuit or sweet drink, if the casualty is conscious, or GlucoGel, a concentrated 40% dextrose gel, can be placed under the tongue, or rubbed into the cheek, or swallowed. Do not put food in the casualty's mouth if they are unconscious because they might aspirate it into their lungs.

Glucagon

If the casualty is unconscious, consider giving glucagon 1 mg intramuscularly (into the shoulder or front of thigh) or IV if access is available.

History

If the casualty is a known diabetes sufferer, find out when their last dose of insulin was given and the time of their last meal. The insulin doses or diabetes tablets may need to be altered. With a casualty who is not known to have diabetes, find out if this has happened before, any history of drugs or illnesses, and contact TMAS. Continue to monitor them until stable.

Treating high blood sugars

With a known diabetes sufferer, this may be due to too little insulin or too few tablets, or it may mean the casualty is unwell; for example, with an infection (this may increase the need for insulin). With a casualty who is not known to have diabetes, it may the first time they have had problems, and they will need medical help as soon as possible. If there are testing sticks for urine on board, test for sugar and ketones and record the results: the medical advisor will want this information. Also ask about increased urination or recent urinary or other infections.

As the casualty improves, the levels of sugar and ketones in the urine should reduce.

Insulin

If insulin is available on board, the best way to treat the casualty is to give insulin injections intramuscularly into the shoulder or front of thigh. Give 20 units at first, then 10 units an hour until the sugar level starts to fall. Contact TMAS early to guide insulin management.

Fluid

The casualty will probably be very dehydrated from passing too much urine (a side effect of the high sugar level in the blood). Start off by giving 1 litre of fluid IV or IO if possible over the first 30 minutes. Then slow down the amount of IV fluid to about 250–500 ml/hour. The aim is to keep urine output at about 50–100 ml/hour. Contact TMAS early to guide fluid management.

If the sugars remain too high after one hour

The situation is very serious if there has been no improvement. TMAS contact is essential. Keep monitoring the blood sugar and vital signs. Continue giving fluids. TMAS may advise:

1. Insertion of a urinary catheter to check on urine output.
2. Insertion of a nasogastric tube (NGT) to empty the stomach (particularly if the casualty is unconscious). This can also be a route for giving fluid.
3. Giving an antibiotic if the casualty's temperature is high (provided they have no antibiotic allergies).
4. Immediate diversion or evacuation.

Be prepared to take these actions.

14 Serious infection and sepsis

Sepsis is a potentially life-threatening condition where an infection affects the whole body. It is sometimes known as septicaemia or blood poisoning. A localised infection, such as in the lungs or in a wound, can occasionally spread rapidly through the bloodstream and cause the body's organs to dysfunction and fail.

The infecting microbe is commonly a bacterium but it could be a virus, fungus or parasite. However, at sea, there is little chance of knowing exactly what microbe is causing the septic episode. The additional problem is that a particular bacterium may not respond to all antibiotics, so if sepsis is suspected, choosing the right antibiotic is not easy. In addition, it is also quite difficult to tell exactly from where the infection originates. The usual originating sites are skin, gastrointestinal tract, urinary system and lungs. Bacteria from each site are known to usually respond to certain types of antibiotics, so at sea this prior knowledge guides the initial choice of antibiotic.

When a septic episode starts, and is first suspected, there is a limited amount of time before the body is overwhelmed by the infection, which becomes irreversible and the casualty may die. Thus early recognition and very prompt treatment (within 30 minutes) with appropriate antibiotics are key to preventing further deterioration and to promote recovery. If you are worried about the possibility of sepsis seek TMAS advice early.

Assess severity
- History
- Examination

Collapsed? / Unconscious? → **Resuscitate ABCDE (Page 2)**

Signs of severe illness
- Sleepy, reduced level of consciousness
- High respiratory rate
- Low blood pressure
- Raised heart rate, little or no urine output
- High or low temperature, above 38.0 °C or below 36.0 °C
- Flushed, or worse – pale, sweaty
- Wound breakdown or non-blanching rash

Likely sources of infection
- Urinary tract
- Skin, wounds, burns
- Gut, intra-abdominal
- Chest
- Ear/nose/throat
- Joints (septic arthritis)
- Genitals (sexual contact diseases)
- Intracranial (meningitis, encephalitis)
- Tropical infections (e.g. malaria; page 162)

Immediate treatment
- ABCDE (oxygen if available)
- Start antibiotics, IM or IV if very unwell (see Antibiotics guide, back flyleaf)
- Encourage oral fluids if possible
- If able, gain IV access and give fluids if very unwell
- If body temperature over 38 °C, keep cool, or actively cool with damp cloths placed on skin, and give paracetamol

Continued monitoring
- Pulse
- Blood pressure
- Temperature
- Conscious state
- Respiratory rate
- Urine dipstick
- Urine output
- Blood sugar

WATCH FOR DETERIORATION

Contact TMAS early

Early recognition of sepsis

Any of the following are at risk of sepsis:

- Anyone complaining of feeling very unwell, but perhaps with no obvious source. Always be vigilant.
- A crew member with an unexplained change in behaviour, undue sleepiness or reduced level of consciousness, with no obvious reason.
- Anyone complaining of feeling unwell, with an increased risk of sepsis (see below).
- Someone with sepsis may not necessarily have a high temperature; it may be low or normal.
- A high respiratory rate (number of breaths per minute), a high heart rate and a low blood pressure are all reliable signs of sepsis, particularly in combination (see page 191).

Someone with sepsis may not pass urine for over 12 hours. Finding this out will be difficult with a casualty who is confused, or has a reduced level of consciousness, so if in doubt, assume they have not done so.

If you have a pulse oximeter on board, check the oxygen saturation by placing the oximeter on a warm finger in order to get a proper reading. An oxygen saturation of 92% or less in someone without previous lung disease (such as chronic obstructive pulmonary disease) is a serious indication of sepsis.

Risk factors for sepsis

The following are at an increased risk of developing sepsis:

- the very young or the very old
- crew members with an impaired immune system, due to inherent disease such as diabetes, sickle cell anaemia, cancer or previous splenectomy
- crew members with an impaired immune system, due to treatments such as recent chemotherapy, stem cell transplants or recent surgery
- crew members with an impaired immune system due to drugs such as immunosuppressants used as treatment for organ transplants, or rheumatoid arthritis
- anyone taking long-term steroids
- recreational drug users, particularly those who inject regularly
- crew members who have suffered accidents where there has been significant skin loss, such as burns, large cuts or skin infections
- women who are pregnant, or who have been so recently; particularly those who have suffered from gestational (pregnancy-related) diabetes or prolonged rupture of the membranes (see page 152).

15 Allergy and anaphylaxis

Certain simple allergic reactions, such as mild asthma and dermatitis, are quite common, preventable and easy to treat. However, the extreme form of allergy, known as anaphylaxis, is much more serious but much less common. Anaphylaxis is where the whole body becomes involved; the mouth and throat may swell, and the casualty collapses because of low blood pressure and an inability to breathe.

The usual causes of anaphylaxis are items of food such as seafood or nuts; other causes include pollen, plants, pets, insect venom (particularly from bee and wasp stings), drugs (e.g. penicillin), latex rubber and vaccines.

Crew members with a history of anaphylaxis from causes that could be present on board may be considered unfit to work at sea. In rare cases where work is permitted, they may be required to carry medications, commonly an adrenaline auto-injector. They should inform the master or responsible officer of their condition and of the known causes so that steps can be taken to avoid exposure.

Assess patient/casualty

- History
- Examination

Collapsed?

Unconscious?

Resuscitate ABCDE

(Page 2)

Watch airway

- Swollen tongue
- Throat constriction
- Shortness of breath

Recognise allergic reaction

Worsening allergic reaction

- General skin flushing, sweating, itchy
- Swelling of lips and eyes
- Wheezy breathing
- Feeling dizzy or faint
- Fast pulse and low blood presssure, shock

Simple allergic reaction

- Itchy skin and eyes
- Localised red rash, wheals, hives
- Runny nose and eyes

Treatment

- Remove cause if identified
- Oral antihistamine: cetirizine or loratadine 10-20mg oral daily for 3 days
- Contact TMAS if the reaction re-occurs

Monitoring

- Pulse and blood pressure
- Respiratory rate/wheeziness
- Temperature
- Oxygen sats if possible
- Extent of rash
- Blood glucose

Anaphylaxis

1 Immediate treatment

- ABCDE and oxygen if available
- Inject adrenaline 0.5 mg to muscle (0.5 ml of 1:1000 solution)
- Lay down, raise legs (shock position)
- Repeat adrenaline injection every 5 minutes if not improving

2 Further treatment

First-line treatment

- Adrenaline: IM injection every 5 minutes as required
- IV fluid if possible, as 500–1000 ml boluses

Second-line treatment

- Antihistamine: chlorphenamine 10–20 mg IM injection
- Steroid: hydrocortisone 100 mg IM or IV injection
- Inhaler: salbutamol 4 puffs. Repeat every 5 minutes if needed

3 Ongoing treatment

- Establish IV access if possible
- Give IV/IO fluids if blood pressure low
- Oral steroid: prednisolone 40–60 mg daily
- Cetirizine or loratadine 10–20 mg daily
- If wheezy, sit up, and also elevate legs as much as practicable

WATCH FOR DETERIORATION

Contact TMAS early

Immediate treatment

1

- Remove the cause if possible.
- Lay the casualty down in a comfortable position, and put the legs up.
- Give oxygen by face mask (5 l/minute) if available.

Adrenaline is the single most important treatment to stop things getting worse:

- Adrenaline injection 0.5 mg (0.5 ml of 1:1000 solution) in the front of the thigh or shoulder. This may be repeated every 5–10 minutes if the casualty is not improving. Use a different limb to inject repeat doses.
- Use pre-filled syringes of adrenaline (auto-injector) if available.
- Adrenaline may make the pulse go faster and increase the blood pressure. Be careful the injection does not go directly into a blood vessel (page 229).

Give IV fluid, if possible in the form of 500–1000 ml boluses.

Further treatment

2

These additional treatments are to dampen the anaphylactic reaction of the body more permanently than adrenaline can, to stop the process starting up again.

Nebuliser:	Adrenaline 5 mg via a nebuliser (if available) may help with breathing difficulties.
Inhaler:	Salbutamol inhaler 4 puffs and repeated as necessary every 5 minutes. This is used to treat the wheeze which may develop with anaphylaxis. Continue for as long as the wheeze is present.
Antihistamine:	Chlorphenamine 20 mg IM injection
Steroid:	Hydrocortisone 100 mg IM or IV injection

Ongoing treatment

3

The goal here is to stabilise the casualty, prevent the anaphylactic reaction from returning, and to get medical help as soon as possible.

IV fluid:	Fluid resuscitation may be required in the early stages if the blood pressure remains dangerously low despite the other treatments (see page 224).
Oral steroids:	Continue oral prednisolone 40–60 mg a day according to symptoms.
Oral antihistamines:	Continue oral loratadine or cetirizine 4 mg 3–6 times a day according to symptoms.

Continue oral treatment until casualty is under medical care
Contact TMAS early

16 Cold injuries and hypothermia

Crew members will be exposed to freezing or near-freezing conditions during deck duties in cold climates and windchill will make this worse. Such exposure may cause both localised cold injury and slower-onset hypothermia. Prevention is fundamental, but if symptoms are recognised they should not be ignored; early treatment will limit the injury and minimise complications. Similar effects are likely on board life rafts and lifeboats in cold conditions. Immersion in cold water will cause acute hypothermia within minutes.

Cold injury

Cold injury may occur after only a few minutes' exposure. Conditions just above 0 °C may cause non-freezing injuries, whereas conditions below 0 °C are more likely to cause freezing injuries.

	Injury	Signs	Treatment
Non-freezing injury	Chilblains and 'Sausage' fingers	• Small, itchy, red, shiny lumps on fingers and toes • Thickened skin on fingers • Reduced sensation	• Keep extremities warm and dry • Pain relief if sore • Care with delicate jobs around the vessel – may drop things
Non-freezing injury	Trench foot	• Prolonged cold and wet feet in tight seaboots • Cold, pale and reduced sensation	• Keep feet dry and warm
Freezing Injury	Frost nip	• Initially painless • White cold firm areas • Affects the fingers, ears, nose tip, feet	• Be vigilant about the risk • Simple warming • May be painful on rewarming • Do not rub
Freezing Injury	Frost bite	• Waxy white or even black • Numbness • Some swelling • May blister on rewarming	• Bathe in water at 40°C • Dress with sterile dressing • Keep elevated, warm and dry • Pain relief

Factors exacerbating cold injury and hypothermia

- Cold temperature
- Damp and/or wet
- Windchill
- Sweating during work
- Drugs and alcohol
- Seasickness
- Dehydration
- Lack of food
- Lack of sleep
- Injury

Hypothermia

The onset of hypothermia may be gradual and may not be noticed until the body core temperature has dropped significantly. The crew member becomes lethargic, confused and withdrawn. This is extremely dangerous and may lead to accidents.

Prevention, early recognition and swift action are required to avoid complications.

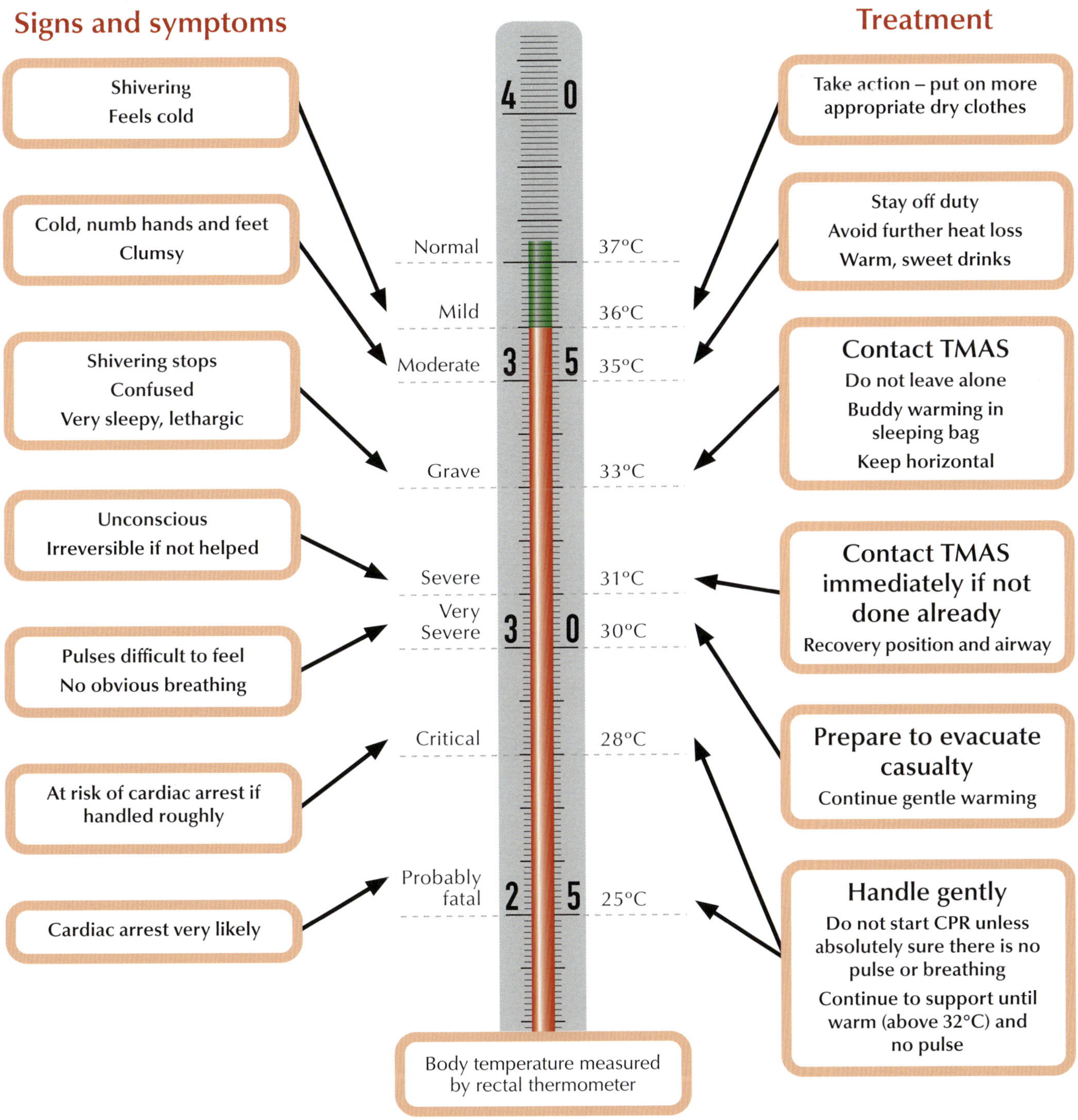

Prevention strategy

- Good nutrition
- Proper hydration
- Limit time on deck
- Heated area below deck
- No alcohol
- Clothing appropriate for conditions:
  - Dry and warm
  - Hat, gloves, mitts, face protection
  - Dry boots and socks, not tight
  - Access to spare clothes

17 Recovery of person overboard

Losing crew or passengers over the side requires a calm, skilled response to effect a rapid recovery. This must be followed by a thorough, structured assessment of the casualty, particularly as sudden illness or injury may have caused the fall initially, or they may have been injured while going over the side. Assessment should start with ABCDE, followed by evaluation for prolonged immersion and drowning, trauma and medical problems. Subsequently, especially in cases of near-drowning, the casualty may deteriorate after being rescued, requiring medical treatment and urgent evacuation.

Locate
Maintain contact with person overboard

- Maintain visual contact
- MOB ('man overboard') position on GPS
- Deploy rescue equipment:
  - Dan buoy
  - Horseshoe buoy
  - Routine use of personal EPIRBs
  - Alarms always on

Retrieval
In horizontal position if possible, to prevent post-rescue collapse

- Use a retrieval cradle, halyard, Lifesling®, bosun's chair or sail sling
- Retrieve via a rescue craft or life raft
- Assistance in the water by a crew member (high risk – use a strop to tether assisting crew member)

Assess
Primary survey
Secondary survey
(Page 4)

Collapsed? Unconscious? → **Resuscitate** ABCDE (Page 2) → **C-spine injury** if unconscious or other injuries present (Page 208)

Treatment and maintenance

- Prolonged immersion (page 49)
- Drowning (page 49)
- Hypothermia (pages 45, 48)
- Trauma (pages 58–117)
- Medical illness (pages 120–84)

Continued monitoring

- Pulse
- Blood pressure
- Respiration rate
- Level of consciousness
- Appearance
- Temperature

WATCH FOR DETERIORATION

Contact TMAS early

18 Immersion and drowning

Cold-water immersion from falling overboard is a constant risk to all those who are at sea in zones of the world where the water temperature is under 28 °C (i.e. the majority of world's seas). Several physiological responses occur in the body following immersion and the casualty's ability to actively cope with them will have a bearing on whether they live or die. If the casualty survives then hypothermia may develop in the ensuing immersion time; this depends upon water temperature and the casualty's fitness level, body build and clothing, and may occur in 15–30 minutes. There are four stages of response to immersion: initial, short-term, long-term and post-immersion (these are explained in more detail below). In addition, a sudden illness (e.g. heart attack) may have caused the crew member to fall over the side, and the event may have also caused injury. These complications will need assessing and treating.

Time from immersion (minutes)	Event	Action
0–3 mins	**Initial response** **Cold shock** • Rapid pulse • Increased blood pressure • Gasping, uncontrolled breathing • Possible inhalation of water	**1** • Don't panic • Escape from entrapment • Inflate lifejacket (manual inflation) • Deploy spray hood • Don't attempt to swim • Hold onto flotsam if possible • Adopt heat escape lessening posture (HELP) position • Wait for cold shock to settle
3–30 mins	**Short-term response** • Manual dexterity impaired • Loss of muscle strength • Body feels numb • Cramps – inability to swim	**2** • Undertake all necessary tasks immediately – Inflate lifejacket – Deploy hood – Fasten clothing – Activate personal EPIRB • Float with back to wind and waves • Do not attempt to swim far
>30 mins	**Long-term response** • Hypothermia • Dehydration • Low pulse and blood pressure • Death if not rescued	**3** • Maintain HELP position • Get as much of the body out of the water as possible on available flotsam • Believe you will be rescued
>60 mins **5** Treatment of drowning ABCDE Page 2	**Post-immersion** • Possibility of deterioration post-rescue • Low blood volume and dehydration • Low pulse rate and blood pressure • Hypothermia • Muscle weakness • Concurrent injury • Psychological stress	**4** • Rescue in horizontal position • Give oxygen if available • Give IV fluids if blood pressure abnormally low • Remove wet clothing and treat hypothermia (page 45) • Treat additional injuries and illnesses • If conscious, administer warm drinks • Handle gently and reassure • Contact TMAS early

Contact TMAS early

Initial response: cold shock (0–3 minutes)

1

Breaths become rapid and gasping, and the fast increase in blood pressure may cause a heart attack or stroke in the vulnerable. Wait for the effects of the sudden immersion to settle, which should happen in a few minutes. Holding onto available flotsam will have a stabilising and reassuring effect.

Short-term response (3–30 minutes)

2

Manual dexterity will become impaired rapidly, so all essential tasks should be completed immediately. The seawater exerts a 'squeeze' on the body, causing dehydration, and the possibility of circulatory collapse on being rescued from the water. Try to get as much of the body out of the water onto flotsam as possible to minimise heat loss. Maintain the HELP position and bunch up close together if with others.

Long-term response (30 minutes and longer)

3

The onset of hypothermia is rapid – more so in colder water – and leads to death if the casualty is not rescued (for treatment see page 48). Believe you will be rescued. However, leave the rescuing to the rescuers and do not attempt to swim any distance.

Post-immersion response (60 minutes and longer)

4

A casualty may collapse at the time of rescue or later on. This is for several reasons:

- loss of hydrostatic support to the lower body, causing circulatory collapse when the casualty is removed from the water
- acute lung injury caused by a significant amount of water entering the lungs
- profound hypothermia
- underlying injury or illness.

The mainstay of treatment is to resuscitate the casualty if they are unconscious (see page 2), treat hypothermia (see page 48) and watch for signs of deterioration. It is vital to check for injuries that may have happened at the same time, and medical illnesses that may have caused the fall. Most importantly, contact TMAS at an early stage.

Treatment of drowning

5

- Carry out ABCDE (see page 2 on resuscitation) immediately (remember any concurrent injury or illness).
- Do not waste time trying to empty water from the lungs.
- Be aware that the casualty may have a lot of water in the stomach and may vomit. If they do, turn them on their side and clear the mouth of vomit to prevent aspiration.
- Remove wet clothing, treat hypothermia and keep them as dry and warm as possible.
- Continue resuscitating until the casualty has a temperature greater than 32 °C, is breathing, medical help arrives, or you are exhausted and cannot continue.
- Any inhaled water will cause an acute lung injury. This may make breathing progressively more difficult over the next 24–48 hours, causing shortness of breath and coughing, a fast respiratory rate and pulse rate, and possible collapse. Give oxygen if available, and urgently evacuate if there is any suspicion of water having entered the lungs.
- In all cases, contact TMAS at an early stage.

19 Heat illnesses

Heat is often an unrecognised hazard, and heat illnesses can be just as dangerous as cold injury and hypothermia.

Tropical environments will increase the risks when crew members are working on deck, and machinery spaces may be hot enough to cause problems at all latitudes. When ventilation and air conditioning systems are not functioning due to failure or maintenance the risks may be greatly increased, particularly for those performing hard physical work in enclosed spaces on board. Also, personnel wearing heavy protective clothing and having to work hard (e.g. firefighting) are more prone to heat illnesses.

However, it is not necessary for the air temperature to be particularly hot; heat illness can be caused by a combination of high humidity (preventing heat loss by sweating), unacclimatised individuals, high work rate and some predisposing factors.

Heat illness is usually preventable, and so safe working practices and a knowledge of who is at risk, and when, are essential. A body core temperature over 40°C is serious.

	Illness	Symptoms/signs	Treatment
Mild heat illness	**Heat cramps** Possibly due to lack of salts	• Usually leg cramps occurring during or after exercise • Casualty may be fit and acclimatised	• Oral rehydration with electrolyte replacement drink • Increase regular salt intake with food while in hot climate
Mild heat illness	**Prickly heat** Blocked, inflamed, infected sweat glands	• Red, raised, itchy spots • On skin usually covered by clothing (hands spared) • May become infected – boils or spots • Reduced sweating due to blocked sweat glands	• Keep skin clean – good hygiene • Keep cool, reduce workload • Relieve itching (loratadine) • Antibiotics may be required to treat infected skin (flucloxacillin)
Mild heat illness	**Heat syncope** Dilated blood vessels reduce brain blood flow	• Sudden fainting on rising from sitting position • May feel lightheaded before • Usually quick recovery	• Recovery position in the shade • Oral rehydration with electrolyte replacement drink • Consider heat exhaustion or heatstroke if no quick recovery
Serious heat illness	**Heat exhaustion** Water and salt loss due to sweating. Water losses may be several litres	• Fatigue, lethargy, weakness • Sweating heavily • Muscle cramps • Rapid pulse • Low blood pressure • Rapid breathing • Low, dark urine output	• Move to cool shade, lay down • Strip off all clothing • Cool with constant wet spray and fanning, to increase evaporation and loss of heat • Oral rehydration with electrolyte replacement drink • A few litres may be required • **Contact TMAS**
Serious heat illness	**Heat stroke** Core temp >40°C Reduced sweating due to high humidity, prickly heat, unacclimatised	• Hot, dry skin • Headache • Nausea, vomiting • Weakness, staggering • Increasing anxiety, confusion, restlessness • Low blood sugar • Fits • Loss of consciousness	• Move to cool shade, lay down • Strip off all clothing • Cool with constant wet spray and fanning to increase evaporation and loss of heat • Ice packs (wrapped in cloths) placed in the axilla and groin • Cool (15–20 °C) IV fluids (see pages 220–1) – 1 l initially. Usually not grossly dehydrated • Measure blood sugar level and correct – often low • **Contact TMAS**

Taking the temperature

Oral temperature readings are likely to be more accurate than those from the rectum or under the armpit. Take great care if the casualty is unconscious. Ear (tympanic) thermometers are increasingly common, easy to use and produce reasonably consistent results.

Severity of hyperthermia

Temperature	Degree of severity	General treatment
>38 °C	Mild hyperthermia	Oral rehydration Keep cool, reduce work
>40 °C	Moderate hyperthermia	Oral rehydration Keep cool, reduce work
>42 °C	Severe hyperthermia	Active cooling (15–20 °C) IV cool fluids Measure blood sugar **Contact TMAS**
>45 °C	Likely death	

Factors increasing the risk of hyperthermia

Personal factors	Dehydration (diarrhoea or menstruation)	Diabetes
	Lack of sleep	Sunburn
	Reduced food intake	Fever, infection
	Alcohol	Old age
	Inappropriate clothing	High body mass index
Environmental factors	Increased air temperature	Increased solar heat
	Increased humidity	Decreased wind speed
Workload	Working at near maximum heart rate for long periods	
Medications	Atropine	Anticholinergics
	Amphetamines	Cocaine
	Antihistamines	Betablockers
	Diuretics	Tricyclic antidepressants
	Prochlorperazine (stemetil)	Theophylline

Prevention

- Identify crew members who are at risk.
- Monitor the work rate of crew members.
- Crew members doing hot work should keep a check on one another to ensure everyone stays well-hydrated.
- Learn to recognise the symptoms early.
- Keep a ready supply of rehydration drinks on deck.
- Encourage crew to take rest breaks away from hot conditions.

Rehydration fluid

It is essential to replace lost salts as well as water. Therefore rehydration should take place using electrolyte replacement drinks. If just water is used on a continual basis, hyponatraemia (low sodium levels in the blood) may occur, causing fits and unconsciousness.

20 Burns

Burns may be caused by the heat from burning gases and flames, very hot liquids, chemicals and electricity. There is plenty of potential for life-threatening burns to occur on a vessel, and commonly there may be other injuries as well. Any significant burn should be recognised as a major injury which affects the whole body. It should be assessed with primary and secondary surveys to ensure that no additional injuries are overlooked (see page 4). The airway may be particularly at risk, especially with fires in enclosed spaces such as the galley, engine room or machinery spaces. The casualty may get worse in the hours after the accident.

The basis of treatment is to stop the burning process as quickly as possible to limit damage. In the case of skin or eye contamination with corrosive chemicals, this requires irrigation of the contaminated area with large amounts of water. After immediate resuscitation of the casualty, appropriate fluid treatment is crucial in reducing the effects of the burn on the rest of the body. The fluid should be of the correct type and quantity.

Approach the casualty safely

- Consider fire/explosion risk
- Turn off electricity supply
- Watch for hot, burning fluids
- Be aware of possible chemical contamination (wear protective clothing)

1

Significant burn

- A burn bigger than palm of hand
- Skin or eyes contaminated with caustic alkalis or strong acids
- Facial burns
- Burns of hands, feet or genitals
- Confined space fire
- Fire with explosion

Collapsed?

Unconscious?

Resuscitate ABCDE
(Page 2)

Airway caution

Signs of airway burn

- Soot in mouth/nose
- Facial burn/blisters
- Hoarse voice
- Noisy breathing

2

Immediate treatment

Stop the destructive burning process in the skin

- Give oxygen if smoke or hot gas inhalation is possible
- Remove burning/hot material (jewellery) from skin
- Cool and wash skin with plenty of cool water
  - Do not use ice on the skin
  - Beware of hypothermia
- If eyes are involved, irrigate copiously (page 81)

Fluid resuscitation

Use fluid resuscitation formula in burns on more than 10% of body surface area

- Fluid resuscitation formula: 4 ml × body weight (kg) × % full-thickness burn over 24 hours
- Give half this amount of Ringer's lactate in the first 8 hours after the time of the accident
- Preferably IV or possibly oral route (if conscious)
- Monitor urine output (30 ml/hour minimum)

3

Dressings and pain relief

Burns are very painful, particularly if partial thickness, and are at risk from infection

- Dress burns to keep sterile and limit fluid loss:
  - Clingfilm
  - Paraffin gauze dressing
  - Silver sulfadiazine cream (not on face)
- Do not burst or remove blisters
- Paracetamol for pain
- Add NSAIDS and morphine as required
- Give anti-sickness medication (e.g. cyclizine)

4

Contact TMAS early

History

- Try to find out exactly what happened as soon as possible. This may give some idea as to the severity of the injury.
- Try to find out exactly when the accident happened (it may be obvious), as this will guide fluid resuscitation.
- More severe burns are likely:
  - if there has been prolonged exposure
  - in enclosed spaces
  - if the casualty has been unconscious for any period
  - if there has been an explosion
  - if there are petrol burns
  - if there are strong alkalis such as caustic soda.

Examination: assessment of burns – area, type and significance

1

Burn area

- The area of a burn is estimated as a percentage of the body surface area (BSA).
- The area of full-thickness burn should be estimated as this type causes more fluid loss and more significant complications.
- Larger burn areas cause more complications.

The area of full-thickness burn is frequently underestimated

- Mildly reddened skin may become an obvious full-thickness burn during the hours following the accident.

Keep monitoring and reassess the type and area of burn

- It is important to know the area of full-thickness burn. There are various ways of estimating it:
  - For small burns, the area can be estimated by assuming that the area of the casualty's palm is 1% of body surface area (BSA), and then 'mapping' the area of burn.
  - For larger burns, there is the 'rule of nines'. This assumes that each region of the body is approximately 9% BSA.

Recognising the type of burn

Type of burn	Characteristics
Superficial burn	Reddened skin, similar to sunburn. This is painful and tender to touch.
Partial-thickness (PT) burn	Blistered skin, with red, healthy soft tissue underneath the blisters. This is very painful and tender as all the nerve endings are still intact.
Full-thickness (FT) burn	Pale, leathery area, burnt through to the underlying layers. It may be charred, involving structures such as muscle, tendon and bone. This tends not to be painful as all the skin nerve endings have been destroyed. The area around the FT burn may be very painful.

Significant burns

- Burns to particular regions of the body, even if they are not large areas, are very significant because of immediate and longer-term complications.
- Particular regions of the body include the following:
  - face (see next page for assessment) and eyes
  - hands
  - feet
  - genitals.

With burns of these types, contact TMAS immediately

Rule of nines

- Each region of the body (arm, front of leg, back of leg, front of chest, back of chest) counts as 9% BSA (see diagram below).
- Count obvious FT burns and blistered skin. Exclude reddened skin, but monitor it as these areas may progress to FT burns and will need including in the total area.

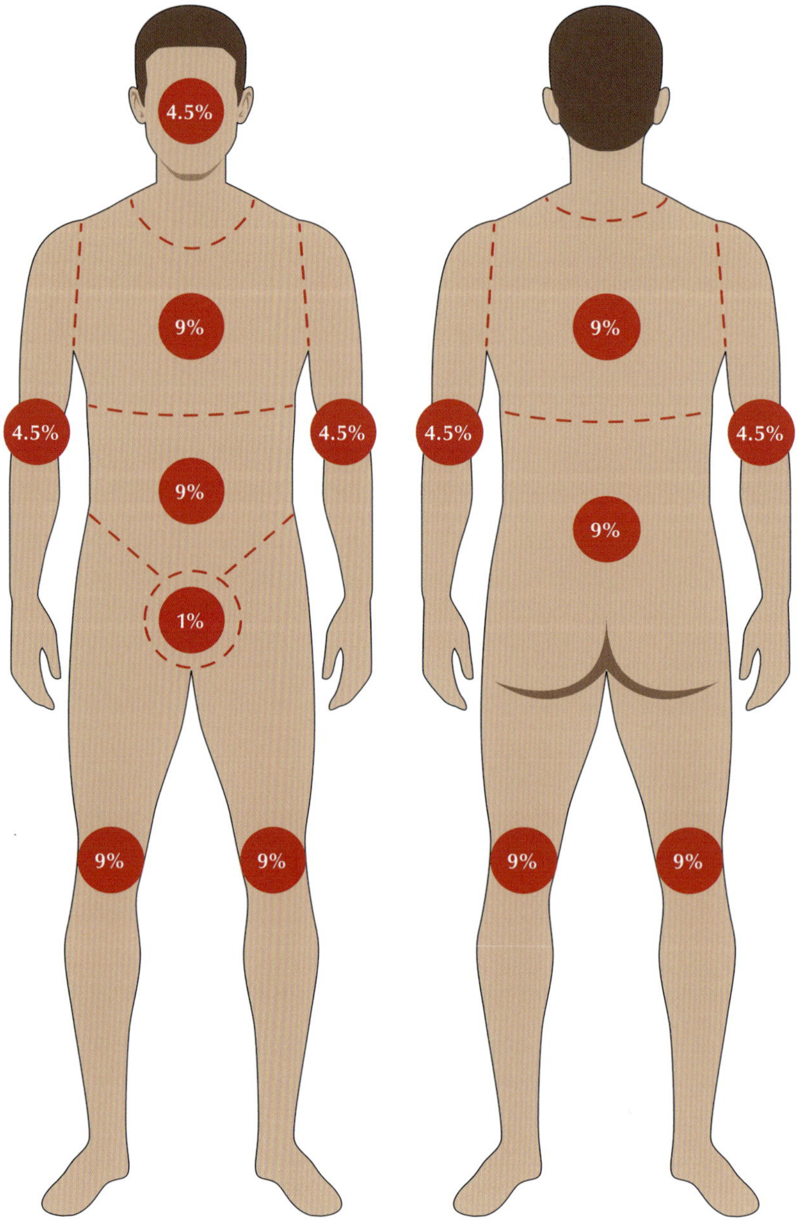

Risks to the airway

2

- The airway is always at risk from significant burns.

The danger to the airway may not be obvious at first

- The burn could become life-threatening as tissue swelling gets worse in the hours after the accident.

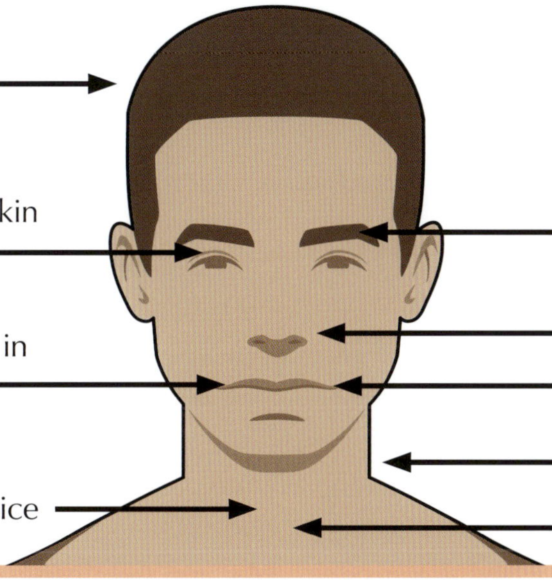

If any of these signs are present, contact TMAS immediately
Prepare to evacuate the casualty without delay

The outlook is very grim if the casualty starts to have difficulty breathing; the only treatment possible on a vessel is to give oxygen, if it is available. Keep the casualty sitting upright for as long as possible to minimise swelling. Resuscitation should be attempted if the casualty collapses, but it is unlikely to be successful.

Intubation or creation of an airway by surgery should be attempted **only** by those who are trained and experienced in the techniques.

Fluid resuscitation

3

- Any FT or PT burn over 10% BSA may need fluid resuscitation. Give IV fluid if the casualty is unconscious. If they are fully conscious, oral rehydration may be acceptable.
- Get IV access in an unburnt part as soon as possible (see page 224).
- The formula for fluid resuscitation is given here:

4 ml × % BSA FT burn × weight (kg)

- Give half this amount in the first 8 hours following the accident.
- Give the remaining half over the next 16 hours.
- Use IV fluid or electrolyte replacement fluid orally if casualty is conscious.

- This is only a guide and the casualty should be reassessed frequently.
- Monitor the casualty's urine output:
  - There should be a minimum of 30 ml urine per hour.
  - If urine output is less than this give a fluid bolus of 250 ml.
  - Put in a urinary catheter if necessary.
- Fluid resuscitation may have to continue for 36 hours or more.

If you are fluid-resuscitating, you must contact TMAS

You need to know:

- what complications may happen
- when to stop.

See page 224 for further information on fluid resuscitation.

Cleaning and dressing burns

Burn dressing should be done using sterile precautions (see page 212, minor operative set-up).

- Burns cause loss of fluid from the body and readily become infected. The dressings reduce this risk.
- Non-adherent material should be removed from the burn area.
- Replace dressings every 2–3 days according to state of burn.
- Burnt hands and feet can be coated in silver sulfadiazine cream and put in plastic bags.
- Genitals and face can be coated in petroleum jelly and not dressed.
- Do not remove blisters as they are excellent sterile dressings.
- Elevate affected areas as much as possible to reduce swelling.
- Use antibiotics if there are signs of infection (see Antibiotics guide, back flyleaf).

Dressings for burns

Dressing	How to use
Clingfilm	Take the exposed part off the roll first, then use the next part for dressing. Do not wind it tightly but just lay it on
Paraffin gauze	A paraffin-impregnated dressing for immediate emergency use. Put a sterile gauze dressing over the top to hold it in place
Silver sulfadiazine	An antiseptic cream used to prevent infection and fluid loss. Do not use it on the face as it may cause grey colouring of the skin
Hydrocolloid	Hold in water and can stay in place for a few days. They can be used for awkward areas
Petroleum jelly	Can be used in an emergency for difficult areas to dress (e.g. face or genitals)
Honey	If nothing else is available, spread honey on pieces of gauze, work it in, and use the gauze as dressings for the burn

Part 2
Trauma

1 Wounds and bleeding

Injuries causing wounds are very common on board vessels. The ability to treat them rapidly and competently is crucial to minimise complications. Measures taken to stem bleeding will stop a drama becoming a crisis.

Dealing with simple injuries and moderate bleeding on a vessel is relatively straightforward, and should be within the capability of the master and medical officer. A structured approach, together with knowledge of how to prevent complications, should give the best chance of success.

Type of injury → **1**

- Laceration/cut
- Abrasion
- Bruising
- High-pressure injection injury
- Bite
- Penetrating
- Amputation

2 Assess severity

- History
- Examination

Collapsed? Unconscious? → **Resuscitate** ABCDE (page 2)

Control of bleeding
Rapidly, to limit overall blood loss → **3**

- Direct wound pressure
- Side wound pressure
- Elevation
- Tourniquet
- Haemostatic agents

Wound cleaning
Thoroughly, sterile, under good light →

- Clean gently
- Wash/irrigate sterile wash
- Remove foreign bodies
- Inspect closely
- Chlorhexidine antiseptic solution wash
- Sterile non-stick dressing

Wound closure
Close ideally within 12 hours → **4**

- Skin glue
- Adhesive wound closure strips (if skin dry)
- Staples (dedicated staple gun)
- Sutures (absorbable/non-absorbable)

Complications
Redress/inspect wound every 24–36 hours → **5**

- Infection
- Bleeding
- Foreign bodies
- Abscess formation
- Non-healing
- Involvement of deep structures:
  - Blood vessels
  - Nerves
  - Tendons
  - Internal organs
  - Bone

6 Further treatment
Pain relief
Antibiotics
Tetanus treatment

Type of injury

1

Cuts and lacerations Cuts are caused by sharp objects (e.g. knives or glass), are usually clean-edged and heal well. Lacerations are caused by blunt objects. They are more ragged, harder to repair, and more prone to infection.

Abrasions Small abrasions (grazes) occur commonly and require simple cleaning. Severe abrasions may result in considerable tissue loss and require surgery when ashore. These should be cleaned thoroughly to prevent dirt causing a permanent 'tattoo' mark. Antibiotics should be used if significant tissue loss has occurred.

Bruising A bruise (haematoma) may appear innocuous, but a collection of blood in the tissues may become infected, causing an abscess, which requires draining. Watch for signs of infection (see page 238).

Bites These may be by humans or animals. They require very thorough cleaning and should always be treated with antibiotics. They are very prone to infection.

Penetrating wounds (including those from projectiles such as bullets) These are very difficult to assess on a vessel, but injury to organs, bones, tendons, nerves and blood vessels underlying the wound is a likely complication. The casualty requires close observation; contact TMAS at the first opportunity.

Amputations Traumatic amputations of fingers and toes on vessels are common. The casualty should be prepared for evacuation as soon as possible, with the amputated digit being kept cool (not frozen). Again, contact TMAS as soon as possible. Traumatic amputation of a limb is life-threatening and a medical emergency.

Crush injuries Crush injuries can be life- or limb-threatening, depending on the forces involved and duration of compression. Tissues (muscle and nerves) may be permanently damaged even if there is no bony injury or obvious wound. Contact TMAS as soon as possible.

High-pressure injection injuries These are injuries caused by high-pressure grease guns, hydraulic oil and other hydrocarbons, paint, solvents, water and gases such as air and oxygen. All these injuries can be limb- and life-threatening. The penetration wound may not look serious but the internal damage can be very extensive. Hydrocarbons and solvents are particularly toxic and urgent surgical intervention is often required to prevent loss of limb or life. Contact TMAS immediately.

Assess the severity

2

History The mechanism of injury may give an idea of the extent and severity of the injury.

Examination Do this in a well-lit, secure place where you can take your time, and be thorough. Proper examination of a penetrating wound at sea is impossible, but try to examine right to the bottom of any wound for contamination. Use a local anaesthetic (see page 214).

Important points in the history

- How did the accident happen? (e.g. knife, glass; energy involved)
- When and where did it happen?
- Was the casualty crushed at all?
- Is there risk of contamination? (seawater is **not** sterile)
- Who else was involved?
- Last tetanus vaccination?

Important points in the examination

- Size and shape of wound
- Contamination and foreign bodies
- Presence of pulses beyond injury
- Signs of nerve damage:
  - Lack of sensation
  - Lack of movement
- Signs of infection:
  - Redness around the wound
  - Painful swelling
  - Swollen lymph nodes in groin, armpit
  - Lymphangitis (red streaks spreading up the arm)

Control of bleeding

3

- Bleeding must be limited or stopped as quickly as possible.
- Bleeding from a vein may be profuse but it can be controlled by raising the limb above the heart.
- Bleeding from an artery may be a pulsatile spurting and needs direct pressure to the wound, or pressure on each side if direct pressure is too painful.
- Use tourniquets only if direct pressure does not work. Perfusion to the distal part of the limb may be dangerously reduced, but this may be necessary if bleeding cannot be controlled otherwise.
- Haemostatic agents (such as gauze impregnated with the agent, or the agent in the form of granules or tranexamic acid IM/IV/IO injection) can be used. Also, strips of gauze soaked in tranexamic acid may reduce bleeding from the nose or tooth sockets. Contact TMAS as soon as possible.

Wound closure (see pages 230–3)

4

- Ideally wounds should be closed within 12–24 hours.
- Wound closure is an effective way of reducing blood loss.
- Wounds of less than 1 cm usually will not require formal closure but a good dressing is needed.
- With larger wounds the principle of closure is to bring and keep the opposing edges together, thus allowing healing to occur.
- A good and quick way to close a wound is to use glue or adhesive wound closure strips. For these techniques to be effective the skin needs to be dry.
- If the wound is under tension and will not stay together with glue or adhesive wound closure use strips, staples or sutures (if possible).
- Absorbable sutures are usually used to close deep layers of tissue below the skin layer. Either non-absorbable or absorbable sutures can be used to close the skin.
- Skin staples from a dedicated skin stapler are rapid to apply, good for damp skin, but require a specialised staple extractor for removal.
- All wounds must be kept clean and dry, and kept covered with a sterile dressing. Inspect for signs of infection every 24–36 hours and more often if there is increasing pain or spreading redness.
- If there is a substantial amount of tissue loss it may be impossible to close a wound. Contact TMAS for advice in these circumstances.

- Healing will be improved, especially of large wounds, if the limb is immobilised to prevent stretching of the skin repair. The casualty should rest as much as possible.

Complications

5

- Infection is likely so wounds should be inspected every 24–36 hours and redressed with a sterile dressing. Any infection should be treated with antibiotics as soon as it is suspected.
- Infection may lead to reoccurrence of bleeding a few days after the initial accident. Thorough cleaning of the infected tissue (under local anaesthetic, which may be only partially effective) is necessary. Contact TMAS if this occurs.
- Foreign bodies (e.g. dirt or grit) may lead to infection if they are not removed initially. They may also cause 'tattooing' of the skin once the wound has healed.
- Damage to structures below the skin may cause a wide variety of complications. If there is ongoing pain, loss of movement or sensation, or bleeding, contact TMAS for advice regarding further treatment, particularly for penetrating wounds anywhere on the body.

Further treatment

6

- Antibiotics are always indicated for:
  - Heavily contaminated wounds
  - Any form of bite
  - Traumatic amputation
  - Fractures where the bone comes through the skin
  - Wounds that become infected.

- Pain relief is essential and should be given as soon as is practicable.
- Local anaesthetic injection (infiltration; see page 214) around the wound will help proper examination and repair.
- Check that the casualty's tetanus vaccination is up to date; if not discuss with TMAS.
- In the event of an animal bite, always consider the possibility of rabies infection and the need for post-exposure vaccination.

2 Head injuries

Minor head injuries are common on vessels and recovery is reasonably quick and complete. Serious head injuries are rarer and are usually devastating, requiring urgent medical attention and evacuation of the casualty. The risk of injury is greater on a small vessel travelling at high speed. The most important piece of advice regarding head injuries is **to avoid them**.

Brain tissue can be permanently damaged or die if blood flow is interrupted for a few minutes. Once a head injury has occurred prompt and appropriate treatment may reduce its severity and prevent further deterioration of the brain due to lack of blood pressure or oxygen (secondary injury)

1 **Assess severity**
- History
- Examination

Collapsed? Unconscious? → **Resuscitate ABCDE** (Page 2) → **C-spine injury** 2

Signs of severe head injury → 3
- Reduced level of consciousness
- Dilated or uneven pupils
- Clear fluid from ears or nose
- Blood from ears
- Prolonged memory loss

Treatment
- Urgent - the brain dies quickly

→ 4
- ABCDE (oxygen if available)
- Immobilise on padded spinal board or scoop stretcher
- Establish IV access if possible (page 224)
- **Check for other injuries**
- Repair scalp lacerations
- Antibiotics, pain relief
- Keep head up at a 30° angle
- Loosen any restrictions around neck
- Insert NG tube only if advised to do so by TMAS and sure there is no basal skull fracture

Complications → 5
- Prolonged unconsciousness
- Seizures
- New neurological symptoms
- Headaches
- Infection
- Memory loss
- Vertigo

Assessment of severity →
- AVPU/GCS
- Respiratory rate
- Pulse
- Temperature
- Blood pressure
- Urine output

WATCH FOR DETERIORATION

6 **Minor head injury**
- Symptoms
- Treatment

Avoidance is the best treatment
- Be aware how fast the vessel is travelling
- Be aware when undertaking work tasks that may incur risk, such as working at height

Contact TMAS early

History and examination

1

- ABCDE takes priority (see page 4).
- **Take particular care of the neck** (see 'Cervical spine (neck) injury' below).
- It is reassuring if the casualty is conscious, **but they may deteriorate**.
- Get as much information as possible from other crew members.

Important points in the history

- How did the accident happen (mechanism of injury)?
- Was there loss of consciousness (and for how long)?
- Does the casualty have any loss of memory (amnesia) and for how long?
- Has the casualty vomited, or do they feel sick?
- Were there any signs of fitting?
- Does the casualty have double vision?

Important points in the examination

- Level of consciousness (see below)
- Size and reactivity of pupils to light (see below)
- Weakness or paralysis of face or limbs
- Heart rate, blood pressure, respiratory rate.

Part 2

Cervical spine (neck) injury

2

Spinal injuries are common when a head injury has happened.

The bones of the neck may be broken and be unstable, but the spinal cord may still be intact.

If in doubt, immobilise the cervical spine (c-spine) with three-point immobilisation (see diagram).

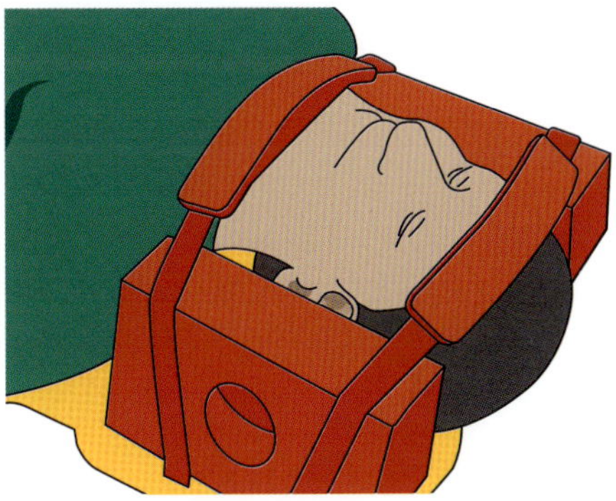

Cervical spine immobilisation

See page 208

Signs of severe head injury

3

Level of consciousness

- In general, the more extreme the depth of unconsciousness, the worse the head injury.
- A casualty may initially appear to be conscious after an injury, but may deteriorate. Therefore, monitor their level of consciousness frequently.
- Initial rapid assessment: AVPU → (page 196)
- More detailed assessment: Glasgow Coma Scale → (page 196)

- If the casualty is less than 'alert' on the AVPU scale, assess them using the Glasgow Coma Scale (GCS; see table below).
- Reassess them every 15 minutes for at least the first few hours.

The Glasgow Coma Scale

GCS	Meaning
9–12	Possible significant head injury
8 or less	Serious head injury
A reduction in score of 2 or more	**A serious deterioration. Contact TMAS**

Appearance of pupils

- Pupils should normally be equal and reactive to light.
- A head injury may cause the pupils to be:
  - unequal in size
  - unreactive to light
  - dilated and unreactive.

Pupil size, response to light and likely cause

Pupil size	Pupil response to light	Likely cause
 **Both pupils equally dilated**	Responsive equally	Fear, alcohol, drugs such as cocaine
 **Both pupils equally constricted**	Responsive equally	Bright light, drugs such as opiates or benzodiazepines
 **Pupils uneven**	Larger pupil unresponsive	Head injury, injury to eye or direct contamination of eye with drugs
 **Both pupils equally dilated**	Both pupils unresponsive	Severe head injury

Cerebrospinal fluid or blood from the ears

- Cerebrospinal fluid (CSF) is clear and can be confused with tears or nasal or mouth secretions. Bear this in mind when you see clear fluid around the head. Blood in the ears may have come from inside the skull, but also may have run into the ears from scalp or facial wounds.
- If you are in any doubt assume the fluid is CSF, and assume that fluid in the ears has come from inside the skull until proven otherwise.

Prolonged post-traumatic amnesia

- A short period of memory loss (amnesia) after an injury to the head is quite common.
- A period of memory loss greater than 30 minutes (prolonged post-traumatic amnesia; PTA) indicates a significant head injury.

Treatment

4

Contact TMAS. They will advise whether a casualty who has a suspected head injury should be evacuated as soon as possible.

Treatment on a vessel remote from land is aimed at preventing secondary injury (see below). Once the casualty has been assessed for ABCDE, and given oxygen if available, immobilise them as securely as possible to protect them from secondary injury due to potential spinal fractures. This could be achieved by using a padded rigid board; the padding is to prevent pressure sores. Limit time on a rigid board to two hours or less if possible. It is important to look for other injuries (the secondary survey; see page 6):

- **A casualty who is head-injured and shocked is likely to have another injury.**
- Scalp lacerations bleed heavily and a lot of blood may be lost in a short time. Repair them as quickly as possible by suturing, stapling or gluing.
- IV fluids (if possible) may be required to restore blood pressure to normal.
- The patient should be kept head-up, if possible, by tilting the rigid board. Remove any tight restrictions around the neck. These manoeuvres help to reduce the pressure in the brain.
- **Insert a nasogastric tube only if advised to do so by TMAS and if there are no signs of a basal skull fracture (i.e. black eyes, blood or CSF from ears or nose) as the tube may end up in the brain (page 216).**
- Avoid giving morphine or tramadol to head-injured patients. If they are conscious regular paracetamol and codeine may be used and should not reduce their level of consciousness.
- Give antibiotics if there is suspicion of a skull fracture.

Complications

5

TMAS should have been contacted by this stage, and MUST be contacted again if there are any signs of complications:

- Managing an unconscious casualty for a prolonged period on board a vessel is a complex and difficult task. The process is described on pages 12–14.
- Seizures are common after relatively minor head injuries. The fits should stop by themselves after a minute or so. Recurrent or prolonged fitting (more than 1–2 minutes) is much more worrying and should be treated (see pages 16–17).
- Any sign of deterioration in the casualty's conscious level, or new signs of paralysis of the face or one side of the body, are ominous signs and the casualty must be evacuated urgently.
- Persistent vomiting is a danger sign. It is likely to indicate that the pressure within the skull is raised.
- Signs of infection (high temperature, flushed, signs of meningism (see page 122) are very serious and IV antibiotics should be used (see Antibiotics guide, back flyleaf).
- Headaches should be treated with non-sedating painkillers if possible. Worsening of the headache may indicate worsening of the head injury, so contact TMAS immediately.
- Lack of coordination is a danger sign; for example, difficulty in balancing or dropping cups.
- Vertigo is common after a head injury and can be treated with prochlorperazine or cyclizine.

Minor head injuries/Concussion

6

The usual definition of a minor head injury is where the period of unconsciousness is less than 1 minute. However, this diminishes the problems that can arise from a seemingly minor blow to the head from a fall, or blow from a fast-moving object (e.g. machinery arms or lifting gear).

Everyone who has had any blow to the head needs to be assessed for their level of responsiveness, mental agility and coordination/balance.

Immediate visible signs of concussion may be:

- Loss of consciousness or responsiveness
- Slow to get up
- Unsteady on feet/balance problems/ incoordination
- Grabbing/clutching of head
- Dazed, blank or vacant look
- Vomiting.

Immediate symptoms of concussion may be:

- Headache
- Irritability
- Constantly repeating the same phrases or questions
- Poor balance
- Dizziness
- Visual disturbance
- Feeling 'in a fog'
- Memory problems (e.g. time of day/where they are/what they were doing).

If anyone is showing any of these signs or symptoms they need to be allowed to rest in a quiet area and be given simple analgesia (e.g. paracetamol). They should be reassessed after 1 hour. If there is any worsening of the signs or symptoms call TMAS.

Concussion may develop over 24 hours, even if there are no immediate signs, and may persist for up to 14 days. Returning to normal activities too quickly may exacerbate them and prolong the recovery.

Typical symptoms are:

- Headaches
- Irritability
- Poor balance
- Feelings of dizziness
- Difficulty concentrating
- Sleep disturbance
- Fatigue
- Restlessness
- Nausea
- Impulsivity and self-control problems
- Sensitivity to light
- Sensitivity to noise
- Feeling depressed, tearful, anxious
- Memory problems
- Difficulties thinking/problem solving
- Feeling 'in a fog'.

Treatment involves rest for the first 24 hours and then a gradual return to activities and work. This is particularly pertinent to safety-critical roles, highly physical activity or using computer screens (for work or leisure). If doing any activity makes the symptoms worse, it should be stopped.

Simple analgesia (paracetamol) for headaches can be used and prochlorperazine or cyclizine can help with dizziness. Alcohol and other stimulants must be avoided.

If symptoms persist or worsen, call TMAS.

Treatment

- Give non-sedating painkillers for headache.
- Advise the casualty to rest for a few days as necessary, avoiding activities that are strenuous or involve concentration, such as using a computer screen.
- The casualty must avoid alcohol.
- Watch for deterioration in their conscious level or vital signs. Give prochlorperazine or cyclizine for dizziness if it is severe.

Outlook

Symptoms should only last a few days at the most. Contact TMAS if they persist longer than this.

Types of head injury

The type of head injury will depend on its cause. Injuries are closed, open, primary or secondary (see diagram).

Closed

This is the commonest type of head injury. The skull is not fractured (or there is only a minor fracture) and the brain is not exposed. This type of injury is usually caused by a blunt blow to the head, such as happens during a fall down stairs.

Open

Open injuries are less common than closed ones, and usually more serious. The brain is exposed, which may be obvious to the untrained eye, but may be difficult to assess with a basal skull fracture (see page 62). This type of injury is usually caused by sharp objects or small, blunt objects (e.g. stanchions). There is a high risk of infection. There are three types of open head injury:

- **Penetrating** With a sharp object such as a marlin spike, going through the skull into the brain
- **Compound depressed skull fracture** Caused by a small, solid object such as by collision with a stanchion top, pushing a bit of the skull bone into the brain
- **Basal skull fracture** Where there is a fracture running across the base of the skull, opening up a communication between the inside of the skull and the ears or nose.

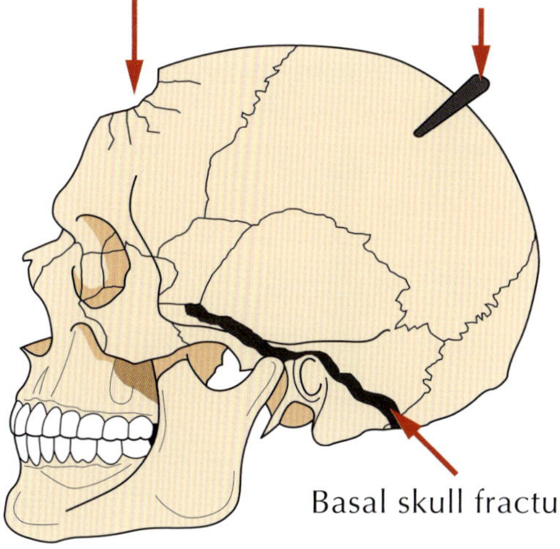

Open head injuries

Primary

A primary injury means the direct result of the blow to the head; for example, a skull fracture, damage to the brain tissue itself or bleeding in the brain.

Secondary

Following a primary injury, there may be deterioration of the brain due to lack of blood flow or oxygen; this is a secondary injury. Although resources on a vessel may be limited, a few straightforward actions may reduce the severity of a secondary injury:

- Maintain blood pressure as near to normal as possible
- Maintain good oxygen saturation
- Keep casualty head up at 30 degrees
- Ensure there are no tight collars or other restrictions around the casualty's neck.

3 Neck and spinal injuries

Spinal injuries are fortunately rare on board, but strains and sprains to the back are much more common. Very occasionally, what looks like a minor back or neck injury is in fact very serious, so if there is any doubt immobilise the casualty until medical advice has been obtained from TMAS. Damage to the spinal cord is devastating and usually irreversible, so make every effort to ensure an existing injury is not made worse, or an unstable spine accidentally damaged by moving a casualty without spinal immobilisation.

The mechanism of the accident gives an indication of the possibility of severe spinal injury. The severity of injury is likely to be greater if more energy is involved (e.g. if a casualty falls from a height or is hit by swinging lifting gear) but seemingly innocuous accidents can still cause fractures of the spine.

Caution is the watchword.

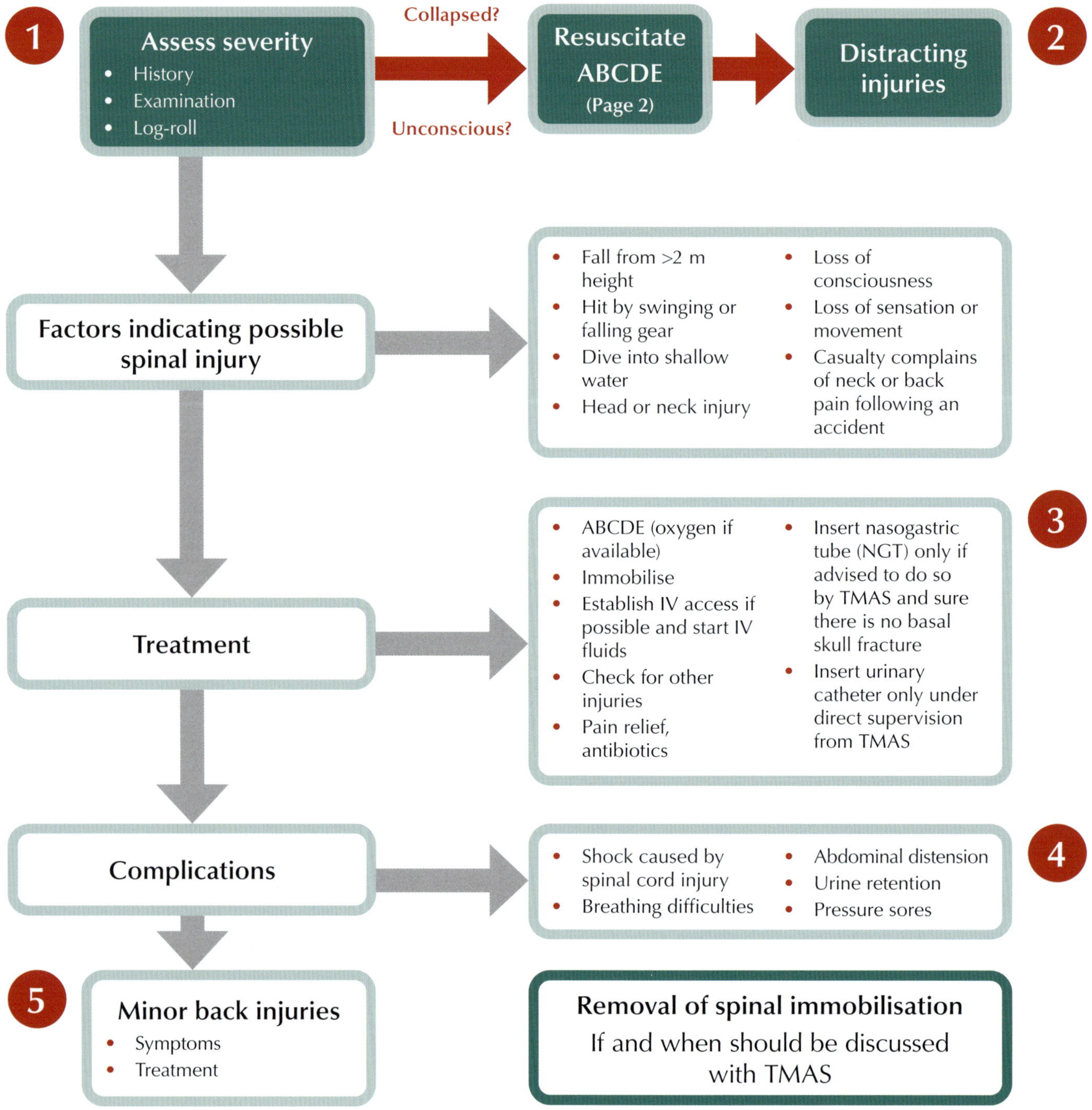

Contact TMAS early

History and examination

1

- ABCDE takes priority.
- A casualty with a head injury may also have a spinal injury.
- A proper examination will require a log-roll (see page 204), which requires three people to turn the casualty and one to examine the back.

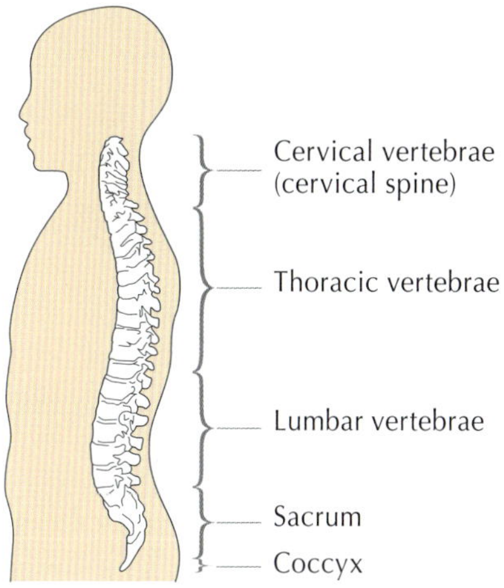

Parts of the spine

Important points in the history

- How did the accident happen (mechanism of injury)?
- Where is the pain?
- Are there any symptoms of nerve damage:
  - Numbness?
  - Pins and needles?
  - Loss of movement?
- Any previous history of back pain or injuries?

Important points in the examination

- **Look** Obvious injuries to head, neck, spine, swelling, bruising, steps in spine
- **Feel** Bony tenderness, steps in spine, can the casualty feel touch or pain?
- **Move** Let the patient move their own body and limbs. Do not move the neck if real suspicion of neck injury
- **Document** Tone, power, sensation for all limbs, and the main body

Cervical spine (neck) injury

Spinal injuries are common when a head injury has happened.

The bones of the neck may be broken and be unstable, but the spinal cord may still be intact.

If in doubt, immobilise the cervical spine (c-spine) with three-point immobilisation (see diagram).

Application of hard cervical collars used to be advised at this time to help immobilise the cervical spine. This is no longer considered appropriate first-line treatment.

Cervical spine immobilisation

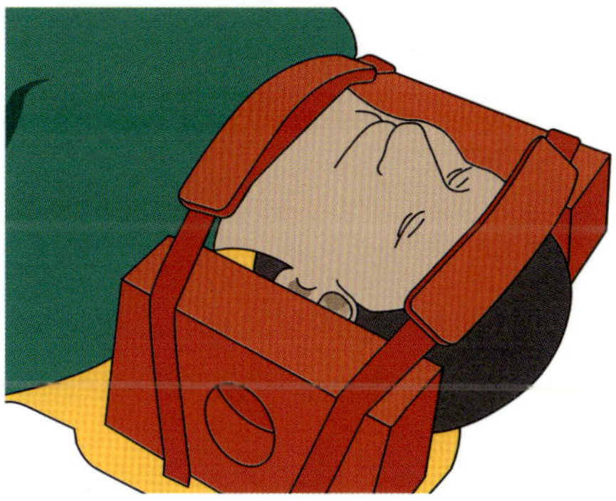

See page 208

Distracting injuries

2

Obvious external injuries, such as a broken leg, or a large laceration losing blood, or the effects of drugs such as alcohol, may distract the casualty and you from a serious spinal injury. Be aware of this, and deal with the casualty according to ABCDE (see page 4).

Treatment

3

- **Evacuation**
  A casualty with a suspected spinal injury should be evacuated as soon as possible.
- **Immobilisation** (see page 208)
  The whole body must be immobilised in the best way possible, with a neck collar, if required, on a padded board. Use a foam mat or layers of cloth if nothing else is available. Use the board for transportation, but aim not to keep a casualty on one for more than two hours if possible.
- **Intravenous access and fluid (if possible)**
  With severe spinal injuries with spinal cord involvement, blood pressure may fall and IV fluids may be necessary.
- **NGT and urinary catheter** **(see pages 216–19)**
  An immobilised patient can be fed and kept hydrated by an NGT and will need a urinary catheter to pass urine, especially if there is spinal cord damage. Insert these only under direct supervision from TMAS.
- **Pain relief and antibiotics**
  Adequate pain relief will settle the casualty, especially if they are immobilised. Give antibiotics if there is any open wound.

Complications

4

- Blood pressure may be low due to blood loss caused by other injuries, or blood vessels may be relaxed due to spinal cord damage. Get advice from TMAS to guide how much fluid to give.
- If the spinal cord injury is high in the chest or in the neck the casualty may not be able to breathe properly. This is ominous. Give oxygen if available, and follow ABC if the patient stops breathing.
- The gut may stop working and the casualty may vomit. Consult TMAS before inserting an NGT. Once the NGT is in place, aspirate all the stomach contents to reduce this risk.
- The casualty may not be able to pass urine and may require a urinary catheter.
- Pressure sores quickly develop on a spinal board, especially if the casualty has low blood pressure. Try to limit the time they are fully immobilised on a hard board.

Minor back injuries

5

Symptoms and signs

- Localised pain
- Pain felt down the leg (sciatica)
- Stiffness
- Muscle spasm
- Abnormal posture
- Worse on straining or coughing

Treatment

- Pain relief to allow mobilisation, preventing stiffness
- Casualty may need to rest in bed if they have sciatica
- Exercises to strengthen back to prevent further injury
- Care with posture when doing physically demanding tasks

4 Facial injuries

Facial injuries are caused by falls and collisions with objects while crew members are living and working on a moving vessel, and trips ashore when in port. They may look bad, but once blood is cleaned up and lacerations repaired, they often turn out to be quite minor.

The face is a complex structure, and bony injuries may be difficult to detect. The immediate risk with facial fractures is danger to the airway, the loss of which results in death within minutes; various manoeuvres will minimise this risk. A less obvious danger is the swelling that may follow a facial injury; this may compromise the airway hours after the initial injury. In addition, vision may be affected by fractures to the orbit.

Other injuries, particularly to the head and neck, often happen at the same time, so the ABCDE approach to assessing the casualty is essential.

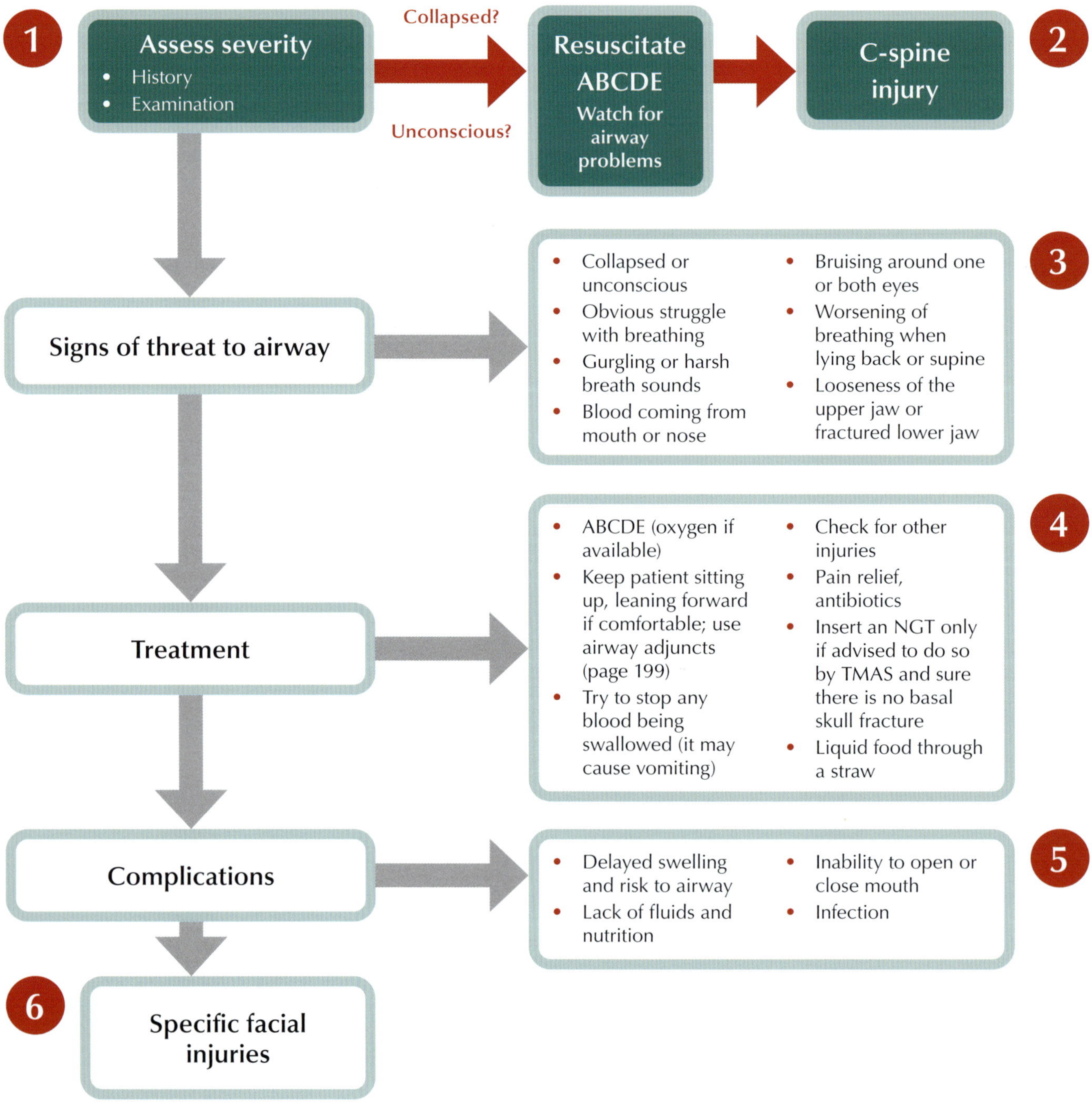

Contact TMAS early

History and examination

1

- Anyone with a facial injury may have other injuries, particularly of the head and neck.
- It may not be easy to get a good account of what happened from the casualty if they have been hit hard in the face, so get as much information as possible from witnesses.

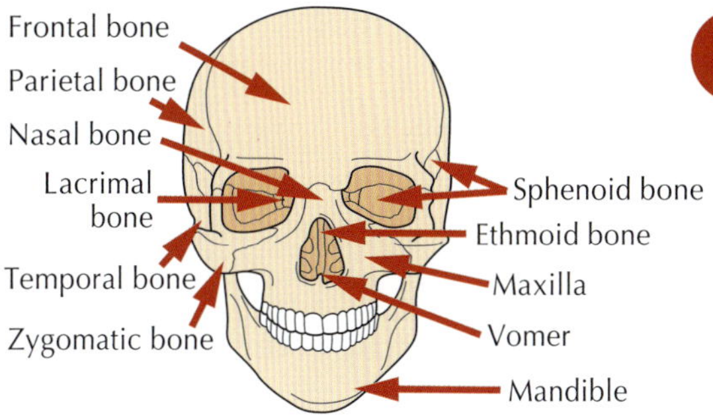

Bones of the face

Important points in the history

- How did the accident happen (mechanism of injury)?
- Was there any loss of consciousness (and for how long)?
- Any difficulty breathing?
- Any problems with vision (e.g. double vision)?

Important points in the examination

- **Look** Obvious injuries to face, deformed nose, swellings or blood
- **Feel** Tenderness over cheeks, jaw, steps in bone edges, crepitus
- **Move** Ask casualty to open and close mouth. Do the teeth line up? Is the upper jaw loose?

Cervical spine (neck) injury

2

Spinal injuries are common when a head injury has happened.

The bones of the neck may be broken and be unstable, but the spinal cord may still be intact.

If in doubt, immobilise the cervical spine (c-spine) with three-point immobilisation (see diagram).

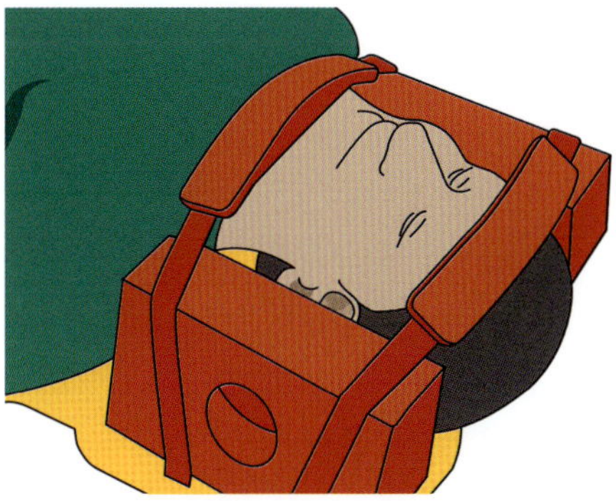

Cervical spine immobilisation

See page 208

Signs of threat to airway

3

Any fracture to the middle of the face or jaw (mandible) is a possible risk to the airway, because the fractured bit of face or jaw may fall back into the airway and partially or entirely block it.

The casualty may be obviously struggling, and making harsh or gurgling sounds when breathing in. Other signs such as pain, swelling, two (i.e. bilateral) black eyes and blood from the mouth are also caused by facial fractures.

If the casualty is conscious, they will be able to describe their problems with breathing, and indicate whether sitting up and leaning forward eases the difficulties. Being upright and leaning forward helps to clear the airway by allowing the broken part of the face or jaw 'hang forward', clearing the airway (see diagram).

A fracture through the mid-part of the face above the upper jaw (through the maxilla) may result in the upper jaw being 'loose'. Test this by firmly holding the upper front teeth with the fingers and gently trying to move the upper jaw in and out. Do this only once, as repeated tests will cause pain, bleeding and further swelling.

Treatment

4

- **A casualty with a suspected facial fracture should be evacuated as soon as possible; call TMAS to discuss.**
- If the patient is conscious, but having difficulty with their airway, try to keep them sitting up and leaning forward, as shown in the diagram.

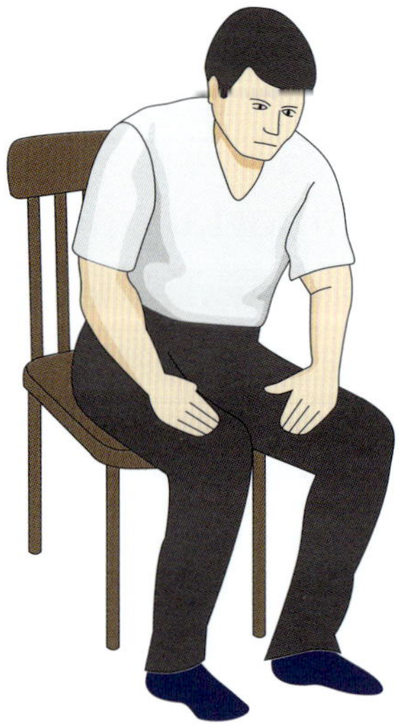

- If the patient is unconscious, lay them in the recovery position if you are confident there are no spinal injuries (see page 204).
- An airway adjunct (oropharyngeal airway; see page 199) may be needed, but insert it very gently. Only insert a nasopharyngeal airway if advised to do so by TMAS. It is essential to be certain there is no basal skull or mid-face fracture.
- Either drain blood from the mouth with the casualty in the recovery position or use suction to remove it, if available. Blood in the stomach is a strong stimulus for vomiting, which may end up in the lungs.
- Fractures are painful, so use non-sedating pain relief (paracetamol, NSAIDs) as required. NSAIDs may help in reducing swelling.
- Insert an NGT only if you are advised to do so by TMAS and you are sure there is no basal skull or mid-face fracture.
- Swallowing or chewing may be painful and difficult. It may be impossible to close the mouth. Liquid food through an NGT or straw may be required.
- Use antibiotics if there are any lacerations, continual blood in the mouth, or if the casualty develops a raised temperature.

Complications

5

- Swelling as a result of a fracture may continue to worsen for a few days after the initial injury. Contact TMAS if there is any doubt regarding the airway, and prepare to evacuate the casualty as soon as possible.
- If oral fluid intake is not sufficient, rehydration by another route may be required (see page 236).
- Fractures or dislocations of the mandible or zygoma may prevent the mouth from opening or closing. A mouth that is jammed open is painful and potentially dangerous (see 'Dislocated mandible' below). Contact TMAS and prepare to evacuate the casualty.
- Infection is a significant risk with facial fractures because fractures that run into the mouth and airway and the airspaces behind the face (the sinuses) are impossible to diagnose on a vessel. Any suspected fracture should be treated with antibiotics initially, until the casualty is evacuated.

Specific facial injuries

6

- **Lacerations of the face and lips**
  Facial lacerations bleed heavily, and look dreadful before being cleaned up. Care must be taken when suturing, applying adhesive wound closure strips or gluing lacerations on the face for cosmetic reasons. If the lips have been lacerated, realign the lip edges as accurately as possible during suturing. In an ordered manner, clean the wound thoroughly and use local anaesthetic (see page 214). Use interrupted sutures with the finest thread possible (see page 232). Use antibiotics for large or dirty wounds.

- **Tongue injuries**
  The tongue may be lacerated by the teeth due to a blow to the face. If there is blood in the mouth, examine the tongue carefully. Contact TMAS if there is a significant injury to the tongue, and keep the casualty sitting up to reduce any swelling that may compromise the airway.
- **Fractured nose**
  A fractured nose will bleed a lot; it may be stopped by firmly squeezing the soft part of the nose. After contacting TMAS it might be necessary to pack the nose with gauze strip soaked in adrenaline, tranexamic acid or petroleum jelly (e.g. Vaseline). Fractures of the nose may cause a haematoma in the nasal septum, which may in turn cause necrosis of the septum.
- **Fractured cheek bone (zygoma)**
  This may cause:
  - a black eye
  - difficulty in opening the mouth and chewing (due to pain and occasionally mechanical locking)
  - a 'step' on the lower ridge of the eye socket
  - double vision and possible pain in the eye.

  Pain relief will be required, and a soft diet, as chewing and mouth opening may be very painful. Arrange to evacuate the casualty as soon as possible.

- **Fractures of the mid-face**
  A large amount of force is required to cause such a fracture, so other injuries are likely (see the diagram). Contact TMAS and prepare to evacuate the casualty as soon as possible.
  Such a fracture may cause:
  - difficulty with the airway and breathing
  - bilateral black eyes
  - a loose upper jaw
  - a step in the teeth of the upper jaw
  - difficulty in opening the mouth.

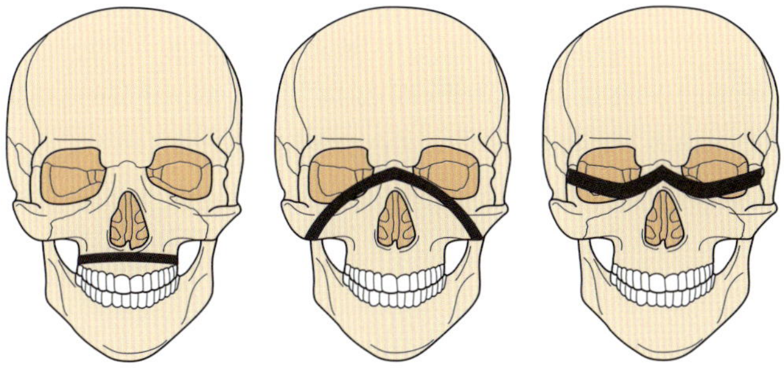

Fractures of the mid-face

  Assess and support the airway. This may be very difficult with an unconscious patient, and may prove impossible on a vessel without specialist equipment and immediate skilled help. Do your best.

  Other supportive treatments are outlined above.

- **Dislocated mandible**
  Dislocation may be caused by a blow to the jaw or opening the mouth very wide, such as during a yawn. It then becomes impossible to close the mouth. The jaw may be twisted off to one side, in which case only one of the joints is dislocated.
  Try to reduce the dislocation as soon as possible. Sedation may be required to relax the casualty sufficiently to get the jaw back into place. Contact TMAS to discuss this.

- **Fractured mandible**

  A reasonable amount of force is required to fracture the mandible (see diagram opposite), and the airway may be compromised if the casualty is laid down. Contact TMAS and prepare to evacuate the casualty as soon as possible. Check to see if any teeth have been lost or damaged by trauma to the lower face (see page 132 for treatment of lost and damaged teeth).

  Such a fracture may cause:
  - difficulty with the airway and breathing
  - obvious deformity of the jaw line
  - a step in the teeth of the lower jaw
  - difficulty in opening the mouth
  - swelling along the jaw and up the side of the head.

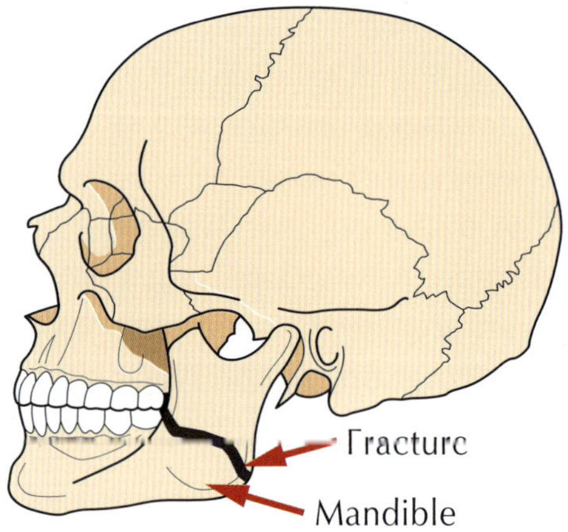

Fractured mandible

Assess and support the airway; this may prove as difficult as with a mid-face fracture.

The mandible may be immobilised by wiring the teeth of the lower jaw to the teeth of the upper jaw, but this requires skill, and a stoical casualty. A Barton bandage may be used (see diagram opposite), and is less invasive and easier than wiring. Be prepared to cut it off quickly should the patient vomit. Contact TMAS for advice on treatment.

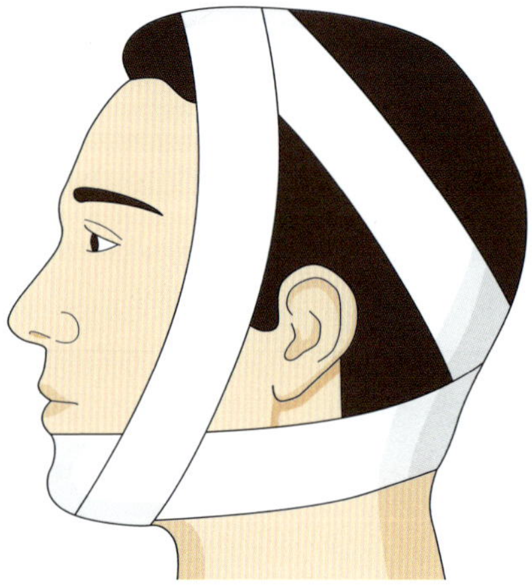
Barton bandage

5 Eye injuries

Good vision is essential for crew members at sea. Simple precautions will avoid eye problems, and some basic treatments will reduce complications and make the casualty more comfortable.

The eyeball is relatively well protected in its bony socket as only about 20% of the eyeball's surface is visible (see diagrams). Direct eye injuries are thus rare but potentially sight-threatening when they do occur. Injuries to the mid-face and cheekbone (zygoma) may be associated with eye injuries and if there are lacerations to the eyelids the eye must be examined closely.

Crew members who normally wear glasses should ideally use plastic lenses to avoid lacerations to the eye caused by shattered glass fragments. Contact lenses can cause problems in a marine environment, particularly with freezing wind and salt spray.

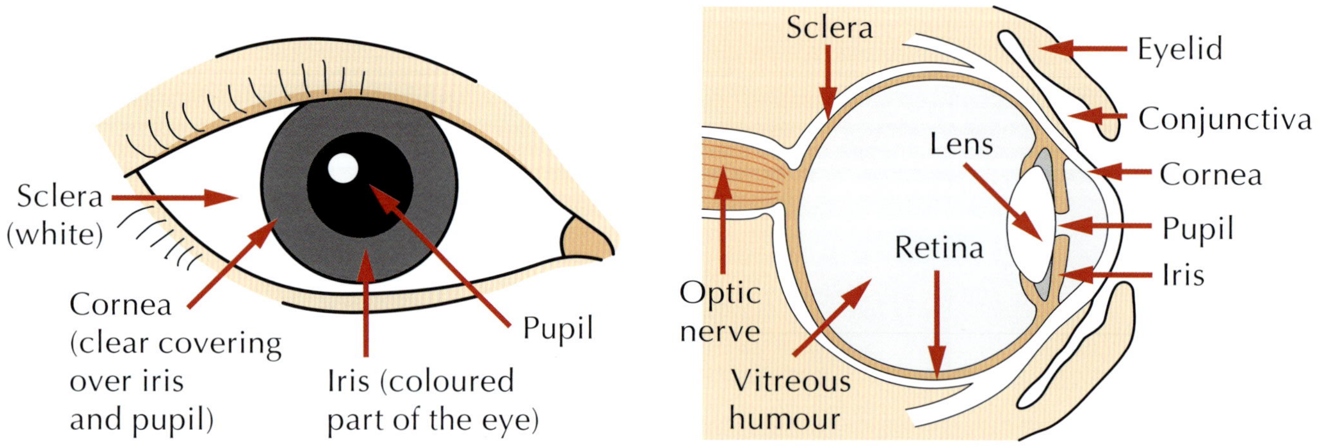

Anatomy of the eye: external (left) and internal (right)

Any splashes into the eye of chemicals, especially strong acids and alkalis, require immediate decontamination and dilution. Wash the eye with a continuous flow of water for at least ten minutes. The eye may need to be forcibly held open as pain will make the casualty try to close it. Do not examine the eye until washing is complete.

History

- If an eye is injured, how and when did it happen?
- Any previous eye/vision problems?
- What is the duration of symptoms?
- Any eye surgery in the past (cataract/laser)?
- Any history of foreign bodies in the eye?
- Are contact lenses or glasses worn?
- Is the eye painful or painless?
- Any known diabetes or glaucoma?

Examination

Examine the eye in a safe and stable place (e.g. with the casualty lying in a bunk), with good lighting (e.g. using a head torch). The casualty should be amenable and pain-free. Give paracetamol or ibuprofen as needed.

Visual acuity

- Ask the casualty whether their eyesight (i.e. visual acuity) is normal or not.
- Test their vision by reading small text from a book at normal distance.
- Examine the cornea using a magnifying glass and fluorescein eye drops (see page 127); these glow in bright light, showing up abrasions. Put local anaesthetic (tetracaine) drops in the eye first.
- **Warn the casualty not to rub their eyes for at least an hour after the anaesthetic as this can cause damage while the eye is numb.**
- Look inside eyelids (gently pull lower lid down and turn out the upper lid; see diagram, method 1).
- Compare one side with the other.
- Examine under the upper lid using either a finger or cotton bud to roll back the upper lid, as shown in the diagram, method 2.

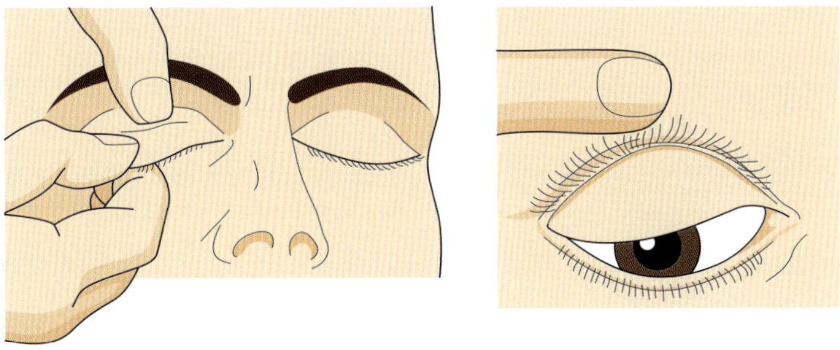

Method 1

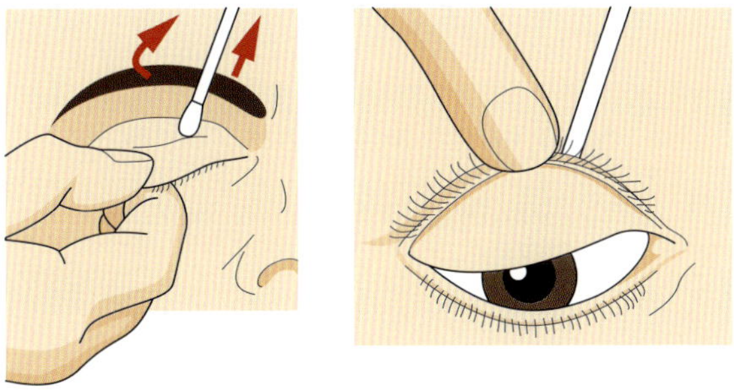

Method 2

Look for

- Obvious bruising, swelling, lacerations
- Foreign bodies (under lids or inside the eye)
- Pupil size and reaction to light
- Reddened sclera
- Tears streaming from the eye
- Blood inside the eye (you may see blood in front of the iris)

Feel

- If there are any bony steps around the edge of the eye socket (orbit)
- The firmness of the eyeball (gently) to get an idea of the intraocular pressure

Move

- Ask the casualty to look at your finger held about 30 cm from their face. Move the finger up and down and from side to side slowly. The casualty should keep their head still. Ask them if they have double vision, and watch their eye movements closely
- Document any pain they feel on moving the eye

Immediate treatment

Contact TMAS regarding any injury where the eyesight is affected, penetrating injuries and chemical burns, or if you are worried

- Assess the casualty for other facial injuries (see page 72)
- Pain relief
- Antibiotics
- Foreign bodies
- Chemicals
- Eye pads

Specific eye problems

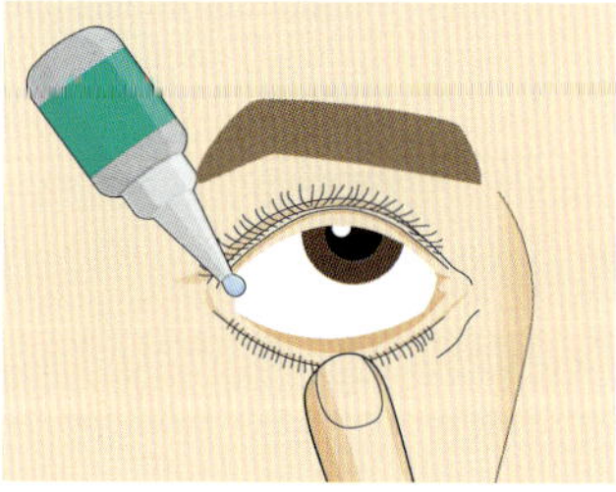

Corneal abrasion

- A corneal abrasion can be caused by a foreign body on the surface of the eye, an object hitting the open eye, or a lack of care with an anaesthetised eye (e.g. when the casualty cannot feel pain or touch).

Symptoms and signs

- Feels as though something is in the eye
- The abrasion may be seen using fluorescein staining (see page 127)

Treatment

- Flush eye to remove any foreign bodies
- Use local anaesthetic drops for pain
- Oral pain relief for accompanying headache
- Use antibiotic ointment (chloramphenicol) to lubricate and soothe
- Pad the eye if particularly painful

Foreign body

- A foreign body can enter the eye following the use of power tools, hammers or grinders without adequate eye protection.
- The object may be under the eyelids or it may even have penetrated the eyeball itself (see 'Penetrating eye injury' below). Discuss treatment of suspected penetrating injuries with TMAS. Urgent evacuation may be recommended to save the casualty's sight.

Symptoms and signs

- Examine eye after local anaesthetic drops
- Examine under the upper and lower eyelids (see methods 1 and 2 above)
- Ask about mechanism of injury
- The eye will produce lots of tears

Treatment

- Pain relief with local anaesthetic eyedrops
- If foreign body is obvious, remove it with clean finger or cotton bud
- Flush eye with sterile water or saline. Use a clean plastic bag with a small hole in it if no syringes are available. Boil water and cool it if nothing else is available
- Antibiotic ointment to soothe and lubricate the eye

Eyelid laceration

- An eyelid laceration is a serious injury, often accompanied by other injures to the eye itself.
- If the eye is left exposed, corneal damage and infection are more likely to occur.
- Contact TMAS regarding repair.

Symptoms and signs

- Examine eye after local anaesthetic drops
- Look carefully for other injuries, particularly if high energy is involved
- Look for foreign bodies in the eye and eyelid
- Particular care is needed if eyelid margin is lacerated

Treatment

- Apply firm and gentle pressure to stop bleeding
- Remove foreign bodies
- Antibiotic ointment and oral antibiotics to stop orbital cellulitis (page 130)
- Contact TMAS regarding attempting repair
- Pad the eye and use artificial tears (if available) if the cornea is left exposed

Chemical burn

- Contact TMAS as soon as possible for all chemical burns.
- Burns with alkaline chemicals are generally worse than those with acids.
- Try to identify which chemical was involved (e.g. caustic solvent used for cleaning or degreasing; engine battery acid).

Symptoms and signs

- Red, painful eye
- Chemical burn to surrounding face
- Eyesight might be blurred
- One or both eyes may be involved

Treatment

- Start flushing eye immediately before chemical penetrates eye
- Use the cleanest water/saline available urgently (preferably sterile)
- Flush for at least 30 minutes
- Antibiotic ointment (chloramphenicol) for lubrication and comfort (also use artificial tears if available on board)
- Local anaesthetic drops if very painful

Non-penetrating eye injury

- A non-penetrating eye injury may be caused by a blunt blow to the face. It may also cause other facial injuries.
- The weakest point of the orbit is the floor (below the eye), and this may 'blow out' into the space (sinus) below.

Symptoms and signs

- Mechanism of injury
- Black eye, swelling, bruising
- Pain on eye movement
- Decreased vision
- Double vision
- Injury to eye itself
- An eyeball that looks sunken
- Compare with the other side
- Assess for other injuries

Treatment

- Thoroughly examine eye before swelling prevents eye opening
- Treat other injuries
- Consider local anaesthetic drops/antibiotic drops to eye if painful
- Pad/cover the eye if double vision causes distress
- Consider ice pack for swelling/bruising
- Contact TMAS if vision is reduced

Penetrating eye injury

- Contact TMAS immediately – the eyesight may be threatened.
- A penetrating eye injury may be obvious (do not remove the object without advice from TMAS), but it may be difficult to see with small objects entering through the cornea – any hole closes up quickly.
- The energy involved in the accident is important – metal fragments moving at high speed are more likely to penetrate the eyeball.

Symptoms and signs

- Mechanism of injury
- Painful, red eye
- Irregular pupil
- Decreased vision
- Visible foreign body in or behind cornea
- Laceration of cornea/sclera
- Soft eye
- Leakage of eye contents

Treatment

- **Contact TMAS immediately**
- Do not remove an object impaled in the eye
- Guard against an impaled object being pushed further in
- Antibiotic ointment
- Local anaesthetic drops
- Oral antibiotics
- Pad over eye with shield to prevent the impaled object moving

6 Chest injuries

Chest injuries are commonly blunt and are caused by falls onto hard edges. Penetrating chest injuries are rare but usually more serious – contact TMAS immediately.

Severe bruising of the chest wall is difficult to distinguish from fractured ribs. Both are disabling and are treated in a similar manner. However, the major concern with chest injury is the possibility of lung or heart involvement and the resulting respiratory or cardiovascular problems. If the casualty already has lung or heart disease this may aggravate the problem.

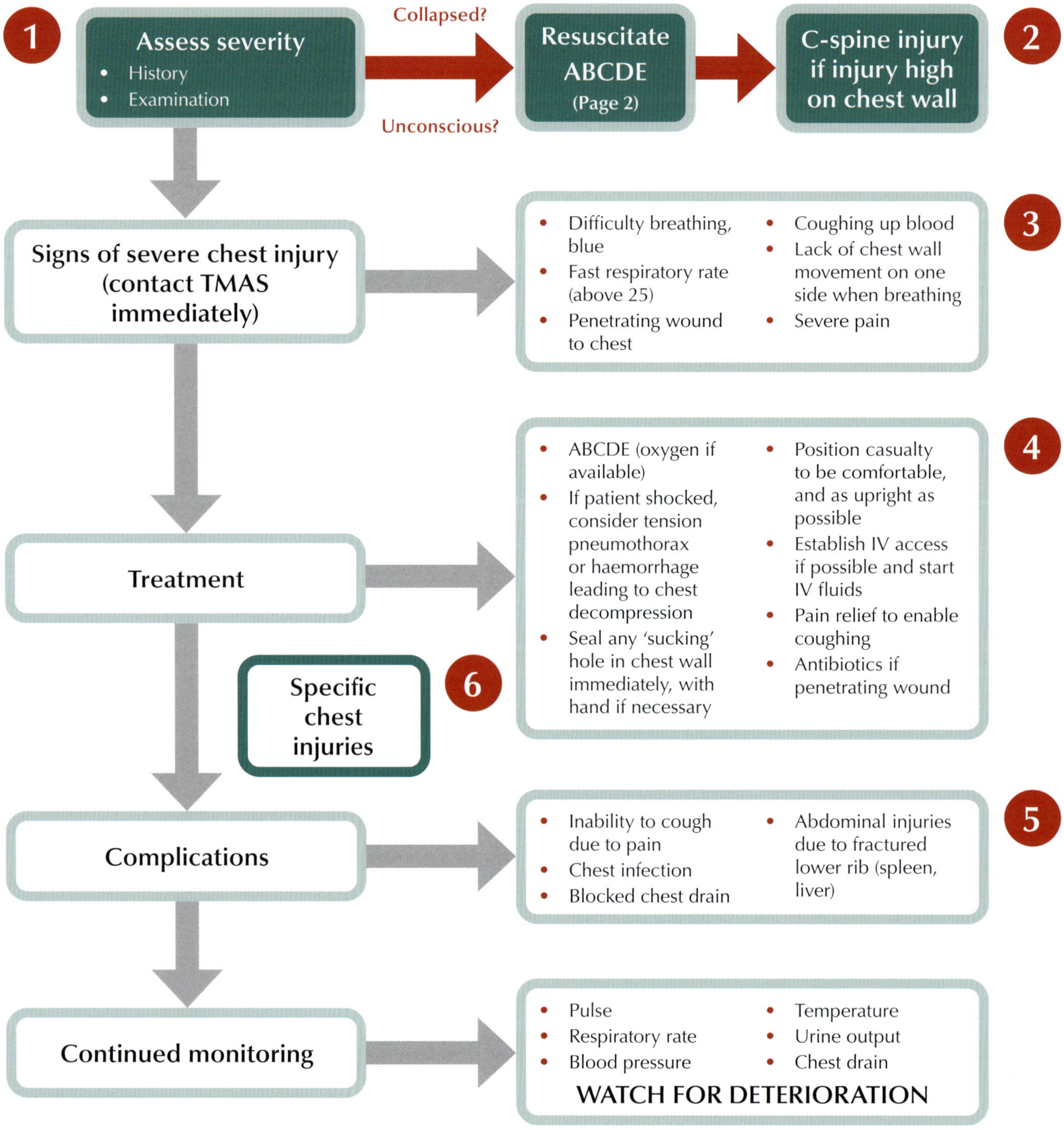

Contact TMAS early

History and examination

1

- ABCDE takes priority.
- **Take particular care of the neck if there is an injury high on the chest wall.**
- A blue patient is a very bad sign – contact TMAS immediately.
- Anticipate problems with breathing, pulse and blood pressure.
- Get as much information as possible from other crew members about what happened.

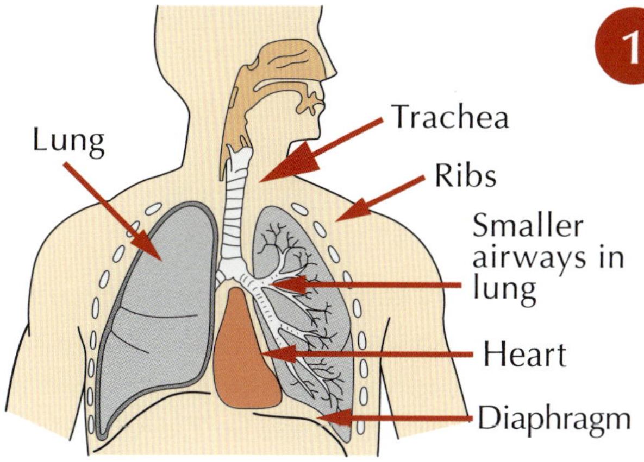

Important points in the history

- How did the accident happen (mechanism of injury)?
- Shortness of breath
- Pain in the chest
  - location?
  - what makes it worse or better?
- Coughing up blood, sputum?
- Previous lung disease (asthma or bronchitis)?
- Other injuries?

Important points in the examination

- **Look**
  - appearance of casualty (blue/white)
  - obvious injuries to chest
  - look for difference in chest wall movement between each side
- **Feel**
  - tenderness over chest wall
  - position of trachea (windpipe)
- **Listen**
  - harsh or gurgling breath sounds
  - breath sounds in the chest (with a stethoscope)
- **Document** Respiratory rate and other vital signs

Cervical spine (neck) injury

2

Injuries high on the chest wall may be associated with injuries to the cervical spine (c-spine).

The bones of the neck may be broken and unstable, but the spinal cord may still be intact.

If in doubt immobilise the cervical spine with three-point immobilisation (see page 208).

Signs of severe chest injury

3

- The casualty may be obviously struggling with their breathing and have a high respiratory rate. They will be very distressed by this.
- Low blood pressure may be caused by loss of blood in to the chest cavity (haemothorax) or by air in the chest cavity under pressure, compressing the lungs, heart and blood vessels (tension pneumothorax; see below).
- Any penetrating wound to the chest is serious. It may have damaged lung, heart and blood vessels and even abdominal organs.
- Coughing up blood indicates damage to both the lung and blood vessels.

- Lack of movement of one side of the chest in comparison with the other indicates that one side does not work properly, probably due to blood or air in the chest cavity. The trachea, which should be in the centre line, may be shifted to the opposite side.
- Pain is subjective; a non-complaining, stoical casualty may in fact have a serious injury.

Immediate treatment 4

- **If the casualty is having obvious difficulty with breathing, or has blue lips or fingers, contact TMAS immediately and prepare for evacuation if possible. Give oxygen if available.**
- **Chest decompression** May be required urgently if a pneumothorax or haemothorax is suspected and, if advised by TMAS, followed by a chest drain (see below and page 234).
- **Sucking chest wound** Should be sealed over urgently, even using a gloved hand, until a proper seal can be made (see page 236).
- **Positioning** The lungs generally work better in an upright position. This may be more comfortable, and the casualty should be wedged in place so they remain upright despite the rolling of the vessel.
- **IV fluid (if possible)** May be required if the chest injury is serious, or the blood pressure low. Seek medical advice from TMAS regarding the type and amount of fluid.
- **Pain relief** Coughing and deep breathing may not be possible because of the pain. Regular paracetamol, NSAIDs and codeine may all be necessary. Morphine may be necessary to adequately control the pain – contact TMAS before using it.
- **Antibiotics** Should be administered for any penetrating, open chest wound, or if the casualty develops a raised temperature and starts to cough up green sputum. Consult TMAS regarding the type of antibiotic.

Complications 5

- **Cough** Inability to cough due to pain is serious. Secretions and any blood from the injury will pool in the lungs, leading to infection, making breathing more difficult. The casualty must be encouraged to breathe deeply and cough for at least one good session of five minutes every hour. Support any damaged ribs with your hands while doing this.
- **Chest infection** Any sign of chest infection (high temperature and/or yellow-green sputum) should be treated with antibiotics.
- **Decompression or chest drain not working** If decompression has been undertaken or a chest drain has been inserted, monitor the casualty very closely. Air may reaccumulate and chest drains block easily, especially if there is blood in the chest. Pressure in the chest may rise again, possibly causing the casualty to collapse. Repeat decompression or use a syringe to flush the chest drain with IV fluid or sterile water (see page 234).
- **Abdominal injury** The lower ribs overlie the upper abdomen, and fractures of these ribs may damage the liver, spleen and other organs.

Specific chest injuries 6

Pneumothorax

This means air in the chest, but outside the lungs, as shown in the diagram below. It can happen because of a blunt injury 'bursting' the lung, a fractured rib piercing the lung, or a penetrating wound to the chest.

A **simple pneumothorax** is air in the chest, causing a small pneumothorax, with little or no effect on the circulation, and making breathing a little difficult. Pain may be variable. A simple pneumothorax may 'tension' (see below).

A **tension pneumothorax** is where the air may be under pressure, causing the lungs and heart to 'collapse', and this is life-threatening. The chest must be decompressed quickly.

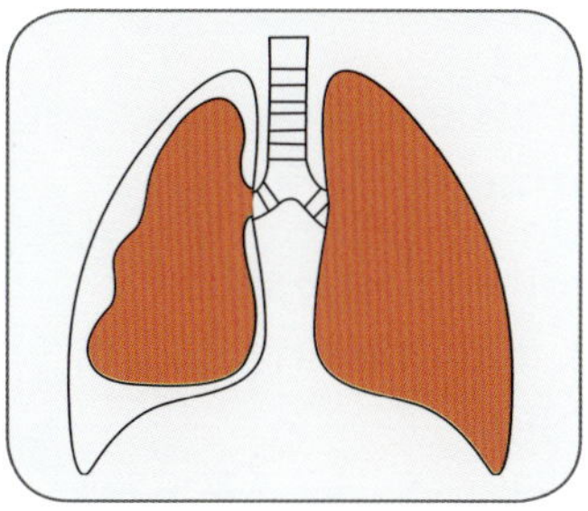

Simple pneumothorax
Air collects between lung and chest wall

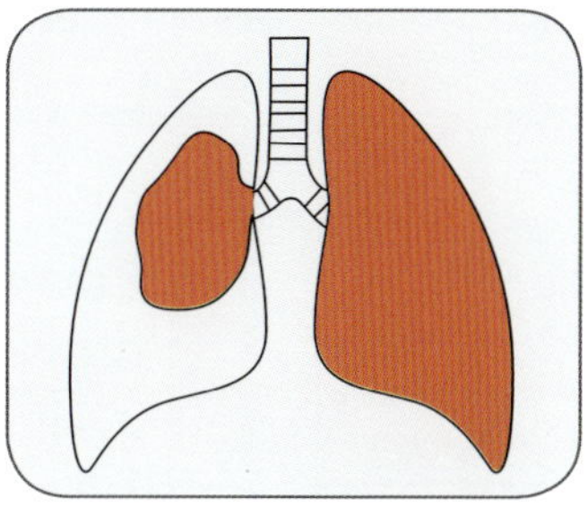

Tension pneumothorax
A lot of air collects and pushes on the lung and heart

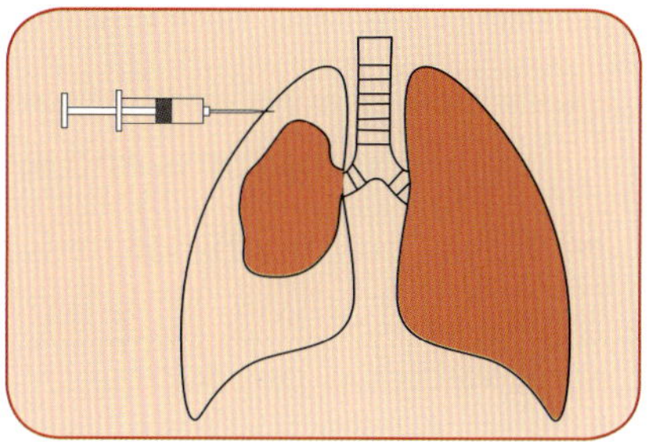

Immediate treatment
Insert needle and decompress

Symptoms and signs

- Difficulty in breathing
- Low blood pressure
- The side of the chest not moving has the air in it (this may be difficult to see)
- The trachea may be shifted away from the side of the chest with the air in it
- Reduced breath sounds on the side of the chest with the air in it
- Use a stethoscope to listen to breath sounds on each side and compare carefully

Treatment

- A needle or cannula should be inserted without delay between the ribs in the upper chest on the affected side (page 235)
- A hiss of air may be heard when the needle enters the chest
- Following decompression, a thoracostomy and application of a chest seal dressing will need to be undertaken, but only by a trained individual (page 235)

Haemothorax

Damage to the ribs or blood vessels in the chest may cause bleeding and the blood may accumulate inside the chest, as shown in the diagram. A significant amount of blood (over 2 litres) may accumulate, causing the casualty to be shocked and the lung to be compressed.

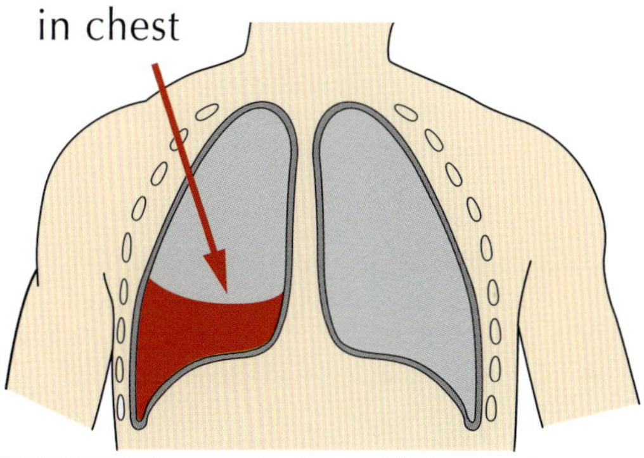

Symptoms and signs

- Difficulty in breathing
- Casualty may be shocked (low blood pressure)
- Reduced breath sounds on the side of the chest with the blood in it

Treatment

- If you suspect a haemothorax, contact TMAS
- An IV line should be inserted if possible and fluids given

Sucking chest wound

A sucking chest wound may cause deterioration in lung function, and there may also be bleeding into the chest that is not obvious externally.

Symptoms and signs

- Casualty may be distressed, struggling with breathing, have blue lips and low blood pressure
- Obvious hissing or gurgling of air through a chest wound when breathing in and out
- Breath sounds may be very harsh on the affected side

Treatment

- Cover the hole with a three-sided dressing or chest seal dressing if available (page 236)

Or

- Only by a trained individual: insert a chest drain through the hole
- Contact TMAS immediately

Broken ribs

It is difficult to distinguish severe bruising from fractured ribs without an x-ray, but both require rest and adequate pain relief. Fractured ribs may cause a pneumothorax or haemothorax. Broken ribs are painful for about 2–3 weeks, and take up to 6 weeks to heal. A flail segment (see diagram), where several ribs are broken in more than one place, may adversely affect lung function and hence breathing.

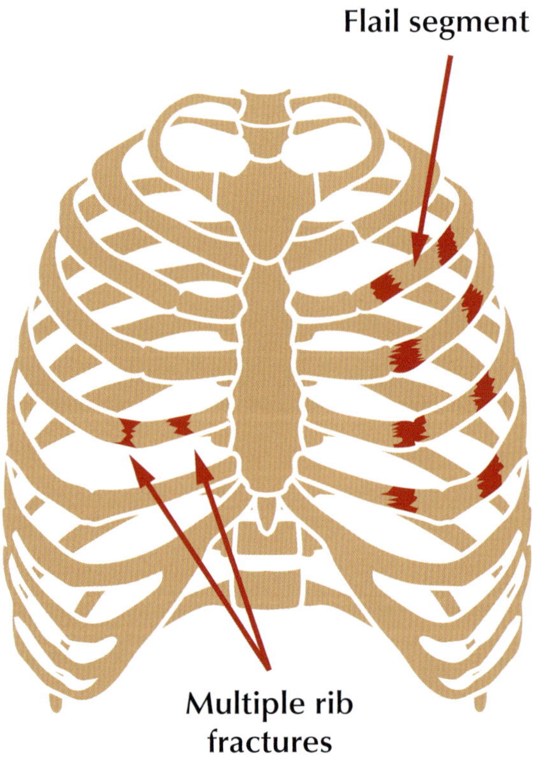

Symptoms and signs

- Tenderness over chest wall at fracture site
- Pain at fracture site if centre of chest is pushed in (be gentle)
- The broken ends of bone may be felt to grate against each other (crepitus)
- A section of chest wall may move in instead of out when the casualty breathes in (a 'flail' segment)

Treatment

- Pain relief to enable the casualty to breathe deeply and cough
- If a flail chest is suspected, give oxygen if possible and contact TMAS
- Do not bind the chest
- Keep comfortable in a bunk, but mobilise as soon as conditions allow

7 Abdominal injuries

Blunt injuries to the abdomen are relatively common on vessels. They are caused by falls above and below decks, usually in bad weather. Penetrating injuries are less common.

Injury to the organs in the abdomen may take some time to cause symptoms, and the abdomen may be easily overlooked if there are other distracting injuries, such as fractured limbs.

Perforation of the bowel, bruising of the internal organs and internal bleeding (commonly from tears to the liver and spleen) are the main abdominal injuries, and may cause infection and shock, causing the bowels to stop working. The kidneys are quite well protected, but may be damaged by a penetrating injury or a severe blow to the flank.

1 Assess severity

- History
- Examination

Collapsed? Unconscious? → **Resuscitate ABCDE** (Page 2) → **Distracting injury** Do not forget possible abdominal injuries

2 Signs of severe abdominal injury (contact TMAS)

- Severe abdominal pain
- Obvious injury – bruising or penetrating/open wound
- Distended abdomen
- Tense, rigid, tender abdomen
- Shocked casualty with no other obvious injury
- Blood in the urine

3 Treatment

- ABCDE (oxygen if available)
- Establish IV access if possible and start IV fluids
- Pain relief
- Anti-sickness medication (cyclizine)
- Consider inserting NGT
- Cover protruding bowel with warm, damp, sterile gauze
- Antibiotics if penetrating wound or develops a raised temperature

5 Specific abdominal injuries

4 Complications

- Shock due to blood loss or infection
- Systemic infection
- Nausea and vomiting (with blood or green bile)
- Continual blood in the urine
- Lack of hydration/ nutrition

Continued monitoring

- Pulse
- Blood pressure
- Respiratory rate
- Temperature
- Urine output
- Abdomen

WATCH FOR DETERIORATION

Contact TMAS early

History and examination

1

- Internal injuries may not be obvious at first, so reassess them frequently if the casualty is unwell.
- Remember to look at the back of the casualty.
- Penetrating injuries in the chest below the nipples may penetrate the abdomen.
- Lower rib fractures may damage the spleen or liver.

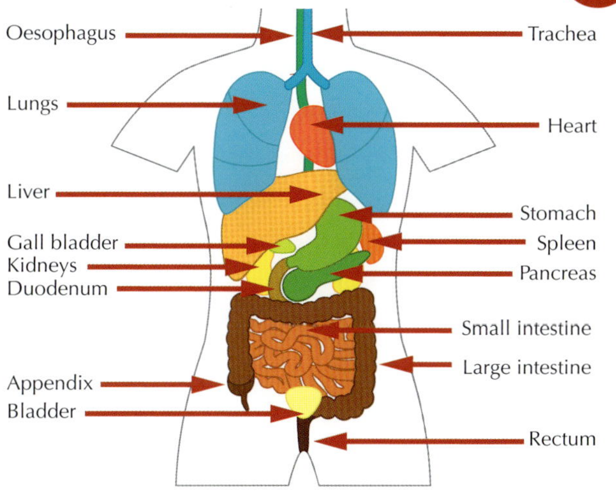

Important points in the history

- How did the accident happen (mechanism of injury)?
- Site and severity of pain
- Any nausea or vomiting
- Any blood or bile in vomit
- Any blood in stool (may be red or tarry black) or urine (may be red, or faintly pink)

Important points in the examination

- **Look**
  - Abdominal wounds or bruising (look around the back)
  - Abdominal distension
  - Old operation scars (e.g. appendix, hernia)
- **Feel**
  - Any masses in the abdomen
  - Tenderness, rigidity
- **Listen**
  - Bowel sounds (over lower right side)

Signs of severe abdominal injury

2

- The casualty may be sweaty and cold from both the effects of pain and blood loss.
- A rigid, tense abdomen is a sign of serious injury.
- Any penetrating wound (even in the chest below the nipples) is serious and may have damaged many internal organs.
- The site and severity of pain give an indication of which internal organs are damaged (see diagram below), and the possible severity of the injury. Remember that people have different pain thresholds, and that the site of pain may be misleading. If in doubt, monitor the casualty closely for signs of deterioration.
- Bruising of the abdomen may be difficult to see initially, so if in doubt, re-examine the casualty every hour or so. Remember to examine the back of the casualty for penetrating wounds and bruising. Flank bruising may indicate injury to the kidneys.
- The abdomen may look normal initially, but may become distended over a period of time (e.g. a few hours).
- Bowel sounds are heard by listening to the abdomen with a stethoscope. They are made by the bowel squeezing gas and liquid around. If the bowel stops working there will be no bowel sounds, and this is a sign of possible serious injury. Sometimes, however, bowel sounds may be difficult to hear even in a normal abdomen.

Immediate treatment

3

Base treatment on TMAS advice whenever possible.

- **Intravenous fluids (if possible)** Will be required if the patient is shocked. Contact TMAS regarding the type and amount of fluid. Insert an IV cannula (see page 225) at an early stage, immediately after assessing the patient, but before they become more shocked.
- **Pain relief** Paracetamol, codeine and even morphine should be used to control the pain to a bearable level. Avoid NSAIDs initially, due to possible complications such as bleeding or bowel perforation.
- **Anti-sickness medication** Should be given to prevent vomiting, which may occur particularly with severe pain and when using morphine. Bad weather at the time of the accident may compound the problem. The medical kit will contain several different types of anti-sickness medications. Medical advice from TMAS will be useful in deciding which ones to use and in which order.
- **Nasogastric tube (NGT)** May be necessary, but only under the direct supervision of TMAS. Abdominal injury can stop the gut from working and the stomach will stop emptying into the lower gut. It will then fill up with gastric secretions and become distended, causing pain to the casualty, who may then be sick. An NGT passed into the stomach (see page 216), attached to a drainage bag, will allow the stomach contents to pass up the tube into the bag, reducing the risk of distension, pain and sickness.
- **Penetrating wounds** Are a serious risk to life; contact TMAS immediately. Protruding foreign bodies should not be removed because they may be plugging a hole in an internal organ or blood vessel. The wound should be cleaned as much as possible, covered with a sterile dressing, examined and redressed every day until evacuation. Any signs of spreading infection, discharge or bad smell from the wound suggests infection and should be reported to TMAS.
- **Protruding bowel** Is both serious and distressing. After transferring the casualty to a safe place, cover the bowel with warm, sterile, damp gauze. Contact TMAS immediately.
- **Antibiotics** Should be used for any penetrating wound and with blunt injuries if the casualty develops a raised temperature.

Complications

4

- **Shock** Could be due to blood loss or increasing infection, causing the casualty to become septic (see pages 28, 40). Both situations are very serious, and the casualty will require fluid to make up for the losses. For a shocked casualty the IV route is preferred.
- **Infection** May only become apparent in the days following either a penetrating or a blunt injury to the abdomen. It may be a sign that the bowel itself is perforated. Antibiotics should be used for all penetrating injuries, and also after blunt injury if the casualty develops a raised temperature, or signs of peritonitis.
- **Nausea and vomiting** May only start hours or days after the injury, and may be a sign of deterioration. An NGT should be inserted if not already in place, and anti-sickness medication given under guidance by TMAS. Examine the abdomen for increasing distension, tenderness, or any masses that may be felt within the abdomen. The casualty should not take anything by mouth.
- **Blood in the urine** May be a sign of injury to one or both kidneys, the tubes from the kidney to the bladder (the ureter), the bladder itself, or the tube from the bladder to the outside (the urethra). At sea, it is not possible to find exactly where the blood is coming from but the danger is that it may clot in the bladder, causing the casualty to go into retention (i.e. the casualty is unable to pass urine). Contact TMAS before considering passing a catheter because this may make matters worse. Continual blood loss over several days may cause the blood pressure to drop and the casualty to become anaemic. Fluid must be replaced and urgent evacuation arranged.

- **Hydration and nutrition** Should be maintained, but may be difficult if the casualty has a distended, painful abdomen and is vomiting; IV fluids may be required. Monitoring urine output will give a good idea about the casualty's state of hydration, and whether more fluid is required. A urinary catheter may be required; aim for a urine output of about 0.5–1 ml per kg body weight per hour. Contact TMAS regarding fluid resuscitation and ongoing fluid requirements.

Sites of abdominal pain and possible related injuries

5

The table below is a general guide relating the site of injury, maximum pain or tenderness to the internal organs that may be damaged (see diagram). The site of pain may change over time or become generalised if peritonitis develops, so frequent reassessment and examination are required.

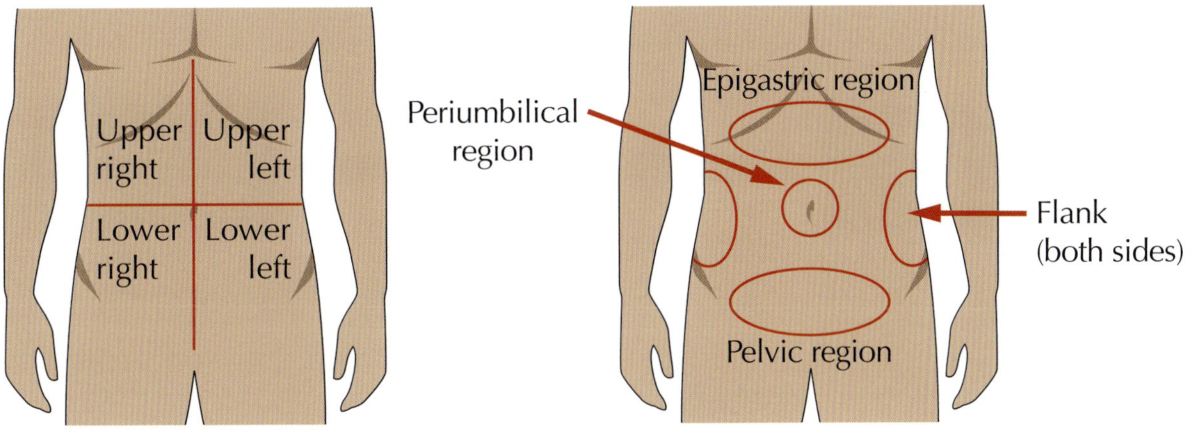

Sites of pain and possible injuries to internal organs

Site of pain	Internal organs that may be injured
Right upper quadrant	Liver; Stomach; Lower rib fractures
Left upper quadrant	Spleen; Pancreas; Stomach; Lower rib fractures
Epigastric region	Stomach; Liver; Small bowel
Right lower quadrant	Bowels; Appendix
Left lower quadrant	Bowels
Periumbilical region	Large bowel; Uterus; Bladder
Flanks	Kidneys
Pelvic region	Bowel/rectum; Bladder; Uterus; Pelvic bones; External genitalia

8 Pelvic and hip injuries

Pelvic and hip fractures are usually caused by high-energy accidents, such as falls from height, people being crushed by a falling object, caught between vessels or caught between a vessel and a quayside. Injuries to other parts of the body often occur at the same time. Falls from more than 2 m causing a hip or pelvic fracture may injure the spine as well.

If the pelvis is fractured the body's organs in the pelvis may be injured as well, notably the bladder, uterus, urethra and blood vessels. Pelvic and hip fractures can cause substantial blood loss which may be life threatening. Contact TMAS at an early stage.

Injuries to the lower part of the body may harm the external genitalia. Any bleeding from the vagina or penis indicates serious injury, so contact TMAS immediately.

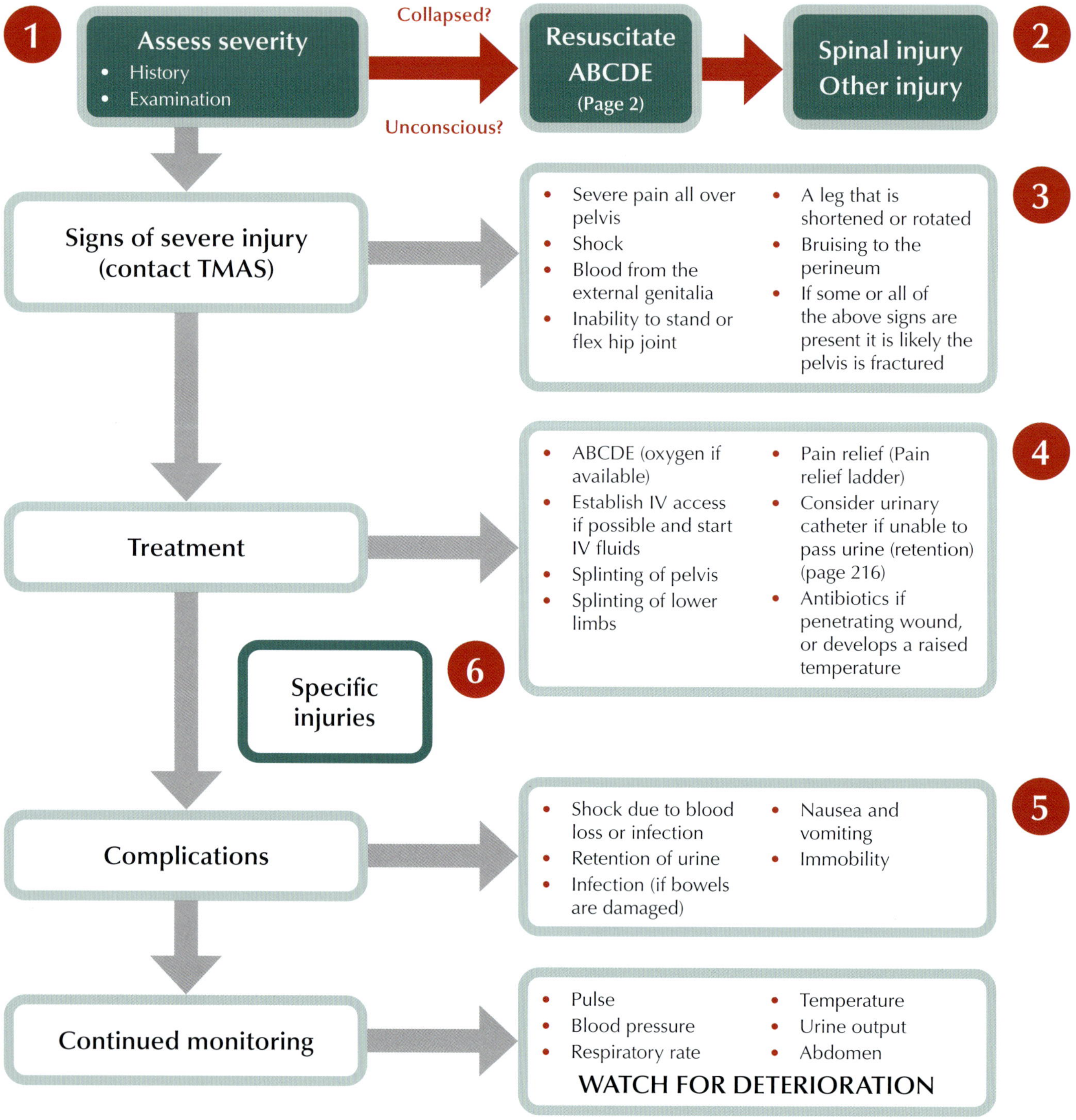

Contact TMAS early

History and examination

1

- Pelvic and hip fractures are life-threatening due to blood loss and possible injury to internal organs (see right diagram) and blood vessels.
- The mechanism of the accident gives an idea of the severity of the injury.
- There may be spinal injuries as well.

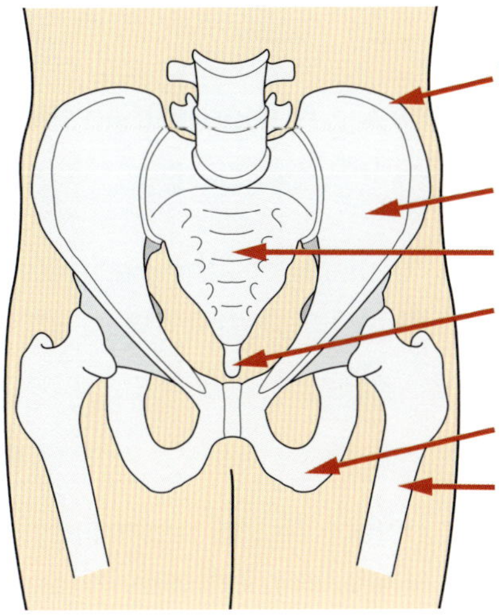

Pelvic bones

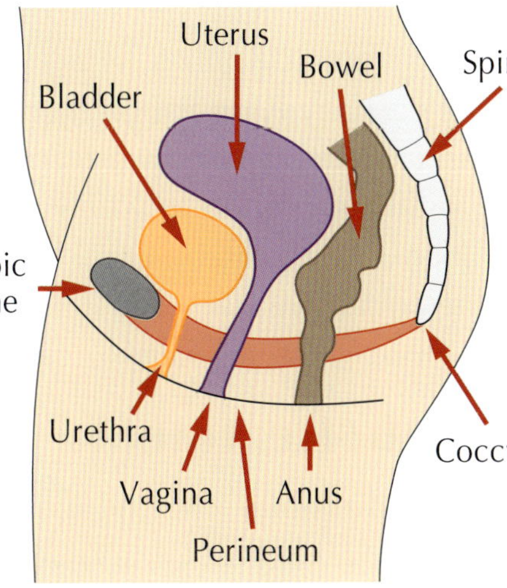

Pelvic organs (female)

Important points in the history

- How did the accident happen (mechanism of injury)?
- What is the site and severity of the pain?
- Can the casualty stand up?
- Any blood in the urine?

Important points in the examination

- **Look**
  - Obvious deformity of pelvis
  - Leg shortened or rotated inwards or outwards
  - Bleeding from vagina or penis
  - Bruising of perineum
- **Feel**
  - Rigid tender abdomen
  - Be careful not to move or disturb the pelvis – it may be fractured and bleed a lot
- **Listen**
  - Bowel sounds (over lower right abdomen)
- **Document** Findings and vital signs

Spinal injury

2

Falls from heights of more than 2 m that cause pelvic or hip fractures may also cause spinal injury and injury to other bones or internal organs (see diagrams above).

The bones of the spine (vertebral column) may be broken and unstable but the spinal cord may still be intact.

If in doubt immobilise the casualty on a spinal board (see page 208) and check for other injuries.

Signs of severe pelvic or hip injury

3

- A fractured pelvis is usually extremely painful, particularly on moving, and the casualty cannot stand up.
- A badly fractured pelvis can cause blood loss of up to 3 litres in a short time, causing life-threatening shock. Moving or pressing down on the pelvis may cause severe bleeding, so splinting of the pelvis should be undertaken quickly (see below).
- Bleeding from the penis or vagina area indicates damage to the bladder or urethra, which can be injured when the pelvis is fractured.
- With the casualty lying flat on their back, it may be obvious that one leg is shorter than the other, and rotated either inwards or outwards. Bending the leg at the hip may cause severe pain. Do this only once as it may cause further bleeding.
- Pelvic injury may cause internal bleeding, which might be seen as 'bruising' to the perineum (see diagram above): the area between the top of the legs, behind the vagina in females and behind the scrotum in males.

Immediate treatment

4

- **IV fluids (if possible)** May be required if the patient is shocked. Contact TMAS regarding how much fluid to give. Insert an IV cannula (see page 225) at an early stage, immediately after assessing the patient, but before they become more shocked.
- **Pain relief** Will be required with moderate to severe pain. Paracetamol, codeine and morphine or tramadol should be used to control the pain to a tolerable level. Initially it may be worthwhile avoiding NSAIDs due to possible worsening of bleeding. Contact TMAS if considering using morphine or tramadol.
- **Splinting of the pelvis** Will reduce blood loss and is relatively simple to do (see page 241). Splinting as soon as possible will reduce complications.
- **Splinting of lower limbs** Is useful for fractures of both the pelvis and hip. Bind the knees and ankles together, putting some padding in between. Keep the patient flat on their back, perhaps with a pillow under their knees if it is more comfortable (see pages 240–1).
- **Urinary catheter** May be required. Pelvic fracture may cause damage to the urethra (see diagram above) or the bladder, preventing the casualty from passing urine. Contact TMAS before inserting a urinary catheter, because the insertion may cause further damage to the urethra.
- **Antibiotics** Should be used for any penetrating wound, and also with blunt injuries if the casualty develops a raised temperature.

Complications

5

- **Shock** Could be due to continuing blood loss or the onset of infection, causing the casualty to become septic. Both situations are very serious, and the casualty will require fluid to make up for the losses. For a shocked casualty, the IV route is preferred.

- **Retention of urine** May not be a problem at first, but might become so during the ensuing hours or days due to blood clots in the bladder or swelling of damaged tissues. Keep a close eye on the amount of urine being passed, and watch for increasing swelling and pain in the lower abdomen, which might be due to an enlarging bladder. Suprapubic aspiration of urine might be required (see page 218).
- **Infection** May only become apparent in the days following the injury. It may be a sign that the bowel itself is perforated. Antibiotics should be used for all penetrating injuries, and also after blunt injury if the casualty develops a raised temperature.
- **Nausea and vomiting** May start hours or days after the injury, and may be a sign of injury to the gut as well as the pelvis. A nasogastric tube should be inserted (under direct guidance by TMAS) if not already in place, and anti-sickness medication given. Examine the abdomen for increasing distension, tenderness or any masses that may be felt within the abdomen. The casualty should not take anything by mouth.
- **Immobility** Will be challenging. Initially the casualty should not move, to reduce the risk of further bleeding. They should be placed in a comfortable position in an accessible bunk, and wedged in place to avoid rolling around. They still need to pass urine (e.g. into a bottle or bedpan), and may need to open their bowels. This is a difficult situation for all concerned, and not a time for shyness. Use a bed pan if available. It may be possible to use a bowl and plastic bag as a modified bedpan. The casualty may not be able to clean themselves so someone may need to do it for them. If the legs and ankles are splinted together, make sure there is some padding in between to reduce the risk of pressure sores forming.

Specific pelvic and hip injuries

6

Pelvic fracture

Any part of the pelvis may be fractured and the pelvis may remain stable, or unstable if there are multiple fractures. The pelvis may be opened up like a book (an 'open-book' fracture) which is dangerous because of the risk of severe bleeding, or it may be compressed together.

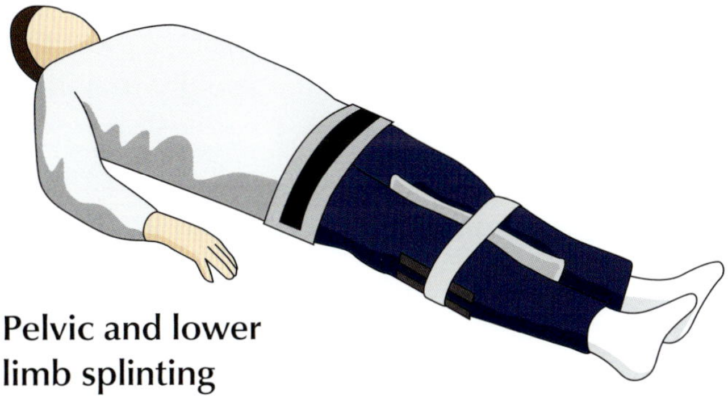

Pelvic and lower limb splinting

Symptoms and signs

- Severe pain in the pelvic/lower abdominal area
- Unable to stand up or flex hip
- Possibly blood from the vagina or penis
- Possible bruised perineum
- Examine very carefully for other injuries (especially spinal injuries)
- There may be signs of bowel injury (rigid tender abdomen, possibly becoming distended after hours/days)

Treatment

- Fluid resuscitation (page 220)
- Pain relief and antibiotics
- Pelvic splinting (see diagram above and page 241)
- Lower limb splinting (see diagram and pages 240–1)
- Place in an accessible bunk, and wedge in a comfortable position
- Minimise all movement and treat like a spinal injury
- Pad all bony prominences and between splinted legs
- Watch for urinary retention, but insert a catheter only on advice from TMAS

Hip fracture or dislocation

A fracture or dislocation of the hip requires a lot of force, especially in the young. Other injuries may also be present. Generally a fractured hip will cause the leg to be shortened and rotated outwards (see diagram opposite) whereas a hip usually dislocates backwards (posteriorly) and the leg will be rotated inwards. A dislocated hip is an emergency because the blood supply may be reduced to the head of the femur. The casualty must be evacuated immediately or an attempt made to reduce (relocate) the dislocation (see page 244). Contact TMAS before doing so.

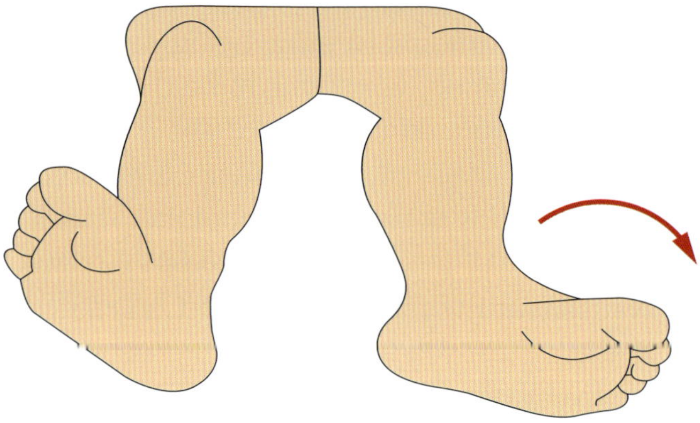

Fractured hip with shortened and externally rotated leg

Symptoms and signs

- Severe pain from the hip or more generalised over the pelvis
- Unable to stand or flex hip
- Inward or outward rotated leg
- Possible loss of sensation to leg

Treatment

- Fluid resuscitation (page 220)
- Pain relief
- If dislocation is suspected, contact TMAS before attempting relocation
- Lower limb splinting (pages 240–1)

Urethral injury

The urethra is the tube by which urine passes from the bladder to the outside. It may be damaged with pelvic fractures, and the casualty may not be able to pass urine, or urine may leak into the pelvic and abdominal cavities.

Symptoms and signs

- Blood from tip of penis or from vagina
- Blood in the urine
- Pain passing urine
- Inability to pass urine
- Bruising of the perineum and scrotum
- Possibly a full and increasingly painful bladder, although urine might leak into the inside of the pelvis and abdomen

Treatment

- A urinary catheter might be needed, but contact TMAS before inserting one – it might make the injury worse
- Antibiotics should be given if a urethral or bladder injury is suspected

Coccyx injury

Injury to the 'tail bone' of the spine is a common injury on a vessel, due to falls down stairs onto the base of the spine. It can be excruciatingly painful, although it will be impossible to differentiate between bad bruising and a fracture. The majority of casualties will get better over a few days or weeks, but the pain can be persistent, and with bad fractures it can result in a chronic pain state.

Symptoms and signs

- Pain and tenderness over the base of the spine, between the top of the buttocks
- Pain on passing stool

Treatment

- Pain relief so the casualty can move around and pass stool
- Use a 'doughnut' cushion to enable the casualty to sit comfortably
- There may be difficulty in passing stool due to pain, so keep well hydrated and use softening laxatives if signs of constipation (page 149)

9 Limbs: fracture and dislocation

Fractures and dislocations of the upper and lower limbs, including the shoulder, are relatively common on vessels, particularly in bad weather. Such injuries are disabling and the casualty will not be able to continue working. Falls into vessels' compartments, to the deck below or when moving heavy machinery, can all cause limb injuries. Other common causes are direct blows to a limb, a fall onto an outstretched arm, being swept along the deck or sometimes quite innocuous accidents where no great energy is involved.

Fractures, particularly of the femur, can cause significant blood loss, resulting in shock. Putting the ends back together and applying direct pressure to the fracture site will limit bleeding and reduce pain. Fractures and dislocations often cause damage to the blood and nerve supply beyond the site of injury, and urgent reduction may be required, following medical advice from TMAS.

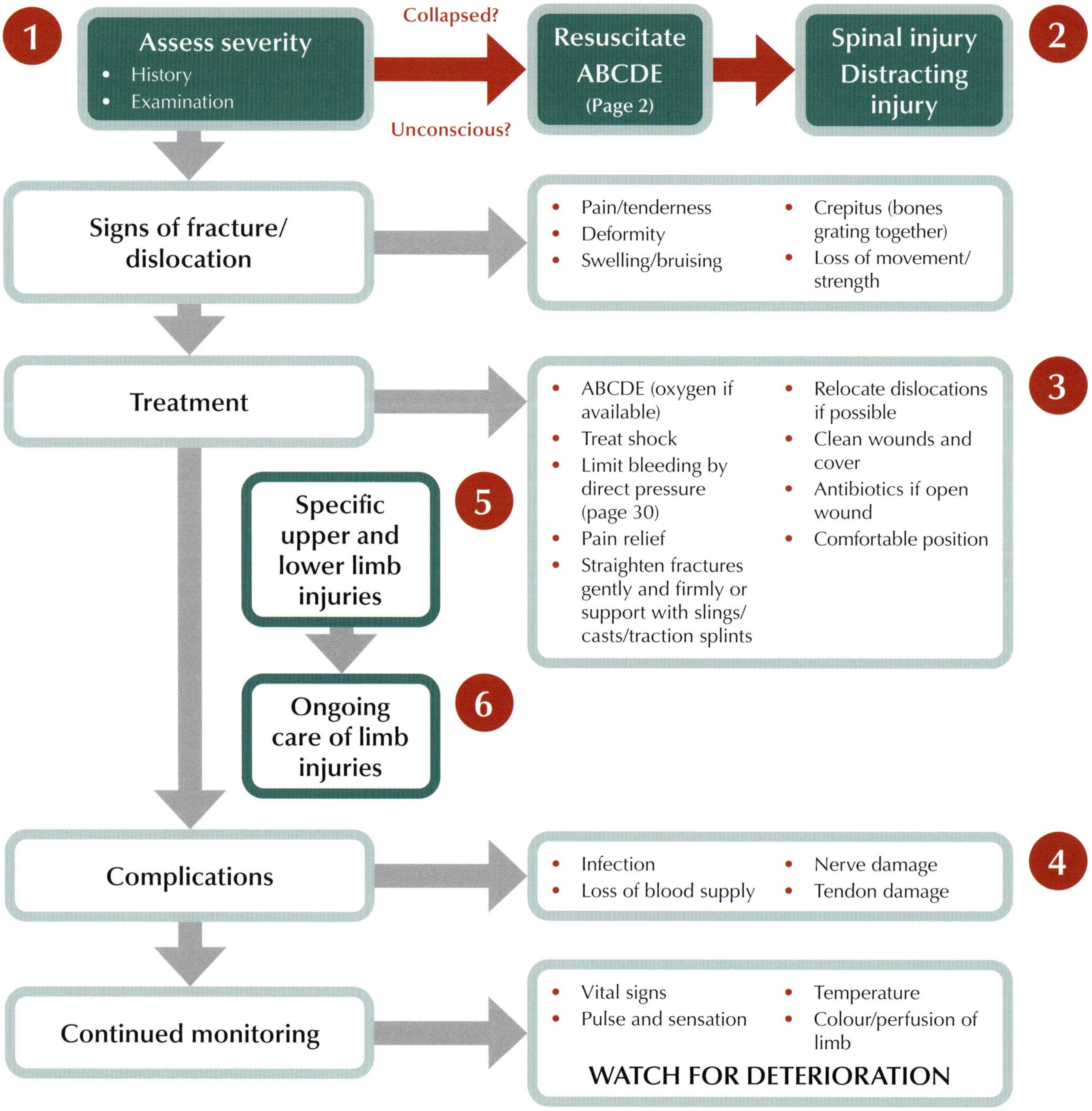

Contact TMAS early

History and examination

1

- Femoral fractures may be life-threatening due to blood loss
- Upper limb injuries are rarely life-threatening
- However, shoulder and collar bone injuries may be associated with spinal injuries
- Painful limb injuries may distract from other more serious injuries

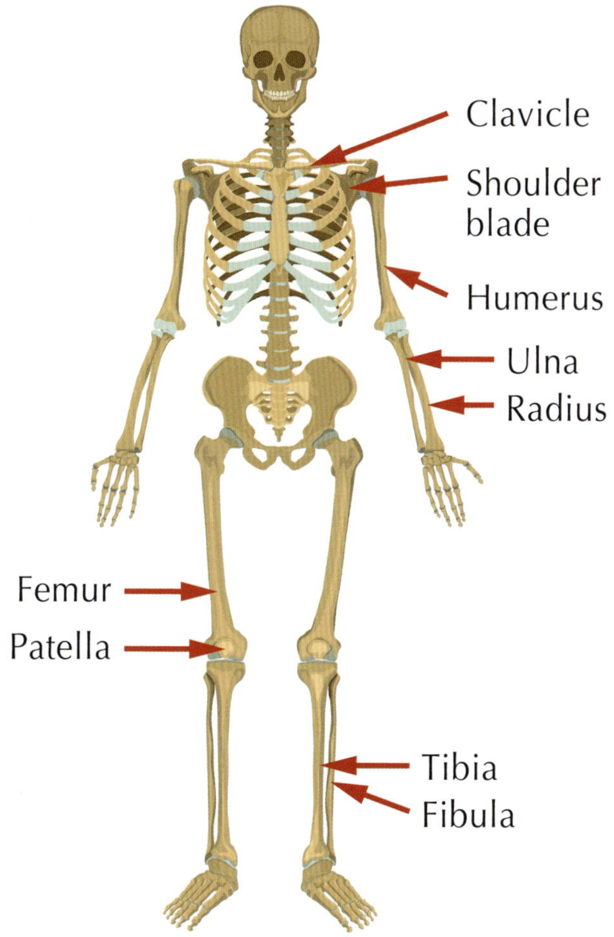

Bones of the limbs

Important points in the history

- How did the accident happen?
- Where and when did it happen?
- Possibility of contamination of wound?
- Any possibility of crushing?
- Any other injuries?
- Any previous fractures or dislocations of the same part?
- Last tetanus vaccination?

Important points in the examination

- **Look**
  - Swelling, bruising
  - Deformity
  - Open wound over fracture site
  - Colour of limb
  - Compare with other limb
- **Feel**
  - Pain, tenderness
  - Bone edges
  - Crepitus (bone edges grating together)
  - Pulses/perfusion beyond fracture
  - Sensation beyond fracture
- **Move**
  - Ask the casualty to move the limb first, as far as possible, in all directions
  - Then move the limb yourself, very gently and stop if causing pain
- **Document** Findings and vital signs

Spinal injury

2

Injuries to the shoulder or clavicle (collar bone) may be very painful and can be associated with fractures of the cervical spine (c-spine). The force required to break the femur may cause spinal injuries.

The bones of the spine may be broken and unstable, but the spinal cord may still be intact.

If in doubt immobilise the cervical spine with three-point immobilisation (see page 208).

Immediate treatment

3

Reducing a fracture

- **Limit bleeding** This is the priority to avoid shock. Bleeding may be internal, or external if the bones protrude through the skin. Apply direct pressure if tolerated (pain), or attempt to reduce the fracture. A traction splint is a good way of stabilising and reducing a femoral fracture, where blood loss may be considerable (see page 240).
- **Pain relief** Will be necessary. Fractures are very painful, and any attempt at reducing the fracture or dislocation will cause more pain. Morphine may be required (see page 301), together with anti-sickness medication.
- **Reduce fractures** If there is obvious deformity (compare with the other side) early reduction may be needed (see page 244).
- **Relocate dislocation** (Usually of the shoulder or elbow). If there is obvious deformity (compare with the other side) early reduction may be needed (see page 244).
- **Clean and cover wounds, give antibiotics** For all wounds anywhere near a suspected fracture. The bone may have come out through the skin and then gone back inside during the accident, potentially contaminating the bone and tissues, or it may still be protruding. The bone ends may go back under the skin during reduction. Clean thoroughly, cover with a sterile dressing, and start antibiotics straightaway.
- **Splinting/support** Will be necessary whether or not it has been possible to reduce the fracture or dislocation (see page 240). This will reduce pain, bleeding and swelling. Swelling is normal after fractures. It is important to regularly check that splints and bandages are not impairing circulation to the distal part of the limb.
- **Keep the casualty in a comfortable position** Wedged in a bunk will be ideal, avoiding pressure on the affected dislocation or fracture.

Complications

4

- **Infection** May start in the days after a fracture where the skin is broken. Inspect any wounds regularly for signs of discharge, spreading red inflammation of the skin, pain or swelling. Contact TMAS regarding antibiotic treatment.
- **Loss of blood supply** May occur immediately after the fracture or dislocation, after attempts to reduce fractures or dislocations, or gradually over a period of hours or days due to swelling of damaged muscles etc. The limb will not survive for very long, and you should contact TMAS urgently. Treat any signs of shock with appropriate fluid to restore blood pressure to normal. Moderate elevation of the limb may help reduce swelling, as will prompt reduction of fractures or dislocations. Keep the limb warm.
- **Nerve damage** May be apparent at the time of the accident, or may become obvious in subsequent hours and days. Loss of motor function or sensation may be reversible and may improve over time. The best treatment is to promptly reduce any fractures or dislocations (checking nerve function before and after each attempt), treat shock to restore blood pressure, and avoid swelling of the limb by elevating it.
- **Tendon damage** Commonly occurs and cannot be treated on board. The limb will be disabled to an extent depending upon which tendons have been damaged, and it may not be possible to flex or extend it properly with full power. Thoroughly clean any open wounds, treat with antibiotics, and splint and immobilise the limb to prevent further injury. Prepare for evacuation urgently.

Types of fracture

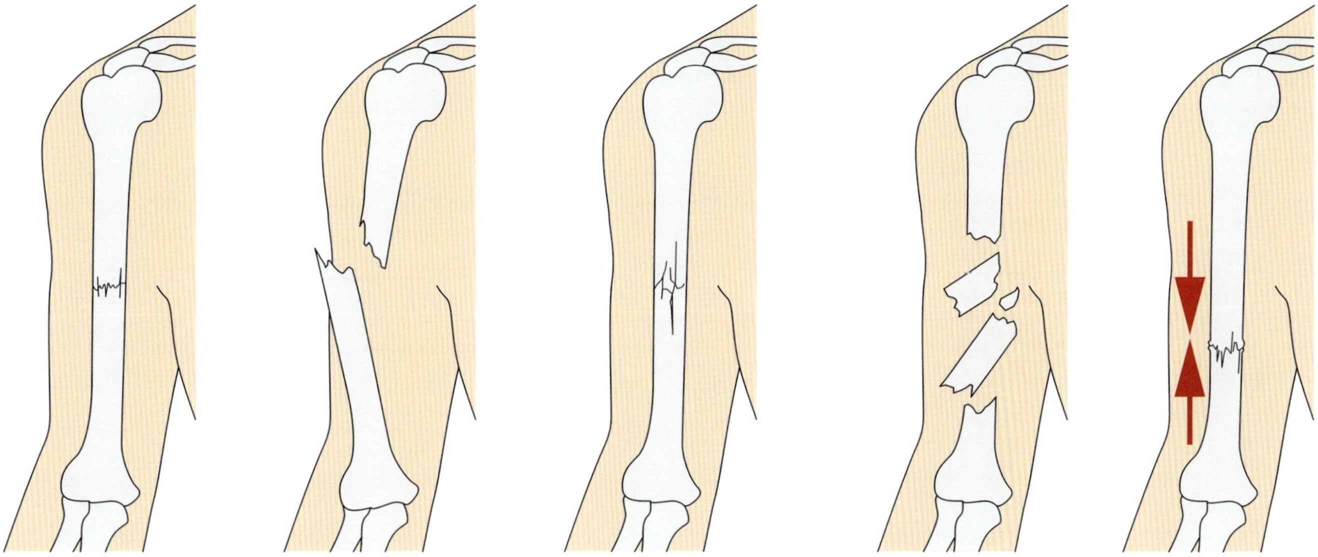

Compound ('open') fractures may not have a bone protruding from the wound when inspected, as the bone ends may have gone back under the skin (see diagram above). Any fracture with a wound near to the fracture site should be considered as compound.

Greenstick fractures happen only in children, whose bones are more flexible, and tend to bend and then splinter rather than fracture.

Upper limb fractures and dislocations

5

Clavicle fracture and dislocation

The shaft of the clavicle may fracture or the end that connects to the shoulder may dislocate (see diagram opposite). A fracture or dislocation may be due to a fall onto, or a direct blow to, the shoulder, or a fall onto an outstretched arm. The ends can protrude through the skin, causing an open fracture.

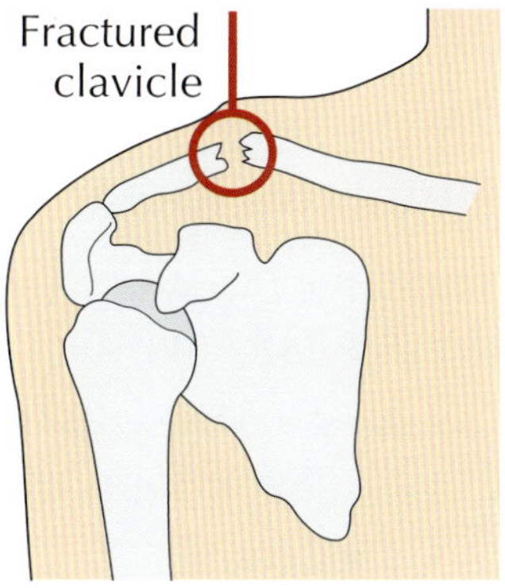

Broken clavicle

Symptoms and signs

- Tenderness over clavicle
- Possible deformity (at the outer end over the shoulder if dislocated)
- Tenting of skin over fractured bone ends
- Reduced and painful shoulder movements

Treatment

- Pain relief
- Immobilise and support the arm with a broad arm sling (see page 243)
- The broken ends of a displaced clavicular fracture may threaten to push through the skin. Gentle traction on the arm pulling away from the centre line may reoppose the ends, reducing the risk of open fracture

Shoulder dislocation

Shoulder dislocations are caused by a moderate amount of force, such as a fall onto an outstretched arm or shoulder, or blows to the upper arm (see diagram below). Less force may cause a dislocation in casualties who have dislocated their shoulder previously. The head of the humerus normally dislocates to the front (anteriorly).

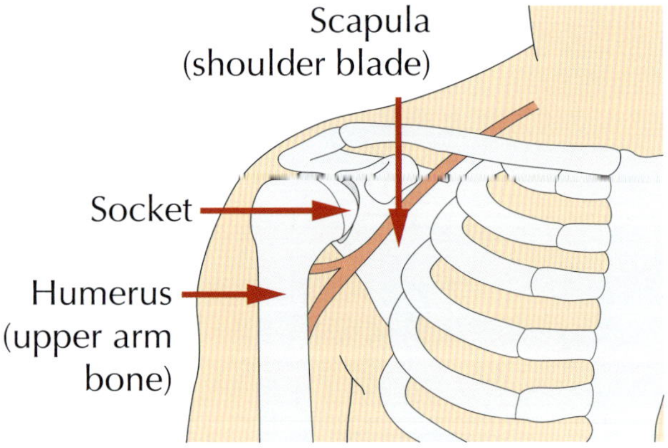

Normal shoulder

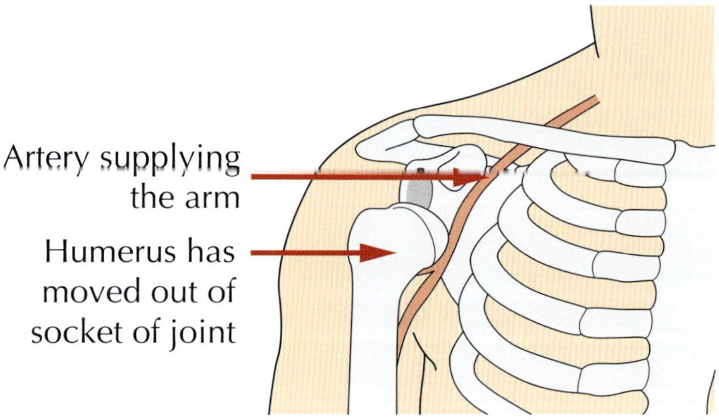

Dislocated shoulder

Symptoms and signs

- Severe pain
- Restricted movement of arm
- 'Squaring' of shoulder (anterior dislocation)
- Loss of blood or nerve supply to arm (pulses and perfusion of skin)
- Crepitus on movement (a sign of possible fracture-dislocation)

Treatment

- Pain relief
- Attempt reduction if blood or nerve supply reduced (contact TMAS and see page 245)
- Support arm with broad arm sling
- Do not attempt reduction of the dislocation if there is crepitus (bones grating together)
- Contact TMAS and prepare to evacuate

Humerus, forearm and wrist fractures

These injuries are normally caused by a fall onto an outstretched hand or an elbow. Blood and nerve supply may be compromised.

Symptoms and signs

- Deformity
- Bruising/swelling
- Crepitus
- Loss of movement
- Open wounds and bleeding
- Loss of pulses/perfusion/nerve supply to distal limb

Treatment

- Pain relief
- Stop bleeding by direct pressure
- Clean and cover wounds
- Reduce and splint (page 246)
- Support with a collar and cuff sling (page 243)
- Antibiotics if open wound

Elbow fracture and dislocation

Dislocation requires considerable force, caused by a direct blow or fall onto an outstretched hand, and is often combined with a fracture (see diagram). Blood vessels and nerves to the lower arm all pass close to the elbow joint and may be damaged.

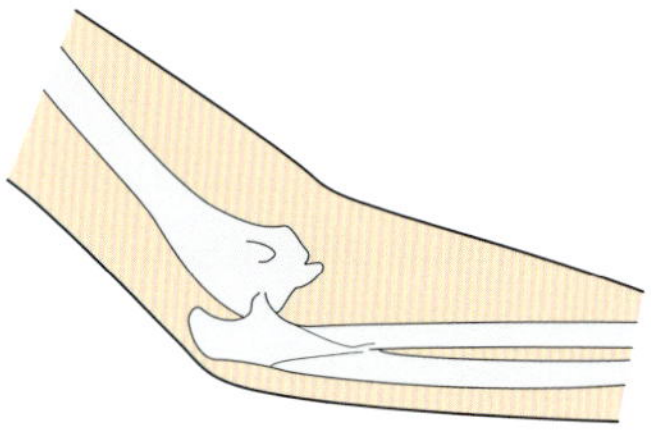

Dislocated elbow

Symptoms and signs

- Pain to elbow and lower arm
- Deformity
- Loss of movement at elbow
- Loss of pulses/perfusion/nerve supply to distal limb

Treatment

- Pain relief
- Attempt reduction if blood or nerve supply is reduced (page 246)
- Support the arm in a broad arm sling (see page 243)

Lower limb fractures and dislocations

Femoral fracture

Substantial force is required to fracture the femur, such as generated by falls from a height, being washed down the deck, or crush injuries between two vessels. Other injuries are common. Contact TMAS immediately and prepare for evacuation.

Symptoms and signs

- Severe pain
- Shock
- Deformity of the thigh (it may appear shortened and thicker than the other side)
- Loss of movement
- Inability to stand
- Loss of blood and nerve supply to lower leg

Treatment

- Limit external bleeding by direct compression
- Treat shock with fluids
- Pain relief
- Apply traction splint; the best way to stabilise the fracture and reduce internal bleeding and pain (see page 240)
- Treat open wounds with antibiotics
- Contact TMAS and prepare for evacuation urgently

Knee injuries

Knee injuries are common on a vessel, usually involving a ligament or meniscus (see knee diagram). The patella (kneecap) may be dislocated laterally (away from the midline), or even fractured by a direct blow or sudden flexion. If there is immediate significant swelling and deformity, fracture of the distal femur or dislocation of the knee is a possibility (these require major force). If in any doubt contact TMAS. Ligament injuries are also included on page 112.

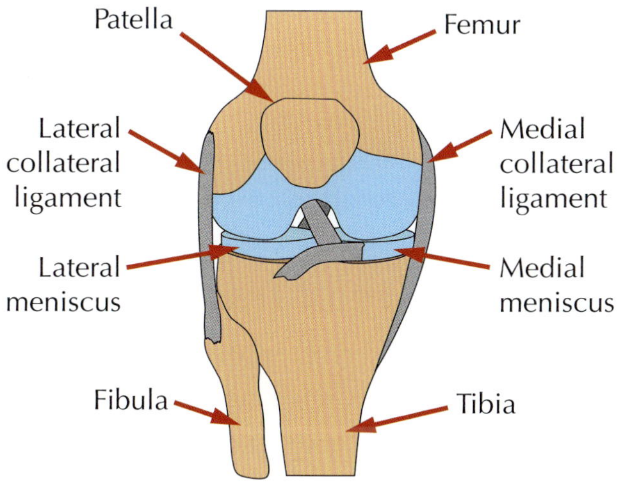

Anatomy of the right knee

Symptoms and signs

- Pain
- Swelling around knee
- Inability to raise a straight leg
- Patella dislocation:
  - Deformity on lateral side of knee
  - Leg held in slight flexion

Treatment

- Pain relief
- Suspected patella fracture:
  - Immobilise using a full leg splint with the knee slightly bent
  - Evacuate urgently
- Suspected patella dislocation:
  - Relocate the patella by straightening the leg, and pushing the patella back into place firmly with thumbs
  - Support the knee with crepe or elastic support bandage

Lower leg fractures

Fracture of the tibia is relatively common on board. High-energy accidents such as falls from height or down stairs, or being swept along the deck, may cause a displaced fracture, which is often open. Badly displaced fractures may cause significant swelling of the lower leg, cutting off blood and nerve supply to the distal limb. Urgent evacuation would be required with such injuries.

Symptoms and signs

- Pain at site of fracture
- Deformity
- Swelling (the calf may become very tense over a few hours or days)
- Crepitus (bones grating together)
- Loss of distal perfusion and pulses
- Reduced distal sensation
- Inability to bear weight

Treatment

- Pain relief
- Stop bleeding by direct pressure
- Clean and cover wounds
- Reduce fracture and splint – a traction splint may be effective in stabilising the fracture
- Antibiotics if open fracture
- Elevate leg to reduce swelling
- Evacuate urgently if open displaced fracture or significant swelling

Ongoing care of fractures and dislocations

6

- Keep the casualty comfortably wedged in a bunk where you can examine the wounds.
- Continue with pain relief, and use more when moving the casualty.
- Elevate the injured limb as much as possible.
- Watch for limb swelling and distal perfusion.
- Encourage the casualty to move around as soon as possible, as pain allows.

10 Hand, foot and ankle injuries

Hands are particularly prone to injury and the loss of use of fingers, or even a hand, seriously handicaps a crew member. Working on deck in sandals or flip-flops may be very comfortable, but such footwear at best provides no protection and at worst may actively cause accidents. Use of appropriate protective gloves and footwear will give protection against most accidents and injuries.

The main injuries to the hands and fingers are rope burns, finger dislocation, crushing, skin de-gloving, and, rarely, mangling or amputation from entrapment in blocks, winches or windlasses. Foot and ankle injuries are less common, especially if proper shoes or boots are worn. Injuries tend to be minor, such as stubbed toes and sprains, but more serious injuries do occur, such as crushing, dislocation of toe or ankle, or amputation by fishing gear or a mooring line bight under load.

Cuts and abrasions to hands and feet are very common. They heal very slowly in a damp environment, and often become infected. The best way to get deep cuts to heal is by suturing them (see pages 230–3), and subsequent protection and immobilisation as far as possible.

History and examination

- Injury to the dominant hand is disabling.
- Injury is usually due to falls, being trapped, a punch or a direct blow.
- Remove rings and bracelets immediately, before swelling occurs.

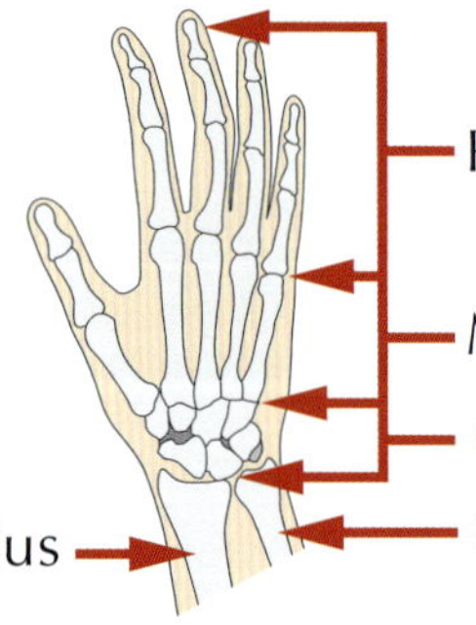

Bones of the hand

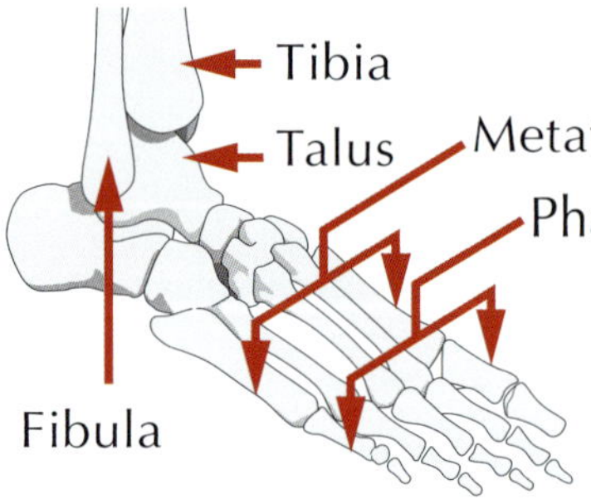

Bones of the foot

Important points in the history

- How did the accident happen?
- Where and when did it happen?
- Possibility of contamination of wound?
- Any possibility of crushing? (page 109)
- Other injuries?
- Previous fractures or dislocations of the same part?
- When was the last tetanus vaccination?

Important points in the examination

- **Look**
  - Swelling or bruising
  - Deformity
  - Open wound over fracture site
  - Colour of toes (with ankle injury)
- **Feel**
  - Pain, tenderness
  - Bone edges
  - Crepitus (bone edges grating together)
  - Perfusion beyond fracture
  - Sensation beyond fracture
- **Move**
  - Ask the casualty to move the hand or foot first, as far as possible, in all directions, testing strength
  - Then move the hand or foot yourself, very gently and stop if causing pain
- **Document** Findings and vital signs

Immediate treatment

- **Stop bleeding** Immediately with direct pressure. Keep this on only until after inspecting the hand or foot, elevation and dressing.
- **Pain relief** Will be required. Consider ring blocks and infiltration with local anaesthetic (see page 215).
- **Clean and cover wounds, consider giving antibiotics** Inspect all wounds for foreign bodies and damage to underlying bones, tendons and nerves.
- **Reduce or relocate** Fractures and dislocations after discussion with TMAS (see page 244).
- **Support and elevate** Use a compression bandage or splint; elevate the hand or foot to reduce swelling.

Specific injuries

Hand and foot fractures and crush injuries

Hand injuries may be serious and require urgent evacuation to prevent permanent damage and loss of vital function. Contact TMAS if in any doubt regarding the severity of the injury. Foot injuries disable the casualty and help will be required getting them moving.

If you are able, take photographs and discuss the injuries with TMAS.

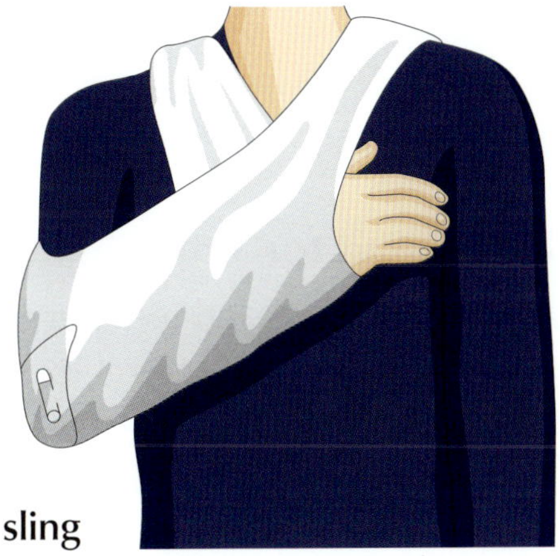

High arm sling

Symptoms and signs

- Deformity, swelling or bruising
- Bent or twisted fingers
- Pain or tenderness (palpate the hand or foot firmly, but do not cause pain)
- Loss of function (grip strength, ability to spread fingers or toes, make fist, bend foot up and down)
- Loss of sensation

Treatment

- Remove rings and bracelets
- Pain relief
- Clean, inspect and cover wounds
- Antibiotics for deep wounds or open fractures
- Compression dressings
- Support arm with high arm sling (see diagram)
- Elevate leg and foot
- Splint if necessary

Finger and toe dislocations and fractures

These wounds are often caused by the finger being forced backward, or toe stubbing. ‘Buddy’ splinting to an adjacent finger or toe (see diagram opposite) is usually sufficient.

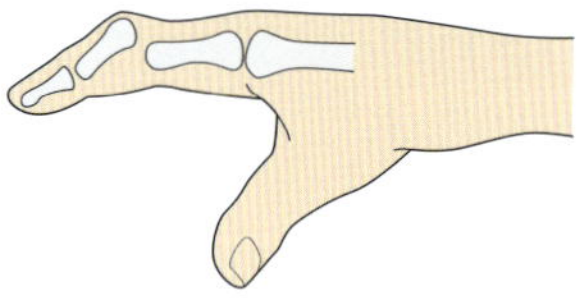

Dislocated finger

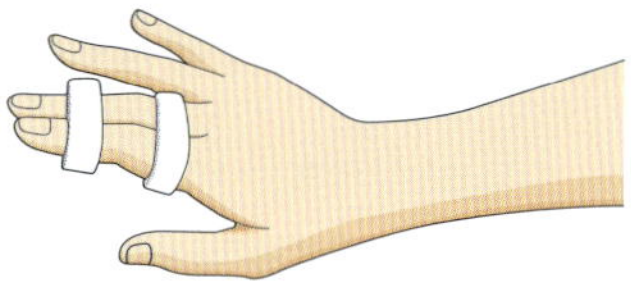

Buddy splint

Symptoms and signs

- Deformity with dislocations and displaced fractures
- Swelling, bruising
- Loss of function

Treatment

- Remove rings
- Pain relief – initially consider nerve block (ring block; page 215)
- Clean, inspect and cover wounds
- Antibiotics for deep wounds or open fractures
- Reduce dislocation and displaced fracture (page 244)
- Buddy splint to next finger or toe (see above)

Finger and toe crush injuries and de-gloving

Injuries to fingers and toes are more common in the cold, when dexterity and sensation will be reduced. Some injuries may become apparent only when the hands and feet warm up. With proper treatment, enough function may be restored to restore the hand or foot to function.

Contact TMAS if there is significant tissue loss or amputation.

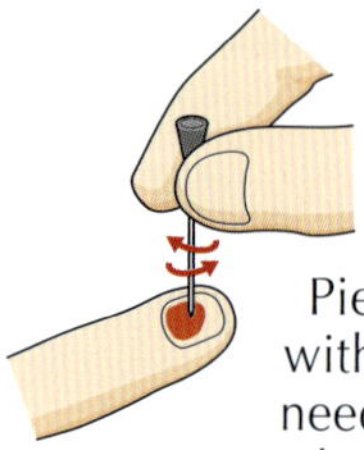

Haematoma under nail bed

Symptoms and signs

- Deformity, bruising and swelling
- Obvious loss of skin with exposed bone if finger de-gloved of skin
- Blood (haematoma) under nail bed – this can become very painful
- Possible tissue loss depending on injury

Treatment

- Remove rings
- Pain relief – consider a local anaesthetic nerve block (ring block; page 215)
- Clean, inspect and cover wounds
- Antibiotics if open wounds
- If finger de-gloved, cover with damp, sterile dressing and contact TMAS
- If blood under nail, use a hot, blunt needle to gently pierce nail to relieve pressure of blood (see diagram above)

Ankle fracture or dislocation

Fractures of the ankle are relatively common, whereas dislocations are less common, but more serious and may require urgent evacuation.

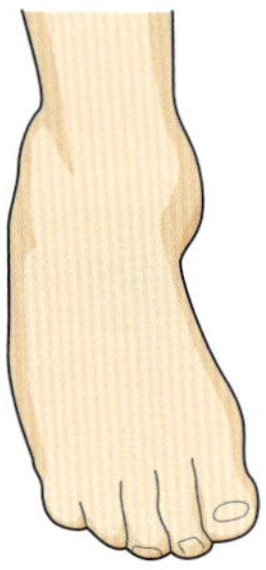

Dislocated ankle

Symptoms and signs

- Deformity of ankle, worse with dislocation
- Pain
- Swelling, bruising
- Loss of function
- Severe deformity may cause loss of blood and nerve supply to foot

Treatment

- Pain relief
- Clean, inspect and cover wounds
- Contact TMAS. If advised, reduce dislocation urgently if nerve and blood supply are reduced (page 244)
- Antibiotics for deep wounds or open fractures
- Compression dressings and supportive splint (page 240)
- Elevate leg and foot
- If advised by TMAS prepare to evacuate

11 Minor soft tissue injuries

Injuries and strains to muscles and joints are common and are the result of impacts, falls, twists, heavy lifting and repetitive overuse. These injuries range from being a slight nuisance to disabling. However, with correct and rapid recognition, initial treatment and early mobilisation, the casualty will regain reasonable function within a short period of time.

Knowing the exact diagnosis is not usually necessary on board because the principles of treatment are the same for most injuries.

As with many medical conditions, prevention is better than cure, so awareness of personal risk, use of protective clothing, and early recognition and treatment of injuries will reduce the crew member's off-watch time.

History and examination

- The injury may be acute (caused by a single incident) or chronic (the result of repetitive trauma).
- The injured part is at risk of further injury.
- Inflammation and infection may complicate the injury and need treatment.
- If in any doubt, treat the injury as a fracture.
- Further investigation may be required at the first port of call.

Important points in the history

- When, where and how did it happen?
- Sudden or gradual onset?
- Site and severity of pain?
- Previous similar injuries?

Definitions

- **Ligament** A fibrous rope connecting bones or cartilages, serving to support and strengthen joints
- **Tendon** A fibrous rope being part of a muscle, and attaching the muscle to bone or cartilage. Inflammation leading to tendonitis/tenosynovitis
- **Cartilage** A piece of fibrous tissue that forms part of the flexible skeleton
- **Bursa** A fluid-filled lubricating sac situated in places in tissues where friction would otherwise occur. Inflammation leading to bursitis

Important points in the examination

- **Look**
  - Deformity
  - Swelling, bruising
  - Redness
- **Feel**
  - Site of tenderness
  - For fluid around joint
  - Crepitus if possible fracture
  - Warmth of joint (may be infected)
- **Move**
  - Ask the casualty to move the injured part, as far as possible, in all directions, testing strength
  - Then move the injured part yourself, very gently, stopping if causing pain
- **Document** Findings such as range of movement, what causes pain

Signs of significant injury

- Severe pain
- Total loss of movement
- Immediate swelling
- Obvious bruising

Immediate treatment

- **Pain relief** Will be required. NSAIDs provide good pain relief and also reduce inflammation. However, if there is severe bruising, it is advisable to avoid NSAIDs for the first 24 hours as they may worsen bleeding. Morphine is rarely required, and if the pain is very bad it usually indicates a more severe injury such as an underlying fracture.
- **Rest** Is required initially (for 24–72 hours depending on the severity of the injury). This is not always possible on board, so immobilisation and support of the affected joint by taping or splinting (see page 240) will be required.
- **Ice** Reduces swelling that occurs immediately after injury, thus speeding recovery. Put crushed ice in a plastic bag, wrap in a damp cloth and hold firmly on the injured part. Do not hold the plastic bag directly on the skin because this may cause a cold injury. Apply the ice pack 4–6 times a day for 15 minutes, and continue for 48 hours if you have to mobilise the casualty with protection or support straight after the injury. The alternatives to ice are cold aerosol spray (e.g Cryogesic if available) and cold packs or even just a cloth soaked in cold water.
- **Compression** Use a crepe or tubular bandage (properly sized to avoid excess compression and reduction in blood flow – check distal limb perfusion), especially when mobilising. This will help support the injury, reducing further damage, and also to remind the casualty to protect the injured part.
- **Elevation** Also reduces swelling. As a rule, an injured arm should be held above the heart (in a high-arm sling; see page 243). An injured leg should be elevated so the foot is higher than the hip. Elevation should be maintained during the initial rest period and between periods of mobilisation.
- **Mobilisation** Of the injured joint or muscle aids recovery as long as it is done in a controlled manner. If the casualty is mobilising immediately after injury, protect the injured part with splinting or taping, and compression. When a casualty is mobilising after 24–72 hours use compression dressings, elevate the injured part when resting, and use it a little more each time.

Specific injuries

Grazes, bruises and rope burns

Symptoms and signs

- Very common injuries, usually acutely painful
- Potentially contaminated
- Large bruises (haematomas) may become infected and form abscesses

Treatment

- Clean thoroughly, remove foreign bodies, and apply sterile dressing
- Watch for infection and treat with antibiotics (cream/ointment/oral)
- Abscesses may need incision and drainage (page 238)

Shoulder injuries

Excessive force and strain can cause damage to the muscles (rotator cuff) around the shoulder.

Repetitive actions can cause inflammation of the tendons and bursae.

Symptoms and signs

- Restricted movement
- Pain on movement
- Sudden onset generally means strains or muscle tears
- Tendonitis and bursitis are usually gradual in onset

Treatment

- Rest and immobilisation in severe cases (broad arm sling)
- NSAIDs
- Gradual return to activity
- Change the way in which the activity is performed

Elbow and wrist injures

These joints are prone to repetitive strain injury. Blows to the point of the elbow may cause bursitis.

Symptoms and signs

- Restricted movement
- Pain on movement and making fist
- Swelling over the elbow (bursitis) which feels boggy and fluctuant – the swelling might become tight and painful
- Infection – redness, swelling, warmth

Treatment

- Rest, reduction in particular activity that provokes pain
- Splinting might be helpful for painful wrists
- Strap around forearm muscles for tennis or golfer's elbow (not too tight)
- A tight fluid swelling may require drainage. Contact TMAS
- Antibiotics for signs of infection

Knee injuries

The knee is a complex structure, with ligaments, bursae, tendons and cartilage all serving to stabilise the joint. Any and all can be damaged.

Knee injuries can be disabling for weeks and the casualty may require evacuation.

Repeated kneeling can cause bursitis in front of the kneecap and is quite common.

Symptoms and signs

- Swelling (the knee may swell rapidly and considerably with severe injury)
- Restricted painful movement
- Instability on weight bearing is a sign of ligament injury
- 'Locking' of the knee on movement is a sign of cartilage damage inside the knee
- Infection – redness, warmth over knee

Treatment

- Rest, ice, compression
- Pain relief (NSAIDs)
- Immobilisation (splinting) for serious injury – evacuate
- A tight fluid swelling may require drainage. Contact TMAS
- Antibiotics for signs of infection
- Careful mobilisation as tolerated

Ankle injuries

Injured ankles tend to lose their stability so take care when mobilising.

It is difficult to tell the difference between a minor undisplaced fracture and a sprain but the treatment is the same.

The large Achilles tendon (see diagram) is at the back of the ankle and can be torn or ruptured when a sudden load is applied to the ankle (e.g. by jumping down onto the quayside). People describe it as a blow to the back of the calf. Such a rupture is disabling.

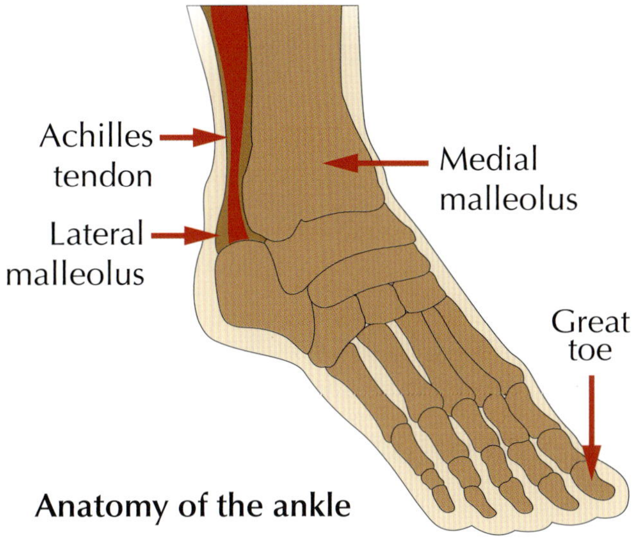

Anatomy of the ankle

Symptoms and signs

- Swelling, bruising
- Pain on movement
- A gap in the Achilles tendon which you may be able to feel
- Tenderness over the ankle bones (medial and lateral malleoli)

Treatment

- Rest, ice, compression (strapping)
- Pain relief (NSAIDs)
- Elevation
- Suspected Achilles tendon injury – splint ankle and seek medical advice
- Careful mobilisation (care with instability)

Lower back pain

Back pain may be linked to a single incident but commonly there is no clear predisposing cause. Recovery usually takes a few days unless there is damage to muscles, ligaments, intervertebral discs or nerves.

Occasionally a back injury may be serious and require evacuation. If there is numbness of legs, severe pain when one leg is raised with the casualty lying down or any problems with passing urine or stool, contact TMAS.

Symptoms and signs

- What movements make the pain worse or better?
- Where is the pain felt – locally in the back, down the legs, one side or both?
- Previous back problems?

Nerve problems

- Any problems with passing water or bowel function?
- Burning pain, numbness or tingling felt in the legs?
- Loss of power in the leg?

Treatment

- Rest but encourage early, careful, gentle mobilisation
- Care with activities (no heavy lifting, keep back straight)
- Pain relief (NSAIDs)
- Use of low-dose benzodiazepine (diazepam 1–5 mg) may help
- If signs of nerve problems, contact TMAS and prepare to evacuate

12 Treating pain

Pain is a very personal matter, and perception of pain varies significantly between individuals. There is no absolute measure of pain, so the casualty's opinion about the pain they are suffering is the main guide to treatment. If the casualty says they are in pain, **believe them**.

Treatment of pain is of paramount importance. Pain demoralises, demotivates and physically stresses the casualty. Controlling pain promotes physical and emotional recovery, enables sleep and mobility, reduces complications and speeds healing. The options for pain relief are detailed in the Pain relief ladder (back flyleaf).

Causes of pain

- Obvious wound
- Swelling
- Organ infection or damage
- Fractures
- Abscess
- Lack of blood flow to an organ (e.g. the heart)
- Infection
- Nerve damage
- Increased sensitivity (previous nerve damage)

Signs

Usually the casualty will be able to say whether they are in pain. Sometimes they may not be able to because of confusion, loss of speech or loss of consciousness. There are signs that give some indication regarding the existence and severity of pain.

- Grimacing
- Cold to touch
- Localising to a point of maximum pain
- Writhing
- Pale
- Raised heart rate
- Confusion
- Sweating
- Raised breathing rate
- Agitation
- Nausea or vomiting
- Increased depth of breathing

Treatment

Immediate control of pain is the first objective, followed by longer-term measures to reduce pain to a bearable level while healing takes place or evacuation for definitive treatment is arranged.

Medications These are listed in the Pain relief ladder (back flyleaf). There is a structure for increasing pain relief according to increasing pain, starting with oral painkillers and progressing to injectable ones. For severe pain morphine or tramadol injected intramuscularly (IM) provides rapid pain control but may make the casualty vomit, so give an anti-emetic at the same time. For longer-term pain relief use regular paracetamol and NSAIDs (see Pain relief ladder). This reduces the use of morphine and tramadol, both of which may cause sickness, constipation and drowsiness, and supplies may run out. Discuss with TMAS if the pain is difficult to control, or repeated doses of morphine or tramadol are required.

Methoxyflurane is an inhaled analgesic agent which is very effective for short-term (up to 30 minutes') treatment of acute pain. This facilitates recovery of a casualty to a place of safety and possible reduction of acute limb fractures.

Local anaesthesia Can be used to numb nerves and reduce pain. It is particularly useful for infiltration around wounds before repairing and also finger (ring) blocks (see page 215).

Limb splinting Immobilises fractures and reduces bone movement, thereby reducing pain.

Reduction Of fractures and dislocations reduces bleeding, swelling and nerve damage.

Elevation Of an injured limb reduces swelling, reducing pain and allowing early mobilisation.

Cool Sprains and muscle injuries to reduce swelling and pain. The same applies to burns (see page 52).

Warmth/heat Eases muscle discomfort in the days following injury. Take care not to cause burns. On a vessel use a hot water bottle (wrapped in a towel) or a hot compress.

Dressings Applied to wounds will reduce pain.

Part 3
Medical disorders

1 Nervous system disorders

When something goes wrong with all or part of the brain it changes the normal way the body works. This may cause the crew member to become unconscious or paralysed, have a fit, develop a headache, or behave differently.

There are a number of disorders that may happen to the brain in addition to trauma (see page 62). Bleeding can occur in and around the brain; infection can affect both the brain itself and the membranes covering it (the meninges); blood clots may cut off the blood supply to part of the brain; and lack of blood pressure, oxygen and glucose in the blood all give rise to problems. Epilepsy, migraine and faints often occur without any obvious brain abnormality.

Nerves both transmit sensations from all parts of the body to the brain and carry instructions to muscles and other organs. Damage to peripheral nerves from either injury or illness can cause weakness, changes in the crew member's ability to feel, and local pain.

1 Assess severity

- History
- Examination

Collapsed? Unconscious? →

Resuscitate
ABCDE (page 4)
Diagnosing loss of consciousness (page 8)
Managing the unconscious crew member (page 12)

Signs of severe illness → **2**

- Loss of consciousness
- Fitting
- High temperature and rash
- Photophobia and neck stiffness
- Paralysis or weakness
- 'Worst ever' headache

Immediate treatment → **3**

- ABCDE (oxygen if available)
- Treat fitting
- Establish IV access
- Give fluid if blood pressure low
- Give sugar if blood sugar level low
- Antibiotics; pain relief if indicated

Specific disorders → **4**

- Headache
- Subarachnoid haemorrhage
- Meningitis
- Epilepsy
- Stroke or transient ischaemic attack
- Local numbness, pain or weakness

Continue monitoring
Watch for deterioration

- Pulse, blood pressure
- Temperature
- Pupils
- Respiration rate
- Blood sugar
- GCS/AVPU

Contact TMAS early

History and examination

1

- It may not be possible to communicate with the crew member if they are confused or have a reduced level of consciousness.
- Use other sources of information; for example, other crew, medical reports, medical alert bracelets.
- Symptoms may take some time to develop and the crew member may deteriorate so re-examine them regularly.

Important points in the history

- Did the symptoms start suddenly or did they develop over a few days?
- 'Worst ever' headache?
- Any neck stiffness?
- Pain when looking at bright light?
- Any rashes on the body?
- Vomiting?
- Weakness in arms or legs?
- Loss of consciousness?
- Fitting (generalised or local)?
- Paralysis or weakness?
- Has this happened before?
- Usual prescription medications?
- Regular use of aspirin, clopidogrel, warfarin?
- Any other medical problems in the past?

Important points in the examination

- **Look:**
  - Obvious signs of illness: pallor, fitting, not moving arms or legs, pain when looking at bright light, rashes anywhere on body?
  - Pupil size and reaction to light? (see page 64)
  - Do they respond to you normally?
  - Do they know where they are?
  - Do they know the date and time?
- **Feel:**
  - Peripheries for perfusion and temperature
- **Move:**
  - Ask the crew member to move their arms and legs; look for weakness or paralysis
  - Move the limbs gently yourself, looking for stiffness or limpness
  - Flex the head forward gently, touching the chin to chest. Stop if it hurts

Signs of severe illness

2

- **Loss of consciousness** has many causes and is an emergency. The priority is ABCDE. See page 4 for causes and treatment.
- **Fitting** must be treated if it does not self-terminate after 5 minutes. See page 16 for causes and treatment.
- **High temperature and rash** may be signs of the infection which causes meningitis. The rash in meningitis does not fade when firmly pressed (use a drinking glass to do this and watch the rash through it).
- **Photophobia and neck stiffness** are other signs of possible meningitis:
  - **photophobia** the crew member will have pain looking into a bright light
  - **neck stiffness** the crew member will get intense neck pain trying to put chin to chest.
- **Paralysis or weakness** may occur down one side of the body or the other. Legs or arms may be involved, or one side of the face. This may be a sign of a stroke or haemorrhage in the head.
- **Headache** is very common; most have simple causes. A very severe headache may be caused by a subarachnoid haemorrhage, meningitis or a stroke (see below).

Immediate treatment

3

- **Fitting** may stop within a few minutes without any treatment. You should treat it if it carries on for more than 5 minutes (see page 17). Fits may be generalised (where the whole body shakes, with possible loss of consciousness, incontinence and tongue biting) or localised (to an arm, leg or part of face, with no loss of consciousness). If in doubt, contact TMAS.
- **IV access (if possible)** is very useful, to give medications to stop fitting and fluids to treat low blood pressure (see page 224).
- **Fluids** may be needed if the crew member has low blood pressure but excess fluids may not be beneficial for certain disorders. Contact TMAS to guide fluid replenishment and further hydration.
- **Blood sugar** should be checked and corrected if it is very low or very high (see page 37).
- **Antibiotics** should preferably be given IV if there are signs of infection and a possibility of meningitis (see below).
- **Pain relief** may be required for severe headaches. Use paracetamol and codeine as required but avoid morphine if possible. NSAIDs can be useful but do not use them if a bleed in the head is suspected as they can make bleeding worse. Use anti-sickness medication such as cyclizine or ondansetron if required and when using codeine.

Specific disorders

4

Headache

Headaches are very common and not usually a problem, but take seriously any severe or persistent headaches (lasting more than 24 hours despite treatment with plenty of fluids, simple pain relief and rest).

Symptoms and signs	Treatment
Serious but rare causes • **Meningitis** • **Subarachnoid haemorrhage** • **Carbon monoxide poisoning**	See below See below See page 181
Less serious, more common causes • **Tension or tiredness** – General headache and sore neck – Lack of sleep – Dehydration	• Efficient rest • Good hydration • Change of repetitive work practice • Pain relief
• **Dehydration** – Thirst – Lethargy, fatigue – Small amount of dark urine – Heavy work, sweating – Tropical climate	• Drink plenty of water or rehydrating drinks, especially in hot climates and when working hard • Work as a team to keep hydrated • Watch colour of urine; if it goes dark, drink more rehydration fluid
• **Sinusitis** – Tender over cheek or eyebrow – Fever – Foul discharge from nose or back of throat	• Antibiotics • Pain relief • Avoid blowing nose • Steam inhalation may help • No diving or air travel
• **Migraine** • Previous history of migraine? • Often pain on one side of head • Visual disturbances (blurring, flashing lights, even blindness)	• Pain relief • Rest in quiet and dark • Keep hydrated • Anti-sickness medication if sick • Avoid chocolate, citrus fruits, cheese
• **Sunstroke** • History of sun exposure without proper protection • Heavy work in direct sun • Reddened, painful, itchy skin, blistering	• Keep out of sun • Wear sun cream, hat, shirt • Cool down (damp clothes and hat) • Pain relief • Keep hydrated • Anti-sickness medication if vomiting

Symptoms and signs

Serious but rare causes

- **Alcohol and drugs**
  - History of heavy alcohol intake
  - Medications such as nitrates (GTN)
  - Dehydration

Treatment

- Hydration
- Avoid certain prescription drugs if they are possibly the cause; contact TMAS
- Reduce alcohol intake

Subarachnoid haemorrhage

Subarachnoid haemorrhage (SAH) is a result of the rupture of a defective blood vessel in the head, causing bleeding and headache. It is immediately life-threatening.

It commonly follows strenuous exercise or trauma to the head. It may result in sudden loss of consciousness.

Symptoms and signs

- Sudden-onset 'worst ever' headache like a blow to the back of head
- Confusion or drowsiness
- Neck pain
- Vomiting
- Possible fitting
- Loss of consciousness

Treatment

- ABCDE and vital signs
- Treat fitting (see page 17)
- Pain relief
- Rest
- Contact TMAS
- Prepare for urgent evacuation

Meningitis

This is inflammation of the membrane covering the brain caused by infection. It is life-threatening if not recognised and treated rapidly with antibiotics.

Symptoms and signs

- The crew member feels and looks unwell
- Fever and headache for several hours
- Stiff neck
- Photophobia
- Possibly a non-blanching rash
- Later, unconsciousness

Treatment

- ABCDE and vital signs
- Antibiotics (preferably IV)
- Pain relief for headache, sore neck
- Establish IV access and consider IV fluids
- Contact TMAS
- Prepare for urgent evacuation

Epilepsy (Control of fitting – see page 17)

Epileptic fits may be generalised (where the crew member's whole body convulses and they lose consciousness), or localised (where perhaps just one set of muscles twitches and the crew member may stay fully conscious).

People known to be suffering from epilepsy and who require medication may be able to work at sea in near-coastal waters. They may be present in other maritime settings and will normally take medication. Seasickness may prevent them from absorbing their normal oral medication, resulting in uncontrolled fitting.

Fitting may also occur in people with heavy alcohol use who suddenly stop drinking. Crew members who have been drinking heavily while on leave are at risk if they subsequently board a 'dry' vessel and abruptly stop drinking.

The crew member will be very sleepy after the fit (the 'post-ictal' period), especially if drugs have been used to terminate the fit. This may last from 30 minutes to a few hours. They need to remain under observation for at least 24 hours after the event in case of a recurrence and should not return to safety-critical duties until they have been medically assessed ashore.

Symptoms and signs

- Generalised or localised fitting
- Incontinence; tongue biting
- Blue around lips, under tongue, finger tips (cyanosis)
- Causes:
  - Non-absorption of normal medication
  - Infection
  - Alcohol withdrawal
  - First fit with no predisposing features

Treatment

- ABCDE and give oxygen
- Do not restrain but prevent injury caused by the convulsions
- Recovery position
- Treat fitting (see page 17)
- Contact TMAS regarding prevention of further fits
- Prepare for urgent evacuation

Stroke and transient ischaemic attack

A stroke or cerebrovascular accident (CVA) may be caused by a bleed in the brain or a blood clot blocking off the supply of blood.

A blood clot may cause a transient ischaemic attack (TIA). This may have similar symptoms to a stroke but the crew member will fully recover from it within an hour or so.

Both are life-threatening events so contact TMAS immediately.

Symptoms and signs

- Paralysis down one side of the body, or just one limb or side of face
- Difficulty speaking and swallowing
- Visual problems
- Lack of coordination
- Altered sensation
- Headache and possible fitting

Treatment

- ABCDE and give oxygen
- Treat fitting (see page 17)
- Recovery position if unconscious
- IV access may be required for fluids
- Pain relief if required
- Contact TMAS regarding giving aspirin 300 mg
- Prepare for urgent evacuation

Peripheral nerve damage

Abnormal nervous sensations, including pain and localised weakness, have a wide range of causes including trauma, pressure on nerves, infections and longer-term degenerative diseases. Most symptoms will resolve over a few days or weeks, but duties may need to be adjusted to take account of any physical limitations. If symptoms worsen rapidly or spread to several parts of the body contact TMAS. Otherwise give pain relief where pain is present and, if the symptoms persist, get medical advice during the next port call.

2 Eye disorders

The eye is relatively well protected within its socket and behind the eyelids, so serious disorders are rare. However, harsh environments can cause significant problems. For example, wind, snow, ultraviolet (UV) glare, fatigue and lack of hygiene all affect the eye, particularly for crew members who wear contact lenses or glasses. Risks to the eyes from work at sea include foreign bodies from chipping and cleaning operations and 'arc eye' from UV light during welding.

Only a few treatments for eye disorders are practicable on a vessel. These include antibiotic drops or ointment, anaesthetic drops, eye lubrication, rest and protection, and are effective for most complaints. However, for some symptoms, such as blindness and a painful red eye, you must contact TMAS and prepare for urgent evacuation.

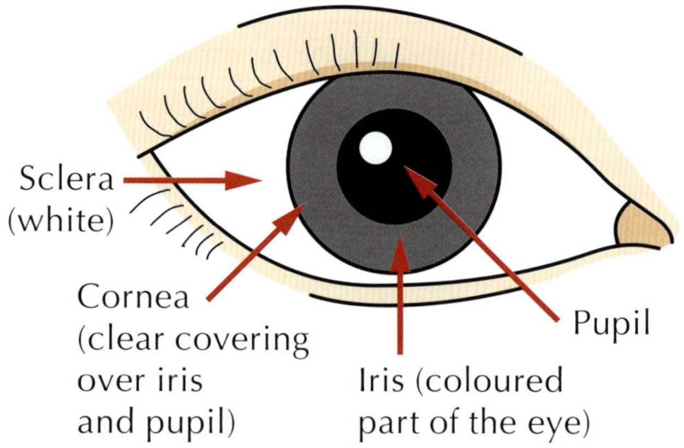

Front view of the eye

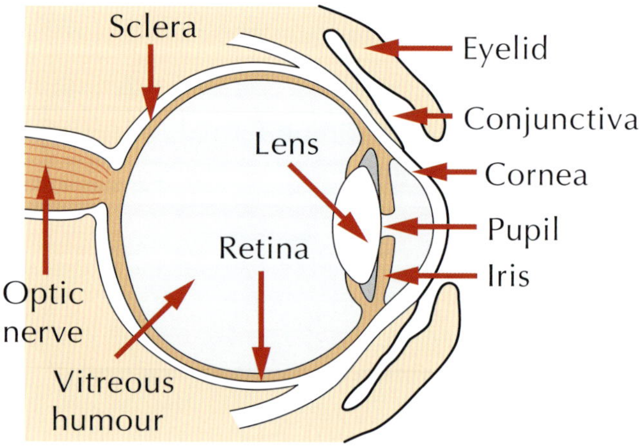

Side view of the eye

History and examination

- The crew member may have a history of eye problems; they should give you some idea of the diagnosis.
- Examine the crew member in a safe and stable place (e.g. lying in bunk). It should be well lit (e.g. head torch). The crew member should be amenable.
- Compare eyes to see if the problem affects both sides.

Important points in the history

- How quickly have the symptoms developed?
- Pain? Worse with light?
- Blurred, poor or double vision?
- Any discharge from eye (stickiness)?
- Recent exposure of eyes to irritants, strong light, welding?
- Previous problems with eyes/vision?
- Eye surgery in past (cataract/laser)?
- Contact lenses or glasses?
- Diabetes, glaucoma, arthritis?
- Medications for eyes?

Important points in the examination

- **Look:** (compare sides)
  - Redness over sclera?
  - Discharge?
  - Swellings around eye and lids?
  - Size and reactivity of pupil?
  - Blood or pus in front of the iris?
  - Cloudiness of cornea or lens (pupil should appear clear black)
  - Look inside eyelids (see page 79)

- **Visual acuity:**
  - Ask the casualty whether their vision is normal or not
  - Test vision by reading small text from book at normal distance
- **Feel:**
  - Press gently on globe of eye – painful or very tense? Compare with other side
  - Tenderness around orbit or eyelids
- **Move:**
  - Ask casualty to look at your finger held about 30 cm from face. Move the finger up and down and from side to side slowly. Keep head still. Ask about double vision, and watch eye movements closely
  - Record which movements cause pain

Using fluorescein drops to help examination of the eye

- Fluorescein stains scratches, abrasions and ulceration of the cornea with a greenish colour when lit by blue light.
- Put a few drops of tetracaine 0.5% local anaesthetic inside the lower eyelid (fluorescein stings).
- After 2 minutes, put a few drops of fluorescein inside the lower eyelid.
- Close the eye for a minute or so, and wipe off the excess fluorescein.
- Examine the cornea with a magnifying glass and bright (preferably blue) light.
- Stain one eye at a time and wait 30 minutes before doing the other one.

Signs of severe eye disorders

- **Blindness** either in one eye or both; may or may not be painful.
- **Reduction in visual acuity** the crew member has blurred vision.
- **Red eye** particularly when the eye itself is painful (see below).
- **Unreactive pupil** to a bright light being shone into the eye.
- **Cloudy cornea or lens** where the pupil should be clear black.

Causes of a 'red eye'

- Serious
  - Acute glaucoma – blurred vision, painful eye
  - Acute iritis – blurred vision, pain, photophobia
  - Corneal inflammation/ulceration (keratitis)
  - Orbital cellulitis – swelling and redness around the eye
  - Trauma to the eye (see page 80)

- Less serious
  - Prolonged contact lens wear
  - Conjunctivitis
  - UV effects from strong sun or welding
  - Foreign body in eye (see page 80)
  - Sub-conjunctival haemorrhage

Specific conditions

Contact lens problems

Being at sea is generally hostile to eyes and contact lenses, due to long periods of use, lack of proper cleaning, and exposure to sea, sun, wind and salt. Crew members should always take glasses on board that can be used in the event of contact lens problems.

Particular problems include:

- **Lens stuck in eye** Wash out with plenty of sterile saline. Someone may need to help extract the lens gently
- **Sore, dry eyes** See below.
- **Conjunctivitis** Stop wearing lenses until infection has completely cleared. Sterilise lenses.
- **Corneal abrasion** A problem with prolonged use. Stop wearing lenses. For treatment see below.
- **Lost lens** It may still be in the eye, but quite difficult to see. Inspect thoroughly inside the lower lid, and particularly the upper lid (see page 79).

Dry eyes

Dry eyes are caused by exposure to sea, sun, salt and wind, and contact lens wearers are particularly at risk.

Symptoms and signs

- Eyes are red and painful, and feel gritty
- Both eyes usually affected
- Long period of wearing contact lenses

→

Treatment

- Use artificial tears if available
- Reduce wearing time of contact lenses
- Wear sunglasses or goggles to protect eyes from glare and wind
- Use antibiotic eye ointment to soothe if particularly bad

Ultraviolet damage

'Sunburn' of the eye can be caused by UV rays from the sun or from welding ('arc eye'). 'Sea blindness' is a particular risk at sea due to surface reflection.

Symptoms and signs

- May happen after only 2–3 hours' exposure
- Very painful red eyes
- Face may be burnt red as well
- Bright light may hurt eye
- Headache is common
- Usually both eyes are affected

→

Treatment

- Prevention is best: sunglasses with good protection from the sides; welding shield
- Assess for foreign bodies
- Local anaesthetic drops for pain, and oral painkillers for headache
- Antibiotic eye ointment may lubricate the eyes and help to relieve pain

Conjunctivitis

Conjunctivitis is a serious problem on vessels because it can be very infective, and the whole crew can catch it. Do not share towels or bedding etc. Usually both eyes are affected.

Symptoms and signs		Treatment
• Red, painful eye (cornea is not red) • Discharge of pus: bacterial infection • Watery discharge: viral infection • Itchy eye: caused by allergy • Vision not affected	→	• Antibiotic drops or ointment for 5 days • Viral conjunctivitis will clear without treatment • Antihistamine eye drops, if available, or oral tablets (loratadine or cetirizine) if allergy or reaction suspected

Sub-conjunctival haemorrhage

Symptoms and signs		Treatment
• One eye may appear alarmingly red • Vision unaffected • No pain or other symptoms • No apparent cause (perhaps minor trauma; recurrent coughing; use of anticoagulants such as aspirin and warfarin)	→	• No specific treatment required • Should clear in 2–3 weeks • If recurrent, check blood pressure and review anticoagulant dose and effect when ashore

Corneal inflammation and ulceration (keratitis)

Inflammation and ulceration of the cornea may cause scarring, which can permanently affect vision.

The causes are infection, contact lens overuse and corneal abrasion.

Do not use steroid drops in the eye if there is any possibility of corneal ulceration because this may make the inflammation much worse.

Symptoms and signs		Treatment
• Red and painful eye • Photophobia • Watery eye • Cloudy cornea with bacterial infection • Blurred vision	→	• Ulcers will glow greenish with fluorescein staining (page 127) • Antibiotic drops or ointment • Contact TMAS as vision may be threatened

Part 3

Orbital cellulitis

Inflammation of the orbit within which the eye sits is a threat to eyesight.

It is also life-threatening if the infection spreads to the brain.

Use IV antibiotics if possible.

Contact TMAS and prepare for evacuation.

Symptoms and signs

- Painful, red eye
- Swelling around eye, possibly causing lids to close
- Possible loss of vision
- Reduced and painful eye movements
- Fever and generally unwell

Treatment

- IV antibiotics
- Monitor vital signs
- Keep well hydrated
- Pain relief as required
- Contact TMAS immediately
- Prepare for urgent evacuation

Acute glaucoma

Acute glaucoma is a serious condition caused by build-up of fluid pressure within the eye.

Just one eye is usually affected, with the other normal.

Sight in the affected eye is threatened.

Treatment on a vessel is limited, but pilocarpine 2% drops may be available for emergency treatment, until evacuation can be arranged.

Symptoms and signs

- Pain may be severe, with nausea and vomiting
- Red eye around cornea, which might be hazy
- Blurred vision, with halos around lights
- Pupil may be semi-dilated and unresponsive to bright light
- History of glaucoma or other eye problems?

Treatment

- Pilocarpine 2% eye drops into affected eye every 15–30 minutes; pupil will constrict
- Rest, and sit upright
- Anti-sickness medications if needed
- Contact TMAS and prepare for urgent evacuation

Acute iritis

Iritis (uveitis) is an acute condition that is often associated with systemic diseases, such as some types of arthritis. The crew member may have had previous attacks.

Symptoms and signs

- Sudden onset of pain
- Reddened eye around cornea
- Watering eyes
- Blurred vision
- Photophobia
- Small, possibly irregular, pupil
- Signs of systemic disease

Treatment

- No specific treatment at sea
- Rest and pain relief
- Contact TMAS
- Urgent evacuation
- Steroid (dexamethasone) eye drops may help but only use under direct supervsion from TMAS

Eyelid infections

Symptoms and signs

- **Stye** – small boil arising from eyelash hair follicle. Usually discharges with no treatment
- **Meibomian cyst** – an infected gland in the eyelid; may develop into an abscess or nodule affecting vision

Treatment

- Similar treatment for both:
  - 'Hot spooning': wrap warm, damp cloth around a small spoon and press to eye; repeat every few hours
  - Antibiotic ointment or drops
- A complicated meibomian cyst may need surgical treatment

3 Dental and mouth disorders

Dental problems and mouth ulcers can be debilitating and can reduce the crew member to the position of passenger.

Most crew members are required to have a medical examination at least every two years, including a dental examination. Even if this is not a mandatory requirement, a thorough dental review is very desirable. All checks should be made in good time so that any dental work can be completed. These precautions should reduce dental problems during voyages but it may not eradicate them completely. Good personal dental care (including regular brushings, flossing and salt-water mouth washes) is also essential to maintain tooth and gum health.

Definitive dental repair work cannot be performed on a vessel, but good first aid can minimise problems until port is reached. The vessel should carry a basic dental repair kit containing temporary filling material and some basic tools for simple dental procedures. The other aspect of care is control of symptoms, such as pain, swelling and infection. Do not extract teeth at sea unless absolutely necessary. Refer to a dentist once in port, for definitive treatment.

History and examination

- Examine teeth in a safe and stable place (e.g. with crew member sitting in a bunk or on a chair) that is well lit (e.g. using a head torch). The crew member should be amenable.
- Examination from behind (as at the dentist) is easier and more effective.
- Procedures are easier if they are carried out from behind the crew member's head.
- The mouth is a dark hole full of saliva. Use a good head torch and sucker if available.
- Be aware that sinusitis can resemble dental pain, and dental pain can be felt in the face and ears.

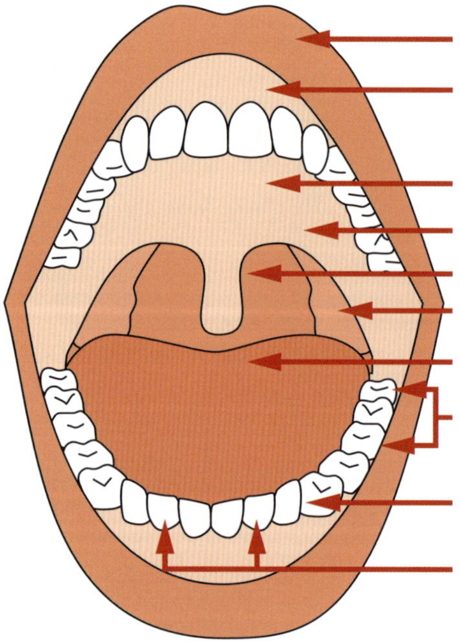

Important points in the history

- Site and severity of pain
- What makes the pain worse?
- Fever, unwell?
- History of trauma?
- Any foul-tasting discharge or smell from mouth or nose?
- Retrieve any knocked-out teeth/dentures (especially if history shows loss of consciousness)
- Previous dental problems, cold sores?

Important points in the examination

- **Look:**
  - Inspect all teeth, noting crowns, fillings
  - Gums, tongue (above and below), lips for inflammation, swelling, discharge
- **Feel:**
  - Each tooth for looseness, tenderness
  - Lips, tongue, cheeks for tenderness, swelling, ulcers
  - Tap over cheek below eye and forehead above eye checking for sinusitis
- **Document** Findings for each tooth

Replacing a filling

- Stable working position, good light, use gauze swabs to keep tooth and hole dry
- Gently probe hole in tooth removing loose bits of filling. Dry the hole as much as possible
- Push in small amount of filling material from dental kit (for mixing follow instructions)
- Pack in firmly, and repeat until hole is full (do not leave proud of tooth surface)
- Bite together with damp cotton wool pad between teeth for a few minutes

Specific conditions

Toothache

Symptoms and signs

- May result from cracked tooth, dislodged filling or gum disease
- Pain with cold/hot drinks
- Pain felt in tooth, in cheek, or as ear ache
- May result in root or gum abscess

→

Treatment

- Pain relief
- Antiseptic mouth wash
- Antibiotics if fever, local inflammation
- Replace filling if lost (see above)

Root and gum abscesses

Symptoms and signs

- Pain on biting firmly
- Swelling/inflammation of gum
- May discharge into mouth
- May spread to cause swelling of cheek, difficulty in opening mouth

→

Treatment

- Pain relief
- Oral antibiotics
- Antiseptic mouth wash
- Lancing the abscess may be possible if it is tense or points
- Contact TMAS if it worsens

Broken or knocked out (avulsed) teeth

Symptoms and signs

- Usually front teeth
- Try to find tooth and keep it in saliva/milk – aim to re-implant within 30 minutes
- Do not handle root of tooth
- Check for other injuries
- Splint broken tooth as for avulsed tooth

→

Treatment

- Clean blood clot from socket
- Clean tooth with sterile saline
- Re-implant to same height as surrounding teeth – hold in place for 10 minutes
- Splint with aluminium foil wrapped over teeth, or filling material squeezed in between thoroughly dried teeth
- Pain relief and antibiotics

Broken crowns, bridges and dentures

Symptoms and signs

- There are different types of crowns
- Bridges are similarly varied and are generally impossible to replace
- Some breaks will leave a sensitive socket
- Denture wearers should take a spare set. A superglue repair may not be successful

Treatment

- It may be possible to reglue a crown – get dental advice at next suitable port if not urgent
- Clean and dry both surfaces. Use dental glue (superglue may be suitable but be very careful)
- Sensitive sockets may require temporary filling for protection

Mouth ulcers and cold sores

Symptoms and signs

- May result from trauma (teeth), bacterial and herpes infection (lots of small ulcers)
- Painful ulcers
- Bleeding gums and bad breath with bacterial infections

Treatment

- Antibiotics if bleeding sore gums and bad breath (bacterial infection)
- Cold sores – aciclovir cream is effective if used early
- Herpes mouth ulcers – oral aciclovir used early (usually a history of similar ulcers)
- Antiseptic mouth wash

4 Ear, nose and throat disorders

Flu-like symptoms of ear, nose and throat disorders, such as a running nose, sore throat and blocked ears, make life miserable for the crew member affected. Treatment is aimed at the relief of symptoms, while the infection, which is usually viral, gets better in its own time. Signs of bacterial infection (a discharge of pus from the nose, ear or tonsils) need treating.

The various tubes and spaces in the head can easily become lodging places for foreign bodies, which can cause complications. Diving and air travel to or from the vessel may cause pain or rupture of the eardrum (barotrauma) and pain in the sinuses if they are blocked. A bleeding nose may sound trivial, but can become life-threatening through loss of blood if it is allowed to continue unabated.

History and examination

- Examination needs to be done in a safe and stable place (e.g. with the crew member lying in their bunk). It needs to be well lit (e.g. with a head torch). The crew member should be amenable.
- Compare both sides.
- Do not stick things in the ear, apart from an otoscope (if one is in the medical kit), and only use this if trained.

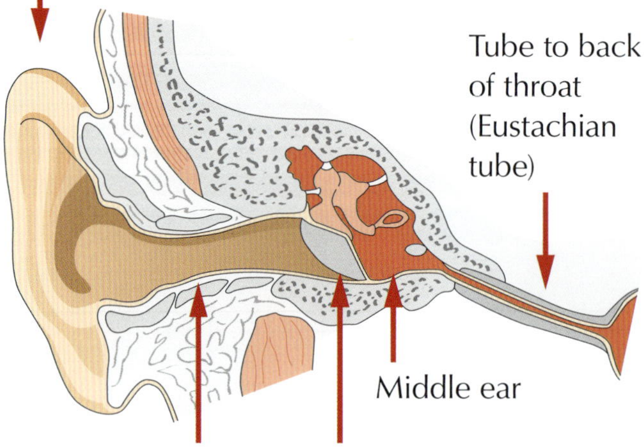

Important points in the history

- Site and severity of pain
- What makes the pain worse (blowing nose, tapping on cheek or forehead)?
- Feeling of deafness?
- Feeling of object stuck in throat?
- History of ear, nose and throat problems?

Important points in the examination

- **Look:**
  - In ears, up nose, in mouth using good light (otoscope in ears only if trained)
  - Pus in ears, on tonsils, in nose
  - Inflamed tonsils, throat, ear canal
  - Foreign bodies, wax in ears
- **Feel:**
  - Tap on cheek and forehead – painful with sinusitis

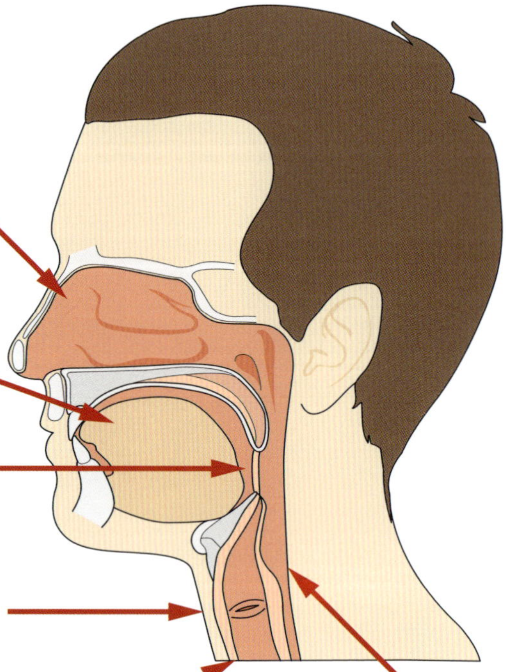

Using an otoscope

- Get proper training if an otoscope is to be used
- Use it gently – stop if you are causing pain
- Gently pull the outer ear back to straighten the canal
- Use a clean tip for each ear and each patient.

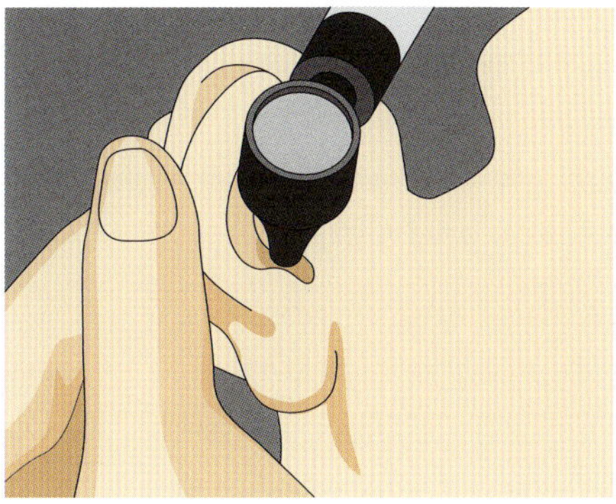

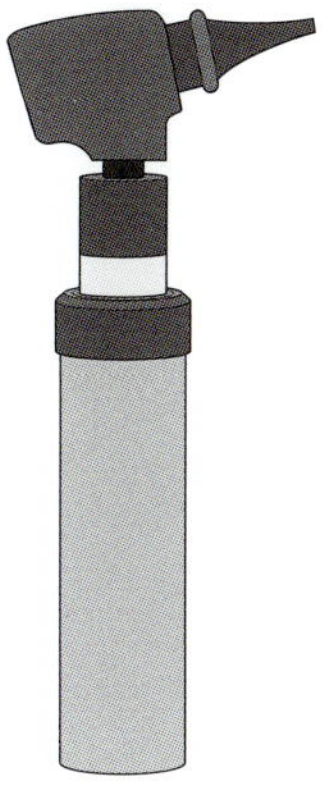

Specific conditions

Build-up of ear wax

Symptoms and signs

- Gradual onset of deafness

Treatment

- A few drops of olive oil (or other ear drops) each day for a few days
- **Do not use cotton buds**
- If persistent, contact TMAS and, if advised, arrange for medical treatment in next port

Outer ear infection

Symptoms and signs

- Pain and discharge from ear
- Inflamed ear canal, possibly blocked with wax, secretions, swelling
- Pulling on the outer ear hurts
- Feels unwell if severe infection

Treatment

- Antibiotic ear drops
- If severe – oral antibiotics
- Gentle cleaning of ear with sterile water
- Avoid diving, swimming, air travel

Middle ear infection

Symptoms and signs

- Pain and deafness
- May feel unwell with cough, cold
- Inflamed ear drum through otoscope
- Ear drum may burst giving relief of pain, discharge of pus

Treatment

- Oral antibiotics
- Pain relief
- Decongestant (pseudoephedrine or proprietary cold remedy) may be helpful
- Avoid diving, swimming, air travel

Ear barotrauma

This may follow air travel, diving and exposure to sudden, intense, low-frequency noise such as an explosion.

Symptoms and signs

- Pain in ear with changing pressure when Eustachian tube blocked
- Ear drum may be red and inflamed
- Drum may rupture – blood from ear
- If dizzy and vomiting contact TMAS

Treatment

- Pain relief
- Oral antibiotics if ruptured drum
- Avoid diving, swimming, air travel until better

Foreign bodies in ear, nose and throat

Contact TMAS as the casualty may need treatment ashore.

Symptoms and signs

- **Ear** – deafness, discharge, irritation. An insect may cause buzzing in ear
- **Nose** – discharge, irritation. Danger of inhalation of foreign body
- **Throat** – coughing, wheezing, may precipitate choking (page 22). A feeling of something lodged in throat may persist. Often stuck at back of tongue, in tonsils

Treatment

- **Ear** – olive oil drops may soften the object. Attempt to remove foreign body if clearly visible. Do not persist and cause injury to the canal
- **Nose** – try to blow out first, or remove under direct vision. Do not persist in trying to remove it.
- **Throat** – use tongue depressor and direct vision. Use forceps

Nose bleeds

Symptoms and signs

- **Shock may develop with continual bleeding**
- Most bleed from inside the front part of nose
- More serious from the back of nose, more difficult to control
- Blood may be swallowed so not seen on outside
- Check for medications such as warfarin, aspirin or clopidogrel – if the crew member is on these, contact TMAS

Treatment

- Sit up, do not swallow blood
- Firmly squeeze nose just below bony part for 10 minutes. Let go and reassess. Reapply pressure if further bleeding
- If bleeding continues, use a strip of paraffin gauze, or soak a gauze strip in adrenaline, tranexamic acid or petroleum jelly (e.g. Vaseline). Pack firmly into nose, but leave a tail hanging out. Contact TMAS. Remove as advised or at 48 hours
- If bleeding is catastrophic pass a lubricated urinary catheter to back of nose. Inflate balloon, and pull firmly forwards. Do this only under direction from TMAS

Sinusitis

Symptoms and signs

- Pain on tapping over cheek below eye, or over forehead above eyebrow
- Fever, headache
- Discharge of pus

Treatment

- Oral antibiotics
- Pain relief
- Nasal decongestants

Sore throat and tonsillitis

Symptoms and signs

- Fever, headache
- Some difficulty swallowing
- Tonsillitis – inflamed tonsils, at either side of mouth, at back of tongue, sometimes with pus visible (use tongue depressor and torch to examine)

Treatment

- Give paracetamol or ibuprofen
- Should clear without antibiotics if throat is just red, with no white pus
- If pus is visible on tonsils, antibiotics may be advisable
- If cannot swallow fluids, contact TMAS

5 Chest disorders

The age of crew members working on vessels at sea is increasing. Older crew members are more likely to have problems with their heart and lungs which may be made worse by their lifestyle. In gruelling conditions previously unknown problems may come to the surface, even in the young and supposedly fit. For instance, asthma is common, and attacks may be brought on by cold and exercise.

Some knowledge of what symptoms are caused by which disorders will guide management on the vessel. This may buy time until you have discussed the clinical situation with TMAS and, if they advise, prepared for evacuation.

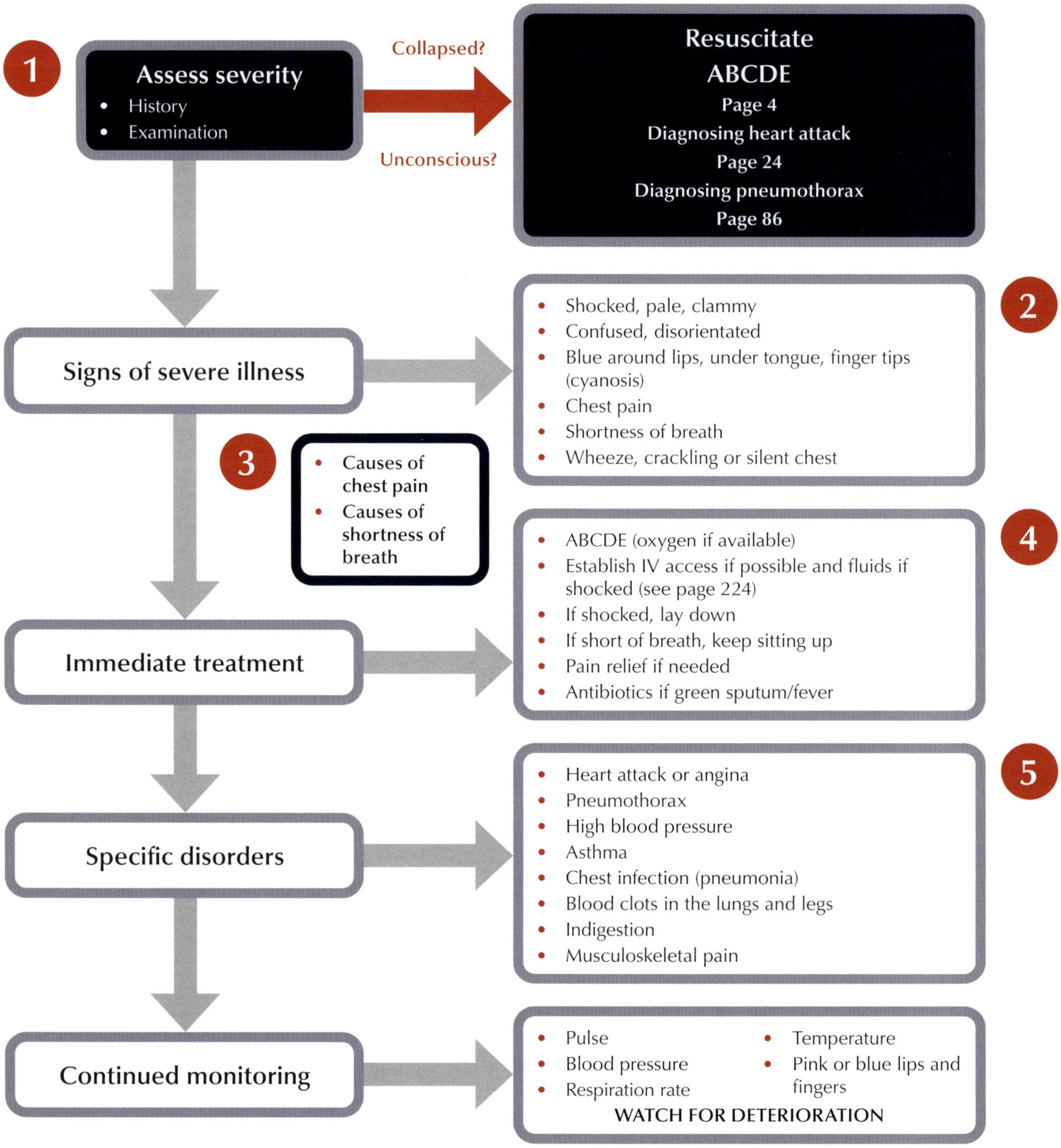

Contact TMAS early

History and examination

1

- ABCDE takes priority over everything.
- A blue or white casualty is a very bad sign; contact TMAS immediately.
- Find out if the casualty has a history of heart or lung problems.
- Find what medications they are taking.
- Exclude any possible trauma (talk to the rest of the crew).

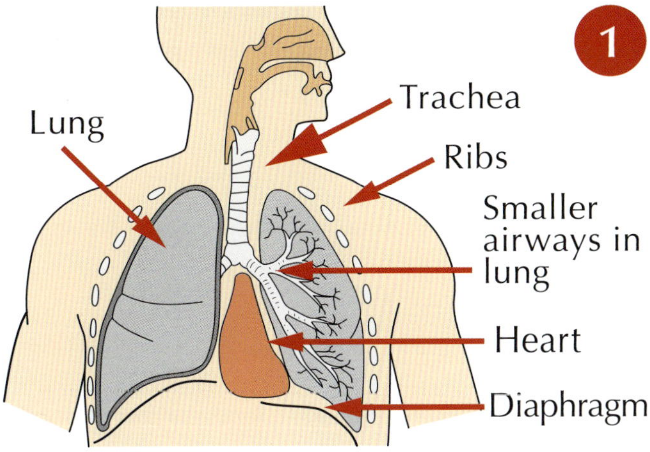

Important points in the history

- Did the symptoms start suddenly or did they come on over a few days?
- Pain in the chest:
  - Location (up to jaw, down arms?)
  - Severity ('worst ever'?)
  - What makes it better or worse?
- Shortness of breath:
  - Does anything make it worse?
  - Did anything obvious bring it on?
  - Can they speak in sentences or just one or two words?
- Any sputum and what colour?
- Any trauma?
- Pain or swelling of legs?
- Recent immobility or air travel?
- Any history of similar attacks?
- Normal medications?

Important points in the examination

- **Look:**
  - appearance of casualty (blue/white/ feverish/sweaty)
  - obvious struggling with breathing – perhaps sitting upright, leaning forward, muscles standing out in neck with effort
  - clutching chest
  - tender swelling of calves
- **Feel:**
  - pulse, perfusion
  - tenderness over chest wall
  - position of trachea (windpipe)
- **Listen:**
  - breath sounds in the chest with a stethoscope (present or absent?)
  - harsh or crackly breath sounds
- **Document** Vital signs; peripheral perfusion

Part 3

Signs of severe illness

2

- **Being shocked, pale and clammy** are symptoms of severe pain or low blood pressure. There are many causes including heart attack (see page 24), pneumothorax (see page 86) or severe indigestion (see below).
- **Confusion and disorientation** may be a sign of very low blood pressure, shortage of oxygen or infection such as meningitis (see page 124).
- **Blue lips or fingers** are symptoms of lack of oxygen in the blood, or low blood pressure.
- **Chest pain** can be felt anywhere in the chest. If it is crushing, central, felt up in the jaw or down the left arm it is likely to be coming from the heart.
- **Shortness of breath** can be seen by an increased rate of breathing and breathing more deeply. In severe cases the crew member will be sitting up, bracing themselves forward with their arms, and the muscles in their neck will stand out with effort.
- **Wheezing** might be heard without a stethoscope. It is usually a sign of asthma, but it can be caused by heart problems and chest infections.
- **Crackling** heard when the crew member is breathing can be a sign of chest infection or heart problems.
- **Silent chest** when you are listening with a stethoscope to a very unwell crew member who is struggling with their breathing is very ominous. Contact TMAS immediately.

Causes of shortness of breath

- Chest infection
- Asthma
- Pneumothorax
- Pulmonary embolus (blood clot in lungs)
- Anxiety
- Heart problems
- Trauma

Causes of chest pain

- Heart attack
- Angina
- Anxiety
- Indigestion
- Pulmonary embolus
- Chest infection
- Trauma
- Pneumothorax

3

Immediate treatment

4

If the casualty is having obvious difficulty with breathing, or has blue lips or fingers, contact TMAS immediately and start to prepare for immediate evacuation if possible. Use oxygen if available.

- **Shock** must be treated immediately. Lay the casualty down and prop their legs up above the heart. Insert an IV cannula if possible (see page 225) and give IV fluids (500 ml initially; measure blood pressure and contact TMAS immediately).
- **For shortness of breath** keep the casualty sitting up as the lungs work better like this. Give oxygen if available. Try to work out why the crew member is short of breath; see list above and symptoms, signs and treatments below.
- **Chest pain** should be treated. If it is very severe use morphine IM injection (see page 25), otherwise paracetamol and NSAIDs (check they have no stomach ulcer or asthma problems first; see pages 33 and 143). Try to work out the cause of the chest pain; see the list above and symptoms, signs and treatments below.
- **Antibiotics** should be used if the casualty is feverish and has green sputum. Give IV if the casualty looks very unwell, their temperature is above 39° C and they are short of breath.

Specific conditions

5

Heart attacks and angina (see page 24)

Heart attacks and angina become more common with increasing age.

Smoking, high blood pressure, diabetes and previous angina or heart attacks make heart attacks more likely.

Angina (pain from the heart) is less severe than a heart attack. It occurs when the crew member is doing heavy work and should stop when they are resting. In simple terms, it is the stage before a heart attack and a sign that the heart is not well. A crew member who suffers from angina should be seen by a doctor, fully assessed and treated. Their statutory fitness certificate should be reviewed by an MCA Approved Doctor or a doctor approved by another recognised maritime authority before they return to sea.

Symptoms and signs		Treatment
• Central, crushing chest pain • May be felt in the left or right arm, jaw, neck or abdomen • Pain is continuous with a heart attack • Pain of angina improves when resting • Sweaty, pale, short of breath • Nausea and vomiting • Possible collapse with either low or very high blood pressure • Pain may be relieved by GTN spray under tongue	→	• **If any doubt, treat as a heart attack (page 24)** • Give 300 mg aspirin orally • Give oxygen if available • Treat pain with morphine 5–10 mg IM injection (page 229) if very severe or casualty is sweaty • Try GTN spray (2 squirts) under tongue (page 25) • Rest and avoid exertion and stress • Contact TMAS and prepare for urgent evacuation

Indigestion

See page 151.

Asthma

Asthma is becoming increasingly common and causes a significant number of deaths; take it seriously.

It can be precipitated by dust, irritant or allergenic substances, animals, pollen, cold air, work, infection and emotion.

It can improve at sea, or it may get worse; it depends on the individual.

Prevention and early treatment are the keys to avoiding problems.

In many maritime sectors periodic medical examinations should reduce the risk of recurrent asthma occurring at sea by excluding those with significant disease. Where such examinations do not occur, any potential traveller (e.g. family or contract engineers, who do not require medical clearance) known to have asthma should be advised to obtain medical clearance before embarkation.

Mild exacerbations of asthma may be treated by regular salbutamol and beclometasone inhalers, possibly at an increased dose. Always discuss with TMAS if symptoms persist.

Symptoms and signs

- Shortness of breath, fast respiratory rate
- Wheeze on breathing out
- There may be very little wheeze in dangerously severe attacks; look at the crew member and if they look very unwell **they are**
- Barrel chest
- Chest infection and cough
- Pale, exhausted, sitting up, braced
- Unable to talk in sentences
- Severe if they cannot manage two words
- Peak flow (if available) less than 50% of normal
- **Do not give NSAIDs or betablockers to asthmatics**

→

Treatment

- Keep sitting up
- Give oxygen if available
- Give salbutamol inhaler – 4 puffs every 15 minutes
- If not improving, use a spacer or improvise one – cut a hole in the bottom of a plastic bottle, insert the inhaler tightly, put in 10 puffs of salbutamol, get crew member to breathe in and out for 6 breaths from the top of the bottle
- Continue with salbutamol until they improve
- Give prednisolone 40 mg orally, or if severe attack, insert an IV line and give hydrocortisone 100 mg IV
- Give antihistamine either IV or orally
- Contact TMAS and prepare to evacuate

Chest infection (pneumonia)

Chest infections may range from a viral infection causing an irritating cough to life-threatening pneumonia where the crew member looks very unwell.

Symptoms and signs

- Feverish, unwell
- Short of breath, fast respiratory rate
- Coughing green sputum
- Possibly wheeze or chest pain
- Crackly, coarse breath sounds
- Oxygen saturation less than 92%
- Blue around lips, under tongue, finger tips (cyanosis)

→

Treatment

- If very unwell, respiratory rate above 25 breaths a minute, cyanotic, oxygen saturation less than 92%, give oxygen if available
- Antibiotics for 5 days (give IV if temperature above 39°C, very unwell)
- If very unwell or not improving, Contact TMAS

High blood pressure (normal below 140/90; severe above 160/110)

Many crew members will have a history of high blood pressure and will take medication, which they should have with them at sea.

Uncontrolled high blood pressure may result from prolonged seasickness (crew members not absorbing tablets), forgetting or losing their normal tablets.

Symptoms and signs

- Headache
- Chest pain
- Nausea or vomiting
- Confusion or fitting if very severe

Treatment

- Seek medical advice if above 160/110, or if symptoms present
- Give anti-sickness and normal medication
- Consider medication from medical stores on board (e.g. metoprolol, atenolol, amlodipine) but consult TMAS prior to treating

Blood clots in the lungs (pulmonary emboli) and legs

Blood clots may form in the leg and thigh veins (deep vein thrombosis). These may then float off (embolise) and lodge in the lungs.

Large pulmonary emboli (PE) can cause severe chest pain.

The risk increases with obesity, smoking, oral contraceptive pill, pelvic and lower limb fractures, immobility and dehydration.

If the crew member collapses with a large PE there is little you can do except attempt resuscitation (see page 2).

Symptoms and signs

- Sudden-onset shortness of breath
- Chest pain on one side
- Cough with bloody sputum
- Shock or even cardiac arrest
- Swollen, tender lower leg or thigh
- Oxygen saturation less than 92%

Treatment

- If collapsed, ABCDE (page 2)
- Give oxygen if available
- Pain relief: IM morphine 5–10 mg or tramadol
- Aspirin 300 mg orally
- Contact TMAS and prepare for urgent evacuation

Pneumothorax

See pages 86, 234.

Musculoskeletal pain

Pain from a particular point on the chest wall may be quite severe but have no obvious cause and the crew member may be otherwise well. Inflammation of rib/cartilage junctions (costochondritis) can be particularly painful.

Symptoms and signs

- Sudden onset at a particular spot
- Pain that can inhibit deep breathing
- Tender over the point of pain

Treatment

- Exclude other causes
- Pain relief
- May take a few days to improve

6 Abdominal disorders

Pain and distension of the abdomen at sea is worrying. There are lots of possible causes; most are minor, but some are more serious. However, on a vessel it is more important to detect early the signs of infection, inflammation (peritonitis) and bowel obstruction, and treat them with antibiotics, than to make a precise diagnosis. Fluid replacement, IV or IO if possible (see page 224), is occasionally necessary, as the gut may stop absorbing oral fluids and food.

Constipation is a common problem at sea, particularly when the diet lacks fresh fruit and vegetables. A healthy diet and good hydration are essential. Diligent hygiene standards must be maintained to prevent infections that can cause vomiting and diarrhoea to spread rapidly among the whole crew.

Other causes of abdominal pain are angina (see page 24), chest infections (see page 144), urinary tract infections (see page 156), gynaecological disorders (see page 152) and diabetic ketoacidosis (see page 36).

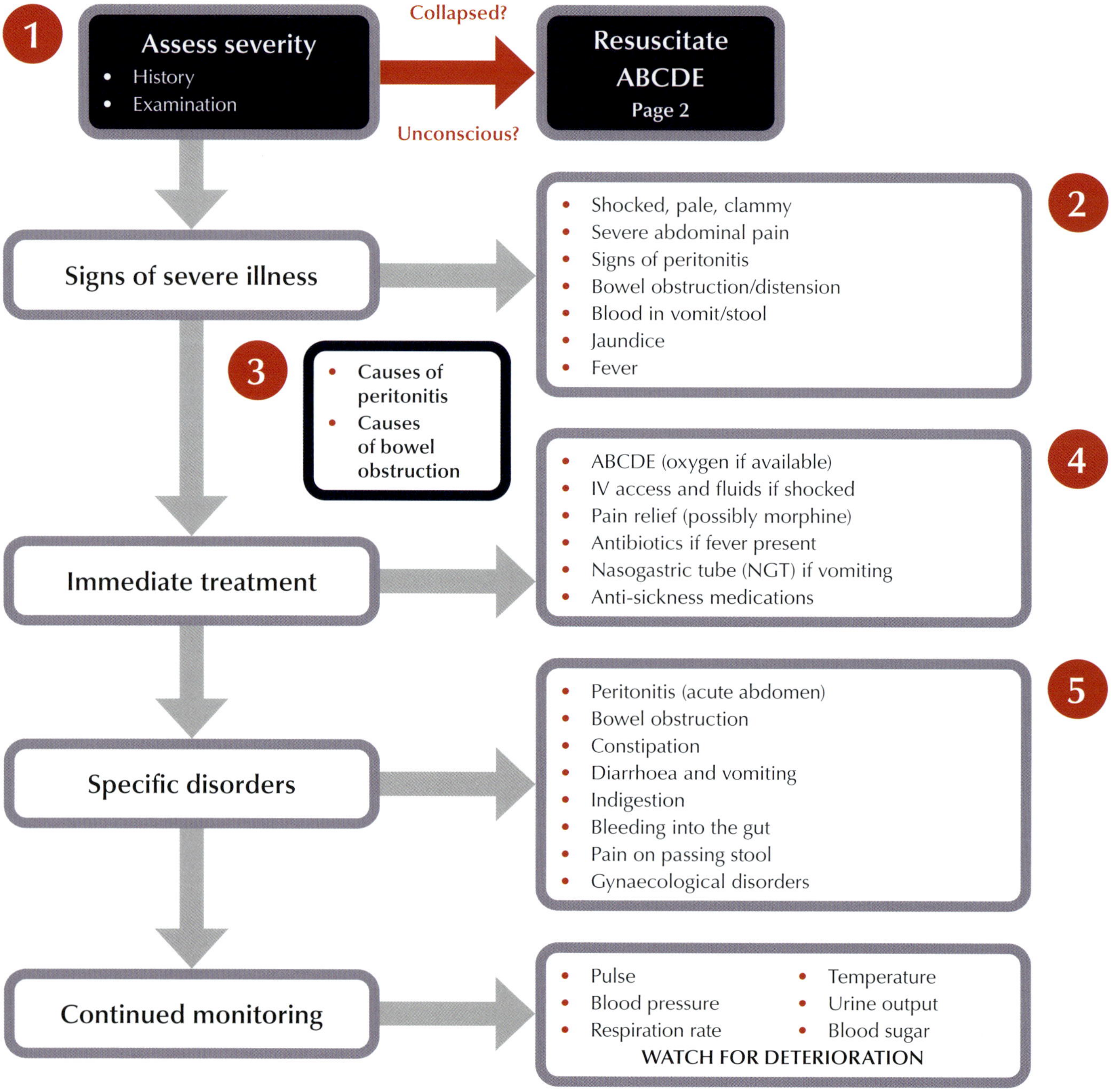

Contact TMAS early

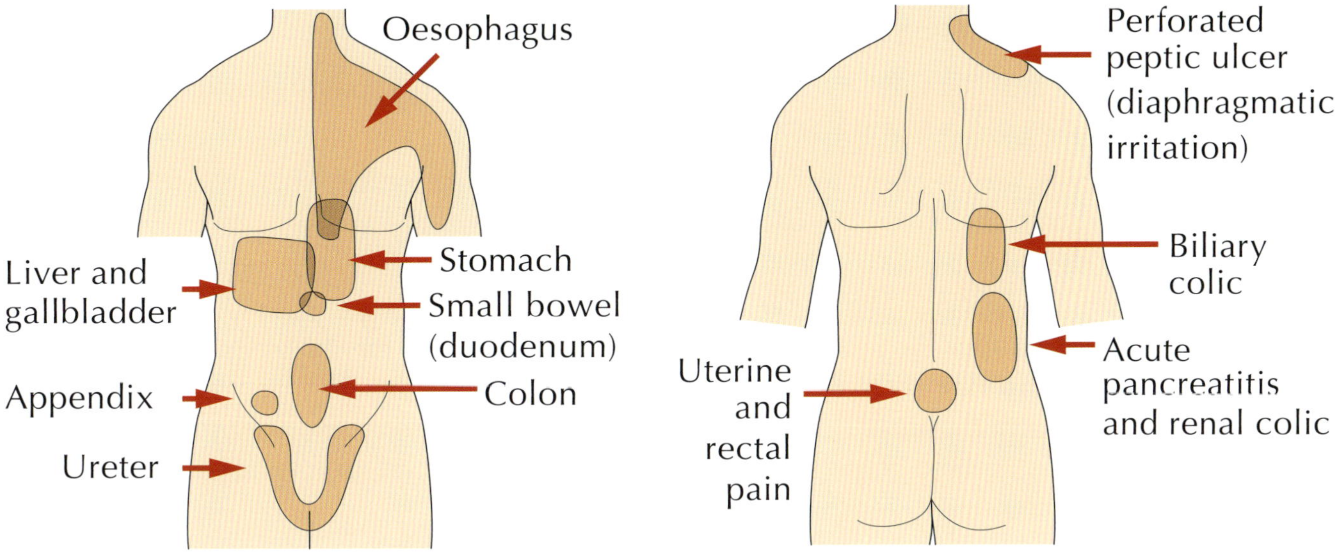

Abdominal pain locations associated with certain organs and disorders

See page 91 for anatomy of abdomen.

History and examination

1

- Symptoms and signs can take a while to develop, so the crew member may deteriorate over hours or days.
- The crew member may have a history of abdominal problems.
- Previous abdominal operations may be significant – look for scars. Remember that the scars of keyhole surgery are small – look around the navel (umbilicus).
- Abdominal pain can be caused by chest infections and angina.
- Do not do a rectal or vaginal examination unless advised by TMAS, and trained to do so.

Important points in the history

- Site and severity of pain
- What makes it better/worse (eating, deep breathing, antacids, vomiting)?
- Any nausea/vomiting/diarrhoea/constipation?
- Women – menstrual history and other gynaecological problems (see page 152)
- Previous abdominal problems and surgery

Important points in the examination

- **Look:**
  - Appearance of crew member (in severe pain, feverish, pale, jaundiced)
  - Abdominal distension
  - Scars (look around the umbilicus)
  - Blood in vomit (might look like coffee grounds) or stools (might be black, tarry and very smelly)
  - Urine offensive smelling or with blood
- **Feel:**
  - Pain when gently pressing abdomen
  - Pain when 'tapping' abdomen
  - Abdomen rigid with pain
  - Any masses
- **Listen:**
  - Bowel sounds with stethoscope
- **Document** Vital signs, blood sugar, urine output, dipstick the urine

Signs of severe illness

2

Being shocked, pale and clammy are symptoms of severe pain or low blood pressure. The cause may be dangerous blood loss into the gut or peritonitis.

- **Signs of peritonitis** are an abdomen that is rigid with pain, very tender when pressed with the hand, or tapped with the finger. For causes see below.
- **Bowel obstruction** will cause vomiting of green bile; no stool or flatulence (wind) being passed; abdominal distension is possible. For causes see below.
- **Blood in vomit/stool** may be a small amount or profuse, which is life-threatening. Blood in the vomit (which may look fresh, or blackish, like coffee grounds) signifies bleeding from the stomach or first part of the small bowel. The stool may be black, tarry and very smelly. Fresh blood in the stool is likely to come from the lower part of the bowel, or haemorrhoids (piles, which are quite common).
- **Jaundice** is usually caused by a problem with the liver, often because of gallstones, liver disease or a problem with the pancreas. Prepare to evacuate urgently.
- **Fever** is caused by infection, which may mean that the bowel is very sick and may have perforated, or that an infection has affected the kidney.

Causes of peritonitis

- Bowel perforation
- Peptic ulcer
- Strangulated hernia
- Diabetes
- Appendicitis
- Pancreatitis
- Gallstones
- Gynaecological problems

Causes of bowel obstruction

3

- Severe constipation
- Previous surgery
- Peritonitis (acute abdomen
- Inflammation of the bowel (colitis)
- Pancreatitis
- Twisted bowel
- Hernia

Immediate treatment

4

The casualty may be extremely unwell, and require urgent resuscitation. Contact TMAS at an early stage and prepare for urgent evacuation.

- **Shock** must be treated immediately. Lay the casualty down and prop their legs up above the heart. Insert an IV cannula (see page 225) if possible, and give IV fluids (500 ml initially; measure blood pressure and contact TMAS immediately).
- **Pain relief** will be required. Morphine 5–10 mg IM can be used to treat severe pain. Do not use NSAIDs until you are sure there is no peptic ulceration or bleeding.
- **Antibiotics** must be given at an early stage if there are any signs of infection (temperature over 37.5 °C; acute abdomen; bowel obstruction). Give IV if the casualty is vomiting or their temperature is over 39 °C. Use antibiotics, including metronidazole (see Antibiotics guide, back flyleaf).
- **Nasogastric tube** must not be inserted unless TMAS directly advise this (see page 216). It will be very useful if the bowel has stopped working and the casualty is vomiting frequently. The tube should be left attached to a bag to allow the stomach to drain, thereby reducing pain, distension and vomiting.
- **Anti-sickness medication** should be given to reduce vomiting, and also when using morphine. The medical kit may contain several anti-sickness medications. Obtain TMAS advice on which ones to use and in which order.

Gynaecological disorders → **see page 152**

Urological disorders → **see page 156**

Specific conditions

5

Peritonitis (acute abdomen)

This is a life-threatening condition which needs to be detected at an early stage.

Treatment on a vessel can be successful by containing the cause (which may not be known) until evacuation can be arranged.

Symptoms and signs

- Severe abdominal pain
- Pain on gently pressing on the abdomen or tapping with a finger
- Rigid abdomen, possibly distended
- Fever
- Vomiting (green bile)
- Check for hernia – painful swelling in groin at top of leg
- Jaundice
- Previous abdominal problems?
- Check blood sugar
- Check chest for signs of angina and infection

Treatment

- ABCDE if collapsed
- IV access and 500 ml fluid
- Treat pain with morphine 5–10 mg IM injection (see page 229) or tramadol if very severe pain, sweaty
- Antibiotics IV
- Anti-sickness medications
- Anti-acid treatment (see below)
- NGT (see page 216) and drain bag
- Watch urine output – aim for minimum 0.5 ml/hour/kg
- Contact TMAS and prepare to evacuate

Constipation

Normal bowel habits vary enormously, from three stools per day to one every 3–4 days. Find out how the current concern differs from the crew member's normal pattern of bowel movements.

Symptoms and signs

- No stools (or very little hard stool) passed for 2–3 days longer than normal for that crew member
- Cramping abdominal discomfort
- Distended abdomen if severe

Treatment

- Avoid by good hydration and high-fibre diet (aim for dilute urine)
- If established, treat with glycerol suppositories, stool softener (lactulose) and stimulants (bisacodyl)

Bowel obstruction

There is little that can be done to solve the causes of bowel obstruction on a vessel at sea. The aim is to maintain the casualty as well as possible and evacuate them urgently. The only exception is constipation, but even this may be untreatable once frank bowel obstruction is present (see above). Fluid resuscitation may require many litres of fluid.

Symptoms and signs

- Vomiting (green bile)
- No stool or flatulence (wind)
- Possibly distended abdomen
- Check for hernia: painful swelling in groin at top of leg or at the navel (umbilicus)
- High-pitched 'tinkly' bowel sounds or silent abdomen
- Fever
- Previous abdominal surgery
- Medications

Treatment

- IV access and 500 ml fluid
- Treat pain with morphine 5–10 mg IM injection (see page 128) if very severe pain, sweaty
- Anti-sickness medications
- Anti-acid treatment (see below)
- NGT (see page 216) and drain bag
- Watch urine output – aim for minimum 0.5 ml/hour/kg
- Antibiotics IV (discuss with TMAS first)
- Contact TMAS and prepare to evacuate

Diarrhoea and vomiting

This is common on vessels, and the cause is usually either food poisoning (often from eating unhygienic food ashore) or a gut infection. More rarely it may be caused by an abdominal disorder. Nausea and vomiting alone may be due to seasickness or pregnancy. Infection is passed via the faecal–oral route. Strict hygiene must be practised at all times to make sure the whole crew do not go down with the same illness. A person with these symptoms should not work in food preparation or service until 48 hours after the symptoms have stopped, and they must practise scrupulous hand washing at all times. If there is more than one case, contact TMAS about further precautions required to stop an infection spreading through the entire crew.

Symptoms and signs

- Vomiting or diarrhoea or both
- Abdominal cramps
- Dehydration
- Vomit may be yellow, green, bloody
- Diarrhoea may be watery, black and tarry, bloody

Treatment

- Keep hydrated (use rehydration drinks)
- IV fluid may be needed if severely dehydrated and still vomiting
- Anti-sickness medications (cyclizine)
- Anti-diarrhoeal medications (loperamide)

Indigestion

Indigestion is frequent on vessels due to a change in diet, irregular and rapidly eaten meals, stress and fatigue. The pain of severe indigestion may be mistaken for a heart attack (and vice versa).

Symptoms and signs

- Pain over upper part of abdomen or in chest
- Pain may be burning or gripping
- Stomach acid may reflux into mouth leaving an unpleasant taste

Treatment

- Adjust diet if possible
- Simple antacids
- Medications that reduce acid in stomach (e.g. lansoprazole). Also use an alginate antacid that creates a barrier for the stomach lining against acid

Bleeding into the gut

Blood in vomit is likely to have come from a bleeding stomach or duodenal ulcer. Blood in or on stool is most likely to have come from bleeding piles or from another part of the lower bowel. Treatment is limited and the casualty should be evacuated. For severe haemorrhage, see page 32.

Symptoms and signs

- Vomit containing fresh blood or 'coffee grounds' (altered blood)
- Fresh blood on the surface of the stool, or tarry black stool (melaena)
- If bleeding is severe, shock may develop (page 28)
- Inspect around anus if blood on stool or on toilet paper
- History of peptic ulcer disease

Treatment

- IV access and 500 ml fluid if shocked
- Medications that reduce acid in stomach (e.g. lansoprazole). Also use an alginate antacid that creates a barrier for the stomach lining against acid
- Watch urine output – aim for minimum 0.5 ml/hour/kg
- Contact TMAS and prepare to evacuate

Pain on passing stool and haemorrhoids (piles)

This is very unpleasant and can be excruciating. It can result in avoidance of passing stool, leading to serious constipation. However, simple treatments can be effective.

Symptoms and signs

- Pain on passing stool, worse with hard formed stool
- Traces of blood on the surface of the stool
- Piles may come out of anus
- An anal fissure may be visible

Treatment

- Keep well hydrated to keep stool soft
- Avoid constipation (see above)
- Pain relief – lidocaine gel rubbed up inside the anus before passing stool may help
- Use specific haemorrhoid preparations if available

7 Gynaecological disorders

There are several disorders associated with the female reproductive organs; these can be either variations in their normal functions (such as menstruation and pregnancy) or diseases (infection and bleeding).

Infection, starting as a simple vaginal irritation or discharge, can ascend through the womb (uterus) and then enter the abdominal cavity through the fallopian tubes, occasionally causing life-threatening sepsis. Early detection and treatment is essential.

Examining another crew member in such a sensitive area requires trust and confidentiality on both sides. Internal digital examination of the vagina is unlikely to be of benefit unless you are trained and have experience. Consult TMAS before any such procedure, and even then do it only under medical direction.

Menstruation (periods) and contraception

Normal menstruation is on a cycle of approximately 4 weeks. Most women will be familiar with their own cycle; however, it may be altered by pregnancy, contraceptive methods, stress or illness. Menstrual symptoms are a normal event, and women will be able to manage their usual occurrence, including pain and other symptoms that they are familiar with. If there are any unexplained significant changes, get advice from TMAS.

There are several methods available for contraception in addition to oral contraceptives, condoms and other barrier methods, and all may have side effects:

- **Depot injection** (e.g. Depo Provera, Noristerat) Provides contraception for three months. Light bleeding ('spotting') may occur in the first three months, followed by menstruation suppression.
- **Implant** (e.g. Implanon) Provides contraception for up to three years and can be removed at any time. Spotting may occur in the first three months, followed by menstruation suppression.
- **Intra-uterine contraceptive device** (e.g. Mirena) Inserted in the uterus, providing contraception and reduction of menstrual bleeding after 3–6 months.
- **Emergency contraception** (morning-after pill) This could be sourced privately and used at sea. There is a risk of significant bleeding if used more than 72 hours after unprotected sex.

Pregnancy

Pregnancy, both known and unexpected, causes profound change in a woman's body, and some symptoms may require treatment on the vessel. Most pregnancies proceed smoothly, but women who know or suspect they are pregnant, and who hold an ENG 1 medical certificate, should obtain medical advice (from an MCA Approved Doctor) before any prolonged period at sea. They will need to cease working at sea well before delivery (currently at 24 weeks in distant waters; see MCA MGN 522).

Complications of pregnancy can occasionally be serious, causing severe abdominal pain and heavy vaginal bleeding. The two main disorders are miscarriage and ectopic pregnancy (see below). Repeated vomiting may occur during pregnancy and seasickness may be worse; seek medical advice from TMAS before using anti-sickness medication as some may adversely affect the foetus.

Contact TMAS immediately if labour starts on board or if the end of a pregnancy is found to be imminent while the vessel is distant from land.

History and examination

- Be diplomatic and respect confidentiality. With the consent of the casualty, and if feasible, another woman can be asked to act as a chaperone during the examination.
- Gynaecological disorders can cause severe abdominal symptoms.
- Do not do a vaginal examination without first seeking advice from TMAS, and even then under medical direction only.
- The casualty may have a long history of gynaecological problems.
- Do a pregnancy test at an early stage if you have a testing kit on board.

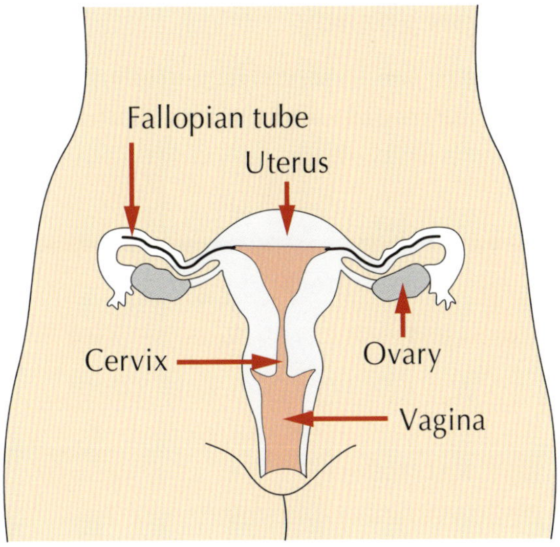

Female reproductive organs

Important points in the history

- Pelvic or abdominal pain
- Genital soreness or ulceration
- Recent sexual history and possibility of pregnancy
- Bleeding or discharge from vagina
- Change to menstrual cycle:
  - no bleeding or bleeding mid-cycle?
  - painful?
  - more blood than normal?
- Pain and frequency passing urine
- Method of contraception
- Previous gynaecological history and number and outcome of previous pregnancies

Important points in the examination

- **Look:**
  - Appearance of crew member (pale, shocked, in pain, feverish)
  - Examine discharge (perhaps on pad) – yellow/green/watery/offensive smell
- **Feel:**
  - Abdomen for tenderness and rigidity, swelling arising out of pelvis
- **Listen:**
  - Bowel sounds with stethoscope
- **Document** Vital signs, do pregnancy test, do urine dipstick test

Specific conditions

Vaginal bleeding

- A small amount of bleeding is normal during menstruation, and the volume of blood may increase for a variety of reasons. The normal cycle may become irregular with stress, fatigue or change of contraception, and will cease during pregnancy.
- Bleeding may be the first sign of miscarriage (even if the pregnancy was not known about), ectopic pregnancy, or post-coital (post-sex) inflammation.
- Bleeding can be catastrophic and life-threatening. Contact TMAS immediately if the crew member is shocked.

Symptoms and signs

- Signs of shock – pale, sweaty, cold
- Tender abdomen
- Try to quantify blood loss – any clots?
- Pregnancy test and urine dipstick

Treatment

- Treat shock with IV fluids
- Consider tranexamic acid (oral, IV/IM/IO) but consult TMAS first
- Pain relief
- Ergometrine and oxytocin may reduce bleeding if miscarrying but contact TMAS before use

Ectopic pregnancy

This is where the fertilised egg implants in the fallopian tube before it gets to the uterus. As it grows it causes pain and eventually may rupture the tube, causing catastrophic bleeding into the abdomen, with perhaps only a little from the vagina.

Symptoms and signs

- Signs of shock – pale, sweaty, cold
- Severe abdominal pain (one-sided)
- Usually happens about week 6–8 after last period
- More common with uterine coils
- Pregnancy test usually positive

Treatment

- Treat shock – lay down, legs up
- Consider tranexamic acid (oral, IV/IM/IO) but consult TMAS first
- Establish IV access and give IV infusion
- Pain relief
- Keep quiet and rest
- Call TMAS and prepare to evacuate

Vaginal discharge

A certain amount of colourless vaginal discharge is normal, and keeps the vagina healthy. Offensive, green, yellow or watery discharge, vaginal discomfort and pain on passing urine are all signs of infection. A thick whitish discharge is probably thrush.

A foul black discharge may be a forgotten tampon. The discharge should settle once the tampon is removed, although antibiotics may be required if the crew member is feverish and unwell.

Symptoms and signs

- Change in colour and amount of normal discharge
- Fever, unwell
- Abdominal pain or discomfort
- Pain, frequency of urination

Treatment

- If white thick discharge, treat for thrush (clotrimazole pessary)
- Treat infections with erythromycin and metronidazole
- Seek TMAS advice

8 Urinary, kidney and genital disorders

Disorders of the male and female genitals are potentially embarrassing. They can also be a serious threat to health.

Infections of the urinary tract are common; more so in women, for anatomical reasons. Both male and female genitalia can also get infected and may become extremely uncomfortable and painful. Some of these infections may be sexually transmitted so it is sensible to practise safe sex and use condoms. Infections affecting the kidney may make the crew member exceedingly unwell, possibly shocked, with a high fever.

For men the testicles in the scrotum are prone to injury, torsion (twisting) and infection, all causing considerable pain. Torsion of the testicles is an emergency, requiring surgery within 12 hours if possible.

Examining another crew member in such a sensitive area requires trust and confidentiality on both sides. If you have any doubt about what you should examine, contact TMAS.

Passing blood can be alarming, particularly when the urine is completely red. This may be caused by relatively little blood, therefore the crew member is unlikely to become shocked because of blood loss in the urine. However, if it carries on for several days, they may start to become anaemic; the symptoms include paleness, lethargy and feeling unwell.

The causes of blood in the urine are:

- Infection of the urinary tract (see below)
- Renal stones (see page 158)
- Vaginal bleeding colouring the urine (see page 153)
- Trauma, such as pelvic fracture (see page 94) or as a result of inserting a urinary catheter, which should settle
- Use of medications such as warfarin, aspirin or clopidogrel; contact TMAS if this is the case
- Other diseases of the kidneys and renal tract.

Red coloration of the urine may also be caused by drugs (e.g. rifampicin) and foods such as beetroot, if eaten in large quantities.

Reassure the crew member and treat them according to possible cause. If their urine stays red for several days and they start to develop signs of anaemia (generally unwell, fatigued, very pale, short of breath, dizzy or faint, chest pain), contact TMAS. Otherwise refer them for medical assessment in the next port unless a clear cause is established.

History and examination

- Be diplomatic and respect confidentiality.
- Do not do a vaginal or rectal examination without first seeking advice from TMAS, and do it only under medical direction.
- If there is a genital infection, any sexual partners may also be infected. On a vessel this may be awkward, but the problem must be dealt with, and as sensitively as possible.

Important points in the history

- Site and severity of pain (including abdomen and testicles in scrotum)
- Amount and colour of discharge
- Pain and frequency of passing urine
- Colour and smell of urine
- Any sores, swellings or ulcers on genitals or around anus
- Any sexual contacts
- Test urine with dipstick
- Pregnancy test for women

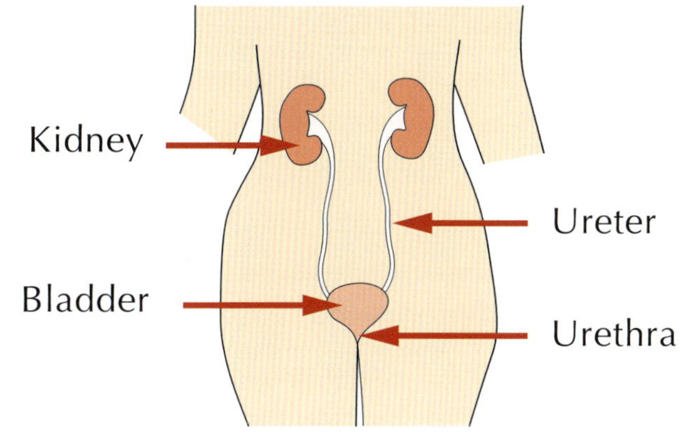

Male and female urinary tract

Important points in the examination

- **Look:**
  - Appearance of crew member (pale, in pain, feverish, shocked)
  - Inflammation, sores, lumps, discharge
  - Swollen, reddish-blue scrotum
- **Feel:**
  - Lower abdomen for tender or swollen bladder
  - Flanks for tenderness over kidney
  - Scrotum and testicles for swelling and tenderness

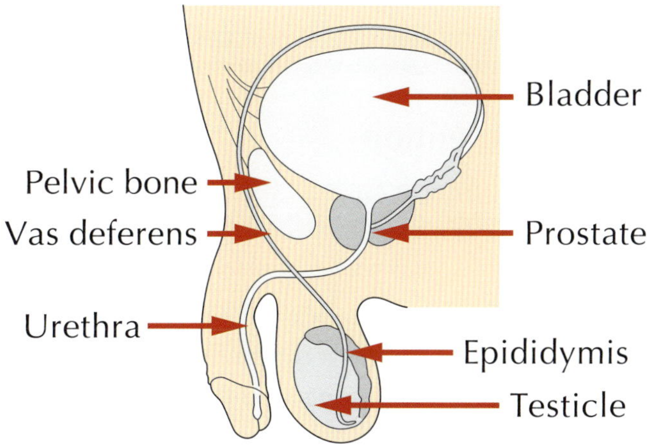

Male genitals and lower urinary tract

Specific conditions

Urinary tract infection

An infection may affect all parts of the urinary tract, from the urethra to the kidney. They are common, especially in women.

Infections of the kidney may cause the crew member to be very unwell, with a high fever, and possibly septic with signs of shock.

Infections of the lower urinary tract tend to produce broadly similar symptoms, but usually less severe, and are treated in much the same way.

Symptoms and signs

- Fever, feeling unwell
- Kidney infections: feeling very unwell, possibly shocked; flank pain
- Pain and frequency on passing urine
- Urine may be cloudy and foul-smelling
- Urine dipstick usually shows protein, blood, white cells, nitrites

Treatment

- If shocked, establish IV access and fluid and seek medical advice
- Pain relief
- Antibiotics (IV if very unwell)
- Keep hydrated: aim for pale, dilute urine

Kidney (renal) stones

Stones from the kidney can cause severe pain in the flank and down to the groin when being passed. They may become lodged in the ureter or bladder, causing obstruction.

Working in a hot climate and becoming regularly dehydrated can cause stones to form.

Stones and infection can cause blood in the urine, which may turn the urine reddish.

Symptoms and signs

- Stones cause sudden severe pain in one flank and down to the groin, and often blood in the urine
- Nausea and vomiting
- Possible fever
- Dipstick testing may show blood, protein, nitrites and white cells

Treatment

- Keep well hydrated
- Pain relief with paracetamol or NSAIDs; morphine is often necessary
- Antibiotics if feverish
- Contact TMAS if the symptoms do not improve

Urinary retention

The most common causes of urinary retention on a vessel are infection, trauma to the pelvis or genitalia, blood clot in the bladder, enlargement of the prostate gland (in older men), drugs (antihistamines and some antidepressants), and loss of consciousness if this is prolonged (see page 8).

A catheter must be passed into the bladder through the urethra (see page 217). Be very cautious if there is blood in the urine and if there is any resistance to inserting the catheter. This is a specialised procedure and you must contact TMAS for guidance.

Symptoms and signs

- Inability to pass urine despite urge to do so
- Fullness and tenderness in lower abdomen
- History of trauma
- Signs of infection

Treatment

- Contact TMAS before attempting to insert a catheter
- If there are any problems with insertion, discuss with TMAS
- Leave catheter in and evacuate

Scrotal pain and testicular torsion (twisting)

The pain of testicular torsion comes on suddenly, is very severe and can cause the crew member to vomit. The pain is caused by lack of blood supply to the testicle due to the twisting. The testicle will die unless the twisting is undone quickly (within 12 hours). Usually this is done surgically, but this is obviously not possible on a vessel. Manual untwisting can be attempted under medical guidance, but may not be successful.

Symptoms and signs

- Sudden-onset severe testicular pain
- Very tender testicle on gentle palpation
- Scrotum may become red and swollen
- No history of trauma; crew member may wake with the pain

Treatment

- Strong pain relief and anti-sickness medication
- Contact TMAS and attempt manual untwisting
- Prepare to evacuate

Manual untwisting of a testicle

- Lay the crew member down in a bunk with scrotum elevated
- Gently but firmly hold the affected testicle in fingers and rotate towards the thigh on that side. In other words, rotate his right testicle anti-clockwise (as you look at it), and his left testicle clockwise. These directions usually work
- Relief of pain will be immediate, but more than one turn may be necessary
- Try rotating in the opposite direction if pain increases

Scrotal pain and epididymitis

Part or all of the testicle may become inflamed. The usual cause is infection, possibly sexually transmitted. Usually only one testicle is involved. It is important to differentiate this from testicular torsion; contact TMAS if in any doubt.

Symptoms and signs

- Gradual onset of pain from one testicle
- Scrotum may become red and swollen
- Fever, and pain passing urine
- Urine dipstick may show blood and protein in the urine

Treatment

- Pain may be relieved by crew member lying down and gently elevating scrotum (on rolled-up towel)
- Pain relief
- Antibiotics if signs of infection

Sexually transmitted infections

Signs of sexually transmitted infections (STIs) may take weeks, months or even years to become apparent.

Some STIs are very serious (e.g. syphilis, HIV), whereas others may be more easily treated (e.g. chlamydia, gonorrhoea), although any STI is a serious matter.

Sexual contacts must be traced and treated, despite the potential embarrassment.

If a crew member has a suspected STI, they should avoid all sexual contact (including oral).

Symptoms and signs

- Green, offensive discharge from penis or vagina
- Pain passing urine
- Sores on genitals

Treatment

- Likely cause will not be known on the vessel
- Treat with antibiotics (ciprofloxacin for 1 week)

Genital sores and lumps

Ulcers, blisters and sores are usually the result of infection, possibly an STI.

Blisters and ulcers caused by herpes tend to be numerous, painful and preceded by mild tingling. Treat them early with aciclovir cream.

Syphilitic ulcers tend to be single, painless, hard-edged and clean.

Bacterial infections may cause swellings and abscesses of the external genitalia that may self-discharge but they may need antibiotics, and even surgical intervention.

Genital warts and the small white lumps of *molluscum contagiosum* do not require treatment at sea. Advise crew members to avoid sexual contact, and not to share towels, bedding etc. Refer them for medical advice in the next port.

Symptoms and signs		Treatment
• Painful or painless sores or ulcers • Pain on passing urine • Swellings may be red and painful; may discharge • Painful swelling in labia	→	• If tingling, treat early with aciclovir cream • Antibiotics for syphilis • Bacterial infections may need lancing and antibiotics

Foreskin problems

The foreskin may become very swollen if it is pulled back over the head of the penis and not put back again. An infection may cause inflammation of the end of the penis under the foreskin, due to an STI or poor personal hygiene.

Symptoms and signs		Treatment
• Swollen, retracted foreskin which may have become alarmingly large • Inflammation and whitish discharge under foreskin; there may be pain on passing urine	→	• Lidocaine gel on the foreskin for pain relief, then gentle, long squeeze to reduce swelling. Return foreskin to normal position over penis end if possible • Applying ice around foreskin may reduce swelling and pain • Infection: thorough regular washing under foreskin. Miconazole cream and antibiotics if not improving or severe

9 Infections

The human body plays host to billions of organisms, most of which are helpful to humans. Some co-exist with us and a small minority are dangerous and cause disease. The immune system normally keeps all infections under control but occasionally a more virulent organism will come along, multiply in the body, and cause unpleasant symptoms. These may range from a simple cough, to shock, collapse and death.

A vessel has an advantage in that once at sea it is an isolated environment and new infections cannot find a way on board. The disadvantage is that **what goes on board stays on board**. Therefore pay attention to vehicles of infection when in port.

Vehicles of infection are the means by which infection may get on board. They include the following:

- **Food and milk** are nutritious so infectious organisms readily grow on them, especially if they are undercooked or untreated.
- **Water** may be contaminated so, where possible, use only properly designated potable water for filling vessel tanks. Make sure all water is clean or treated before it goes into the tanks. Follow procedures for maintaining water quality on board (and hence freedom from infection).
- **Clothing and bedding** may harbour micro-organisms and larger pests.
- **Crew members** may be harbouring an infection which they bring on board; for example, food poisoning organisms (take care with what and where you eat before joining the vessel and when on shore leave), sexually transmitted infections (see page 159), flu, COVID-19 or tuberculosis.

Prevention

Prevention is by far the best approach and is mostly common sense:

- **Vaccinations and anti-malarial medications** The vessel operator is responsible for arranging crew immunisations and anti-malarial medications when appropriate. However, compliance with the use of anti-malarial medications is the responsibility of every crew member.
- **Vaccinations** For travel to most countries vaccinations and boosters are recommended. A certificate of yellow fever immunisation is required for entry into some ports (see MCA MGN 399(M)). Vaccinations are essential for pandemic infections such as COVID-19.
- **Behaviour** Maintain a high level of personal hygiene on the vessel, such as washing hands after using the toilet, and being scrupulously clean when cooking food. Practise safe sex and avoid unsafe contacts in port.
- **Cleanliness** This is essential. Roles for crew members need to be very clear so that the allocation of responsibilities for cleaning on board is followed. However, all crew have a personal responsibility both for cleanliness on the vessel and for good personal hygiene.
- **Travel** Crew may travel away from port and visit areas where malaria, rabies and other tropical diseases are common. Ensure they are aware of the risks and that they take precautions.
- **Anti-bite measures**
  - On board: insect screens on vessel doors and other openings, and filtered air conditioning systems.
  - On deck and ashore: long trousers, long-sleeved shirts and insect repellent (N,N-Diethyl-meta-toluamide (DEET)) may be required in some ports, and certainly when travelling to mosquito areas.

- **Contamination** Avoid contamination by the bodily fluids of fellow crew members (particularly blood). Take care and wear gloves if dealing with wounds.
- **Wound care** Dressings must be as sterile as possible to prevent wounds becoming infected. In general, inspect and redress wounds each day (with clean hands, sterile gloves and a sterile dressing).
- **Antibiotics** These are the last line of defence against infection, after all the above precautions have been taken. In general, early signs of infection should be treated more readily on a vessel in the middle of the ocean than on shore. This is because the consequences of leaving an infection untreated when isolated are higher than on land.

Treatment

Treatment on a vessel is limited but can be very effective. It is aimed at controlling the infection in the crew member and preventing its transmission to other crew members:

- **Isolation** is not easy to achieve on a small vessel, but avoiding use of the same bedding, towels and clothes may reduce the transmission risk. If a particular crew member has immunity to the disease (e.g. chickenpox), only they should attend to the sick casualty.
- **Hygiene** is absolutely essential to stop infection spreading throughout the crew. Skin infections such as impetigo can spread rapidly if hygiene is substandard.
- **Nutrition and hydration** must be maintained as far as possible as this improves recovery. Various methods of hydration may be possible (see page 220).
- **Antibiotics** will contain and possibly cure bacterial infection (see Antibiotics guide, back flyleaf).

Common rapid-onset infectious diseases and infestations are listed in the table on the next page. In recent years a number of new infections have emerged, most of which are viral, including new strains of influenza. This pattern is expected to continue into the future. If the vessel is going to an area where these infections are reported it is essential to obtain definitive advice, usually from national centres of expertise in infectious disease.

Precautions in the event of a pandemic

The pandemic caused by COVID-19 caused widespread disruption of living and working conditions for the entire world population, and millions of deaths. In the event of another pandemic, it is essential for crew and passenger welfare that all advice on disease spread and treatment is followed closely, in a very volatile situation.

Infection	Type of organism	Geographical location	Transmission	Incubation
Chicken pox (varicella)	Viral	Widespread	Airborne droplet spread, direct contact. Adults with shingles can be a source of infection	14–16 days
COVID-19	Viral	Widespread	Airborne droplet spread, direct contact	5–10 days
Dengue fever	Virus	South-east Asia, South America, Caribbean	Mosquito	4–10 days
German measles (rubella)	Viral	Widespread	Airborne droplet spread, direct contact	12–23 days
Glandular fever	Viral	Widespread	Airborne droplet spread, direct contact	4–6 weeks
Hepatitis A	Virus	Mostly developing countries	Faecal–oral route (unwashed food)	7–45 days
Infestations	Lice, fleas and mites (scabies), ticks	Widespread	Clothes, bedding, sexual contact, animals (domestic, pets and wild)	Variable
Influenza	Viral	Worldwide but intermittent	Airborne droplet spread, direct contact	1–4 days
Malaria	Protozoa	Africa, Americas, Asia, southern Europe	Mosquito	7 days to several months
Measles	Viral	Widespread	Airborne droplet spread, direct contact	7–21 days
Meningitis, meningococcal septicaemia	Bacteria	Widespread in close communities	Airborne droplet spread, direct contact	Generally 24 hours but depends on infecting agent
Mumps	Viral	Widespread	Airborne droplet spread, direct contact	14–25 days
Rabies	Virus	Widespread	Bite and saliva from infected animal e.g. dog, cat, cattle, sheep. For any bite from a sick-looking dog, assume rabies	2–12 months or more
Typhoid/ paratyphoid	Bacteria	Widespread (common in Asia)	Faecal–oral route (unwashed food and vessel sewage systems)	8–21 days
Worm infections	Various worms	Americas, Asia, Africa	Infected water, lakes, rivers. Skin and faecal–oral route	Variable
Yellow fever	Virus	Africa, South America	Mosquito	3–7 days

Symptoms	Treatment	Available vaccine
Unwell, small raised blisters which crust over. Immunity gained in childhood in some countries, but can be a disease of adults in those not previously exposed (often from Asia)	Isolate if feasible. Look out for other cases in crew. Symptomatic treatment with NSAIDs for fever and for any skin itching	Yes
Fever, headache, fatigue, cough, shortness of breath, change in sense of taste/smell	Supportive care, regular paracetamol. Seek medical advice if severe symptoms	Yes
Fever, headache, muscle and bone aches, red blotchy rash that blanches. Rarely, bleeding from nose and gut, shock	Supportive, control fever, hydration. **Contact TMAS and prepare to evacuate if severe and bleeding**. Avoid mosquitos	No
Unwell and feverish, fine red rash a day or two later. Immunity usually gained in childhood by infection or immunisation. Highly contagious. Risks of abnormal birth if caught in pregnancy	Isolate if feasible. Look out for other cases in crew. Symptomatic treatment with NSAIDs for fever	Yes
Low fever and prolonged period of feeling unwell. Often spread in late teens	Isolate if feasible. Look out for other cases in crew	No
Fever, chills, vomiting, fatigue, jaundice, pale stool, dark urine	Supportive, hydration, isolation until improving, no alcohol. Refer for medical assessment when next in port	Yes
Itching of head, groin, skin, infected bites, scabies (long burrows between fingers or wrists). Other diseases may be transmitted by fleas, lice and ticks (e.g. typhus, Lyme disease, plague, tick-borne encephalitis (TBE)	Good hygiene and avoid vectors. Permethrin or malathion topically for scabies and lice. Antihistamine for itch. Thorough treatment with long-acting insecticide to kill fleas in living accommodation and regular work areas. Gently remove ticks with tweezers. Watch for other symptoms of disease	No (vaccine available for Lyme disease and TBE)
High temperature, unwell, headache and cough/ cold symptoms. Some strains may predispose to pneumonia	Isolation rarely practical. Likely to have spread among crew. Symptomatic treatment with NSAIDs for fever and headache. Strains of virus change rapidly and some may be immune because of past exposure to related strains	Yes, but not usually to new epidemic strains
Recurrent episodes of high fever, sweating, headache, muscle aches, diarrhoea, jaundice, shock, fits, coma, heart failure	**If there are symptoms, contact TMAS and prepare to evacuate urgently**. Avoid mosquito bites. Consider quinine, artesunate, proguanil, atovaquone, artemethur, mefloquine or doxycycline. Seek advice for local area	No, but prophylaxis recommended. Seek advice
Unwell and feverish, fine red rash a day or two later. May be complicated by pneumonia. Immunity usually gained in childhood by infection or immunisation. Highly contagious	Isolate if feasible. Look out for other cases in crew. Symptomatic treatment with NSAIDs for fever, and headache	Yes
Fever, headache, photophobia, neck ache, non-blanching rash (sepsis), shock, coma	Urgent antibiotics (ceftriaxone or co-amoxiclav, IV or IM). Pain relief, IV fluids to treat shock. **Contact TMAS and prepare to evacuate urgently**	Yes, for some causes
Unwell and feverish. Painful swelling of salivary glands in cheek. May be complicated by painful swelling of testicles and sometimes by infection of brain	Isolate if feasible. Look out for other cases in crew. Symptomatic treatment with NSAIDs for fever and pain	Yes
Itching at site of bite, headache, fever, confusion, hallucinations, hydrophobia (spasm of throat when attempting to drink), loss of consciousness	If bitten, scrub wound thoroughly with antiseptic (even gin/whisky). Antibiotics for other possible infections. Check tetanus status. Even if they had previous tetanus vaccinations **contact TMAS**. Check previous rabies vaccinations, but **prepare to evacuate urgently** for rabies immunoglobulin/post-exposure vaccination	Yes
Fever, headache, cough, abdominal pain, diarrhoea/constipation, blanching rash on abdomen. Later, gut bleed, shock	Isolation. Strict hygiene to prevent spread. Antibiotics – ciprofloxacin. **Contact TMAS (symptoms similar to malaria) and prepare to evacuate urgently**	Yes
Worms seen in stool, vomit. Skin rashes, anal itching at night. Some worms cause serious illness	Do not bathe in sluggish, infected water. Strict hygiene and food preparation. For known infections, praziquantel (if available), mebendazole	No
Headache, fever, chills, aches, vomiting, stomach pain, jaundice, gut bleeding, shock	No direct treatment, supportive of symptoms, treatment of shock. **Contact TMAS and prepare to evacuate urgently**	Yes, mandatory in some countries

10 Seasickness

Seasickness among crew is not only debilitating for the individual. It may seriously impair the running of the vessel and even place it and its crew in danger. Experienced crew members will have strategies for managing their own symptoms. It is more likely to be a problem in new crew members and people on board with little or no previous sea time, such as technical staff and passengers. Beginning management before departure from port can reduce symptoms, and in 95% of people seasickness can be prevented or treated effectively. Most people will have gained their 'sea legs' within 72 hours.

Once seasickness has become established, frequent reassessment and appropriate action will usually prevent a drama becoming a crisis.

Structured assessment

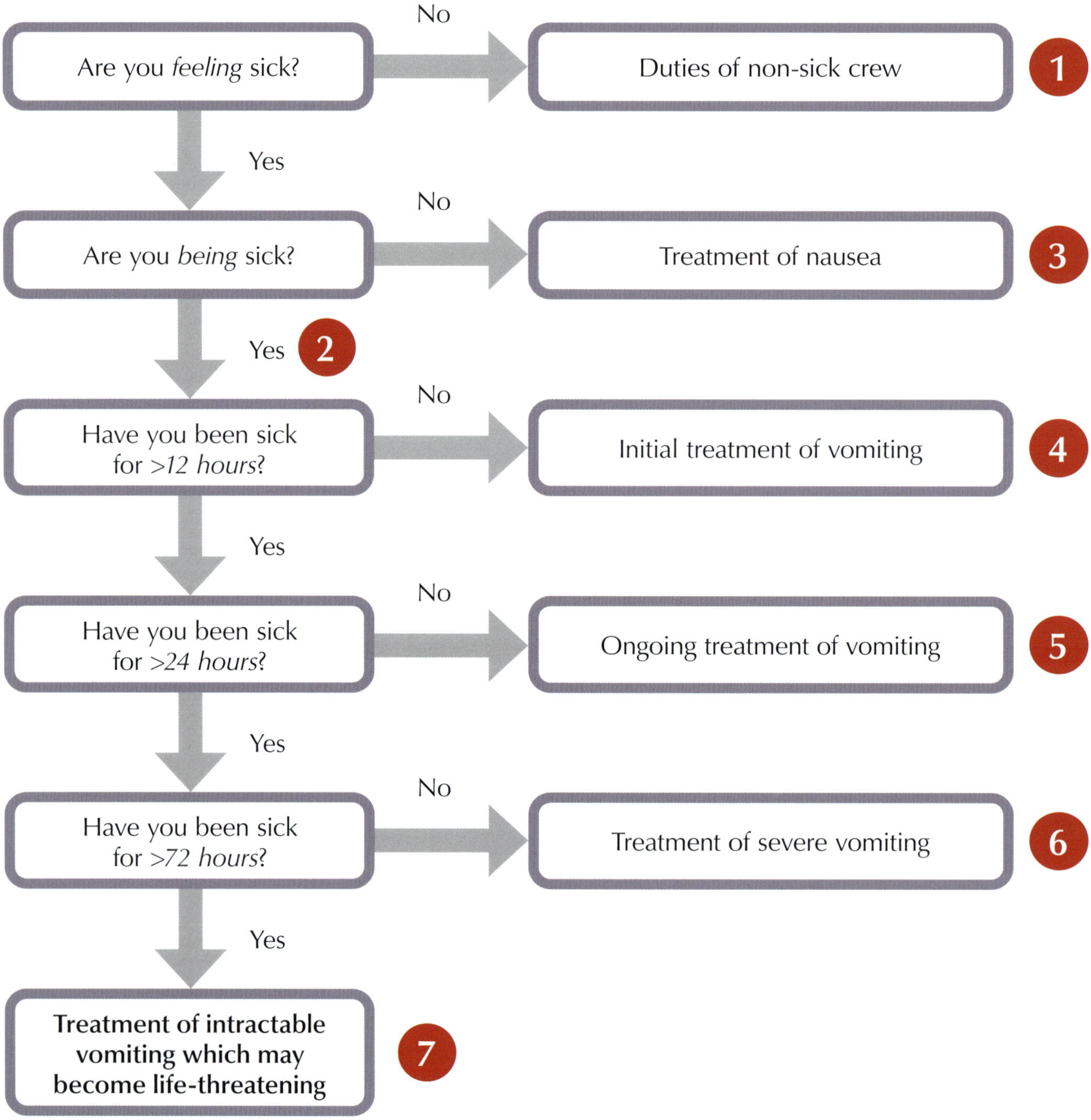

Duties of the non-sick crew

1

Crew members who are resistant to seasickness should look out for those who are suffering. They may have to take on the duties of crew who are too sick to work; for example, deck work, bridge duties and galley work. Sufferers require sympathy and support, and having a 'buddy' system on board can hasten recovery. Sufferers are not only ill but may also lack coordination. In severe cases they are disorientated and a danger to themselves. They often need help with the simplest tasks such as dressing appropriately when going on deck.

2

It is important that a fellow crew member is delegated to ensure that their safety gear is correct at all times, look after them if they vomit, and make sure they do not fall down stairs etc. The fellow crew member can supply a bucket, tissues, a water bottle and some dry biscuits. However, encourage seasick crew members to undertake some task that takes their mind off their plight; even concentrating on watching the horizon helps.

Treatment of nausea

3

- Take oral anti-seasickness medication in good time (page 169).
- Avoid activities such as cooking, navigating and working in engine rooms.
- Keep well hydrated.
- Take small meals and often.
- Get adequate rest.
- Some sufferers find that lying down helps; others find that concentrating on the horizon or some other external fixed point reduces nausea.
- Be positive and believe in a rapid recovery.

Initial treatment of vomiting

4

- Continue taking oral medications.
- Continue to take at least fluids by mouth, and dry biscuits if possible.
- Stay warm and dry.
- Loss of concentration and judgement increases accident risks, especially on deck. Close supervision is mandatory.
- Keep busy if it helps.
- The sight and smell of vomit can promptly cause symptoms in others, so all vomiting should be into toilets or over the lee side (safely) if possible.

Ongoing treatment of vomiting

5

- Prolonged vomiting is miserable and support from others is helpful. There is usually less motion low down in the centre of the vessel; consider moving the sufferer to a bunk in this location. Additional types of anti-seasickness medications should be taken if possible.

Treatment of severe vomiting

6

- Oral medications are unlikely to be effective at this point.
- Use either tablets that melt and are absorbed in the mouth, medicines by IM injection, or suppositories.
- Use oral electrolyte replacement fluids (page 221).

Treatment of intractable vomiting

7

- This situation is serious, and may require evacuation from the vessel. However, you may be able to avoid this with proper treatment.
- The risks are:
  - severe dehydration leading to shock
  - hypothermia
  - weakness and debilitation
  - severe constipation.
- Undertake a thorough assessment of the casualty, including peripheral perfusion, pulse, blood pressure and urine output.
- Use injectable forms of anti-seasickness medications.
- If necessary give fluid rehydration via IV (if possible) (page 225).
- Contact TMAS early.

Prevention and treatment

Seasickness can be effectively controlled in the vast majority of people. In a few it is severe and intractable, making a career at sea impracticable.

Cause

Seasickness is caused by the response of the brain to motion. Gut symptoms are a secondary phenomenon so special diets have little effect in preventing the condition. Do not consume alcohol (which has a direct effect on balance) or other recreational drugs before sailing. A meal comprising a large amount of fatty food will slow gastric emptying, exacerbating feelings of nausea.

Seasickness mechanism

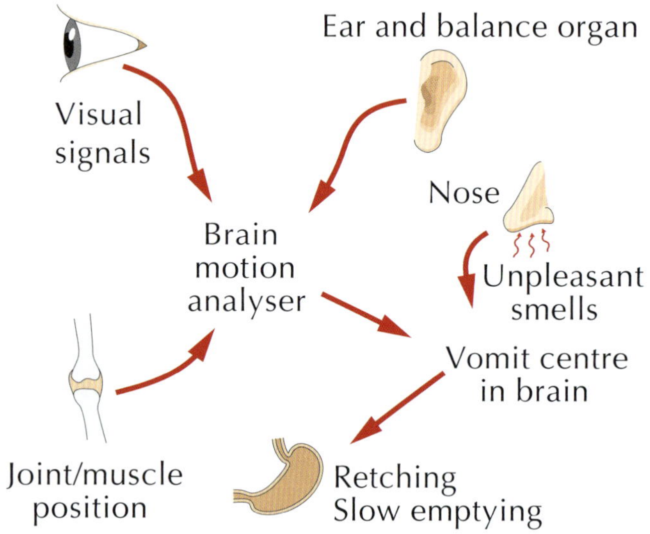

Symptoms and signs of seasickness

Stomach

- Loss of appetite
- Fullness of stomach
- Nausea
- Vomiting/retching
- Occasional blood in vomit

Brain

- Pallor and sweating
- Dizziness, drowsiness
- Yawning, excessive breathing
- Headache, malaise
- Dry mouth or increase in saliva

Prevention

There is no single preventive measure for seasickness. The following tips have been found to be helpful for novice crew members, especially on small craft such as yachts and fishing vessels. Although not all of them will be possible, it is worth trying those that are:

- **Start anti-seasickness remedies 12–24 hours before embarking.** It is important that the most effective drugs have been established before an extended voyage.
- Avoid heavy, fatty meals, alcohol and recreational drugs before leaving port.
- Board the night before departure and try to get a good night's sleep.
- Dress appropriately when leaving port for the open sea. Wear more rather than less clothing to keep warm and dry and to avoid going below later.
- Keep occupied and do not read, write, do chart work, navigate, go below or cook.
- Stay in the fresh air. Fix your gaze on land, clouds, stars or the horizon, which provide a stable reference point. Taking the helm on a vessel can help, if safe to do so.
- Keep hydrated, taking small amounts of water (or sugary drink), and small, frequent snacks, even if continuing to vomit; there will still be some benefit in this.
- Finally, believe that seasickness is not going to take over; be positive and hopeful of a rapid recovery.

Treatment

There are many medications that aim to control seasickness. They work on a variety of chemical pathways (controlled by acetylcholine, histamine, dopamine and serotonin neurotransmitters) in the brain and gut, and each produces a slightly different effect in individuals. Some will be helpful for some crew members, and others will produce unpleasant side-effects. Each individual will find a particular medication (or combination) that works for them, with minimal side-effects.

The most commonly used medications are shown in the table below. Individuals who are concerned about seasickness will have considered remedies in advance. The table is provided to both guide them and help medical officers who need to give treatments. Start at the top of the table and work down until an effective remedy is found.

- Do not combine medications that have the same action, for instance two antihistamines such as cinnarizine and cyclizine.
- Do not take in pregnancy without either medical advice prior to embarkation or after contacting TMAS if at sea.
- If a crew member is taking seasickness remedies for the first time, in conjunction with routine prescription medication, obtain prior clearance from the prescribing doctor (or seek advice from TMAS), to confirm that there are no adverse interactions.

Medication	Route	Dose	How it works	Notes
Cinnarizine	Oral	30 mg 6–12 hours before leaving then 15 mg every 8 hours	Antihistamine	Although it is an antihistamine, cinnarizine usually has little sedative effect
Domperidone	Oral	10–20 mg every 6 hours 30 mg every 6 hours	Peripheral anti-dopamine	Well tolerated and non-sedating
Prochloperazine	Oral Under tongue IM injection	10 mg every 6 hours 3 mg every 6 hours 12.5 mg injection, then oral therapy 6 hours later	Central anti-dopamine	Some sedative properties, dry mouth; rarely, causes abnormal movements, tremor and restlessness
Hyoscine hydrobromide	Patch behind ear Oral	Replace patch every 72 hours, on the opposite side 0.3 mg every 8 hours	Anti-cholinergic	Some sedative effects, confusion in older people, dry mouth; rarely, difficulty in passing urine. Take care with patch as contaminating eye will dilate pupil and blur vision. Wash hands after touching. Suppresses symptoms but prevents development of 'sea legs'
Ondansetron	Oral Under tongue (melts)	4–8 mg every 8 hours 4–8 mg every 8 hours	Anti-serotonin	Non-sedating. Occasional constipation
Cyclizine	Oral IM injection	50 mg every 8 hours 50 mg every 8 hours	Antihistamine	Slight sedation only. Painful injection
Promethazine teoclate	Oral	25 mg once daily for 3 days	Antihistamine	Commonly causes drowsiness. May also cause a dry mouth and, rarely, urinary retention
Promethazine hydrochloride	IM injection	25–50 mg once only	Antihistamine	Commonly causes drowsiness. May also cause a dry mouth and, rarely, urinary retention

Alternative treatments

Several alternative treatments may work well with some crew members. Ginger root (*Zingiber officinale*) 1 g every 8 hours may also be effective.

11 Skin disorders

The skin is the protective barrier between the inner body and the outer world, and sun, salt water, heat, cold, damp and friction all have a damaging effect on it. As a response to manual work, cold and friction, skin tends to get thicker and less sensitive, particularly on the fingers.

Despite this natural adaptive response by the skin, it is still prone to problems such as sunburn, infection, sores, rashes and itching. Some forms of infection can spread to other crew members in a short time if good hygiene is not strictly followed, and if any established infections are not treated promptly.

It is wise to protect the skin as much as possible. Most of this is common sense, but it is worth having a structured approach. Use simple methods before more expensive, invasive treatments become necessary.

Protection measures

- **Reduce time of sun exposure** Always keep in mind how long you have been in the sun.
- **Protective clothing when exposed to the sun** Wear a wide-brimmed hat, long sleeves and long trousers.
- **Sunscreen** Use a physical screen such as a zinc- or titanium oxide-based cream or a chemical screen with a high sun protection factor (e.g. SPF 50) containing para-aminobenzoic acid or cinnamates. Water-resistant agents are ideal.
- **Sunglasses** Wear sunglasses with side protection. The *MCA Code of Safe Working Practices for Merchant Seafarers* (section 3.13) covers the requirements for sunglasses used when performing safety-critical tasks.
- **Gloves and other recommended protective clothing** Wear these when doing deck work and using substances that may damage the skin.
- **Shoes or boots** Wear them at all times on deck and on shore.
- **Regular moisturiser** Use a moisturiser such as a petroleum jelly-based cream for hands after undertaking manual work or being exposed to skin-damaging substances. This should not be seen as a 'soft' thing to do; it keeps the hands and fingers in good shape so they function better.
- **Vessel hygiene** Good hygiene on the vessel is essential in reducing infections (see page 162).
- **Personal hygiene** This is a personal responsibility. Pay particular attention to feet and groin; these areas are prone to fungal infections. Dry yourself as thoroughly as possible and keep all parts aired.
- **Clothing** Wash and change clothing regularly, especially if you are hot and sweaty.
- **Infections** Keep an eye on your own skin and that of others. Intervene early if there are signs of inflammation, rash, itching, spots, boils or bites.

Specific conditions

Sunburn

Wind, and reflection of ultraviolet light from the surface of the sea, combined with a lack of natural shade, increase the risk of severe sunburn when working on deck. Sunburn is easy to prevent, less easy to treat.

Symptoms and signs

- Red, painful skin on exposed parts
- Dehydration, malaise, nausea
- Feels chilly but hot to touch
- Blisters and swelling if severe

→

Treatment

- Keep hydrated and in shade where possible
- Paracetamol and NSAIDs
- Hydrocortisone 1% cream may help
- Do not burst blisters

Rashes (including heat rash)

Infection, allergic reactions and abrasive conditions on board are the most common causes of rashes of varying appearance. Non-blanching rashes are serious (see page 124). Rashes may be the symptom of infections such as chicken pox, measles or viral infections (see page 164, infectious disease table). It will usually be necessary to contact TMAS, providing a photograph of the rash. They will need a good quality, well-lit, in-focus image to make a potential diagnosis.

Symptoms and signs

- Red, raised, blotchy itchy lumps (hives) are likely to be an allergic reaction
- Rashes that include sores that exude pus or in groin/feet are likely to be infective
- A rash in armpits, on waist, chest or back may be prickly heat, a particular problem in the tropics

→

Treatment

- Look for source of allergy and treat accordingly (see page 42)
- Infection may be bacterial, viral or fungal (see below)
- Heat rash – keep area dry and clean as much as possible. Calamine lotion or hydrocortisone cream

Skin infections

Impetigo in particular is a skin infection that can run through a crew very quickly.

Symptoms and signs

- **Viral (shingles)** – very painful blisters that erupt in one area of body usually. Burst and crust. Unwell beforehand
- **Bacterial**
  - **Impetigo** – crusting blisters that spread in patches. Itchy, red, painful, increasing numbers of patches
  - **Cellulitis** – painful, red, inflamed spreading area from a wound site
- **Fungal** – generally in groin, under breasts or between toes. Reddish discoloured, cracking skin, spreading outwards

→

Treatment

- **Shingles** – pain relief, antibiotics only if blisters become infected
- **Impetigo** – strict hygiene (no sharing towels etc). Antibiotics – flucloxacillin and fusidic acid or mupirocin cream. Seek medical advice if not improving after 3 days
- **Cellulitis** – antibiotics such as co-amoxiclav. Watch carefully to ensure improvement – contact TMAS if no improvement after 2 days
- **Fungal infection** – terbinafine or fluconazole tablets or miconazole cream for 1 week. Keep clean and dry

Salt-water boils and tropical ulcers

Tropical ulcers start from a trivial scratch or similar on the shin, over which a pustule forms; this then discharges after some days, forming a painful, hard-edged ulcer.

Symptoms and signs

- **Salt water boil** – a collection of smaller boils that join together. May form an abscess. Usually on arms or hands
- **Tropical ulcer** – a non-healing ulcer

Treatment

- **Saltwater boil** – if large and not draining, may need lancing to let pus out. Antibiotics – co-amoxiclav
- **Tropical ulcer** – antibiotics – Co-amoxiclav and/or metronidazole

Itchy skin

This may be due to an ongoing condition (e.g. eczema) or exposure to new substances. Scabies (see below) is a particular problem on board, and can spread.

Symptoms and signs

- Known condition or allergy
- New exposure (saltwater, sun, oil or fuel)

Treatment

- Avoid exposure to substance if known
- Antihistamine (such as loratadine or cetirizine), aqueous creams, emollients

Personal infestations

Scabies, head lice, fleas and bed bugs may prove to be an uncomfortable problem on a vessel, exacerbated by the close living quarters in crew accommodation. Spread may be from close human contact or through bedding and other linen. Continual vigilance is required to prevent an individual introducing such an infestation onto a vessel or to eradicate an outbreak promptly.

Symptoms and signs

- **Scabies** – reddish lines and spots, often around fingers. Can spread over the entire body. Very itchy at night

Treatment

- Treat contacts on board if there is an outbreak. If the crew is small this means everyone
- Wash bedding and linen at over 60 °C
- Permethrin 5% cream rinse or malathion cream to skin
- Avoid close personal contact

Symptoms and signs

- **Head lice** – itchy scalp and visible small blackish insects or whitish eggs in hair

Treatment

- Medicated shampoo (malathion)
- Use a nit comb to remove insects/eggs
- Check everyone on board

Symptoms and signs	Treatment
• **Fleas** – small itchy red lumps, sometimes in lines or clumps. Often hosted by animals such as pets	• Thorough cleaning of all areas • Removal of animals • Bites may need antihistamines to reduce itch from allergic reactions
• **Bed bugs** – bites are usually small red lumps, sometimes in lines, usually on face, arms and hands. Bites can become infected and blister. Bed bugs can be found in bedding and linen	• Hydrocortisone cream and antihistamines may reduce the itch from the bites • Wash all bedding at over 60 °C • Thoroughly clean all mattresses, cabin furniture and fittings

12 Bites and stings

The marine world is full of animals that may sting, jab and bite any crew member who comes within range. While the vessel is crossing the deep oceans the crew are not likely to encounter these animals. Problems arise when the vessel is close to land or in port and the crew come ashore or swim in the sea. Unpleasant insects may also visit unless discouraged from doing so. A range of venomous and irritant sea creatures may be brought aboard and cause harm when fish catches are handled and processed. Cargo may also harbour venomous animals, such as tropical spiders in bunches of bananas.

Most injuries will cause a little pain, itching, localised swelling and some ongoing discomfort. Treatment comprises removing stings and tentacles that may still inject venom, and relief of symptoms. However, there is always a very small chance that, particularly with stings that inject venom, the body will respond with an overwhelming allergic response known as anaphylaxis. This is immediately life-threatening with a grave outlook if you do not start treatment promptly (see page 42).

The species of animal that crew members may encounter depends upon geographical location, although some species, such as sharks and jellyfish, are widespread and can be found anywhere from the tropics to the high latitudes.

Geographical spread

Animals that sting	Regions where most prevalent
• Bees, wasps, hornets	All areas
• Mosquitoes and midges	All areas. Disease transmission in tropical and subtropical areas
• Jellyfish	All areas (except Arctic and Antarctic)
• Sea anemones	All areas (except Arctic and Antarctic)
• Fire coral	Tropical and subtropical
• Portuguese man-of-war	All areas (except Arctic and Antarctic)
Animals that jab with spines	
• Catfish	Marine, estuarine, fresh water
• Cone shells	Tropical and subtropical
• Sea urchins	Tropical and subtropical
• Stinging fish (lionfish, scorpionfish, stonefish, needlefish, weeverfish)	Tropical and subtropical (weeverfish – temperate)
• Stingrays	Atlantic, Pacific and Indian Oceans Freshwater (South America)
Animals that bite	
• Sharks	All areas (except Arctic and Antarctic)
• Moray eels	Tropical
• Barracudas	Tropical and subtropical
• Sea snakes	Tropical and subtropical (fresh and sea)
• Crocodiles, alligators	Tropical and subtropical

Particularly dangerous marine animals that have caused fatalities

• **Box jellyfish** (sea wasp) – South-East Asia and North Australia	• **Needlefish** – Caribbean, West Africa, Japan, Indian Ocean
• **Irukandji jellyfish** – South-East Asia and North Australia	• **Blue-ringed and spotted octopuses** – Indian and Pacific tropical areas
• **Flower sea urchin** – Indian and Pacific tropical areas	• **Stingrays and sea snakes** • **Larger animals that bite**

Symptoms of anaphylaxis (page 42)

Symptoms and signs

- General skin flushing
- Swelling of lips and eyes
- Fast pulse
- Faintness
- Wheezy chest
- Shock

Treatment

- ABCDE if collapsed
- Adrenaline 0.5 mg IM (0.5 ml of 1:1000 solution) every 5 minutes
- IV access and IV fluids (500 ml immediately)
- Further treatment – see page 43
- Steroid: hydrocortisone 100 mg IM or IV
- Antihistamine: chlorphenamine 10–20 mg IM

General symptoms of bites and stings

Typical symptoms	Unusual symptoms
• Pain	• Headache
• Stinging	• Weakness
• Itching	• Sweating
• Rash	• Nausea and vomiting
• Redness	• Muscle pain
• Swelling	• Chest pain

Commonly, the animal causing the injury will not be known

Immediate treatment

- **If the casualty has collapsed and has difficulty breathing see pages 8 and 43**
- **If they have large bites, retrieve from water and treat as trauma – see page 48**
- **Stings:**
  - Avoid getting the stings or tentacles on yourself – use gloves.
  - Soak the area in very warm seawater (as warm as tolerated) for 60–90 minutes. This will encourage the breakdown of venom in the skin. This is preferable to using vinegar.
  - Alternatively soak the area in vinegar for 10 minutes. This may neutralise the venom **but be careful** because occasionally it may make matters worse; stop if the pain increases.

- Cover the area with shaving cream, flour, or a paste of sand and seawater. Scrape a knife across to remove stingers; this avoids any further injection of venom.
- Thoroughly wash the area and put sterile dressings on wounds.
- For relief of pain ibuprofen (NSAID) gel and lidocaine 2% gel are effective.
- For itching give an oral antihistamine (loratadine or cetirizine).
- For inflammation hydrocortisone 1% cream is effective.
- Observe the casualty and their wounds for signs of infection and deterioration.

• **Bites and penetrating wounds:**

  Wash the wound thoroughly with soap and hot water (sterile if possible).
- Remove embedded spines if possible. **Do not** remove large spines (e.g. from a stingray) embedded in the chest, head, neck or abdomen because bleeding may worsen. Call TMAS for advice.
- Stop bleeding with direct pressure (not a tourniquet if possible – see page 30).
- If there is intense pain from venom, soak the wound in very warm water (as warm as tolerated) for 60–90 minutes.
- Cover the wound with a sterile dressing and check daily for infection.
- Start antibiotics (co-amoxiclav or ciprofloxacin).
- **Check the casualty's tetanus vaccination status and, if venomous, the availability of an anti-venom.**

Prevention

- Insects – see page 162
- Splash or shuffle feet in shallow water
- Do not wear bright clothing or carry bright objects in the water
- Take care if diving using a flashlight at night
- Do not swim with open wounds
- Do not touch anything (e.g. animals or corals)
- Wear dive suits and shoes at all times
- Do not harass animals at any time
- Make sure tetanus vaccination is up to date
- Carry anti-venom in high-risk areas

13 Poisoning

Poisons may enter the body through a variety of routes:

- **Airway and lungs** gases and dust (usually from occupational exposure); illicit drugs
- **Mouth and stomach** contaminated food, medications (accidental or intentional overdose; illicit drugs)
- **Absorption through the skin** certain liquids; usually occupational exposure
- **Injection** using a needle for drugs; high-pressure fluid or gas; venomous animals.

Poisons may cause local effects, related to the nature of exposure (irritant and inflammation in the airway, on the skin or in the eyes). They may also have systemic effects in the body, causing problems with body organs such as the brain, heart, lungs and kidneys. The severity of poisoning may become obvious immediately after one exposure, or it may be gradual, after prolonged or repeated exposure.

Generally, the greater the amount of toxic agent enters the body, the greater the severity of symptoms. Therefore the priority for initial treatment is directed at reducing absorption, encouraging breakdown and excretion. Support for body organ systems may also be needed. If poisoning is suspected, contact TMAS immediately, particularly if the vessel is carrying a potentially dangerous cargo (see page 174).

An up-to-date Material Safety Data Sheet (MSDS) supplied by the manufacturer/shipper will contain information on poisoning risks from chemicals used or carried on board, and how to deal with an event. It is essential that an MSDS is supplied before loading the chemicals or cargo.

The International Maritime Organization *Medical First Aid Guide (MFAG)* from the International Maritime Dangerous Goods Code provides information on the risks from dangerous cargoes in addition to an MSDS. Vessels are required to carry it if they are transporting such cargoes. It also contains a supplementary list of medical stores that must be carried.

1 **Assess severity**
- History
- Examination

Collapsed? / Unconscious? → **Resuscitate ABCDE** Page 2

Signs of severe illness **2**
- Loss of consciousness or confusion
- Very slow or very fast heart rate
- Low blood pressure
- Low or very high respiratory rate
- Dilated or pinpoint pupils

Care of the unconscious crew member **(page 12)**

Immediate treatment
- Remove from harm – watch yourself
- ABCDE (oxygen if available)
- Care of airway if vomiting
- Establish IV access and fluids if low blood pressure
- Specific antidotes (see below)

Specific poisons or overdoses **3**
- Paracetamol
- Antidepressants
- Sleeping pills (benzodiazepines)
- Alcohol
- Cocaine or amphetamines
- Heroin, morphine, other opiates
- Carbon monoxide
- Chlorine
- Solvents
- Dangerous cargoes

Continued monitoring
- Pulse
- Blood pressure
- Respiration rate
- Conscious state
- Blood sugar
- Urine output

WATCH FOR DETERIORATION

Contact TMAS early

History and examination

1

- Make sure you do not get poisoned yourself.
- If there are multiple casualties and no apparent cause, likely reasons are either the presence of an undetectable gas such as carbon monoxide, or contamination of food.
- Look around for empty pill bottles, packets, prescriptions, syringes, needles etc.

Important points in the history

- The crew member may be able to tell you everything
- Have they worked recently with any toxic substances or been in enclosed spaces on board where contaminants may build up?
- Find out about previous medical problems
- Normal medications – check whether any are 'slow-release' forms – the crew member may get worse
- Often alcohol is taken at the same time as a deliberate overdose

Important points in the examination

- **Look:**
  - Level of consciousness and whether confused
  - Very pink or pale
  - Pupils – large or small/reactive
- **Feel:**
  - Peripheral perfusion
  - Muscle stiffness, brisk reflexes, tremor
- **Document:** Level of consciousness, blood sugar

Signs of poisoning

2

- **Loss of consciousness (LOC), low blood pressure, low respiration rate, very small pupils** possible opiates (morphine or heroin)
- **LOC, fast heart rate, large pupils, brisk reflexes** possible antidepressants (tricyclic antidepressants)
- **LOC, low blood pressure, low respiration rate, smallish pupils, limp limbs** possibly sleeping pills (benzodiazepine), alcohol, severe tricyclic antidepressant overdose, over-exposure to solvents/inert refrigerants or fire suppressants (halons, hypoxia from work in a confined space that is short of oxygen)
- **Agitation, tremor, sweating, fast heart rate, nausea, fever, dilated pupils** cocaine, amphetamine
- **LOC, low blood pressure, fast respiration rate, stiff muscles, brisk reflexes, pale or flushed/ cherry red** possibly carbon monoxide poisoning
- **Shortness of breath, wheezing** inhalation of a respiratory irritant such as chlorine or ammonia.

Specific conditions

3

In all cases, if the casualty is symptomatic, contact TMAS and prepare to evacuate urgently

Paracetamol

Paracetamol is a dangerous drug in overdose. It has no initial effect (the crew member appears normal), but it poisons the liver over several days. If there is a suspicion that more than 8 tablets (4 g) have been taken within the past 24 hours, contact TMAS and prepare for evacuation.

Antidepressants

These come in many different forms, but most have similar effects in overdose.

Symptoms and signs

- LOC, confusion, large pupils, fever
- Fast heart rate but low blood pressure with large overdose

Treatment

- Supportive – keep airway clear and ensure vomit is not inhaled
- May need IV fluid if low blood pressure

Sleeping pills (benzodiazepines: temazepam, diazepam, nitrazepam)

Benzodiazepines in overdose effectively anaesthetise the crew member.

Symptoms and signs

- Sleepy, then LOC
- Low blood pressure and respiration rate
- Smallish pupils, limp limbs

Treatment

- Supportive – keep airway clear and ensure vomit is not inhaled
- Await recovery from overdose, and call TMAS for advice regarding care

Alcohol

Alcohol is very common in overdose; usually spirits. It is often taken with pills.

Symptoms and signs

- Sleepy then LOC, smallish pupils
- Low blood pressure and respiration rate
- Low blood glucose
- Look for other poisoning

Treatment

- Supportive – keep airway clear and ensure vomit is not inhaled
- May need IV fluid if low blood pressure
- May need sugar (not orally if LOC)

Cocaine and amphetamines

Very large overdoses may result in LOC, which is very grave.

Symptoms and signs

- Agitation, tremor, sweating, hot
- Fast heart rate, dilated pupils
- Fitting in large overdose

Treatment

- Keep cool – tepid cloths, fan etc
- Establish IV access and fluids
- Contact TMAS

Opiates (morphine, heroin etc)

These drugs may be taken by mouth, smoked or injected.

Symptoms and signs

- Sleepy then LOC
- Pinpoint pupils
- Low blood pressure and respiration rate
- Look for injection marks, needles etc

Treatment

- Supportive – keep airway clear and ensure vomit is not inhaled
- Naloxone is an antidote if available, but should only be given on direct advice from TMAS

Carbon monoxide

Insidious in onset; all the crew may be affected. May come from incomplete combustion in faulty gas and oil heaters, and as a gas released from wood pellet cargoes.

Symptoms and signs

- Lethargy, headache, nausea, vomiting
- Fast respiration rate, chest pain
- Low blood pressure and LOC; possible fits
- May be pale, or worse, flushed
- Outlook is grave if LOC

Treatment

- Do not endanger yourself
- Evacuate crew member into an area of clean air; give oxygen
- Supportive – keep airway clear and ensure vomit is not inhaled
- Treat fits (page 16)

Chlorine

Chlorine poisoning is a risk on vessels from water treatment, disinfection and leaking batteries.

Symptoms and signs

- Wheeze, cough, breathlessness
- Chest pain
- Watering, sore eyes
- Breathlessness may get worse over several hours

Treatment

- Do not endanger yourself
- Move crew member out into open air, give oxygen
- Salbutamol inhaler 2 puffs/15 minutes
- Prednisolone 60 mg orally
- Contact TMAS and prepare to evacuate

Solvents (methanol, ethylene glycol etc)

Solvents are widely used for cleaning and degreasing and in paints. They are also taken in deliberate and accidental overdose.

Symptoms and signs

- Nausea, vomiting
- Confusion, possible fits, then LOC
- Low blood pressure
- Low or high blood sugars
- Effects may be delayed by up to 36 hours

Treatment

- Supportive – keep airway clear and ensure vomit is not inhaled
- Check blood sugar and give sugar if level is below 3 mmol/l (see page 37)
- If methanol or ethylene glycol poisoning, give 150 ml spirit drink (e.g. gin, vodka) if carried (only if conscious)

14 Mental health disorders

A significant proportion of the population will experience a mental health disorder at some time in their lives. Such problems may occur on a vessel, given the occasionally arduous and isolated working environment. 'Mental health disorder' is a broad term and includes states such as anxiety, depression, suicide, mania, psychosis and substance misuse.

Mental health disorders still carry a social stigma, and crew members may try to hide such problems, especially if they fear disclosure may affect their certification as fit to work at sea. There are also significant cultural differences in how mental health disorders are regarded, and this can create difficulties in a multinational crew.

These problems should be approached with compassion, understanding, and as much confidentiality as is possible.

Prevention

Working at sea can be physically and emotionally stressful, which may exacerbate tension between crew members. The master and medical officer need to be alert to any possible problems and take the initiative in good time to avert difficulties between crew members.

It is useful to know about any problems that crew members may have had in the past, such as depression requiring treatment or anxiety attacks. Knowing there are people around who can help, empathise, or even just talk, is enough for most.

Particular strategies to prevent problems and maintain a well-balanced crew include:

- Recognising tiredness and getting enough sleep
- Eating and drinking properly
- Understanding that everything does not always run smoothly and that plans change
- Making sure a crew member does not become isolated and withdrawn
- Assigning appropriate roles to crew members that are within their capability, with supervision where necessary
- Keeping a sense of humour and a sense of proportion.

Particular mental health disorders

Anxiety and panic attacks

Extremely bad weather, accidents, the unknown and the unexpected cause anxiety in most people. However, acute anxiety is an exaggerated response with tearfulness, feelings of dread and doom and lack of control. It also causes physical symptoms such as a fast heart rate, breathlessness and dizziness. Once you have recognised these symptoms as acute anxiety, put the crew member in a safe place (a quiet bunk if possible) until the crisis is over, and then talk things over with them. Diazepam may be required to control the symptoms until the emergency passes. They may require continual reassurance, or at least frequent review until they are calm and back to their normal self.

Disordered sleep

Watch or shift systems, long flights to the vessel, change of time zones, hard work and disturbed sleep all combine to cause fatigue. This quickly saps morale and decreases performance. It is important to avoid the downward spiral of poor sleep leading to more poor sleep, so try to start any sea voyage well rested. Maintaining an organised watch system will increase the likelihood that crew members will get adequate rest and sleep. It requires discipline to come off watch and go to bed and sleep straightaway, rather than staying up and being distracted by entertainment from other crew members or electronic devices. After a few days, the body usually adjusts to the altered sleep pattern of a watch or shift system. Longer periods of sleep may be required occasionally.

Depressive problems

Depressive problems range from low mood, through reactive and endogenous depression (where there is no obvious cause) to suicide.

- **Low mood**
  Everybody experiences low mood from time to time and it is not a medical diagnosis. This only becomes an issue when it is prolonged (for more than 3 weeks) or interferes with daily work and living.

- **Depression**
  This is a persistent low mood, which interferes with normal life and work patterns.

Potential causes

- Significant life events:
  - bereavement
  - relationship problems
  - financial problems
- Interpersonal relationships on board
- Bullying
- Poor sleep
- Irregular working and shift patterns
- Alcohol or drug abuse
- Previous episodes of depression

Symptoms

- Withdrawal from contact with others
- Lack of interaction
- Poor sleep and/or early morning waking
- Tearfulness
- Poor appetite
- Lethargy
- Little eye contact
- Slow speech
- Inability to feel joy
- Alcohol or drug abuse

Treatment

Ensure the crew member is not isolated and has a friend in whom they can confide. Find out if there is a particular reason for the symptoms. If the depression is felt to be due to conditions on board then every effort should be made to improve them.

If the crew member is taking antidepressive medication they should continue at their normal dose. You will need to contact TMAS if they become worse and actively contemplate suicide.

Suicide

This is a tragedy for the casualty and a disaster for all those who surround them. Prevention is obviously paramount and there are several 'red flags' of behaviour which may give forewarning, raising the opportunity for intervention.

Act immediately on any evidence of severe depression, suicidal thoughts, active plans to put thoughts into action (e.g. hoarding tablets or obtaining and concealing sharp implements). In these circumstances it is essential to get early medical advice from TMAS.

Keeping the casualty safe is the priority, although on a vessel this is not easy. Confine the person to a cabin and keep them there under supervision. Do not leave them alone, even when they appear to be sleeping. The person must be escorted at all times, even to the toilet (leave the door discreetly ajar but respect their privacy). The deck is a dangerous place and they may be tempted to jump overboard. Remove all drugs and medicines from their cabin. Also remove all cord, rope and sharp or potentially sharp objects from sight and access. Contact TMAS and prepare for evacuation.

Mania, delirium and psychosis

These three disorders cover a very wide range of abnormal behaviour, and there is some overlap between them. They represent a significant challenge on a vessel at sea, and medical advice from TMAS is essential if a crew member starts to behave in an abnormal manner. Remember that recreational drugs such as amphetamines, cannabis and ketamine may contribute to the development of these disorders.

- **Mania** The person appears to be hyperactive; their speech is very fast, with illogical jumps. They will claim not to need sleep and may either take no food or eat excessively. They may also be uninhibited and drink alcohol excessively or use drugs. They can have grandiose ideas, and while initially they may appear amusing, the ideas can be very dangerous if they try to act them out; for example, believing they can fly. An alternating pattern of mania and depression indicates a bipolar disorder.
- **Delirium** This represents a general deterioration in a casualty's normal mental state. The symptoms can include the acute onset of confusion, attention deficit, disordered behaviour, detachment from reality (delusions) and hallucinations. In many cases this is a consequence of an underlying illness (see page 20).
- **Psychosis** This includes schizophrenia but it can also be a result of drug abuse. The person hears voices or sees objects that others do not hear or see. They may believe, for example, that other powers are trying to influence them through the TV or radio. They can harm themselves or others if they 'obey the voices' or if they try to escape them.

Treatment

The general approach is the same for all the above disorders: get medical advice from TMAS immediately. This will aid assessment, determine the best method to manage the casualty, and gauge whether they require urgent evacuation.

Keep the casualty in a safe place, away from vessel controls or machinery, or any circumstance where they may harm themselves or others. They should not be allowed on the open deck and they should be supervised at all times. They may need to be confined to their cabin. Chlorpromazine may be used to control excesses of dangerous behaviour, but only under immediate medical direction from TMAS.

The casualty is likely to require evacuation if the vessel is in a suitable position. In extreme cases it may be very difficult to evacuate as the casualty's behaviour may be unpredictable; this is obviously a problem in a helicopter. Contact TMAS to determine how an evacuation will be managed, and which medications may be required to make this possible.

Part 4
Medical procedures

1 Taking a history from a casualty

The first step in finding out what is wrong with the injured or sick casualty is to understand what has happened; both the immediate events and further back in the past. This is difficult on land in a hospital, and even more so at sea.

It is vital to remember that resuscitation and treatment of life-threatening injuries or illnesses take precedence over a detailed history. However, a history of sorts is still necessary in emergencies. The section on emergency assessment explains how to do this (see page 4).

It is useful to have a structure for taking a history, for both medics and non-medics. Such an approach will minimise the chance that essential information is missed. It also enables medical information to be sent to shore logically and comprehensibly. Avoid medical jargon, which may be misleading if not used correctly.

It is usually impossible to get the whole history in one go; it may come together from any possible sources, not just the casualty, over a few hours or even days.

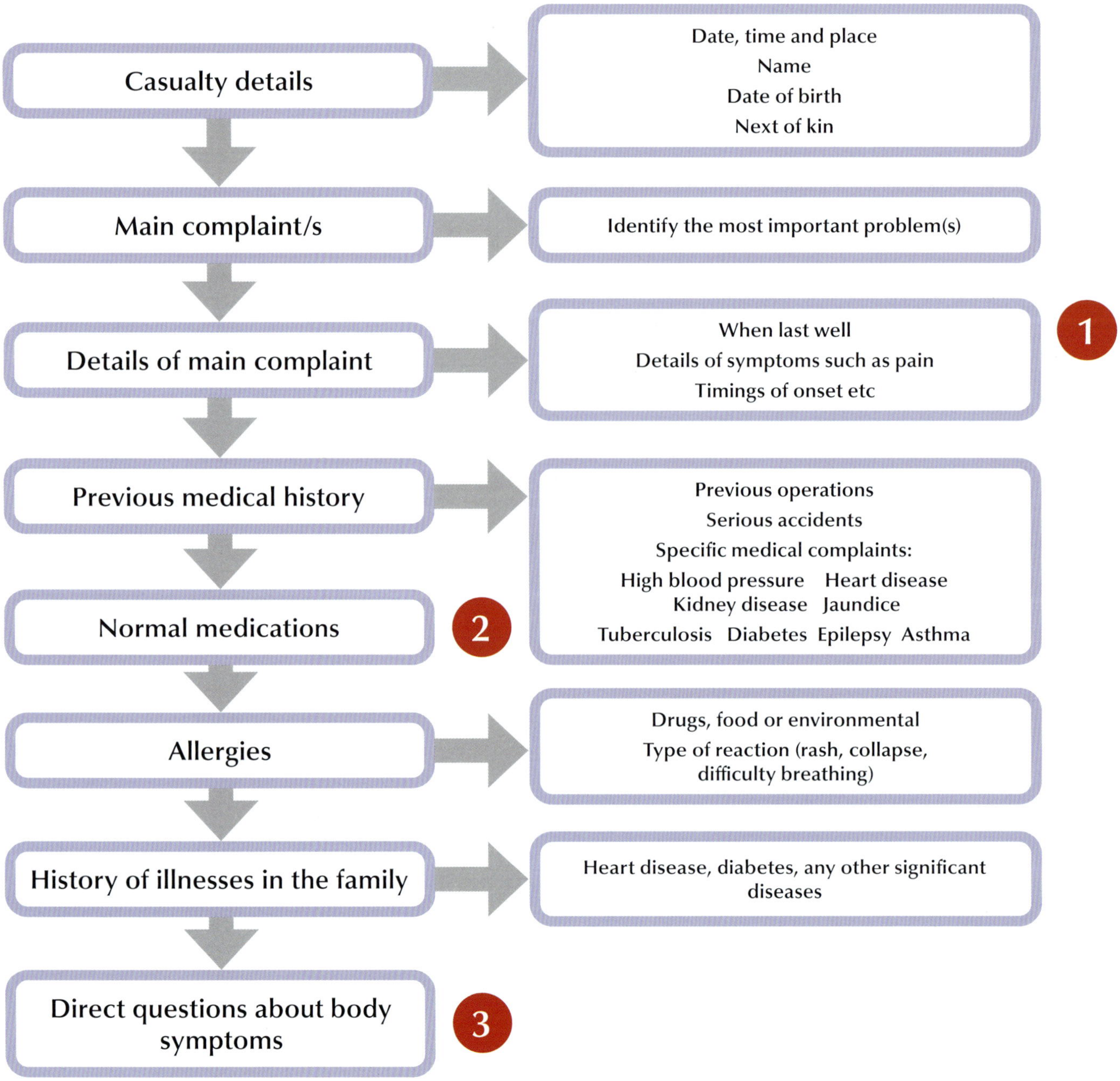

Details of main complaint

1

- What happened?
- What is wrong now?
- When did it first start?
- What makes it better now?
- Do you know what it is?
- When were you last well?
- Have you had this before?
- How long did it last?
- What makes it worse now?
- What treatment worked last time?

Pain

- Where is the pain worst?
- Do you feel it anywhere else?
- Is it sharp, dull, constant?
- How severe is the pain (1–10)?
- What makes it worse?
- What makes it better?
- Anything else linked to the pain?

Normal medications

2

Ask specifically if the casualty takes any heart medications, anticoagulants, inhalers, medications for epilepsy or diabetes, anti-malarial medications or oral contraceptives.

Get details of the casualty's immunisations, prophylactic medications and foreign travel, including port visits and transit airports.

Ask about any alternative medicines they may have taken, such as any homoeopathic remedies, recreational drugs and alcohol, smoking.

Direct questions about body symptoms

3

Heart and circulation

- Chest pain
- Palpitations
- Shortness of breath
- Swelling of the ankles
- Pain in the legs when walking

Lungs

- Shortness of breath
- Pain related to breathing
- Cough
- Wheeze
- Sputum – amount and colour

Mouth, throat and intestines

- Nausea and vomiting
- Indigestion
- Abdominal pain
- Distension of abdomen
- Last bowel movement
- Nature of stool – colour, blood
- Appetite, weight loss

Kidneys, bladder and genitals

- Pain on passing urine
- Passing urine frequently in large volume
- Colour of urine
- Loin pain
- Discharge from genitals
- Date of last menstrual period
- Any miscarriages

Musculoskeletal system/skin

- Pain or stiffness on moving limbs
- Muscle pains or swelling
- Joint pain or swelling
- Stability while walking
- Skin diseases/problems
- Skin allergic reactions

Nervous system

- Headache
- Pain at looking at light
- Stiff neck
- Vision
- Hearing
- Fits and faints
- Weakness or numbness in limbs

Record keeping

It is essential to keep details of the history and examination **as you go along**. These records may be needed to follow progress, to inform TMAS when seeking advice, and most importantly, to accompany the casualty if they are transferred ashore for treatment.

Contemporaneous records may also be important if there are any subsequent concerns about the adequacy of treatment on board. Facts and figures are very easily forgotten, and such a medical record may be valuable in establishing a true record of assessment and treatment (see page 258).

2 Examining a casualty

Once the casualty's history has been taken (see page 186) a thorough examination is needed. This is the second stage in finding out what is wrong with the casualty. The examination is best performed in the vessel's sick bay (if available), or on a bunk or bench seat, unless the initial assessment has identified reasons for not moving the casualty. It may not be possible to undertake a thorough examination in cramped or dangerous conditions, so the examination must be repeated in more detail once the casualty is in a more controlled environment.

Procedures for moving casualties from working or living spaces to the designated treatment area should have been developed and practised in advance (see Appendix III, page 282). Depending on the situation, moving by stretcher is the preferred option in the event of serious injury or illness.

Examining a fellow crew member is a very sensitive activity but it is absolutely essential if they are seriously injured or sick. If an injury is clearly localised, you need to examine only the injured part. However, if the casualty has fallen from height or is unconscious, the examination should cover the whole body, including the back.

Undressing (exposing) a part or whole of the body is necessary when examining thoroughly. This may not only be inconvenient and difficult to achieve with a sick or injured casualty; it may also be detrimental because the casualty could become very cold whilst uncovered. Minimising the exposure time, and making best use of it, is imperative.

The basis for examination is **look**, **feel**, **listen**, **move**, and compare left with right.

Look

- Make sure the area is well lit, and that you can see a reasonable amount of the casualty
- General appearance – well or unwell?
- Skin colour, rashes
- Obvious injury:
  - Deformity
  - Wounds
  - Blood or fluid from orifices

Feel

- Try not to cause pain
- Find a comfortable, stable position for the casualty and you
- Warm, firm but gentle hands
- Feel for:
  - Tenderness
  - Broken bones (gently)
  - Pulses (page 192)

Listen

- Breathing sounds:
  - Noisy or silent?
  - On inspiration or expiration?
- Voice – has it changed in any way?
- With a stethoscope:
  - Chest:
  - Silent (no breath sounds)?
  - Wheeze (on expiration)?
  - Harsh (on inspiration or expiration)?
  - Abdomen: Sounds of gas moving in the bowel (bowel sounds)

Move

- First ask the casualty to move each limb
- Then move the limb yourself very carefully
- Look for range of movement of joints
- Is movement limited by pain or mechanical locking?

Examining body systems

This should be done in a methodical manner, examining each body system in turn. It is common sense to start with the body system which appears to be the main problem.

The only exception to this is in the case of major trauma or collapse, where the resuscitation and emergency assessment guidelines should be followed (pages 2, 4). A procedure for examining the body systems in these emergency circumstances, with the essential requirements for each, is included on page 5.

Monitoring of vital signs

Monitoring of vital signs (see table) starts when the casualty is first examined and should continue until they are better or evacuated. Routine monitoring of unwell casualties should be hourly, and increase to at least every 15 minutes if the casualty is very unwell.

Vital sign	Normal range	Seriously unwell
Pulse (beats per minute)	50–100	<40 or>120
Systolic blood pressure (mmHg)	100–140	<90
Skin blanch test (seconds) (Capillary refill test)	<2	>4
Breathing rate (breaths per minute)	10–20	<8 or >24
Temperature (°C)	36–37.5	<35 or >38.5
Urine output (ml/hour)	40–100	<20

If any measured value lies outside the normal range, or there is any doubt, contact TMAS. If the casualty looks unwell, they probably are, despite apparently normal vital signs.

An example of a monitoring chart for vital signs is included in Appendix VI (page 294).

Testing

The following simple but effective tests can easily be performed on board, and may contribute significantly to making a diagnosis and aiding treatment:

- Blood glucose
- Urine analysis (dipstick)
- Pregnancy test
- Oxygen saturation – pulse oximeter
- Stool colour/consistency
- Sputum colour/amount
- Temperature
- Malaria

Always be aware that a test may give a false positive or false negative result. Contact TMAS to interpret test results accurately.

Record keeping

It is essential to keep details of the history and examination **as you go along**. Facts and figures are easily forgotten, and the medical record may be of considerable importance for the shore medical team (page 258).

An example of a medical assessment form is included in Appendix IV (page 288).

3 Pulse and blood pressure

There are several quick ways to assess how the casualty's heart (more accurately the 'cardiovascular system') is performing:

- General appearance A sick casualty tends to look pale and will have cold hands and feet. A casualty who has a cardiac arrest will look grey or white.
- Pulse May be very slow (<40 beats/minute) or very fast (>120 beats/minute).
- Blood pressure May be low (<90 mmHg systolic pressure) or very high (>160 mmHg).
- Perfusion of the skin May be low, with a capillary refill time (CRT) of >4 seconds).

Pulse and blood pressure are vital signs, and it is essential to be able to measure them accurately.

Measuring the pulse

- The pulse can be felt anywhere in the body where an artery lies close to the skin. Typical sites are described below.
- Use two fingers to feel for the pulse. Do this firmly but not too hard or you might block off the blood supply.
- Use a watch or clock with a second hand and count over a period of 60 seconds.
- Do not estimate a rate – you could be significantly wrong, and this will affect treatment.

In an emergency

- Measure the carotid pulse
  Feel for the pulse in the groove between the larynx (voice box) and the muscles of the neck (see diagram).

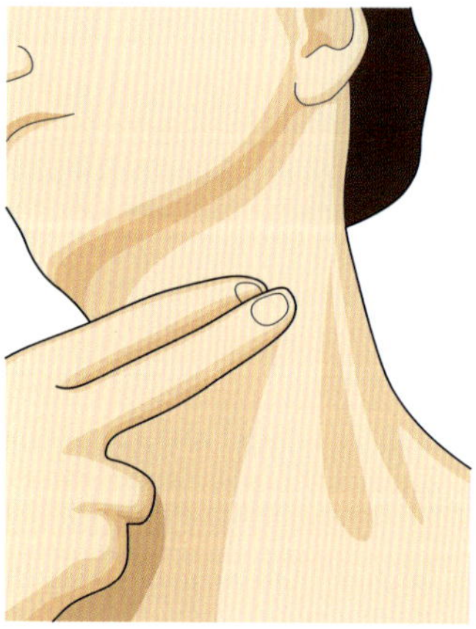

- Measure the femoral pulse
  Feel for the pulse in the skin groove in the groin at the top of the leg (see diagram).

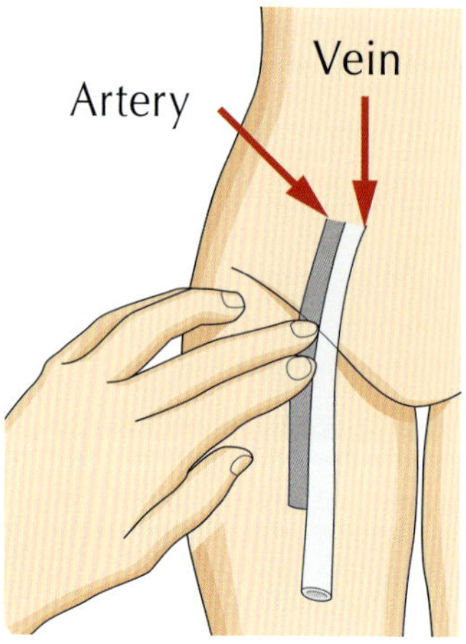

Routinely

- Measure the radial pulse
  Feel for the pulse at the wrist, about 3 cm up the arm from the base of the thumb (see diagram).

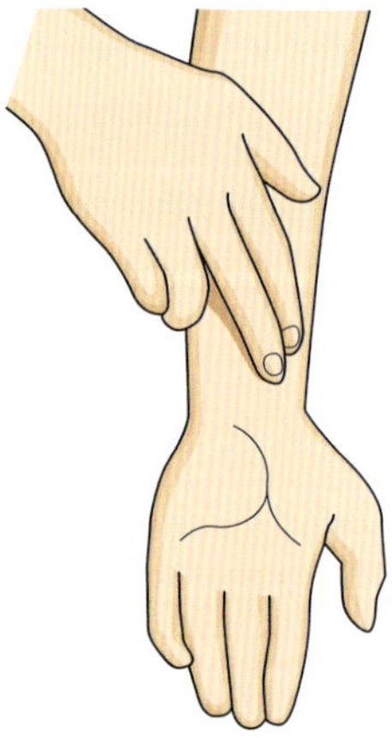

- Measure the brachial pulse
  Feel for the pulse at the elbow, on the inside edge of the biceps muscle (see diagram).

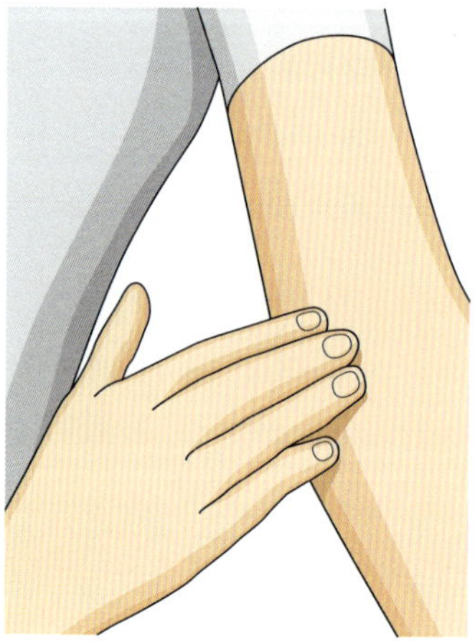

Measuring the blood pressure

The blood pressure has two values:

- Systolic blood pressure (SBP) – this is the higher value
- Diastolic blood pressure (DBP) – this is the lower value.

For example, a blood pressure of 120/70 mmHg has an SBP of 120 mmHg and a DBP of 70 mmHg.

Position

- The casualty should preferably be sitting, or if they cannot sit up, lying down.

Methods

A blood pressure monitoring device that uses a cuff around the arm is known as a 'sphygmomanometer' (see diagram).

Automatic devices are simple to use and give a quick result. A manual monitor usually has a dial to show the measurement of blood pressure. This type is known as an 'aneroid' blood pressure monitor.

A manually inflated blood pressure cuff can also be used as an effective tourniquet for control of a bleeding limb.

For large people, standard cuffs do not fit right round the arms, so the results can be inaccurate, unless an appropriate larger cuff is carried.

Manual

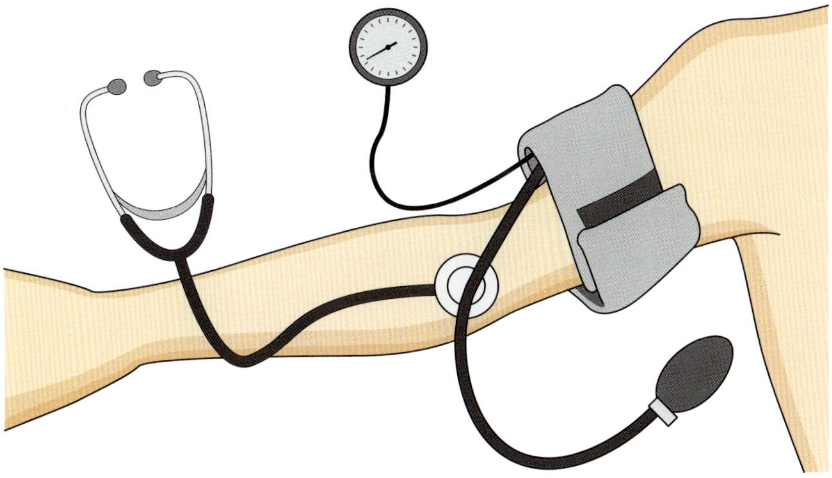

- Fasten the blood pressure cuff around the upper arm.
- Pump up the cuff while feeling the radial pulse. Make sure you can definitely feel the pulse before starting to pump.
- Note the pressure on the dial (in mmHg) when you lose the pulse. Inflate the cuff another 20–30 mmHg and very slowly, while feeling the pulse, let the air out of the cuff with the screw valve.
- The pressure at which the pulse reappears is the systolic blood pressure.
- Inflate the cuff to about 20–30 above the SBP, and listen with a stethoscope over the brachial artery. Let the air out slowly.
- At about the SBP, you will hear a tapping noise made by the pulse reappearing in the brachial artery.
- Continue to let the air slowly out of the cuff, listening to the tapping noise. When the tapping disappears, note the pressure. This is the diastolic blood pressure.

Automatic (using an automatic blood pressure device)

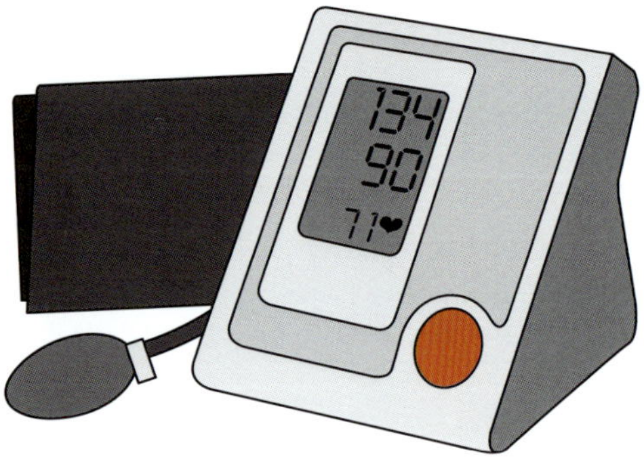

- Once the cuff is in position snugly on the arm, press the 'Go' button on the auto-sphygmomanometer.
- The machine should give a reading within a minute (see diagram). If it does not, it may be that the blood pressure is very low, or there is an irregular pulse, or the batteries are low.

Estimating the blood pressure

Sometimes, it will not be practicable or possible to measure the blood pressure properly, as shown above. An estimate can be made of the systolic blood pressure by feeling various pulses, shown below:

- If a radial pulse is present SBP > 70 mmHg
- If a brachial pulse is present SBP > 60 mmHg
- If a carotid pulse is present SBP > 50 mmHg.

These are only estimates. Look at the casualty as a whole, and measure the blood pressure as explained above, as soon as possible.

Capillary refill time (CRT) – measuring skin perfusion

This is a method for assessing blood flow through the skin (perfusion). It gives an evaluation of the degree of shock in the casualty:

- Press on the fleshy part at the end of a finger (or in the centre of the forehead) for 4 seconds.
- Release and time how long it takes for the white 'blanch' mark to return to normal colour.
- This should not take more than 2 seconds. Any longer than 4 seconds indicates the casualty may require IV fluids (see page 224).
- If the casualty is very cold, this may cause a longer CRT, which could be normal. Therefore, interpret the result in context. If in doubt, discuss with TMAS.

4 Assessing conscious state: Glasgow Coma Scale and AVPU

The conscious state of the sick or injured casualty may range from being completely awake and alert to deeply unconscious and impossible to rouse. Over time they may vary between these two extremes, getting better or worse.

AVPU and Glasgow Coma Scale (GCS) are ways of measuring the conscious level and giving it a numeric value. Repeating the measurement over time enables detection of deterioration or improvement in conscious level, and appropriate action to be taken.

AVPU is a simplified system of scoring conscious state that is very quick. GCS is more comprehensive and sensitive but takes more skill and time. A small deterioration in conscious state is easier to spot with GCS.

AVPU stands for:

A Alert

V Responds to Vocal stimuli

P Responds to Painful stimuli

U Unresponsive to all stimuli.

- Alert means the casualty knows who and where they are, and opens their eyes spontaneously.
- Responsive to Vocal stimulus means the casualty opens their eyes or responds verbally to a question (be aware that their hearing may be impaired).
- Responsive to Painful stimuli means the casualty opens their eyes, responds verbally or moves, in response to a painful stimulus. This could be squeezing a pen on the fingernail bed, pressing hard on the underside of the eyebrow just above the eye, or rubbing firmly on the centre of the chest (if not injured). Try the stimulus on yourself first to make sure it is not too painful.
- Unresponsive means no movement, eye opening or verbal response to any stimulus.

Document the time and conscious level

Glasgow Coma Scale

- GCS is the combination of eye, motor and verbal responses to stimulation.
- The response that should be counted is the best one the casualty gives. That means if the casualty has an injured arm, but can move the other arm, this is the response that is counted.
- Poking the tongue out or closing or opening eyes to command counts as obeying commands.
- Talking clearly in a foreign language counts as talking normally even if you cannot understand.

	Best response	Score
Eyes	Eyes open spontaneously	4
	Eyes open when being asked a question	3
	Eyes open on painful stimulus	2
	Eyes stay shut	1
Motor	Obeys commands (squeezes hands, pokes tongue out)	6
	Moves hand to stop painful stimulus (localises)	5
	Withdraws hand/arm or leg from painful stimulus	4
	Bends up arms and legs to painful stimulus	3
	Straightens arms and legs to painful stimulus	2
	No movement of any part of the body to any stimulus	1
Verbal	Proper answers to questions, orientated in time and place	5
	Answers questions but confused	4
	Single words, no sentences	3
	Incomprehensible sounds	2
	No verbal response	1

The maximum GCS is 15 Fully awake and not confused.

The minimum GCS is 3 Deeply unconscious and unresponsive.

Notes

- A GCS of 8 or less implies the casualty is unconscious, seriously injured, and may not protect their airway. They may inhale vomit or secretions into the lungs, or the tongue may obstruct the airway and prevent breathing. Put the casualty into the recovery position (see page 204).
- Check whether there is a good reason why the casualty cannot respond to you properly. For example, limbs may be paralysed, eyes swollen and not able to open, mouth injured and not able to open.
- If pain is applied above the clavicle (collar bone), and the patient responds by raising an arm, this is counted as 'localising' for determination of the motor score for GCS assessment.

Document the time and the total score.

Note each response score as well.

5 Resuscitation procedures

The process of resuscitating a casualty involves some relatively straightforward skills, which are illustrated here. The skills are easily learnt and can make a real difference to the survival of the casualty.

It is essential to:

- keep training up to date (see page 2)
- practise frequently
- be prepared when you have to deal with an unconscious casualty.

Opening the airway and checking for breathing

To open the casualty's airway and check whether they are breathing there are three basic manoeuvres which you should try in the following order:

- Start with the head tilt, combined with the chin lift (see diagrams below).
- Assess whether you have opened the airway and whether the casualty is breathing:
  - Look at the chest for movement.
  - Listen with your ear next to the mouth for breath sounds.
  - Feel with your cheek next to the mouth for movement of air.
- If there are no signs of breathing, try the jaw thrust (see diagram below), and reassess for breathing.

Control and stabilisation of the cervical spine in cases of trauma

- In many trauma situations, there may be injury to the cervical spine which is not obvious, and can be missed in the early stages of a complex resuscitation.
- Avoid unnecessary movement of the head and cervical spine (c-spine) and immobilise it as soon as possible.
- When removing the casualty from a hazardous position, some movement may be unavoidable. Try to minimise it and immobilise them as soon as possible.
- Manual immobilisation of the c-spine is only the first stage of immobilisation. Keep manual immobilisation in place until the casualty is secured on a rigid board with appropriate head immobilisation in place (straps/blocks/rolled towels). See page 208.
- In the event of extraction from a difficult or confined space, consider using a semi-rigid cervical immobilisation collar.

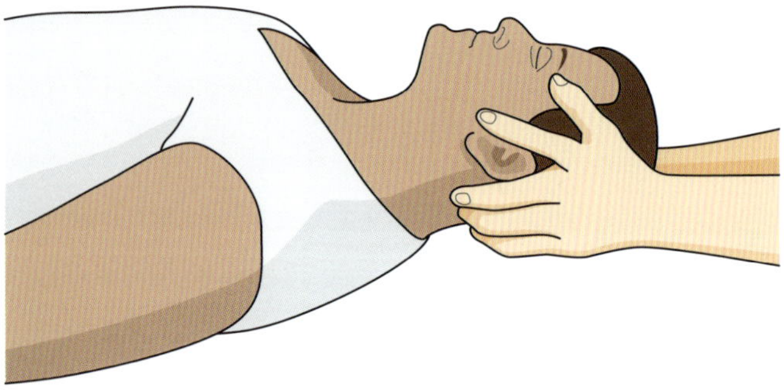

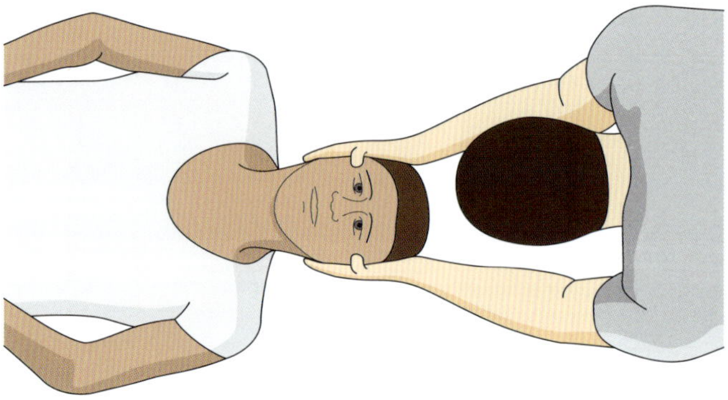

Immobilising the c-spine with your hands

- Do this firmly but gently. If the casualty is conscious let them know what you are doing.
- Do not let go – you are in charge of any movements.
- Do not cover the casualty's ears with your hands – this is claustrophobic and unsettling for them.

Head tilt and chin lift

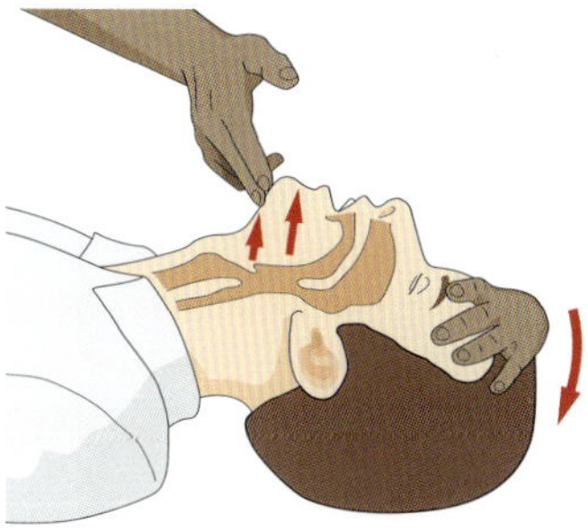

- Place two fingers under the chin and pull the chin up.
- Put your hand on the forehead and push backwards so the head is tilted as in the diagram.
- Do these manoeuvres preferably with a pillow or similar object under the head.

Jaw thrust

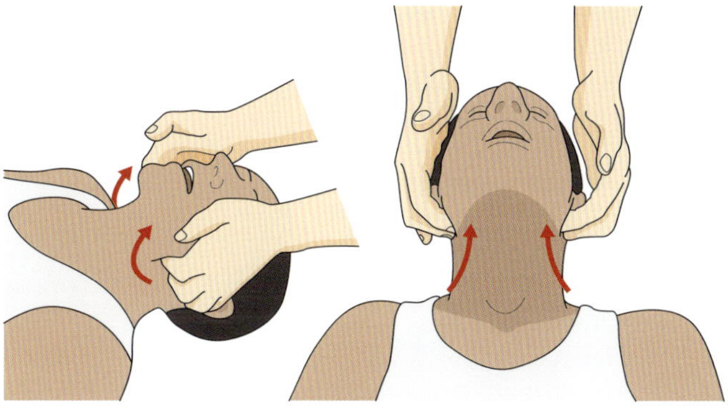

- Put two fingers behind the 'corner' of the jaw on each side (see diagram).
- Push the jaw 'forward' so the lower teeth sit in front of the upper teeth.
- Reassess the casualty for breathing.

Using equipment to keep the airway open with an unconscious casualty

If you have managed to open the casualty's airway you will now need your hands for doing other things:

- There are two simple airway 'adjuncts' (oropharyngeal and nasopharyngeal airways) that are easy to insert in the airway and may keep it open.
- When you have inserted one, you need to reassess to see if the casualty is still breathing.
- Start with an oropharyngeal airway but if that is not tolerated (if the casualty is gagging but still not supporting their own airway) try a nasopharyngeal airway if one is available.

Inserting an oropharyngeal airway

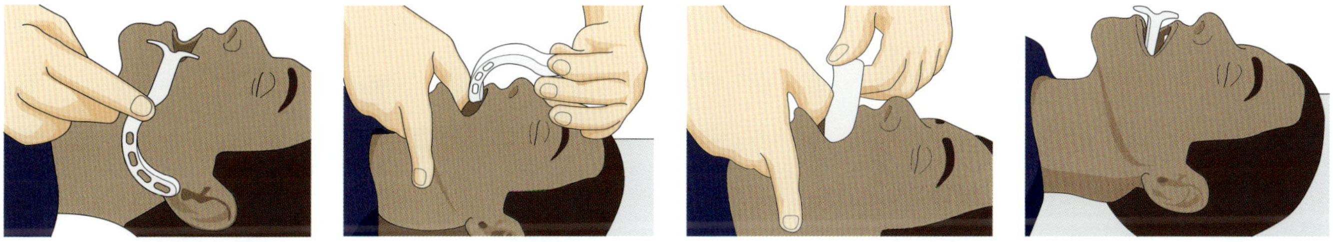

1. Sizing the airway: length from corner of mouth to ear lobe
2. Insert upside down initially. Do not force
3. Gradually turn the right way up as you insert it
4. The flange should sit in the front teeth once in place

- Do not push the tongue back in the mouth.
- Do not insert an oropharyngeal airway in a semi-conscious casualty – they may vomit.

Inserting a nasopharyngeal airway

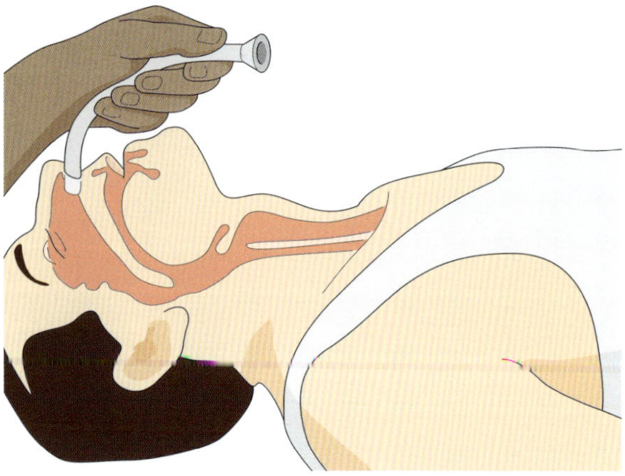

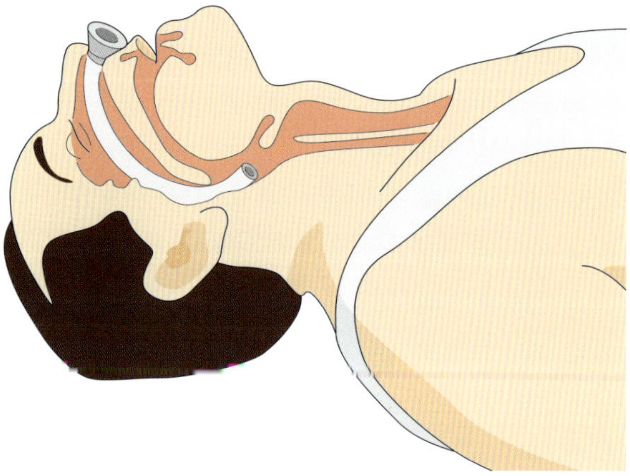

- The length of the airway should be the same as that from the side of the nose to the ear lobe.
- Use some lubricant for the airway.
- Insert the airway heading straight towards the back of the head, not up towards the brain.
- The flange on the end should lie against the nostril.
- Sometimes a safety pin is provided to insert into the flange to make sure the airway does not disappear up the nose.
- Insert the pin into the flange before you put the airway in.

Note: Never insert a nasopharyngeal airway into a casualty with a suspected basal skull fracture (symptoms include obvious injury to the face, bruising around the eyes, bruising behind ears, and clear fluid coming from the nose).

How to give rescue breaths

- Use the manoeuvres and equipment above to ensure the airway is open.
- Check for breathing as explained above.
- For mouth-to-mouth, preferably use a pocket mask as illustrated, to prevent infection. Use oxygen if available via a tube under the side of the mask.
- Mouth-to mouth can be done from the side or from the top, while continuing to maintain head tilt, chin lift or jaw thrust.

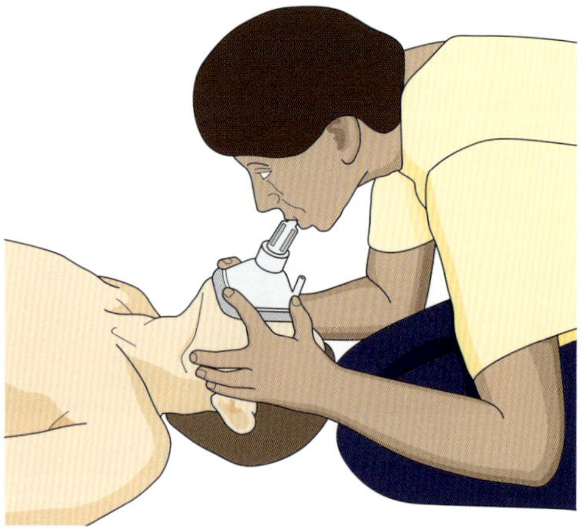

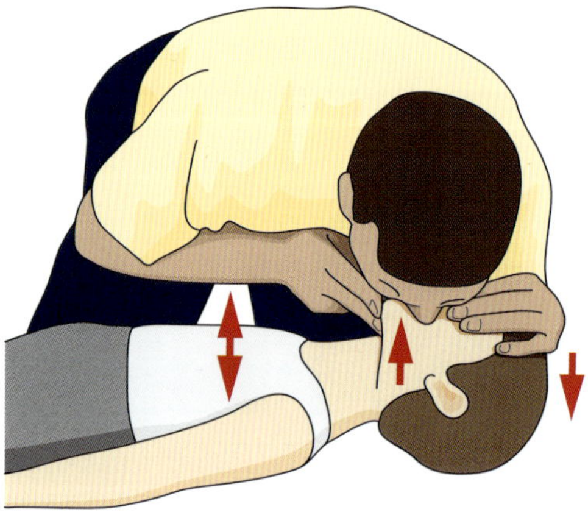

- Blow into the mask or mouth firmly but gently for 1–2 seconds and watch for the chest rising. Hold the nose at the same time, to stop the air coming out (see diagram).
- Aim for the chest to rise 2–4 cm or so, then stop blowing and watch it fall.
- If you have to blow very hard to get air in, and the chest does not rise and fall easily, the airway is not open. Adjust the position you are holding the head to open the airway.

How to give chest compressions

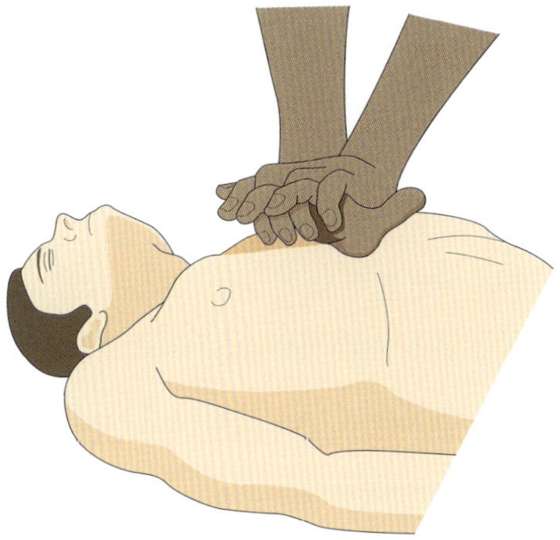

- Lay the casualty on their back on a firm surface, taking care of their cervical spine if appropriate.
- Assess the casualty for breathing and pulse (see page 4).
- Put your hands together as shown, with the heel of the lower hand on the centre of the chest in between the nipples.
- With straight arms, push down on the chest, aiming to depress the centre of the chest by about half the depth of the chest. Do this at a rate of 100–120 times per minute.
- After 30 compressions, 2 rescue breaths should be given. Continue with a ratio of 30 compressions to 2 rescue breaths.

How to defibrillate safely with an automated external defibrillator (AED)

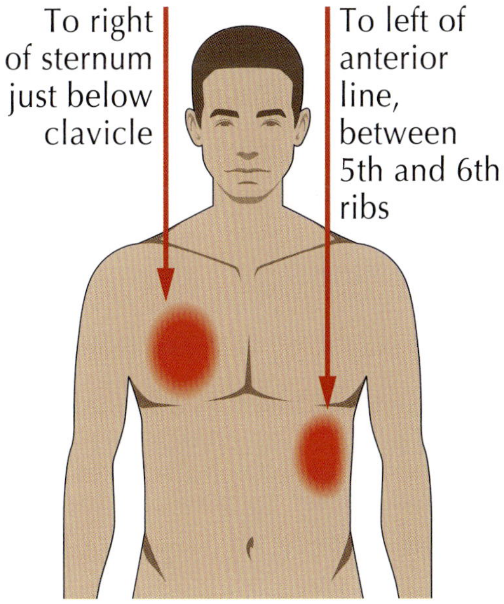

- Lay the casualty on their back on a firm surface, taking care of their cervical spine if appropriate.
- Assess the casualty for breathing and pulse (see page 4). Do chest compressions continuously until the AED is attached.
- Make sure that everything is dry: you, the casualty and the surface upon which they are lying.
- Attach the defibrillator pads as shown, one just below the clavicle on the right chest, and the other below and to the side of the left nipple (not on the breast) as shown in the diagram.
- Remove the oxygen mask and place it well away.
- Turn on the AED and follow the instructions. See diagram for typical arrangement.
- Make sure everyone is well away from the casualty before defibrillating or they will get a shock as well.
- After defibrillation, continue with life support and follow the instructions given by the AED.

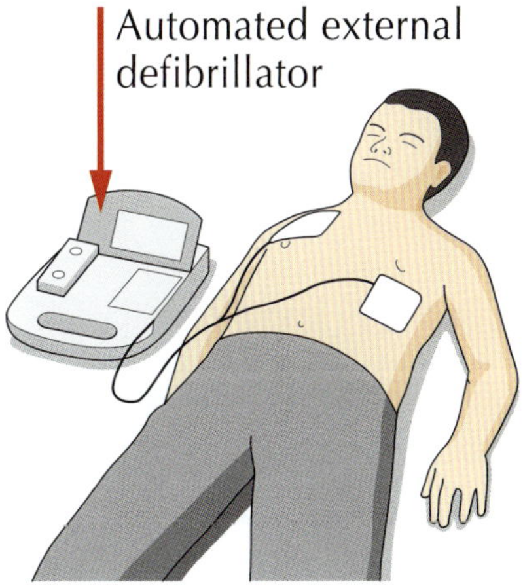

6 Oxygen therapy

Oxygen is a medication. As such, it has very beneficial effects, but also some risks to its usage. Therefore, oxygen should be used appropriately, and the response of the casualty monitored while it is being administered.

If oxygen is being administered to a casualty on board the vessel, obtain medical advice and direct supervision from TMAS as soon as possible.

Uses of oxygen therapy

- Resuscitation
- Initial response to major trauma
- Lung problems causing shortness of breath
- Initial response to a medical disorder
- Cardiac problems, such as chest pain, suspected heart attack
- Shock – whatever the cause (anaphylaxis, sepsis etc)
- Unconsciousness (whatever the cause)
- Convulsions/fitting
- Cerebrovascular accident (stroke)
- Carbon monoxide poisoning (suspected)
- Hypothermia
- Diving accidents.

The aim for oxygen therapy – target oxygen saturation

For healthy people the usual target oxygen percentage saturation is 92–98%. However, for some people with pre-existing lung or heart conditions, the target oxygen saturation may be 88–92%. However, these people are unlikely to be employed crew members, but could still be found at sea as passengers.

Measuring response to oxygen therapy

There are various ways to monitor the response of a casualty to oxygen therapy, but one of the best is to use a pulse oximeter, as described below.

There are other ways which are useful if there is no usable pulse oximeter on the vessel. These involve assessing the casualty directly:

- How a patient looks – normal (e.g. pink) colour, rather than blue or pale.
- Conscious state – the brain requires a reasonable level of oxygen to function properly.
- Pulse rate – this may go up if the casualty is short of oxygen.
- Respiratory rate – this may go up if the casualty is short of oxygen.
- If a casualty is severely short of oxygen, the respiratory rate or pulse rate may in fact reduce. This is a very serious situation.

Pulse oximeter

A pulse oximeter works by shining a red light through the end of a finger, toe, or other part of the body. The red light detects the pulsing blood in the tissue, and can then calculate how much of the blood is properly saturated with oxygen.

The device will report not only the percentage oxygen saturation, but usually the pulse rate as well.

Problems with using pulse oximeters include:

- cold peripheries, so the pulse oximeter cannot detect a pulse
- non-functioning – flat battery or broken equipment

- poisoning with carbon monoxide or cyanide, which may cause an inaccurate result
- cardiac arrhythmias such as atrial fibrillation
- light interference
- low blood pressure
- painted fingernails.

Amount of oxygen on board a vessel

The standard cylinder of oxygen on board a vessel with either an MCA Category A or MCA Category B kit on board is 2 litres in size, and contains 400 litres of compressed oxygen.

This lasts approximately 30 minutes at a flow rate of 10 litres/minute – the typical flow rate when resuscitating a casualty. **Hence it is only sufficient for immediate treatment**.

An alternative source of oxygen is an oxygen concentrator. This is powered by electricity, and provides a sustainable, continuous flow of oxygen by taking in air and filtering out the nitrogen. Flow rates of 2 litres/minute to 10 litres/minute are possible.

How to administer oxygen

Oxygen can be administered to a casualty in a variety of ways. On board a vessel this is usually by the use of an oxygen mask or nasal cannula. The various types are described in the table. In an emergency use the non-rebreather reservoir mask. TMAS will advise if a different method of administration is needed.

Devices for administering oxygen to a casualty who is breathing

Device	Percentage oxygen	Flow rate l/min	Use	Image
Nasal cannula	24–30%	1–4 l/min	Non-acute, mildly short of oxygen, max flow rate usually 1–2 l/min	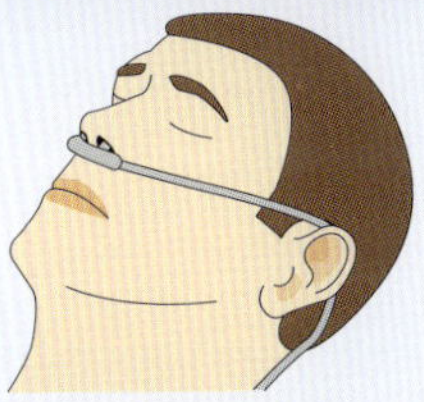
Hudson mask	30–40%	5–10 l/min	Emergency use, simple to set up	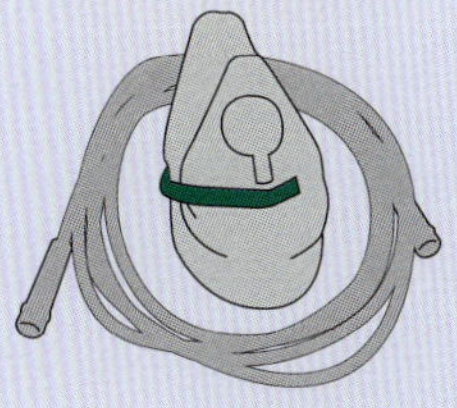
Venturi mask	24–60%	2– 15 l/min	For longer-term oxygen, to control saturations closely. Various colours provide different percentages of oxygen	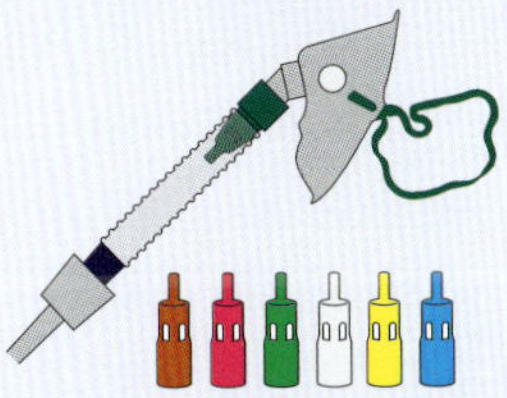
Non-rebreather reservoir mask	85–90%	15 l/min	Used for acutely unwell casualties. Short-term emergency use only	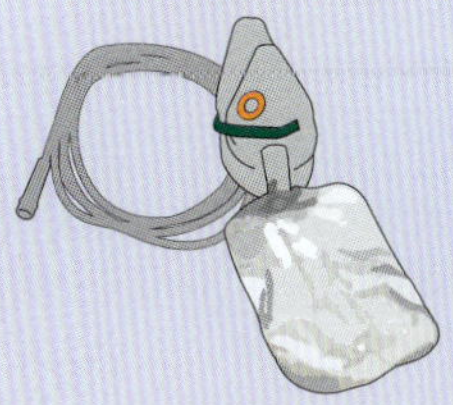

7 Recovery position and log-roll

How to place a casualty in the recovery position

After an accident or medical illness, an unconscious or semi-conscious casualty may not be able to protect their own airway properly. This means:

- They will not be able to control their tongue, so it may fall back and block their airway.
- Saliva may trickle down into the trachea (windpipe) and lungs.
- Refluxing stomach acid and vomit may also pass into the lungs.

Contamination of the lungs with secretions or vomit will cause a chest infection and reduce the casualty's chance of survival. Particularly in an unconscious casualty, stomach acid can reflux quietly up into the mouth and into the lungs without any external sign.

Placing an unconscious casualty in the recovery position will reduce the possibility of secretions and vomit entering the lung, and also encourage the tongue to hang forward, so not blocking the airway (see diagrams 1 to 4):

- Make sure the casualty is stable, has an airway, is breathing and has a pulse.
- Any airway adjunct should be left in place (see page 199).
- Use the log-roll if there is any suspicion of spinal injury.
- The arms and upper leg should form right angles, for best support.

1 Straighten the casualty's arms and legs, taking appropriate care of the spine. Bring the arm on your side up so the hand is alongside the head.

1

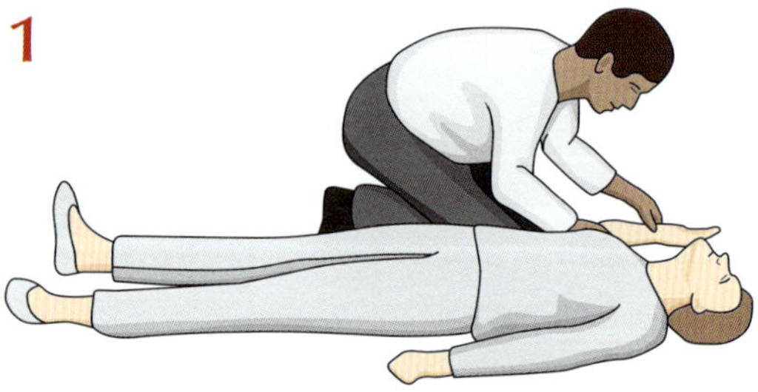

2 Bring the opposite arm over, and place the hand with its back against the cheek on your side. Bend the opposite leg up at the knee.

2

3 With one hand on the knee, use the bent leg as a lever to gently rotate the casualty over towards you. With your other hand, bring the shoulder over at the same time. Control the rotation with your knees.

3

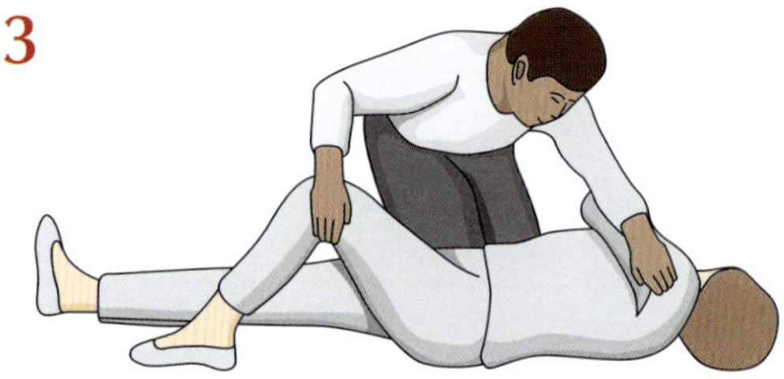

4 Position the head comfortably on the back of the hand, and bring the bent upper leg over sufficiently to stop the body from turning over too much.

4

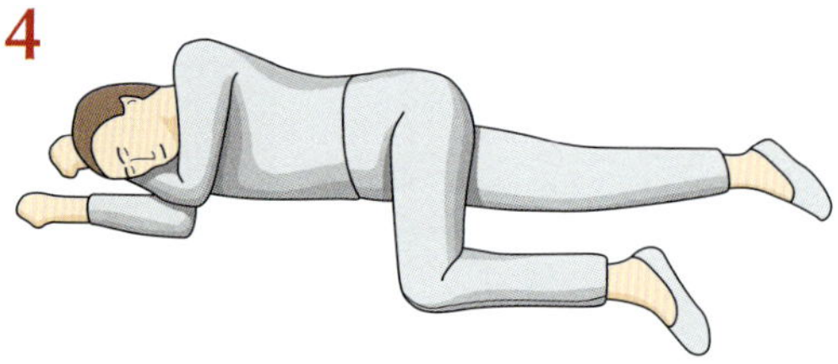

Notes

- Putting a casualty in the recovery position in a bunk is difficult. Use the principles above, but modify them as necessary. It is important to leave the casualty facing outwards so you can see their face and assess them for breathing, vomit and secretions.
- Recheck the casualty's airway, breathing and circulation frequently.
- The recovery position is stable and the casualty can stay there for a few hours. If the vessel is rolling, place rolled-up sleeping bags or other padding on both sides of the casualty.
- Injured limbs may need extra support with something firm but not hard such as a rolled towel.
- Turn the casualty every few hours to relieve pressure areas.

When and how to log-roll a casualty

- Always log-roll the casualty if you suspect there is a spinal injury.
- Log-rolling is carried out for the following reasons:
  - To inspect the back of the casualty for injuries.
  - To place the casualty in a modified recovery position while awaiting evacuation.
  - To place a recovery stretcher under the casualty.
- It takes three people to log-roll (although it might be possible with only two; see below). Ideally you need four people so the fourth one can examine the casualty, particularly the back.
- The aim of the log-roll is to keep the entire spine in one line (not just the neck), without bending the body in any direction.
- A semi-rigid collar should be fitted, if indicated in high-risk cases, before the log-roll – it helps to protect the cervical spine.

Method

- Position yourselves as in the figure, kneeling and stable.
- Person 1 keeps control and immobilises the c-spine, with or without a hard collar. Their hands should not cover the ears, so the casualty can hear.
- Person 1 controls all movements and must be very clear with their instructions to the others.
- Person 2 puts one hand on the casualty's shoulder, and one hand on the top of the thigh.
- Person 3 puts one hand on the top of the pelvis, above the lower hand of the second person. The other hand is put on the lower leg just below the knee.
- On the command of person 1, the casualty is smoothly rotated by 90° to come to rest against the knees of person 2 and person 3.
- Hold the casualty in that position until the examination is complete, or a spinal board/stretcher is in place.
- On the command of person 1, smoothly rotate the casualty back down to the original position.

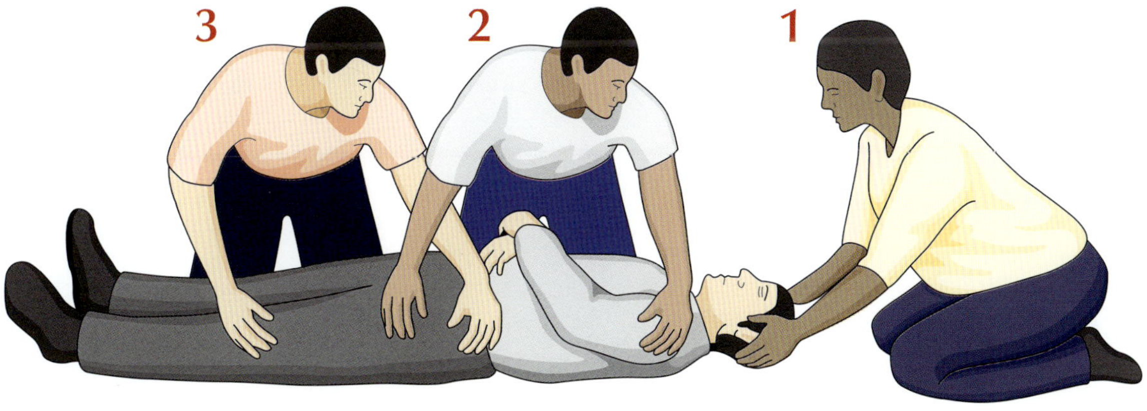

Notes

- If there are only three people in total, two may have to log-roll while the third examines the casualty (see diagram).

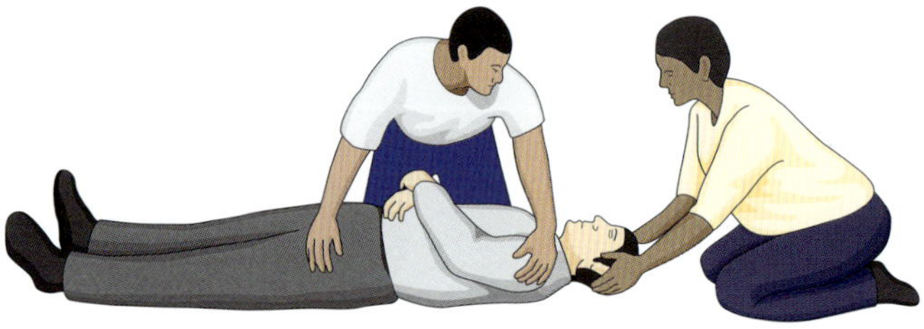

Modified recovery position

A modified recovery position is used when there is a suspicion of spinal injury and the casualty is unconscious (see diagram). This position keeps the spine more in line than the normal recovery position. To put a casualty in the modified recovery position:

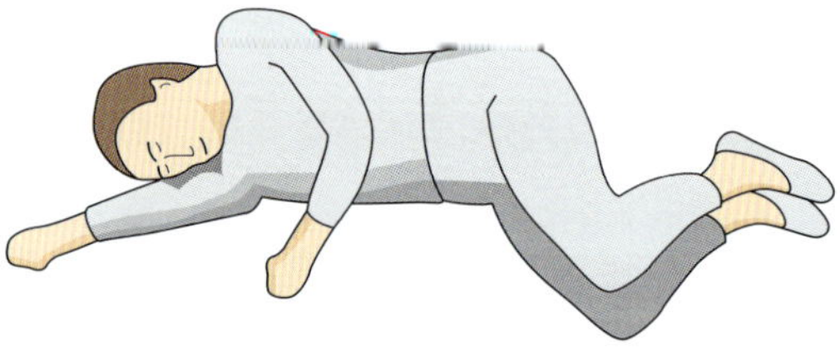

- Extend the arm on your side to straight above the head.
- Log-roll the casualty onto their side and rest their head on their extended arm.
- Either keep the legs straight or bend them as in the diagram to improve stability.
- Support the casualty in place with padding such as sleeping bags, bedding or sails.
- Turn the casualty every few hours to prevent pressure sores.

8 Spinal immobilisation

When a casualty suffers a spinal injury, their spine must be fully immobilised (from the neck to the coccyx) to protect it from further damage. Immobilisation involves fitting a semi-rigid collar, if indicated, to the casualty's neck, then securing them to a stiff stretcher or board, such as a scoop stretcher. Only then is the spine fully immobilised and protected from further damage.

Spinal immobilisation is always required when moving or evacuating a casualty with a suspected spinal injury. However, a casualty should never be left on a spinal board for an extended period (less than two hours if possible), as spinal boards are uncomfortable, and immobilisation on one may cause pressure sores.

Indications for immobilising the spine

- Obvious neck trauma
- Injury to the upper chest
- Injury to another part of the spine
- Injury to the pelvis
- Numbness or tingling in arms or legs following an accident
- An accident where much energy has been involved (e.g. hit by moving machinery, falls from >2 m height)
- Multi-trauma, where many other parts are injured.

If in doubt, immobilise the casualty with manual in-line stabilisation (MILS) and then block and tapes.

Cervical spine immobilisation

- This requires at least two people.
- One person needs to be kneeling at the patient's head with their hands placed at the ears on both sides with gentle pressure to prevent the casualty from moving their head (1). The rescuer needs to stay in this position until the casualty has been placed on a stretcher, with blocks and tapes then taking over the role of immobilising the neck.
- If another person needs to take over the role of manual in-line stabilisation, this is done in a controlled manner by placing their hands over the first rescuer's hands as they remove their hands (2).
- There are commercial blocks and straps which can then be applied to hold the neck still. An improvised alternative of a rolled towel placed each side of the casualty's head can be equally effective (3).
- These are held in place with a strip of tape or strap going over the forehead and a second strip under the chin (3). Ensure this does not impinge on the casualty's ability to breathe or swallow.

1

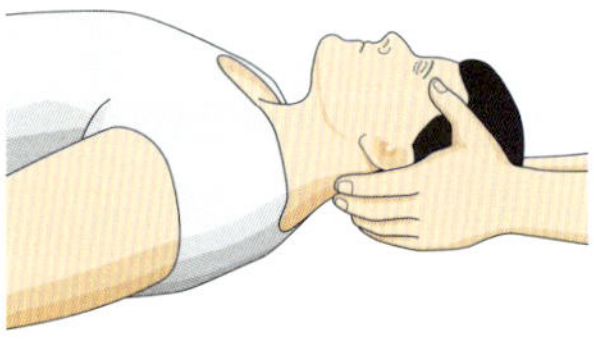

2

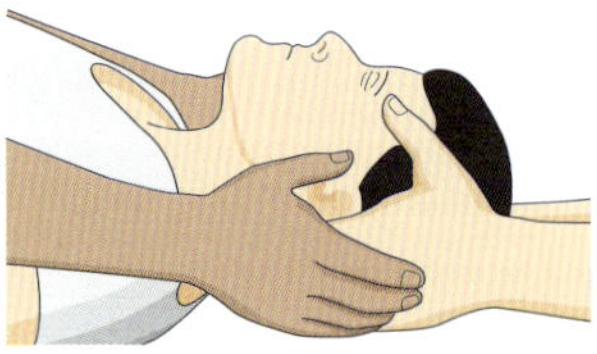

3

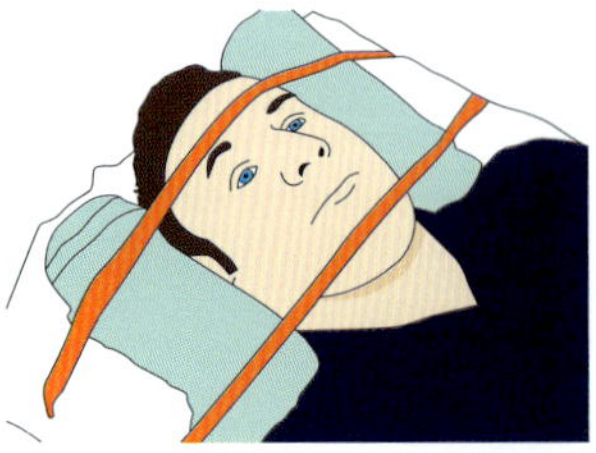

Immobilising a casualty on a scoop stretcher

ABCD takes priority over getting the casualty onto a stretcher. The best stretcher to use is a scoop stretcher if it is available. If not, a rigid board can be used.

Remember to keep the neck immobilised with one person holding the neck in manual in-line stabilisation (MILS).

Once these actions are completed, move the casualty onto the stretcher as soon as possible.

Method:

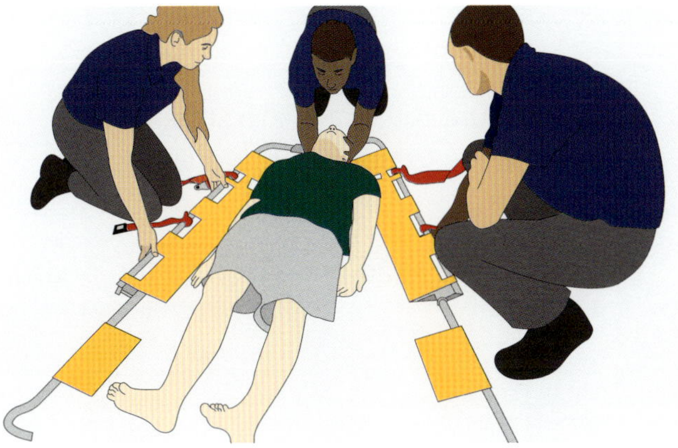

1. The scoop comes in two halves that join together at the head and feet ends of the casualty. The scoop can be adjusted in length, so it needs to be measured against the casualty before placing the casualty on the scoop.
2. It can be applied by two people using the 'scissors' method. While one rescuer continues to apply MILS, slide one half in against the casualty. Fix the other half at the head end and then manoeuvre it under the casualty with minimal movement, and clip the halves together at the bottom.
3. If you have a team capable of log-rolling the casualty (i.e. a minimum of 4 people) it is better to apply the scoop using the log-roll method.
4. Log-roll the casualty onto one side to 20 degrees (see page 204).

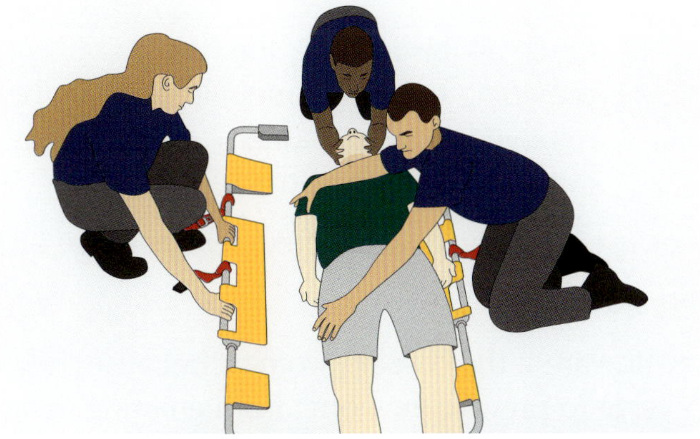

5. Place one half of the scoop under that side of the casualty. Roll back (see opposite).
6. Repeat the procedure with the log-roll team moving to the other side, and place the other half of the scoop stretcher under the casualty.

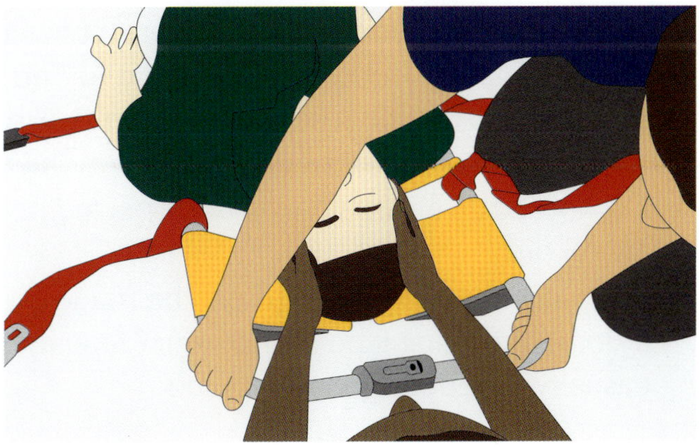

7. Click the top and bottom ends of the scoop together (see opposite).

8. While maintaining cervical spine immobilisation, put straps in the following positions (see opposite):
   - around the upper chest, including the arms
   - around the pelvis, including the arms
   - around the thighs
   - around the calves.

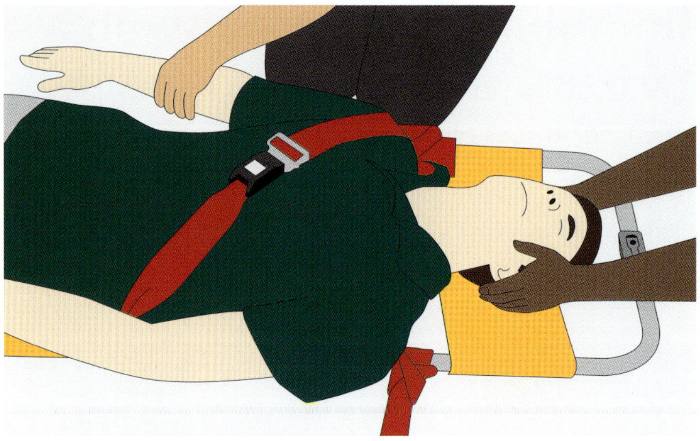

9. Make sure the straps are snug but not so tight as to impede breathing (see opposite).
10. Secure the head and collar to the board.

11. Fix padded blocks or rolled towels on each side of the head (see opposite).
12. Fix straps:
    - over the forehead
    - under the chin.
13. Once all this is done, the hands providing manual immobilisation can be removed, and the casualty can be safely transported on the board.

For use of an evacuation stretcher, see page 281.

Notes

- Beware if the casualty vomits, because they cannot move. Turn the board immediately on its side to prevent the vomit from entering their lungs.
- Being immobilised is claustrophobic for the casualty and they may struggle, especially if confused. If they struggle it is better not to strap them to a board as they may worsen an injury. It may be better to allow them to find a comfortable position and keep them as calm as possible. A small dose of diazepam (1–2 mg IV or IM every 30 minutes as needed) may be required to keep control of the situation but you must seek advice from TMAS first.
- Do not sedate a casualty with a suspected brain injury without seeking advice from TMAS first.
- An improvised spinal board can be made from any long, rigid board on the vessel (such as a door) and using tape such as duct tape for securing. Use a foam mat or blankets under the casualty to reduce pressure points.

- The casualty should stay on a scoop stretcher only to enable safe transfer. If they can be rapidly evacuated to hospital (i.e. within 2 hours), keep them on the scoop. Otherwise, transfer the casualty onto a bed (with padding to minimise any movements), either in the vessel's sick bay, or on a firm bunk mattress until transfer ashore is possible.
- Scoop stretchers are good devices for extracting casualties and can be used for a short carry. However, for transporting a casualty any distance the casualty and scoop should be placed on a trolley or firmer board. There is no need to remove the scoop stretcher.

9 Minor operative set-up

Small medical procedures may need to be undertaken on a vessel, usually under sterile conditions.

This can be complicated because of the working environment. Sterile conditions may be difficult to achieve on a vessel, but make every effort to do so. Proper preparation of the casualty, yourself, the vessel and the equipment you will need will improve the outcome for both of you. A similar approach to set-up is also useful when non-sterile procedures are to be performed.

Ask for advice from TMAS before you start a minor operation, not during or afterwards.

Types of procedures that might be required on a vessel

- Wound repair (cleaning, suturing/stapling, dressing)
- Incising, draining and wicking an abscess
- Inserting a chest drain
- Inserting a urinary catheter
- Inserting an intravenous cannula
- Injecting local anaesthetic
- Cleaning, reducing and dressing an open fracture

Preparing the casualty

- Explain to the casualty exactly what you are going to do. Let them know if you might hurt them, and be truthful.
- Find a comfortable and stable position for the casualty where they can relax as much as possible.
- Make sure the casualty has as much pain relief as required or possible (local anaesthesia and longer-acting painkillers).
- Keep the casualty warm, especially if they are partly uncovered for the procedure.
- Maintain their privacy and dignity (you may be inserting a catheter or incising an abscess close to the genitals).
- Despite the need for privacy and warmth, you must get good exposure of the area with which you are dealing, including shaving the immediate area if necessary. If anything, expose more so you do not have to make adjustments while wearing sterile gloves.
- Finally, once everything is ready, clean a good area around the operation site with sterilising skin preparation fluid, such as iodine or chlorhexidine. Make sure the casualty is not allergic to the sterilising fluid.

Preparing yourself

- Make sure you will have a comfortable and stable working position. This depends on the state of the casualty, but will normally be in the vessel's sick bay or in a cabin – choose one with good lighting and with an accessible bunk.
- If you suffer from seasickness take some anti-sickness medication before you start.
- Make sure your arms are bare to above the elbow, and wash thoroughly with soap and water. If there is alcohol or chlorhexidine fluid on board use it to sterilise your hands.
- Recruit an assistant in case you need another pair of hands or a chaperone, and do not be afraid to ask for help.
- Once ready, put on a sterile pair of gloves that fit. If there are no sterile gloves on board, put on some non-sterile gloves and rub your gloved hands in sterilising skin preparation fluid.

- Take universal precautions, which means making sure you protect yourself and others from potential risks of coming into contact with bodily fluids, from either yourself or the casualty. This involves the use of gloves (sterile or non-sterile), aprons and masks for large, invasive procedures, and safe disposal of contaminated waste and needles.

Preparing the vessel

- Make sure that the motion of the vessel is reduced as far as this is possible.
- Make sure the operative site is well lit, either in a sick bay or cabin. Head torches provide excellent lighting conditions if ambient lighting is poor.

Preparing the equipment

- Get out all the equipment you might need before starting.
- Instruments can be sterilised by boiling for 20 minutes and then allowing them to cool, or washing in sterilising skin preparation fluid if nothing else is available. Some medical kits may have specific instrument sterilising fluid in them, or you could use sterile procedure packs which contain a collection of sterile equipment.
- Each procedure requires a specific set of equipment, but below is a checklist of potential basic items that may be required (check the section covering the procedure to be performed for additional required items):
  - Sterile forceps
  - Sterile scissors
  - Sutures or staples and stapler
  - Disposable razor (for removing hair)
  - Sterile skin drape for around the site
  - Sterile pot for fluid
  - Sterile haemostatic clamp
  - Sterile scalpel
  - Sterile swabs
  - Sterilising skin preparation fluid
  - Sterile drape for set-up
  - Sterile tweezers.
- Use one sterile drape to make a sterile field on which everything else that should be sterile can be placed.
- Make sure it is in a secure, stable place, so it does not fall on the floor with everything else if the vessel rolls. The diagram shows an example of a minor operative set-up on a sterile field.

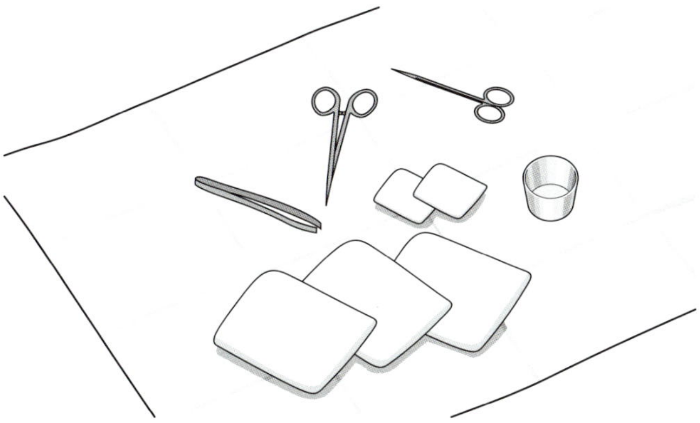

Clearing away after the procedure

- Once you have completed the procedure, all waste that may be contaminated with body fluids must be disposed of safely.
- Disposal is normally by incineration, or marking it as clinical waste and storing it safely until it can be disposed of ashore.
- Wash instruments thoroughly and re-sterilise them if possible.
- Clean the area used for the procedure with antiseptic cleaning fluid.

10 Local anaesthesia

Local anaesthetics (LAs) are very useful on a vessel to treat pain. Procedures such as suturing, resetting dislocated fingers and incising abscesses can be made bearable.

There are some risks to using LAs, and injecting an LA may cause considerable pain, so small procedures probably do not warrant their use.

LA can be injected into the skin in several places around a wound (infiltration), or around specific nerves supplying a limb, finger or toe, to anaesthetise the whole region (termed a 'nerve block'). LA drops can be used in the eye and LA gel can be used to insert urinary catheters and for a variety of other procedures.

There are many types of LA agents, but the one most commonly used in medical kits is lidocaine, and this will be considered here. It is usually supplied as a 1% solution but occasionally a stronger 2% solution may be supplied, so check carefully. This has implications for what volume can be safely injected into an average sized adult of about 70 kg (see below).

Safe dose of local anaesthetics

All LAs are potentially toxic if too much is given too quickly. The maximum safe dose of lidocaine is as follows:

For a 70 kg crew member: 20 ml 1% lidocaine or 10 ml 2% lidocaine

Give proportionally **more** for a larger casualty or **less** for a smaller casualty.

Uses for local anaesthetics

- Cleaning, suturing, stapling wounds
- Incising abscesses
- Drops for the eye
- Nerve block for damaged finger/toe
- Gel for inserting urinary catheters, stings, bites, piles, mouth ulcers/trauma

Risks

- Allergy
- Toxicity
- Pain on injection

Toxicity

Toxicity is rare, but it may occur either because too much LA agent was given, or the correct dose was given but directly into a blood vessel.

Initial signs of toxicity

- Tingling around the mouth
- Blurred vision
- Slurred speech

Late signs of toxicity

- Low blood pressure
- Fits/coma
- Cardiac arrest

Treatment of toxicity

- Seek advice from TMAS immediately if you suspect this.
- Stop giving the LA if the casualty has any of the above signs or symptoms.
- In the event of fitting, consider giving diazepam 10 mg IV (see page 228).
- In the event of cardiac arrest see page 24.

Reducing pain on injection

- Warm the LA vial up to body temperature before injecting it.
- When infiltrating around a wound, inject through an area already anaesthetised.
- Spray the skin first with ethyl chloride cold spray (if available) or use ice.

Infiltration of local anaesthetic

The aim is to leave a complete ring of anaesthetic around the wound or site for operation (see diagram):

- Preferably insert an IV cannula first if possible, in case of a bad reaction to the LA.
- Set up for a sterile procedure (see page 212) and wear sterile gloves.
- Draw up the required amount of lidocaine and check it with a suitably trained colleague.
- Insert the needle (usually 25 gauge orange) about 5 mm under the skin and run it in up to the hub of the needle. Pull back on the plunger as you go to make sure the needle does not go directly into a blood vessel. If the needle is in a blood vessel, blood will appear in the syringe.
- When you are sure the needle is not in a blood vessel, start injecting and slowly pull the needle back, leaving a trail of LA.
- Continue, using the pattern shown in the diagram, until the wound is encircled with LA.
- Leave for 10 minutes and test for sensation and pain before you start.
- Once you start operating, more LA may be needed directly into the wound edge.

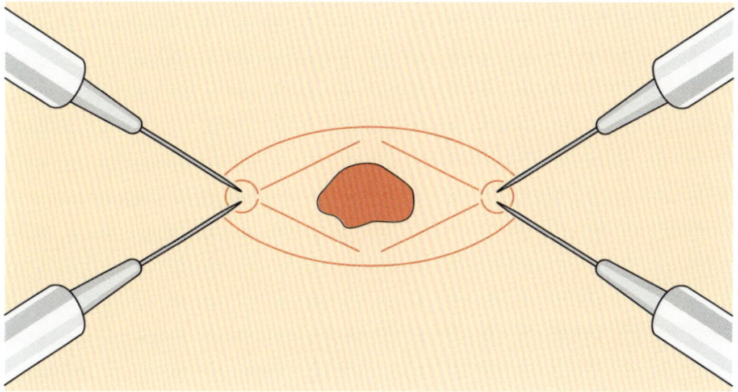

Finger and toe nerve blocks (ring blocks)

The technique is the same for fingers and toes. Never use adrenaline in the lidocaine for these injections. Ampoules containing a mixture of adrenaline and lidocaine may occasionally be included in medical kits in error.

Indications

- Any wound or dislocation of finger or toe.

How to use a finger or toe nerve block

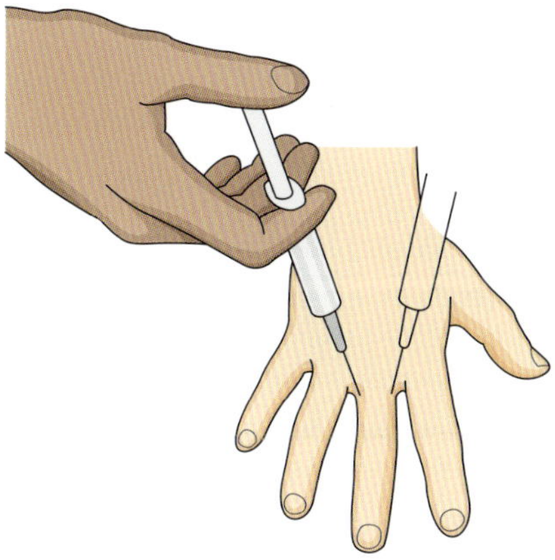

- Prepare as for infiltration of LA (see above).
- Use an orange (25 gauge) needle.
- Insert the needle on either side of the base of the finger or toe, almost through to the other side (see diagram).
- Pull back on the plunger to make sure the needle is not in a blood vessel (see above under Infiltration of local anaesthetic).
- Inject 2–3 ml 1% lidocaine on each side as you withdraw the needle.
- Leave for about 10 minutes and test for sensation.
- More LA may be required under the skin on top and underneath the finger or toe.

11 Insertion of catheters and tubes

Insertion of a nasogastric tube (NGT)

You must only undertake this procedure under the direct advice of TMAS.

Indications

- Persistent vomiting
- Distended or rigid abdomen
- An unconscious casualty to deflate stomach, to reduce vomiting risk
- For hydration and feeding in a casualty who cannot swallow

Do not insert an NGT if the casualty:

- has severe facial injuries
- is taking warfarin or other blood thinning medicine
- has a suspected basal skull fracture
- In addition, take care when inserting an NGT in a semi- or unconscious casualty – they may vomit, and the vomit may end up in the lungs.

How to insert an NGT

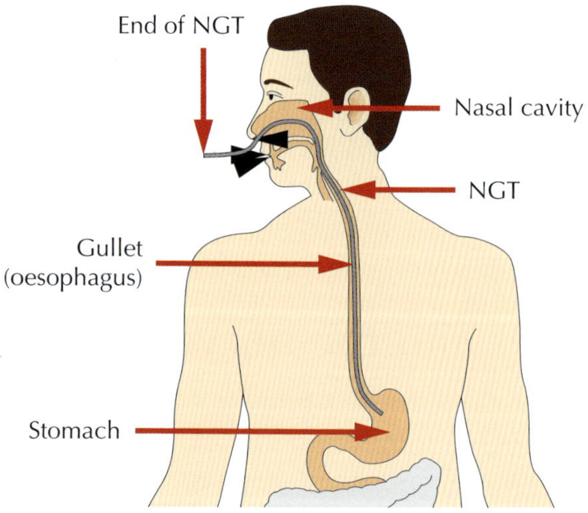

- Set up for a procedure (see page 212). You do not need a sterile field, just a clean one. Wear gloves.
- With the casualty sitting upright, give them a cup of water to sip.
- Lubricate the NGT with petroleum jelly, cooking oil or something similar.
- Introduce the NGT to the nostril, directing it straight back, not upwards (see diagram).
- As the NGT passes into the nose, get the casualty to take sips of water continually.
- Continue to feed the NGT in. You should start to feel it being 'pulled in' by the action of the swallowing.
- Encourage more sipping if the casualty gags, which is quite likely.
- Aim to insert 50–55 cm of tube in an average sized adult. Distance measurements are marked on the tube.
- Constant coughing indicates the NGT has gone into the lungs. Pull it back and try again.
- To make sure the NGT is in the right place, suck some fluid up the tube. This should look greenish/yellow. Test the acidity with urine dipsticks – the acid level (pH) should usually be less than 6. If in doubt do not put anything down the tube and seek medical advice from TMAS.
- Secure the NGT firmly to the end of the nose with tape, then also to the side of the face, to make sure it does not come out.
- Attach a bag to the NGT (e.g. a plastic bag or urine drainage bag) unless the casualty is going to be fed down the tube, in which case put a bung in the tube after feeding to prevent the feed or fluid coming back up the tube.

Insertion of a urinary catheter

It is appropriate to have a chaperone present, if the casualty requests it, for both females and males.

Indications

- The casualty is conscious but cannot pass urine despite having a full bladder.
- The casualty is unconscious.

Do not insert a urinary catheter if the casualty:

- has pelvic trauma where there blood is coming from the penis or vagina.

How to insert a urinary catheter into a male

- Set up for a minor operative sterile procedure (see page 212) and wear sterile gloves.
- Position the casualty on his back and put a bowl between his legs.
- Gently retract the foreskin and use skin sterilising fluid to clean the end of the penis.
- Slowly insert some local anaesthetic (lidocaine) gel into the urethra and leave it for 5 minutes to work.
- While you are waiting, open the catheter packet, and look at the injection port. It should say how much water to inject into the balloon, which stops the catheter falling out. Fill a syringe with the right amount of water (usually 5–10 ml).
- Hold up the penis, gently putting some tension on it, and insert the catheter into the urethra. Feed the catheter in up to the end of the thinner part of the tube. Urine should flow out into the bowl.
- Inject the water into the catheter balloon. Stop if it causes pain and make sure the catheter is in all the way. Try injecting again.
- Connect the catheter to the drainage bag.
- Make sure the foreskin is put back into the normal position.
- Start antibiotics while awaiting evacuation (e.g. ciprofloxacin).

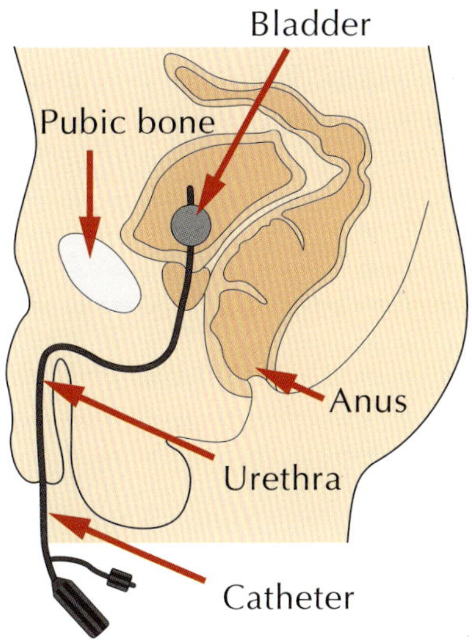

Male urinary tract with catheter in place

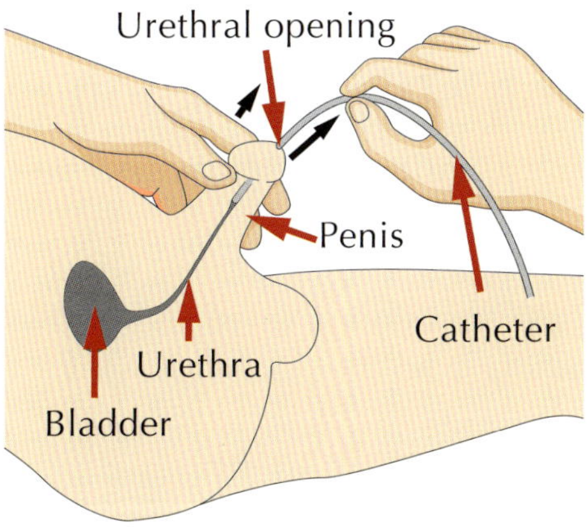

Urinary catheter in a male - insertion

Part 4

How to insert a urinary catheter into a female

The anatomy can be more difficult to identify than for a male, but the procedure is essentially the same except for the following:

- Position the casualty lying on her back with legs apart.
- Spread the entrance to the vagina apart using two fingers, and clean around the entrance with the sterile fluid, if available. Otherwise, use clean water.
- The entrance to the urethra is just above the entrance to the vagina.
- Slowly insert some local anaesthetic (lidocaine) gel into the urethra and leave it for 5 minutes to work.
- The rest of the procedure is the same as for a male.

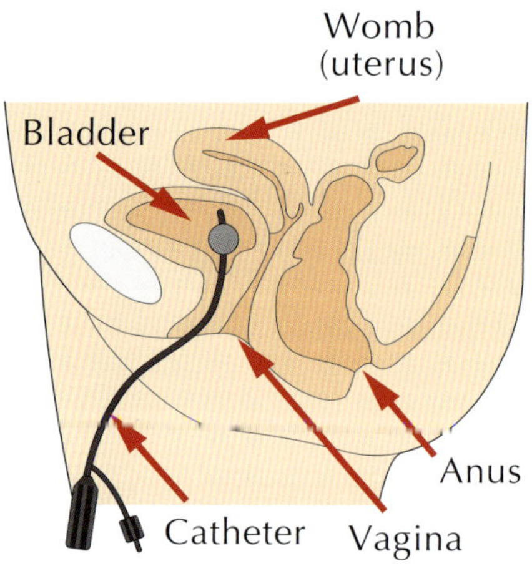

Urinary catheter in a female - side view

Problems with catheters

The main problem is if the catheter will not pass into the bladder. There are many reasons for this. If the bladder is full and painful a suprapubic aspiration of urine may be necessary (see below).

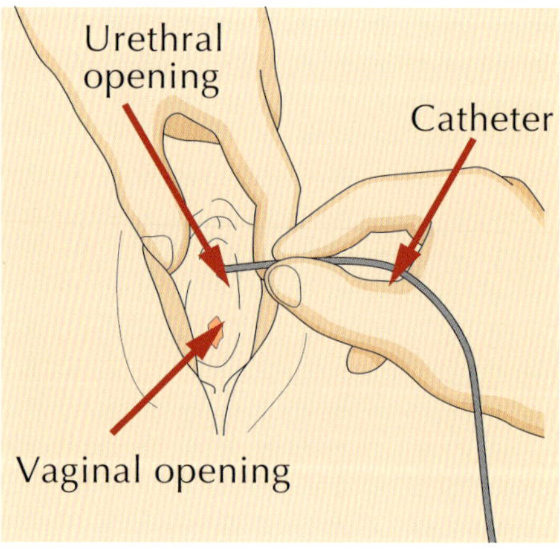

Urinary catheter in a female - insertion

Suprapubic aspiration of urine

You must undertake this procedure only under the direct advice of TMAS.

Indication

- Acute retention of urine and inability to pass a normal catheter or pelvic trauma with blood coming from the penis or vagina.

How to aspirate urine

- Set up for a minor operative sterile procedure (see page 212) and wear sterile gloves.
- Position the casualty on their back. Only if necessary give them sedation to calm them (diazepam 5 mg orally). Put a bowl between the casualty's legs.
- Feel for the pubic bone (just above the base of the penis or in front of the vagina). The distended and painful bladder should be palpable above this point. If it is not palpable, reconsider what you are doing.
- Clean the area and infiltrate with 5 ml 1% lidocaine.

- Use a green needle (size 21 gauge) with a 50 ml syringe (or 20 ml if not available). If there is an IV cannula in the kit, use it instead (see diagram).
- Insert the needle through the skin 2 cm above the pubic bone in the midline, directing downwards (see diagram), pulling back on the syringe as you go.
- Urine should appear in the syringe. If it does not, check you are using the correct technique. After three attempts, stop and seek medical advice from TMAS.
- Once urine appears in the syringe, fill up the syringe, disconnect it and squeeze the urine into the bowl. Reconnect it and repeat the process until no more urine comes out. The casualty should feel relieved, with less pain.
- Remove the needle and apply a sterile dressing to the site.

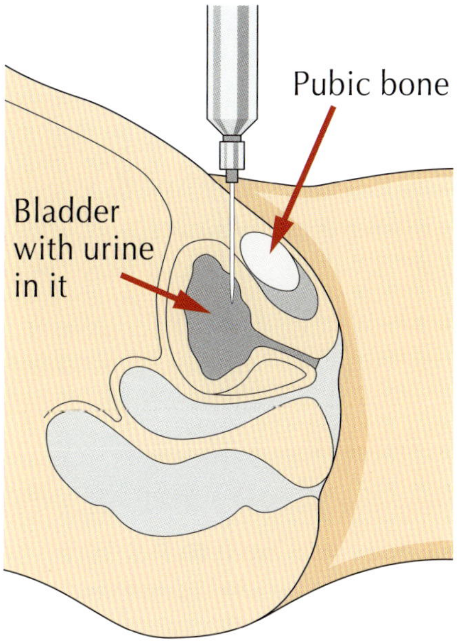

Needle aspiration of urine

- Start antibiotics (ciprofloxacin) until the casualty has been evacuated.
- If urine reaccumulates (as it will) and the casualty still cannot urinate, you may have to repeat the procedure.

12 Rehydration

The body normally controls its own level of hydration very well. However, trauma and illness can upset this balance. In hospital, specific sterile fluid can be given directly into the casualty's blood vessels, using a cannula inserted into a vein (IV) (see page 224) or by the intraosseous (IO) route (see page 226). On board it may be possible to do this depending on the contents of the medical kit, but the kit and expertise may not be available.

There are other methods for getting fluid into the casualty's body:

Oral route

- Getting the casualty to drink is the best and most convenient way of achieving hydration.
- Fluid does not have to be sterile, just clean.
- Do not use water alone if there is a large amount of diarrhoea, vomiting, or sweating. Use a rehydration solution that will also replace the chemicals lost (see below).
- Do not use the oral route if the casualty has reduced consciousness – they may vomit and aspirate it into the lungs.
- If the casualty is awake and vomiting only occasionally, it may be worth persisting with oral fluids – encourage them to drink small amounts frequently. Use anti-sickness medications to prevent vomiting.

Nasogastric tube (NGT) (see page 216)

- An NGT requires considerable skill to insert properly. Only do so with direct advice from TMAS. A misplaced NGT can cause fluid to enter the lungs, resulting in respiratory failure and possible death of the casualty.
- The same types of fluid can be used as for the oral route.
- An NGT can be used in an unconscious patient but not if they are vomiting. Use anti-sickness medication.

Routine fluid losses per day (for a typical 70 kg crew member)

Route of loss	Amount lost per day (ml)
Perspiration (no work)	700
Breath	500
Urine	1300
Stool	100
Total	**2600 ml/day**

Note: the losses due to sweating (particularly in hot climates and when working hard) may increase to above 5000 ml.

Routine daily fluid requirements

- For the average sized male: 3000 ml/day
- For the average sized female: 2200 ml/day

Note: These amounts replace the body's normal requirements. See below for guidance on extra fluid that might be required.

Reasons to give emergency rehydration

- Severe vomiting
- Blood loss
- Burns
- Routine hydration if unconscious
- Profuse diarrhoea
- Severe heat illness
- Diabetic crisis with high blood sugar
- Shock (other causes)

How to give emergency rehydration

The amount of fluid that should be given by any route depends on what has happened to the casualty:

- **Immediately** Give 500 ml fluid by the easiest route available (IV or IO (if possible) if the casualty is unconscious).
- **Assess** The casualty's level of hydration/shock (see below).
- **Check the casualty's medical history** If they have heart, lung or kidney disease, seek medical advice from TMAS before giving more than 1 litre of fluid.
- **Continue giving fluid until the signs of shock reduce** If the casualty still looks shocked after 1.5 litres of fluid, seek medical advice from TMAS before giving them further fluid.
- **Continue giving the casualty their routine daily fluid requirements** Until they are drinking normally, or have been evacuated.
- **A casualty with burns** Will require more fluids (see page 55).

Blood loss due to trauma or bleeding into the gastrointestinal tract

- Estimating blood loss is very difficult and a relatively small amount of blood (such as 500 ml, the amount given in one blood donation) looks much more when spilt on the deck.
- In the event of sudden, large blood loss, it is an emergency requirement to give IV or IO fluid only if the patient becomes unconscious, or if it is not possible to feel the radial pulse in the wrist.
- Giving too much IV or IO fluid may increase blood loss by stopping the blood clotting properly, or by increasing blood pressure too much.
- If fluid is required, initially give 250 ml IV or IO fluid and reassess the casualty.
- Further amounts of 250 ml can be given until you can feel a radial pulse.
- You must seek advice from TMAS in these circumstances.

Assessing level of hydration

- Examining the casualty may indicate whether more fluid is required. Check for the following warning signs:
  - Fast pulse rate (>100bpm)
  - Skin colour may be paler than normal
  - Blood pressure may be lower than normal
  - Skin temperature may be cold on distal arms and legs
  - Urine colour may be dark. It should be pale or colourless
  - Urine output may be <50 ml/hour (for an average sized adult).
- Giving more fluid (250 ml at a time) should improve the above signs (pulse rate will decrease, blood pressure will increase, skin will be warm and normal colour, urine output will increase and be pale in colour).

Emergency fluid mixture for oral and nasogastric rehydration

- Use pre-made oral rehydration salts (ORS) such as WHO ORS or other versions if available. Give 1 litre ORS and 1 litre water in alternating order.

or

- Make up an emergency ORS solution as follows:
  - Take 1 litre of clean water.
  - Add 6 level teaspoons of normal (white or brown) sugar, or 2 teaspoons of honey).
  - Add exactly half a level teaspoon of table salt.
  - Add a generous squeeze of lemon, orange, lime or grapefruit juice.
- Try the drink yourself before giving it to the casualty; it should taste like tears. If it does not, make up the mixture again, paying accurate attention to the amount of ingredients.

13 Venous and intraosseous access and setting up an infusion

These are potentially life-saving procedures but they should only be undertaken by trained crew members and if the correct equipment is available.

Intravenous access

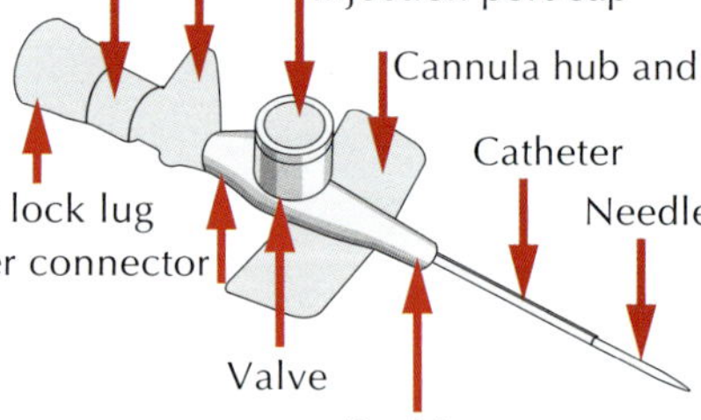

- The intravenous (IV) route is very effective for giving fluids and drugs. Both go directly into the circulation and can start having an effect within minutes.
- Inserting a cannula requires training and regular practice to maintain the skill.
- A cannula is a needle with a plastic pipe around it (see diagram). The needle pierces the skin, then the vein. The plastic tube is advanced over the needle into the vein and the needle is then withdrawn, leaving just the plastic tube in the vein. The cannula has a fitting for a bung which stops blood leaking out. The bung can be removed when attaching tubing to give fluids.
- There are risks involved in inserting a cannula, and also in using it for drugs and fluids (see below).
- Wear gloves when inserting a cannula, and take universal precautions (see page 212).

Cautions and complications

- Larger cannulas allow greater fluid flow rate but are more difficult to insert.
- Inject into the cannula only sterile fluid meant for IV use.
- Ensure that no air can get into the cannula or else the casualty may have a cardiac arrest or stroke.
- Do not touch the cannula or connect tubing with dirty hands. Be sterile if possible.
- Fix the cannula securely so it does not become dislodged.
- Watch for infection around the cannula – redness of the skin, pain on injection, swelling, blockage. If any of these signs occur, remove the cannula and insert a new one in a different place.
- A cannula can stay in place for 5 days and then should be replaced, unless infected, painful, or blocked, in which case take it out earlier and insert a new one in a different place.

Sites for inserting a cannula

Cannulas can be inserted in the following places (see diagram):

- Back of hand Good for normal IV fluids and drugs.
- Wrist Good for resuscitating fluids and larger cannulas.
- Inside of elbow Larger veins, easier to get a cannula in, but the arm has to stay straight.

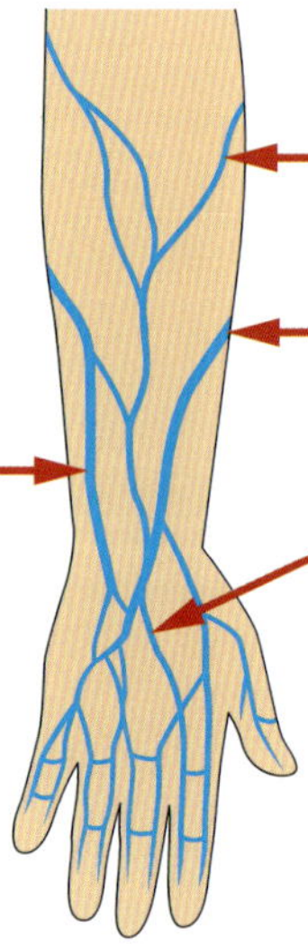

Back of hand

How to insert a cannula (see diagrams 1 to 5)

- **Non-dominant arm** Preferably use this for the casualty's comfort.
- **Veins in the feet/lower leg** Can be used but can be more difficult to cannulate.

- Put a tourniquet firmly around the upper arm (1). If a tourniquet is not available another person can put their hands around the arm instead.
- Wait for a few minutes for the veins to appear. They will be more visible if the casualty is warm and well hydrated:
  - Get the casualty to repeatedly make a fist.
  - Tap the veins to make them expand.
  - Hang their arm down the side of the bed or bunk and let gravity fill the veins.
- Clean the skin over a suitable vein with antiseptic swab or solution.
- Gently stretch the skin on each side of the vein apart and towards you between two fingers (2).
- Line up the cannula with the vein at an angle of about 30° to the skin.
- Insert the tip of the cannula through the skin (3), and then reduce the angle to about 15°.
- Advance slowly into the vein. Watch the back end of the cannula very carefully. Stop advancing it immediately when you see a flash of blood.
- Hold the back end of the needle very still and advance the wings or hub of the cannula so the plastic tube goes into the vein. It should go easily; if not start again at another location.
- Release the tourniquet.
- Take the bung off the back end of the needle and screw it to the end of the cannula (4).
- Fix the cannula securely in place with a special fixing dressing or tape (5).
- Flush the cannula with a 5 ml syringe of IV fluid (Ringer's lactate); this should go in easily without causing swelling or pain.

1

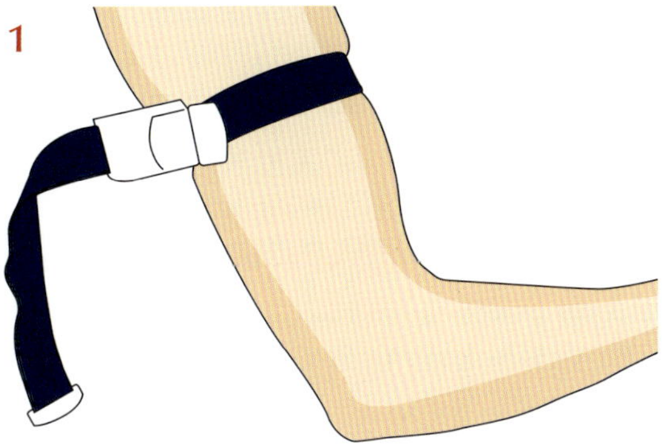

2

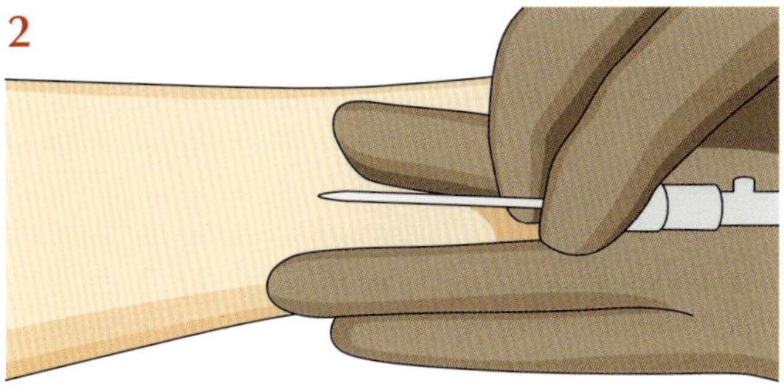

3

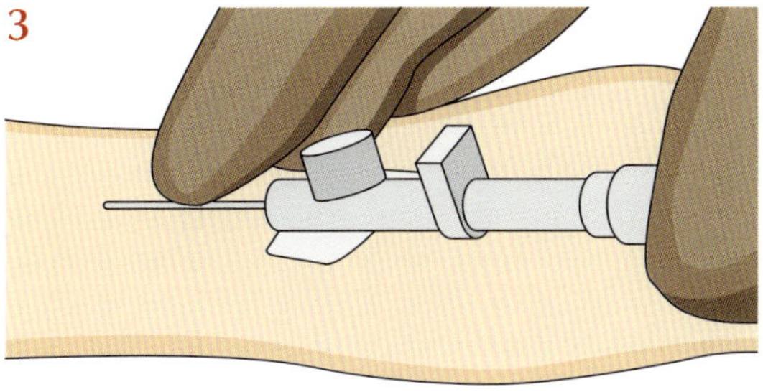

4

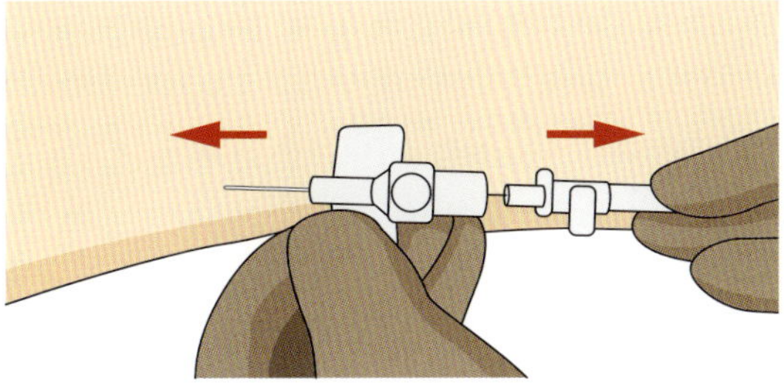

5

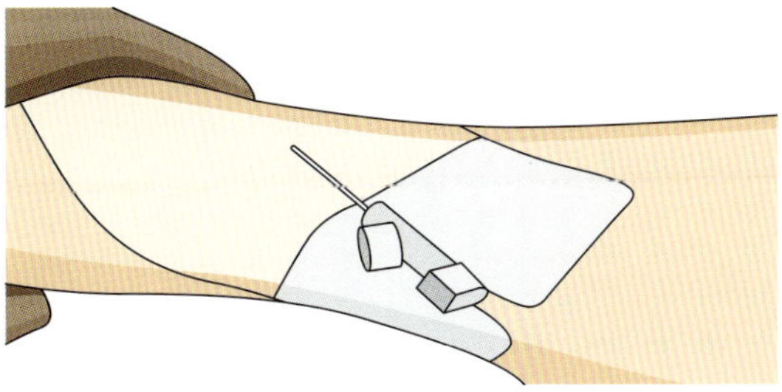

Intraosseous (IO) access

- If you cannot establish IV access in an emergency, consider using IO access.
- Fluid can be given quickly (at least 1 litre every 30 minutes) via the IO route, as can adrenaline and other medicines. They will reach the venous system just as quickly as with direct IV access.
- IO access involves putting a needle directly into the marrow in the centre of a bone, usually just below the knee on the inner (medial) side of the tibia (shin bone).
- IO access can be used for several hours but it should be replaced by IV access as soon as possible.
- A special device called a 'trocar' is used as a manual method. This comprises a hollow tube, with a needle inside it, which enables penetration through skin and bone.
- Alternatively, there are several specialised devices for gaining quick IO access (e.g. Bone Injection Gun (B.I.G.), FAST1®, EZ-IO®) which 'fire' or 'drill' the needle into the bone.
- Do not use IO access in a leg with a suspected fracture, infected skin or open wound, infected bone, or known osteoporosis.

Method for inserting IO access (see diagrams 1 to 4)

- This should be a sterile technique – wear sterile gloves and clean the skin with sterile cleaning fluid (povidone-iodine or chlorhexidine; see page 212).
- Identify the site for needle insertion on the flat of the inside of the tibia (shin bone; see diagram 1), about 5 cm below the knee (in an average sized adult).
- Support the leg behind the knee, with the leg slightly bent.
- For all devices (manual, fire and drill devices), hold the device at 90° to the skin, so the needle enters the skin at the correct angle (diagram 2).
- For the manual trocar device, insert the needle through the skin, and advance the needle into the bone using a twisting action, until you feel a 'give' (this may not be too obvious; see diagram 3).
- With the drill device, drill into the bone firmly, until you feel a 'give'.
- Remove the needle for all devices, leaving behind a tube now inserted into the bone.
- The tube should remain upright in the bone by itself.
- Flush the tube with 5 ml IV fluid (Ringer's lactate), which should go in easily.
- Connect the infusion line and tape it to the leg as shown in diagram 4 (see page 227 for infusions).

1

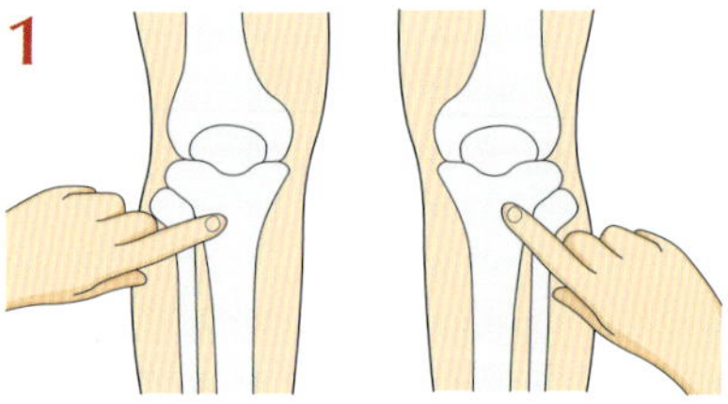

2

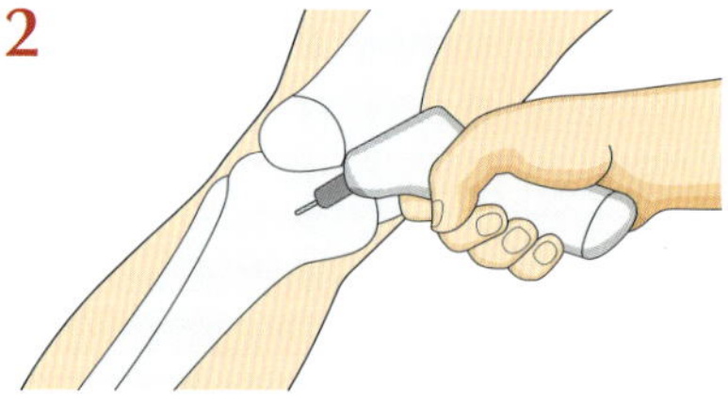

3

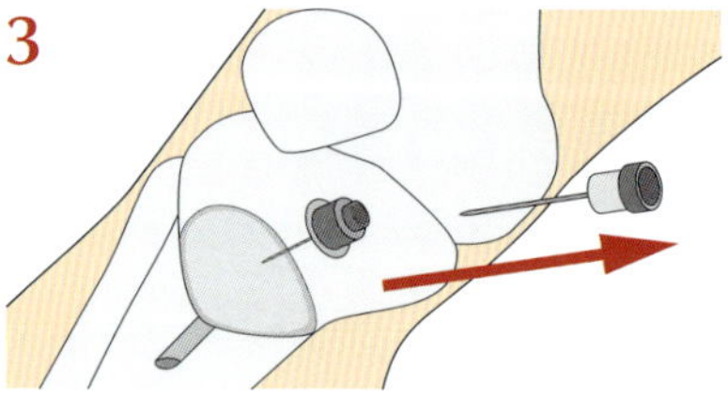

4

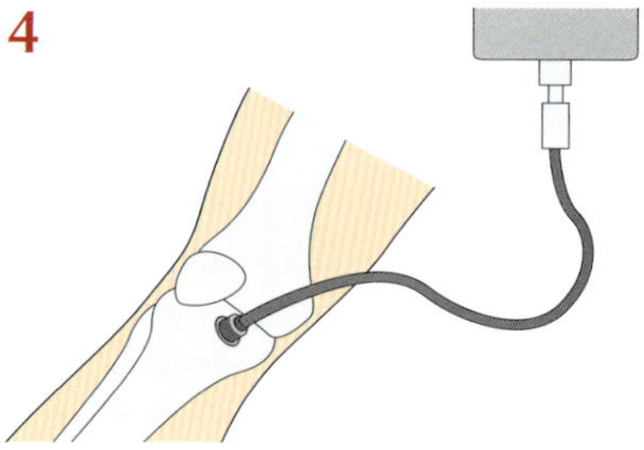

Cautions and complications

- The leg may swell, either around the needle (which means the needle is not correctly sited within the bone) or generally. In either case stop the infusion and take the needle out.
- Infection may affect the skin or bone. Watch for redness, swelling and pain. Remove the needle and treat the casualty with antibiotics.

Setting up an intravenous or intraosseous infusion

An infusion is where specialised fluid is fed directly into the body via an IV cannula or IO needle, via a giving set, which is a plastic tube designed specifically for this purpose. Gravity may not be enough to enable an adequate fluid flow through an IO needle. In this case a large syringe may be required to inject boluses of fluid into the IO needle.

- This is a sterile procedure so avoid touching the connectors. There is no need to wear sterile gloves, but certainly non-sterile gloves are always a good idea when dealing with any procedure like this.
- The giving set has a roller valve. Shut this off at the start.
- The giving set has a sharp, piercing end which should be inserted into the special port of the bag or bottle of fluid (see diagram 1).
- Hang the bag or bottle upside down, and squeeze the drip chamber so it half-fills with fluid (see diagram 2).
- Open the roller valve and watch the fluid flow down the tubing to the end. Keep flushing through until all the air bubbles have gone and the tubing is full of fluid only. Shut off the roller valve (see diagram 3).
- Connect the tubing to the cannula sited in the vein or the IO needle.
- Open the roller valve and adjust the drip rate to give the desired flow rate.
- Tape the tubing to the arm or leg twice to avoid pulling out the cannula or the IO needle.

1

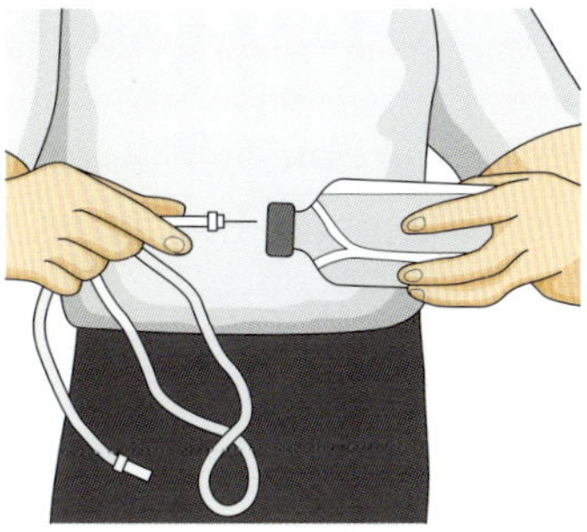

2

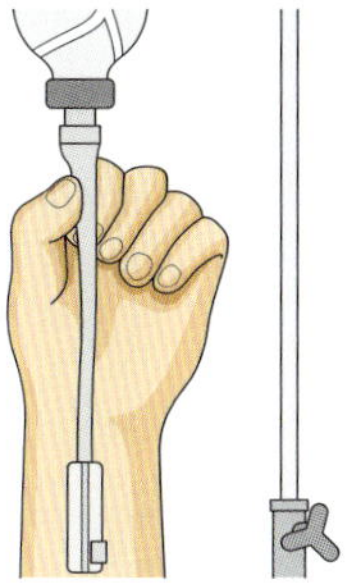

3

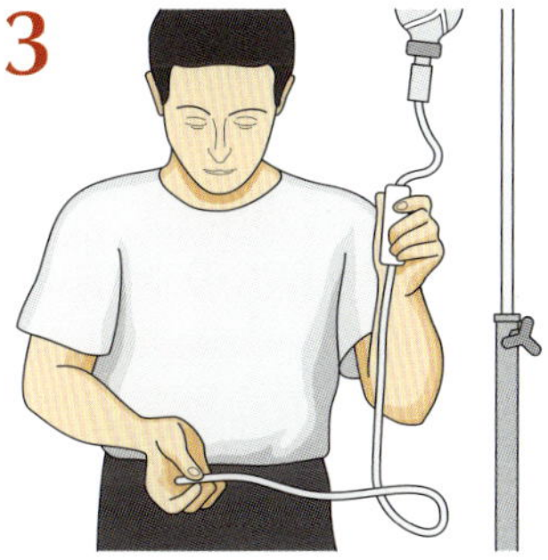

14 Injections: intravenous, intramuscular and subcutaneous

Injections are a way of giving a drug to a casualty, either directly into a vein (intravenously; IV), into a muscle (intramuscularly; IM), or into the skin (subcutaneously; S/C). A syringe and needle are used for injections (see diagrams below). Not all injectable medicines can be given in all three ways, so check the instructions that come with the medicines or seek medical advice from TMAS.

Medicines that are labelled as suitable for IV injection can also be given via an IV or intraosseous (IO) infusion if one has been set up (see page 224).

General rules for giving injections

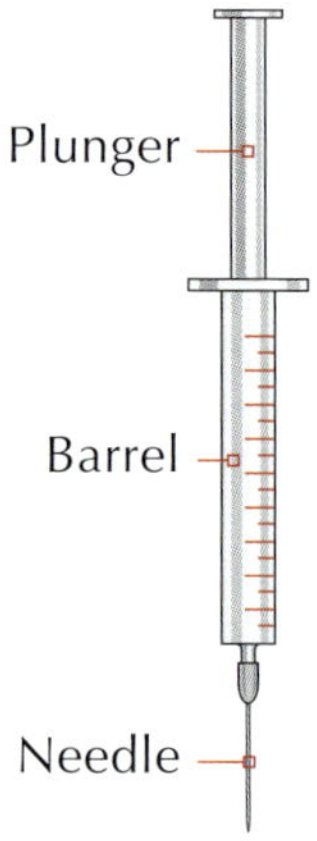

Hypodermic needle

- Make sure you have the right drug in the right dosage for the patient. Double-check it with a suitably trained colleague. It is easy to make a mistake because drugs from different sources may vary in the appearance of the packaging, and also dose and concentration.
- Double-check if the casualty has any allergies before giving the injection.
- Keep the procedure sterile. Do not contaminate the end of the syringe or needle before injecting. Before injecting clean the skin or cannula with an alcohol wipe designed for the purpose, or a cotton wool swab soaked in an antiseptic such as chlorhexidine.
- When drawing up the drug make sure there is no air in the syringe. To expel any air hold the syringe needle upwards and slowly push the plunger in, expelling the air.
- Check the casualty after giving the injection for any signs of allergic reaction (see page 42).
- Dispose of all needles and other sharps safely in a sharps box to avoid needle stick injuries.

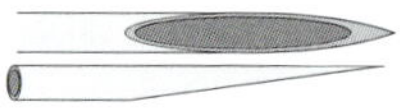
A hollow hypodermic needle tip

Intravenous injections

Note: If repeated IV injections or an infusion are required, it may be better to insert a venous cannula (see page 225).

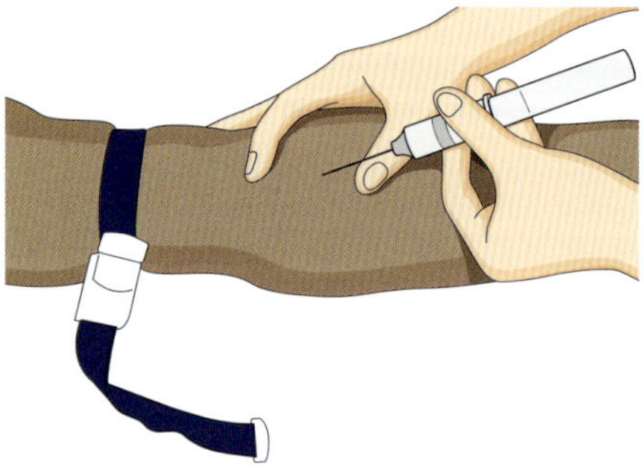

- The best veins to use are the ones on the inner side of the elbow, but look for others if you cannot find these.
- Prepare the drug and clean the skin.
- Put a tourniquet around the upper arm, and let the arm hang down to fill the veins.
- Put a finger each side of the vein where you want to inject and pull the skin a little apart and towards you (see diagram opposite).
- Insert the needle, hole upwards, at an angle of 30° to the skin, pointing up the arm (towards the heart). Once the tip is inside the skin, pull back on the plunger slightly.
- When the tip of the needle enters the vein, blood will appear in the syringe barrel. Stop advancing the needle and give another little pull on the plunger to make sure blood still comes back. Release the tourniquet before injecting. You might need an assistant to do this.

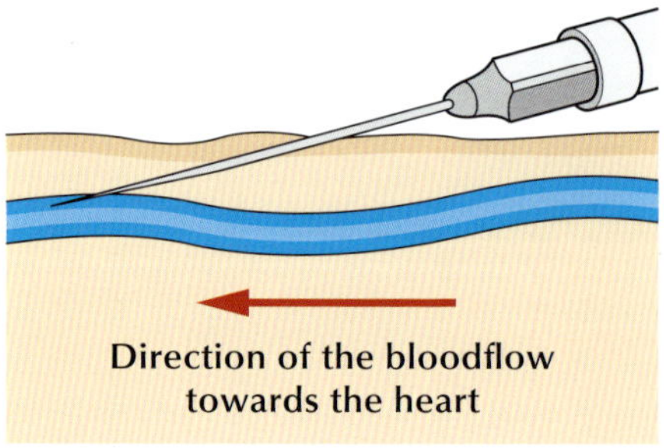

- Inject the drug slowly and smoothly, checking for any swelling around the tip of the needle. A swelling means the tip is not in the vein so you will need to start again.
- Once you have finished, smoothly remove the needle from the skin. Press down firmly on the injection site with a cotton swab for a couple of minutes. Then apply a plaster.

Intramuscular injections

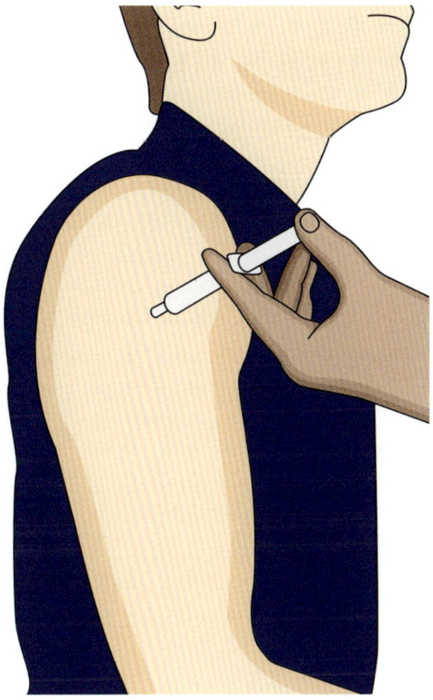

- IM injections are easier to give than IV injections.
- Do not give an IM injection if the casualty normally takes warfarin or another blood thinning agent. They will bleed heavily.
- The two main sites for IM injections are the shoulder (see diagram) and the outer upper part of the buttock.
- Use a green needle (size 21 gauge) for an average sized adult.
- Clean the skin over the injection site.
- Hold the syringe firmly by the barrel like a dart, and aim it at 90° to the skin.
- In one 'stabbing' movement, push the needle fully into the skin.
- Pull back on the plunger. If blood comes up into the syringe, it means the needle is in a blood vessel. Withdraw it 10 mm, angle the needle to one side, and push it in again. Do this until you are sure the needle is not in a blood vessel.
- Inject the plunger smoothly over a period of five seconds.
- Pull the needle out and press on the site with a cotton swab until it has stopped bleeding. Rub the site gently a few times to reduce pain.

Subcutaneous injections

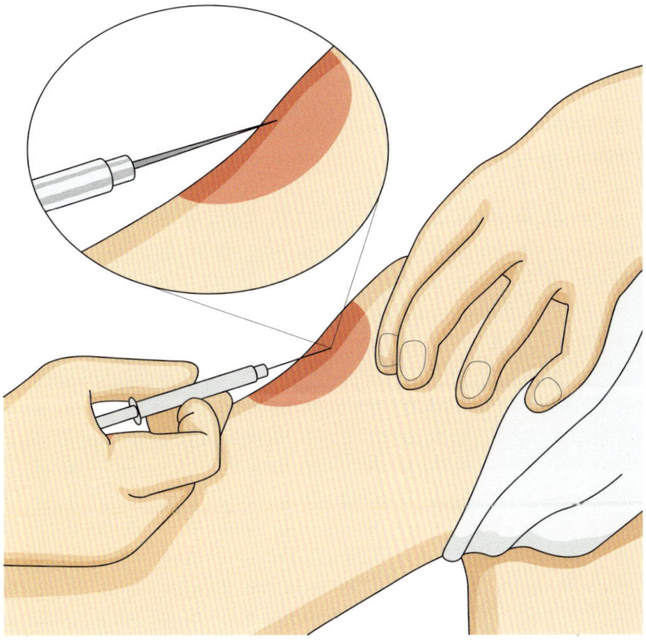

- These are similar to IM injections but the needle does not go in as far. Follow the same general rules above for preparation as for IV and IM injections (see diagram).
- Absorption of the drug may be very slow if the casualty is cold and the blood supply to the skin is shut down.
- Use an orange needle (size 25 gauge) for these injections.
- Pinch the skin gently over the shoulder between the thumb and forefinger, pulling up a ridge of skin.
- Push the needle at a low angle into the skin on the top of the ridge, to about 10 mm.
- Smoothly inject for a period of a few seconds.
- Withdraw the needle, press on the site with a cotton swab and gently rub the site a few times to reduce pain.

15 Repairing the skin

Skin wounds are common on vessels, and if they are deep and gaping, the two edges of the skin should be brought together to aid healing. A wound left open to heal by itself will leave a large scar, whereas a wound neatly closed using one of the methods described below will heal with a smaller scar. However, not all wounds should be closed.

Wounds that should not be closed

- A gaping wound where there has been substantial loss of tissue and the edges will not come together easily.
- A wound that has been open for a while and there is now obvious infection (pus) in the wound.
- A wound that has been open for more than 12–18 hours.
- A wound that is heavily contaminated and cannot be properly cleaned. It is likely to become infected, and if it is closed, the sutures will have to be removed to let the pus out. This includes wounds due to bites (animal or human) unless they are on the face or hands. If this is the case, get advice from TMAS as to the most appropriate management.

These wounds should be cleaned gently but as thoroughly as possible, then dressed with sterile gauze and bandaging. The wound should be inspected each day, and cleaned with sterile fluid if it is looking infected. In this case oral antibiotics should be started straightaway (see Antibiotics guide, back flyleaf).

Methods for repairing skin wounds

Method	Ease of use	Indications	Cautions
Adhesive wound closure strips	Easy	Small incisions less than 10 cm in length Shin wounds	Not good in the damp or over joints
Skin stapler	Difficult	Wounds on the trunk, scalp, arms and legs Not affected by damp	Do not use on face and neck
Tissue adhesive (skin glue)	Moderate	Small incisions less than 10 cm in length Clean edges	Not good in the damp or over joints Do not get it in the eye
Sutures	Difficult	Large wounds, ragged edges, over joints Persistently bleeding wounds	Use on the face or lips

Infiltration with local anaesthetic is usually needed if staples or sutures are used (see page 215).

Adhesive wound closure strips (e.g. Steri-Strips®, Leukostrips®)

- Make sure the wound has stopped bleeding and is absolutely dry and clean.
- Wear sterile gloves and prepare for a minor operative procedure (see page 212).
- Start at one end of the wound (unless the edges are jagged, in which case bring together matching parts of the wound and stick in place).
- To apply an adhesive strip, take off part of the backing material leaving an end free. Stick it to the skin on one side of the wound.
- Gently use the adhesive strip to pull the edges of the wound together and then stick down the other side (see diagram 1).
- Move on to the next point, about 8–10 mm from the first. Depending on how many strips are available, one can be stuck parallel to the wound on both sides (see diagram 2).
- It is possibly beneficial to put tissue adhesive over the entire area covered by the wound closure strips. This is effective in keeping the strips in place whilst the wound heals.
- Put a dressing over the wound to keep it dry and clean.
- Leave the strips on until they fall off. Some may need replacing before the wound has healed properly.

1

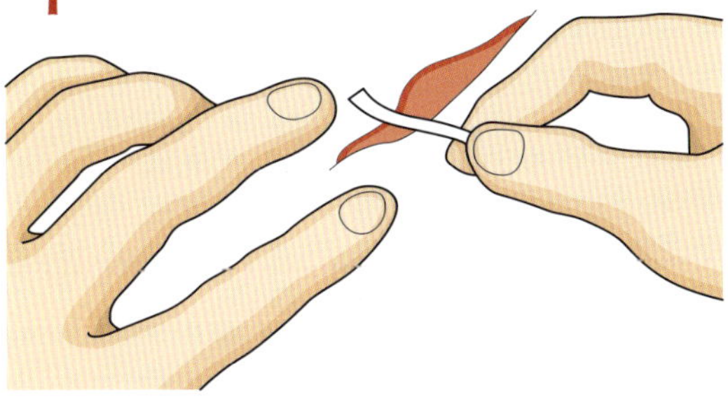

2

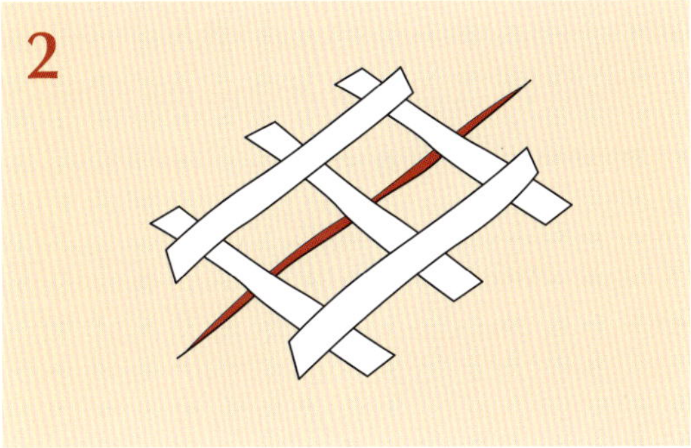

Skin stapler

- The stapler is usually in a sterile pack with the staples already loaded, and should come with instructions.
- Wear sterile gloves and prepare for a minor operative procedure (see page 212).
- When stapling the skin, position the skin edges together with the cut edges pointing to the outside (see diagram), to avoid stapling outer skin inside the wound. 'Toothed' forceps are good for this because they hold the skin well.
- Once the edges are in position, position the stapler as in the first diagram and staple the skin.
- Place the staples about 7–10 mm apart.
- With jagged wounds, start by stapling matching pieces together in several places, then start stapling from one end.
- Place a sterile dressing over the wound.
- Leave the staples in as for sutures (see below). Inspect the wound every other day for infection (swelling). You may need to remove the staples to let pus out.

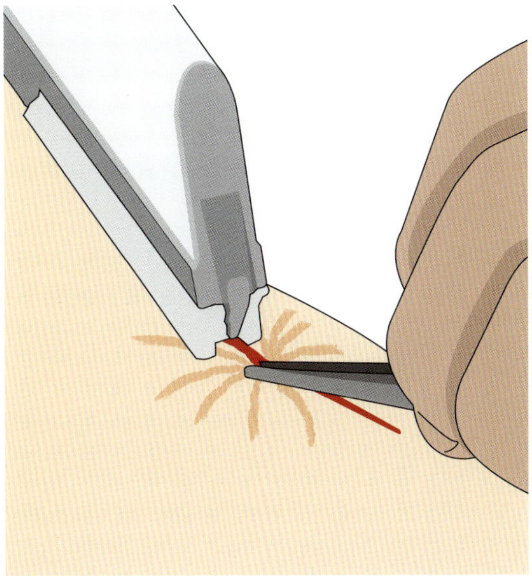

Tissue adhesive (e.g. Dermabond®, Histoacryl®, LiquiBand®, Indermil®)

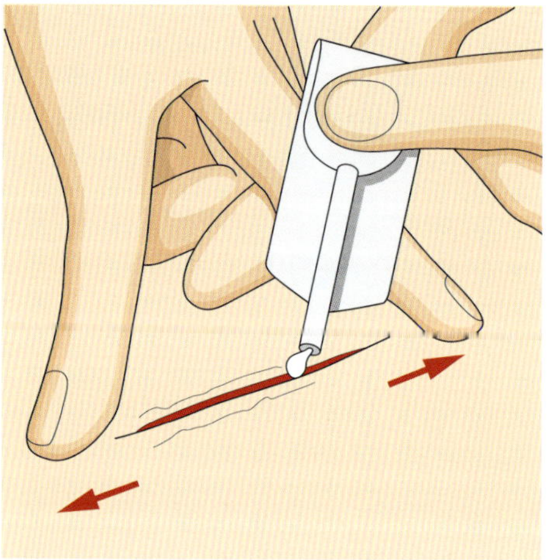

- These are cyanoacrylate glues that stick to everything in seconds, so be very careful not to contaminate eyes etc. Petroleum jelly can be used to soften the bond to separate skin stuck to other things.
- Tissue adhesive is best used on straight, dry, non-bleeding cuts, not on joints.
- Wear sterile gloves and prepare a sterile field (see page 213).
- Hold the skin together and run the glue along the surface of wound edges (see diagram).
- Apply up to three layers (see individual adhesive instructions).
- Do not get glue inside the cut; it may come apart later.
- Hold the edges together for 30 seconds. Full bond strength should develop in 2–3 minutes.
- No dressing is required for most adhesives, but keep the wound dry.
- The adhesive should come off by itself after about 7–10 days.
- For scalp wounds the hair may be used to bring the edges together and then the skin bonded with adhesive.

Sutures (see diagrams 1 to 4)

1 2 3 4

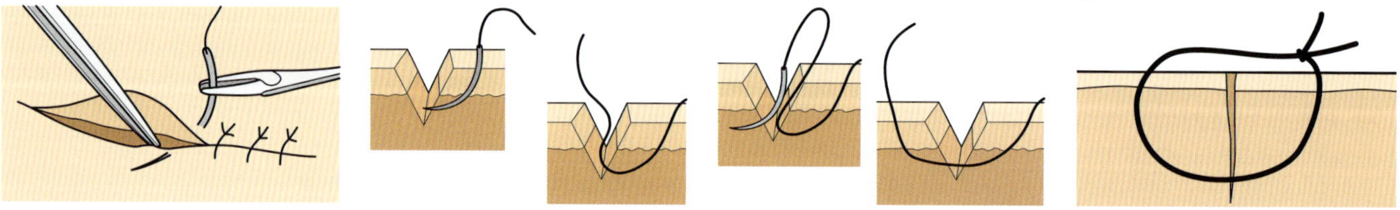

- This is a skill that requires practice, but is effective at closing damp, jagged cuts that are persistently bleeding.
- Most medical kits on a vessel will contain silk, polyester or polyamide sutures (needle bonded to the thread) in a range of sizes. All are suitable for the skin. Use silk if it is in the kit. On the face use thinner thread if you have it (or glue/strips). Discuss the choice of suture with TMAS.
- Wear sterile gloves and prepare for a minor operative procedure (see page 212).
- Use local anaesthetic (up to 20 ml 1% lidocaine) if you are putting in more than two sutures.
- Start by putting in a suture halfway along the wound, then in each quarter. Then fill in the gaps, with about 5–10 mm between each suture.
- If the wound has jagged edges, match these up first and suture in place.
- When suturing, use interrupted sutures as in the diagram (1). Use a pair of forceps ('toothed' ones are ideal) to hold the skin edges up while you put the needle through the skin. Put the needle in about 5 mm back from the wound edge and curve it deeply into the skin (2), and then through the opposite edge (3), aiming to come up 5 mm from the wound on the other side.
- Cut the thread, leaving enough thread to tie the knot. You should be able to do 4 to 6 sutures with one needle and thread.
- Tie with a reef knot (4), but after the first throw pull the knot just as tight as is needed to bring the skin edges together and no tighter, otherwise the wound will break down over time.

- Make sure the edges of the wound match up. You may need to poke some bits down, or pull other bits up.
- If you are not happy with a suture (for instance, the skin does not come together neatly, the suture is tied too tightly or not tightly enough), take it out and start again.
- Clean the wound when you have finished and place a sterile dressing over the wound.
- Inspect the wound every two days or so. If it looks red and swollen, release a suture at that point and see if pus comes out. Leave the suture out and reapply a fresh dressing.

Removing sutures and clips

When the time comes for potential suture removal, as indicated below, remove the dressing and inspect the wound. If it looks ready (dry, not reddened, no discharge of pus), it probably is, so start removing the sutures:

- Snip with scissors and remove with forceps.
- If the wound gapes, do not take any more out and wait a few days.
- Tissue adhesive and adhesive strips can be used to keep the wound together, if it starts to come apart.
- When to remove sutures and staples:
  - Face: 3–5 days
  - Scalp: 7–10 days
  - Limbs: 10–14 days
  - Joints: 14 days
  - Trunk: 7–10 days.

16 Chest decompression

A tension pneumothorax is a very rare event on a vessel (see page 87), but prompt action in releasing the pressure build-up inside the chest may prevent the casualty collapsing and possibly dying. A tension pneumothorax may occur spontaneously or may follow serious injury to the chest.

Once the chest cavity has been decompressed (see below), a thoracostomy should be undertaken and a chest seal dressing placed over the opening in the chest wall. If appropriate equipment is available in the medical kit, a chest drain could be inserted as an alternative to a thoracostomy.

In all circumstances, TMAS must be consulted and any procedures performed under direct supervision of TMAS, as all these procedures carry a significant degree of risk, as well as potential benefit.

After a chest injury there may be blood in the chest (haemothorax; see page 87). This condition should not require emergency decompression, but it does require IV or IO fluids if possible, to resuscitate the casualty.

Signs of a tension pneumothorax

- Difficulty in breathing
- Low blood pressure
- The side of the chest not moving has the air in it (this may be difficult to see)
- The trachea may be shifted away from the side of the chest with the air in it
- Reduced breath sounds on the side of the chest with the air in it

Signs of a haemothorax

- Difficulty in breathing
- Low blood pressure
- Reduced breath sounds on the side of the chest with the blood in it

Monitoring vital signs

Monitoring of vital signs before, during and after all of the procedures described below, is mandatory. There is a risk of the casualty deteriorating at any time, and close monitoring improves the chance of detecting such a deterioration at an early stage.

Vital signs monitoring for these procedures includes:

- Pulse rate
- Blood pressure
- Respiratory rate
- Conscious state
- Pulse oximetry

Emergency chest decompression

A cannula is inserted into the front of the chest **on the side you suspect has the problem**:

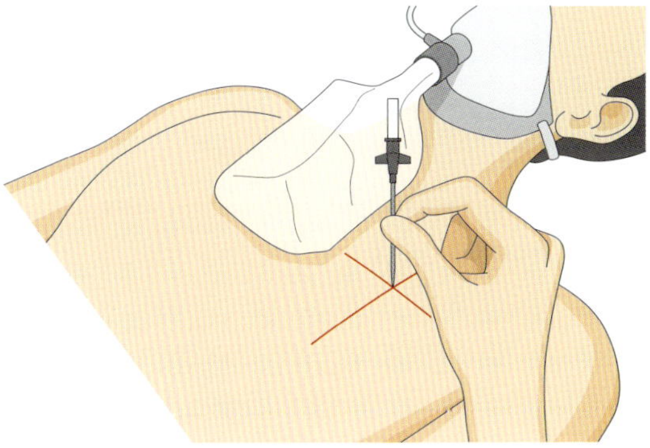

- Position the casualty sitting up at 30° if possible, in a stable position.
- Use sterile gloves and prepare for a sterile minor operative procedure (see page 212).
- Use the largest IV cannula in the medical kit (usually 14- or 16-gauge).
- Locate the position to insert the cannula:
  - Draw an imaginary line down the chest from the midpoint of the clavicle (see diagram).
  - Locate the second space between the ribs along this line. It should be about 5–8 cm below the clavicle in an average sized casualty.
- Do not use local anaesthetic as decompression needs to be undertaken as quickly as possible. Warn the casualty that this may be painful.
- Remove any bung or stopper from the end of the cannula before inserting.
- Insert the cannula at 90° to the skin, up to the hilt.
- When the tip penetrates the pleural space, if there is air in there, a hiss may be heard as it escapes (see diagram).
- Leave the cannula (and needle) in position, and remove it only if a chest drain is inserted.
- If blood comes out instead of air, leave the cannula where it is, and contact TMAS immediately.

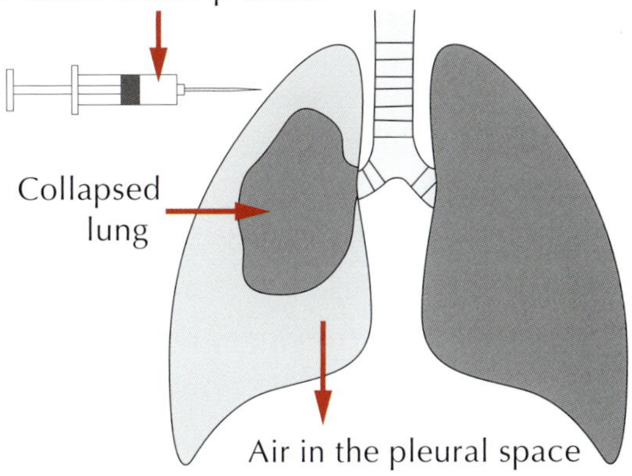

Part 4

Thoracostomy ('slit thoracostomy')

The cannula inserted into the chest to decompress a tension pneumothorax (as above) may work for only a few minutes. A more effective and durable method must be put in place to keep the chest decompressed and the casualty alive.

Put simply, a 'thoracostomy' is an opening from outside the chest, through the chest wall, between the ribs, and into the cavity of the chest, but not into the lungs themselves. Thus, the opening allows out any air or fluid that may be under pressure (such as in a tension pneumothorax), and relieves the pressure compressing the lungs or the heart. It should stay open more reliably than the cannula used for the initial decompression.

This must be undertaken only under direct supervision of TMAS:

- Insert IV access (if possible) before starting, in case it is needed because of bleeding or collapse.
- Position the casualty sitting up at 30° if possible, in a stable position.
- Use sterile gloves and prepare a sterile field for a minor operative procedure (see page 212).

- Locate the point at which to make the thoracostomy:
  - The point should be on an imaginary line down the chest, from the middle of the armpit, in the 'safe triangle'. This is the area between the chest muscle (pectoralis major) and the main muscle at the side of the back (latissimus dorsi) above the level of the nipple (see diagram).

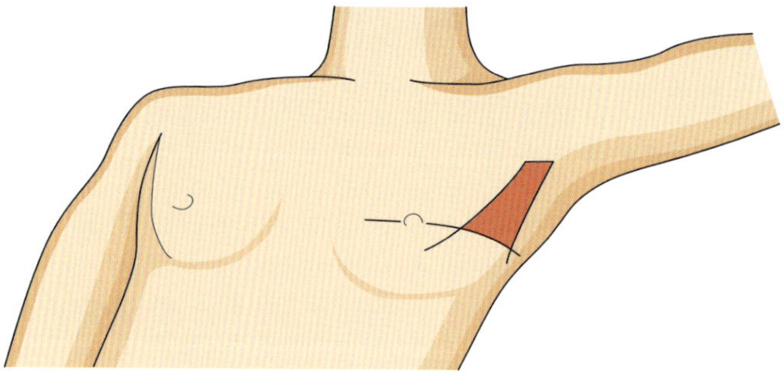

- Clean the area and inject local anaesthetic into the skin (5–10 ml 1% lidocaine) at this point.
- Make a firm incision just above a rib, and along the line of the rib, in the safe triangle, about 3 cm long. The initial incision should be about 1 cm deep, into the underlying fat layer.
- Use an arterial clamp or needle holder to dissect bluntly by pushing in the closed end of the arterial clamp, opening the end, and pulling it back out of the incision, making the opening progressively larger.
- Blunt dissect the track over the top of the lower rib.
- Eventually there will be a 'give' when inserting the arterial clamp as the end of the clamp enters the chest cavity.
- Remove the arterial clamp, and insert a gloved finger firmly, so that the end of the finger eventually enters the chest cavity.
- Make sure that the opening is large enough to allow easy passage of an index finger.
- Clean the skin around the opening, and apply the chest seal, centred on the opening, as described below.
- Occasionally the opening may close up and the pressure may reaccumulate in the chest. The casualty may then deteriorate. If this happens, remove the chest seal and re-insert a gloved finger into the chest to reopen the tract.

Chest seal dressing for a thoracostomy, or an open or penetrating chest wound

- Chest seal dressings incorporate a one-way valve which allows air and fluid out of the chest but not back in (see diagram).
- Clean as much blood and other material off the skin as possible.
- Apply the dressing firmly over the open chest wound.
- Follow the instructions included with the chest seal as different models may require differing methods for managing the injury.

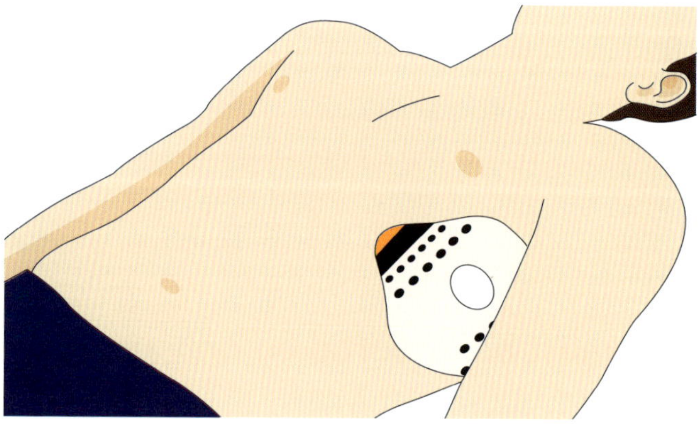

Flutter valve for an open chest wound (alternative to a chest seal; see page 236)

- Take a gauze dressing swab and soak it thoroughly in petroleum jelly.
- Clean the wound with sterilising fluid.
- Place the dressing over the holes and tape it down firmly on three sides, leaving the fourth side open (see diagram).
- This flap acts as a valve, letting air out, but not back in again.
- Consider inserting a chest drain through the wound but you MUST seek TMAS advice first.

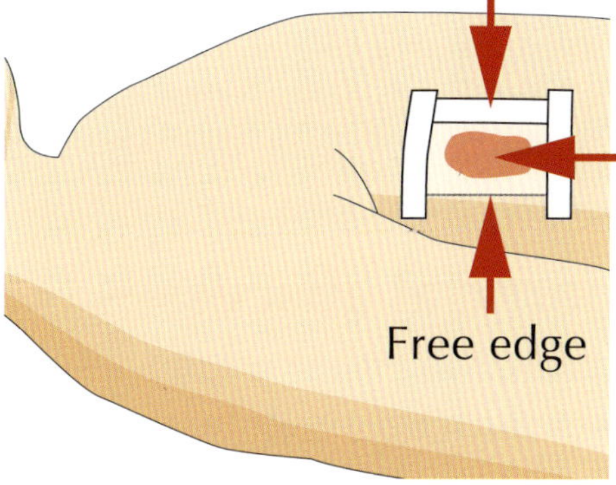

17 Treatment of an abscess

An abscess is a localised collection of pus in the body's tissue, normally as a reaction to infection. On a vessel, abscesses commonly form in a bruise (haematoma) where blood has accumulated under the skin, which then becomes infected. These are relatively easy to open up and drain. Abscesses that form elsewhere (e.g. buttocks, breast, perianal area) may be more deep-seated, requiring a more invasive approach that cannot be safely achieved on the vessel; if this happens contact TMAS for advice on treatment. Abscesses may also form around hair follicles; these may not require incision and drainage, but a less invasive approach.

Small, superficial abscesses (<5mm in diameter)

- Use a hot compress to encourage the abscess to 'point'.
- It may then self-discharge or get better without further treatment.
- A compress with magnesium sulphate paste may also encourage the abscess to self-discharge.
- A dressing may not be needed after the abscess has self-discharged, if there is no further discharge.
- Watch the site for signs of spreading infection, in which case start antibiotics. See Antibiotics guide (back flyleaf) for appropriate antibiotics.
- If it continues to get worse, seek advice from TMAS.

Larger abscesses that can be easily felt under the skin

Seek advice from TMAS before starting on this procedure.

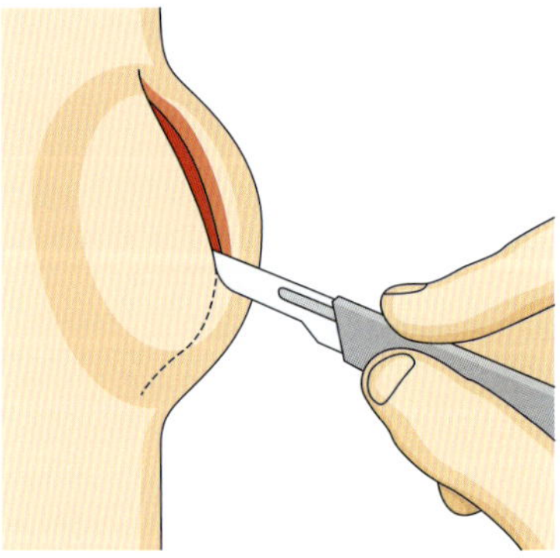

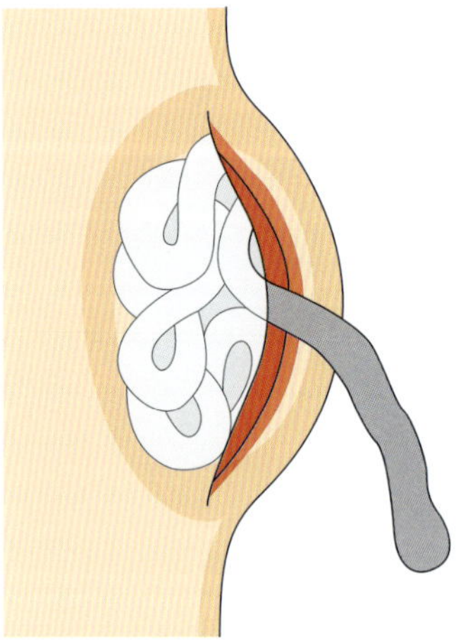

- Make sure the casualty is in a comfortable position, and explain to them what you are going to do; it may be quite painful.
- Wear sterile gloves and prepare for a sterile minor operative procedure (see page 212).
- Clean the area and infiltrate around the abscess with local anaesthetic (10 ml 1% lidocaine). This will dull some of the pain, but local anaesthetic does not work well around an abscess so warn the casualty. An alternative is to use ethyl chloride cold spray (if available) or ice cubes to freeze the skin over the abscess.
- Using a sterile scalpel incise firmly over the abscess and into the cavity to let the pus out (see upper diagram). Be prepared with a gauze swab to catch the pus. Incise along the natural skin folds to minimise the scar. The pus may have an offensive smell.
- You may need to 'sweep' the abscess cavity to break down any walled-off areas to make sure all the pus is out. Use the handle of the scalpel or the end of a pair of sterile forceps. Be firm doing this and warn the casualty that it may hurt.
- Prepare a long strip of gauze soaked in iodine. Squeeze it dry. If no iodine is available a plain, dry strip of gauze can be used.
- Pack the gauze into the abscess cavity until it is quite firm, leaving a tail of gauze hanging out (see lower diagram).
- Apply a sterile dressing and inspect the wound daily.
- On the third day remove the gauze strip. If the wound looks clean and is not leaking pus, apply a sterile dressing. Inspect the wound daily, and allow the cavity to heal from the inside out. If it becomes infected again, clean the cavity, repack and repeat the process.
- Start oral antibiotics after the procedure (co-amoxiclav if casualty is not allergic; see Antibiotics guide, back flyleaf).

Deep-seated abscesses or abscesses in sensitive areas (e.g. around the anus or vagina)

- If the vessel is in a remote location, it may not be safe to incise and drain such an abscess.
- Start oral antibiotics (co-amoxiclav if the casualty is not allergic to penicillin (see Antibiotics guide, back flyleaf) and seek advice from TMAS.
- If the casualty becomes unwell with a high temperature, consider changing to IV antibiotics and arrange urgent evacuation.

18 Using splints and slings

Splints

The vessel's medical kit may contain a variety of splints which are used to immobilise a limb or finger following fractures or other injuries. There are also plenty of other items on board that can be used as improvised but effective splints. Conventional types of splints and suggestions for improvised splints are described below.

General rules for splints

- The splint should immobilise the joint above and below the fracture or injury site.
- Pressure points should be well padded.
- Always check the casualty's circulation before and after applying a splint, and make adjustments if the splint has made matters worse.
- Remove all jewellery before applying the splint because the extremities will swell.
- Elevate the limb as far as practicable after splinting.
- Periodically check the casualty's peripheral perfusion and pressure points of the immobilised limb.

Types of splints

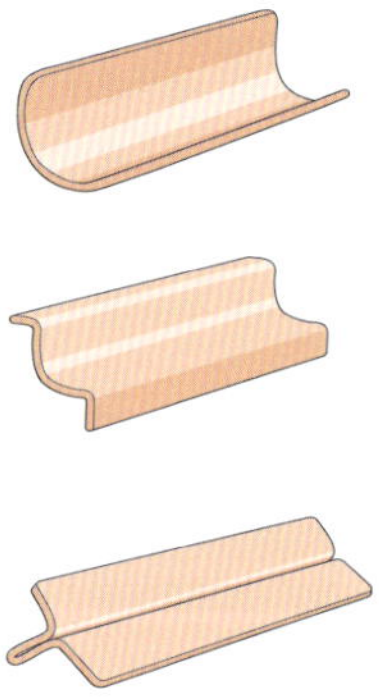

Malleable splint

A malleable splint (e.g. SAM, Redi) is a very effective foam-covered aluminium splint that can be moulded, trimmed to size, and combined with other splints. Pad pressure points such as the ankle, wrist and elbow with gauze swabs. When trimming, peel back the foam and trim the aluminium underneath, then cover the end with the foam. Folding the splint into various shapes increases rigidity (see diagram).

Traction splint

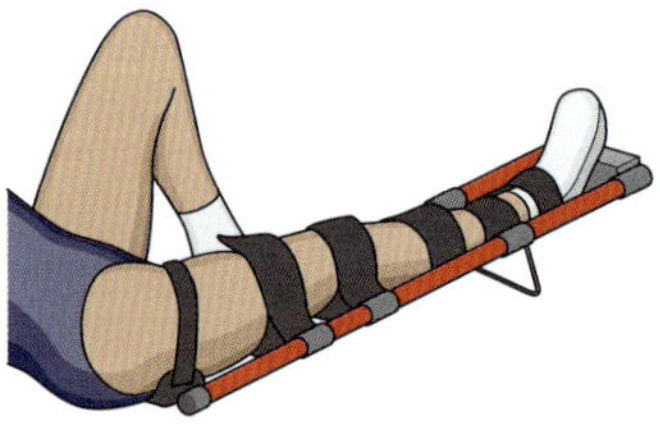

There are various versions of the traction splint (see diagram). These are very useful for reducing and stabilising femoral, hip and lower leg fractures, particularly for transport. The more sophisticated splints have a gauge enabling the amount of traction force applied to be measured. Traction splints can be either unilateral or bilateral, the latter being more stable. When fitting a traction splint, it is essential to refer to the specific instructions to avoid further injury to the leg.

Vacuum splint

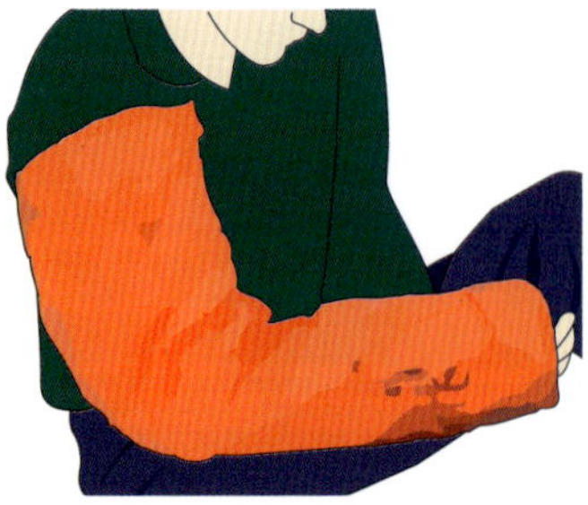

This is a polymer bag containing polystyrene beads in multiple compartments. There are different size splints for upper limb (see diagram), lower limb and whole-body immobilisation. The splint is placed around the site and air is sucked out, using a special pump. The splint becomes rigid but comfortable, moulded to the limb or body. Vacuum splints can be left in place for up to 24 hours.

Inflatable splint

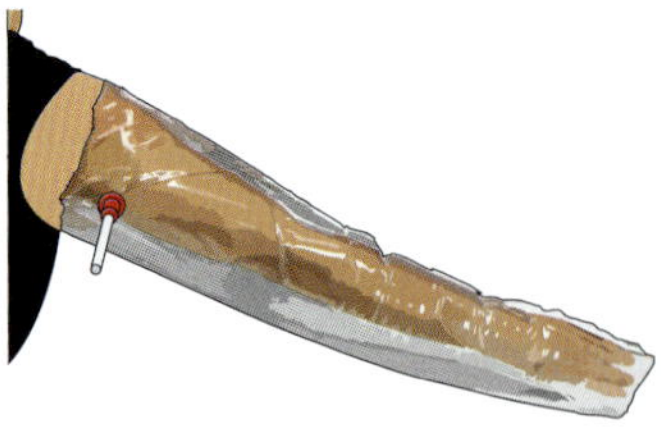

These are very compact to carry and simpler to use than the vacuum splints (see diagram). However, prolonged use is complicated by pressure sores and swelling of the extremities.

Box splints

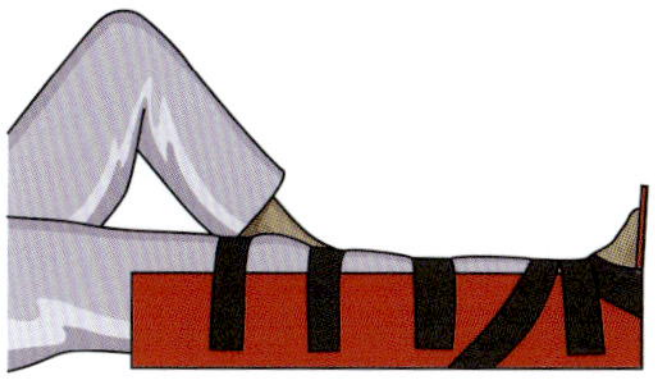

Lower limb and ankle fractures can be stabilised in a box splint (see diagram), following initial treatment. A box-type splint can easily be improvised, following the basic design.

Improvised splints

The vessel's medical kit may not contain a formal splinting device. However, there will be material on board that can be improvised to make effective immobilising devices. Some examples are described here.

Foam sleeping mattress

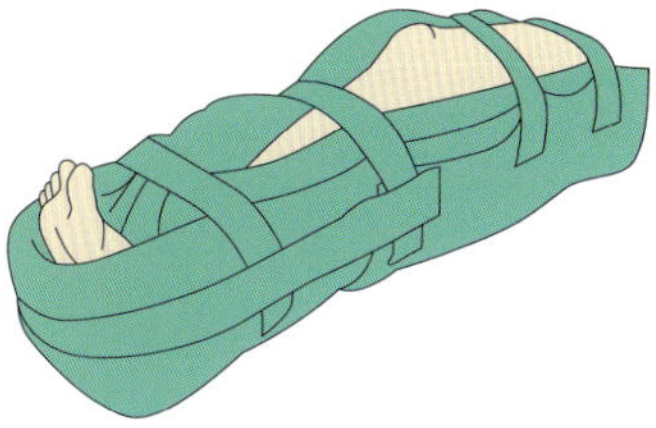

A foam sleeping mattress (e.g. Karrimat) is very effective and comfortable when it is rolled up and strapped around the limb or pelvis (see diagram).

Inflatable sleeping mattress

An inflatable sleeping mattress (e.g. Thermarest) can be used in a similar manner to a foam mattress. A further advantage is that once it is strapped in place it can then be inflated, adding support (see diagram). Take care with pressure points, which should be regularly inspected.

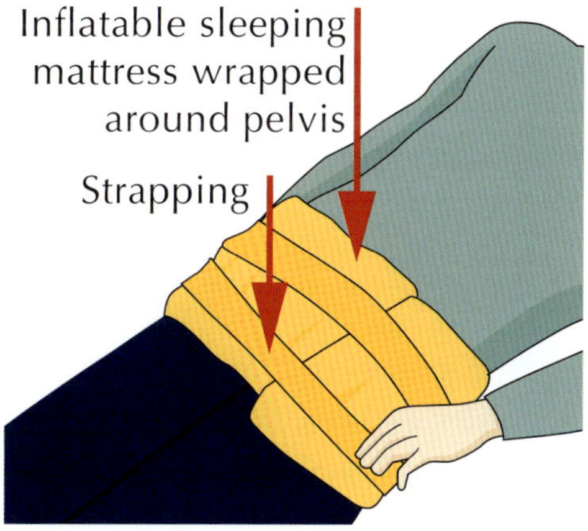

Timber boarding

Timber boarding can be used as a spinal board (covered with foam padding), or cut down for arm and leg splints. Using straps or ropes, these splints can be strapped to the leg and used for a temporary traction splint (see below).

Temporary traction splint

To make a temporary traction splint you need a rigid pole or board longer than the leg. The top should be fastened firmly with a broad strap and plenty of padding around the top of the thigh. A strap should be fastened around the ankle (pay attention to pressure and perfusion). It is a good idea to leave the casualty's work boot on (cut down if necessary) to cushion the ankle and foot. Two loops of strap or rope are a good arrangement (see diagram showing an improvised pelvic splint). The splint is tensioned by fastening the ankle strap to the rigid splint, using a pulley system, and making fast. Gradual increase in tension will slowly reduce the fracture, overcoming the large thigh muscles which may have gone into spasm, and will take a while to relax.

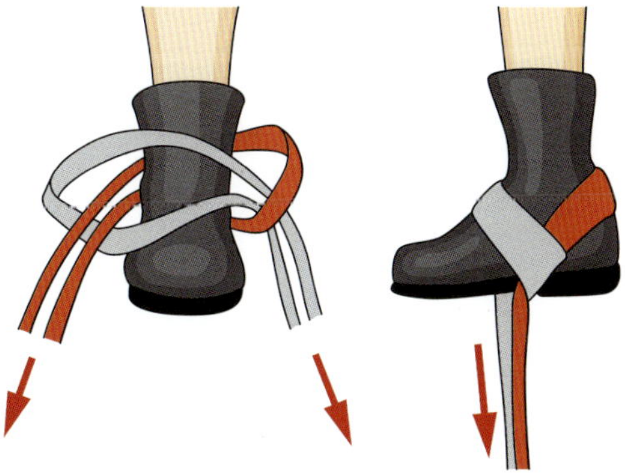

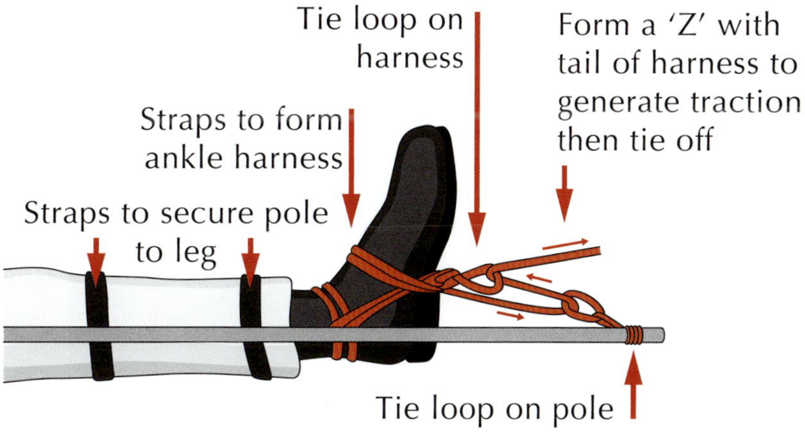

Casts

Casts have traditionally been made from plaster of paris, but this has been replaced by synthetic resin casting material which is soaked in warm water and then applied to the limb before the material becomes rigid.

Always seek TMAS advice regarding application of a cast before going ahead, to ensure it is the appropriate intervention.

General rules for casts

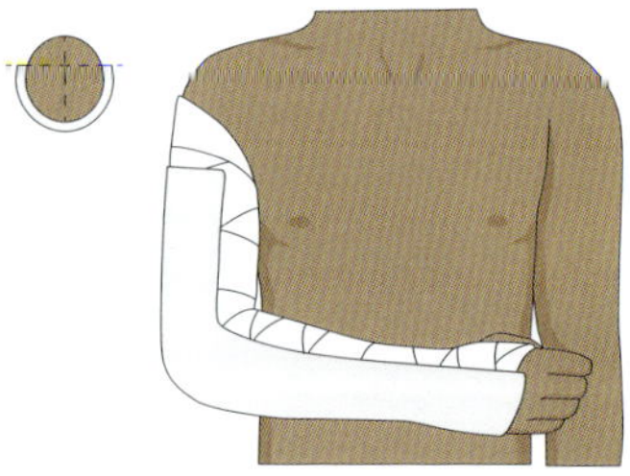

- If it will be several days before the casualty can be evacuated, consider applying a back-slab cast, which will better support the fracture.
- To immobilise a freshly fractured limb it is essential to use only a back-slab cast. There will be considerable swelling around the fracture, and a back-slab cast allows the limb to expand without constricting it and thus restricting blood supply (see diagram).
- Reduce fractures and dislocations, and check peripheral circulation before applying the back-slab cast.
- Do not apply the back-slab cast directly on the skin. Use a foam underwrap, or even a tubular bandage, but not tightly.
- Apply the back-slab cast to the arm firmly, over the foam underwrap. Mould it to fit before it becomes rigid.
- Check the circulation after applying, and regularly thereafter.
- Elevate the limb as far as practicable, to reduce swelling (see diagram).
- If the peripheral circulation becomes worse (which it might if swelling continues inside the cast), undo the crepe bandage, and reapply it slightly more loosely. This may improve circulation; if not, reassess and loosen it further.
- Continue to monitor the casualty's peripheral circulation every few hours, more frequently with bad fractures, and particularly if the casualty complains of worsening pain.

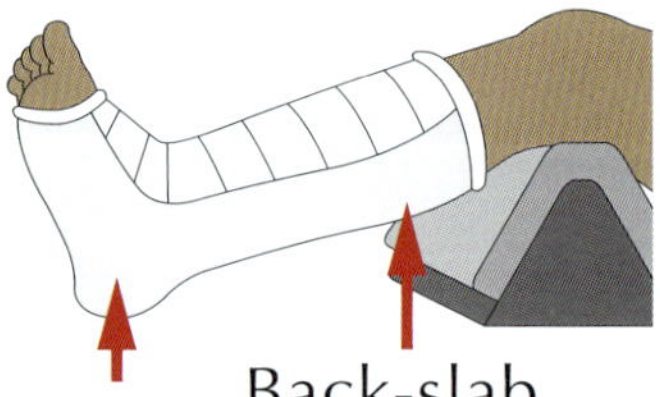

Slings

Slings are used to support the arm after fractures or dislocations, in addition to splints and casts. The vessel's medical kit may contain a triangular bandage, which is ideal for making slings. However, any cloth can be used, such as a towel. Slings may also reduce swelling by keeping a limb elevated, and can help to slowly reduce fractures, using the natural weight of a limb for traction.

Temporary sling

A temporary sling can be made by pinning the bottom of the casualty's top (or the sleeve) to the upper chest of the top, with the arm inside (see diagram).

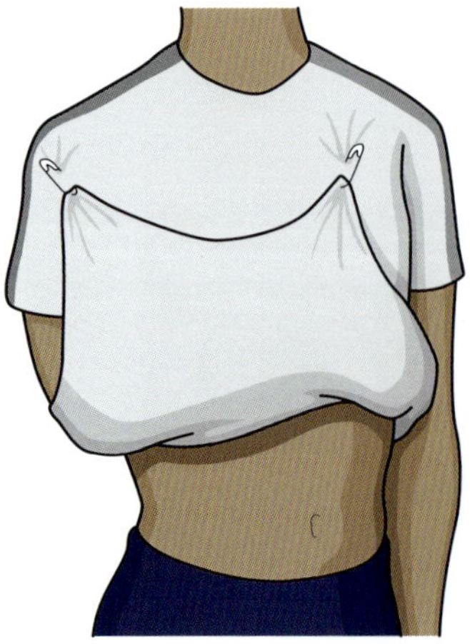

Broad arm sling (see diagrams 1 to 4)

A broad arm sling is used for fractures and dislocations of the shoulder, clavicle, upper and lower arms, including the elbow (see diagrams 1 to 4).

1. Slide the sling up inside the arm, with the 90° pointed end towards the elbow, and the other pointed end around the neck, on the opposite side to the injured arm.
2. Pick up the apex, which is hanging down, and feed it around the side of the neck, on the side of the injured arm.
3. Tie both pointed ends together behind the neck.
4. Using a safety pin, tether the 90° pointed end around the elbow and fasten it to the front of the sling.

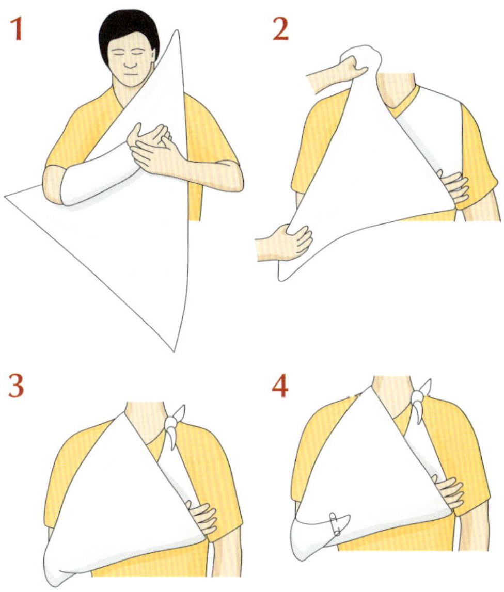

High arm sling

A high arm sling is used for wrist or hand fractures to reduce swelling by keeping the injured part elevated (see diagrams 1 to 4).

1. Slide the sling up inside the arm, with the 90° pointed end towards the elbow, and the other pointed end around the neck, on the same side as the injured arm.
2. Pick up the apex, which is hanging down, and feed it around the side of the neck, on the opposite side of the injured arm.
3. Tie both pointed ends together behind the neck.
4. Using a safety pin, tether the 90° pointed end around the elbow and fasten it to the front of the sling.

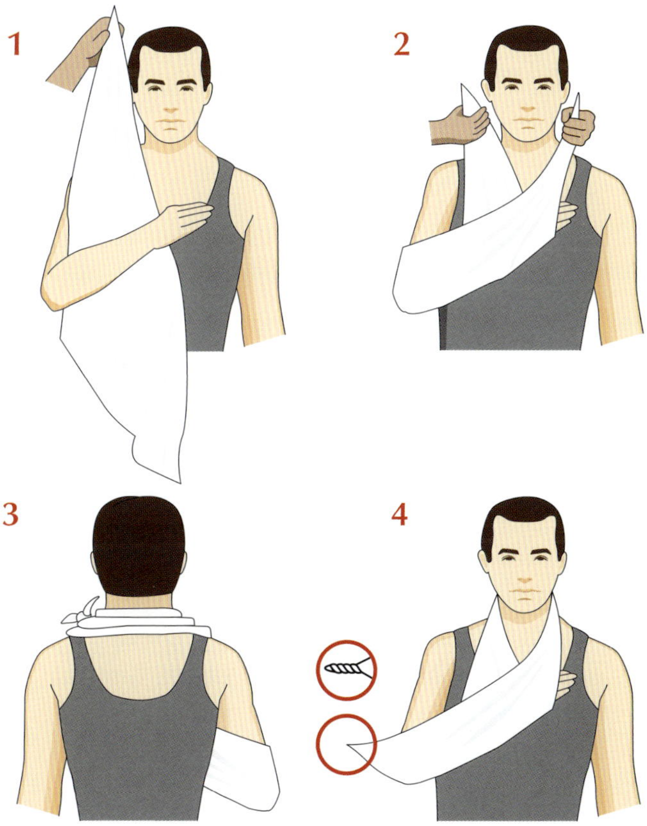

Collar and cuff sling

The collar and cuff sling (see diagram) is used for fractures of the humerus (upper arm). Fractures may slowly reduce with the gentle weight of the lower arm. On a moving vessel, adequate support may not be given, so bandaging around the whole upper body, going around the sling, will be helpful.

19 Fractures and dislocations

Fractures and dislocations are common on vessels and effective emergency treatment is a valuable skill. Treatment comprises prompt realignment of fractures and relocation of dislocations (termed 'reduction' of the fracture or dislocation) when possible; cleaning and dressing of wounds, especially those involving fractured bones (page 100); and applying splints, casts and traction (page 240).

The aim for all fractures and dislocations is to return the bones to their normal position. Doing this should reduce pain and increase mobility, reduce the risk to the blood and nerve supply of the limb, and reduce the risk of infection with open fractures.

Fractures may be:

- Undisplaced The alignment of the broken bones is normal (see diagram).
- Displaced The ends of the bones are put out of place to either side (see diagram).
- Angulated The ends of the bone are at an angle to each other (see diagram).
- Rotated One end is turned in the opposite direction to the other. This can happen when lines or other ropes become wrapped around a limb which then comes under load (see diagram).

Undisplaced fracture

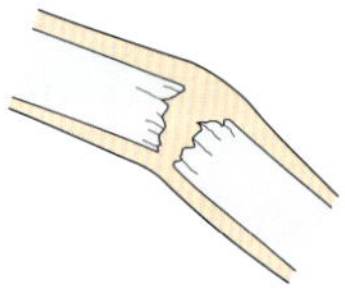

Angulated fracture

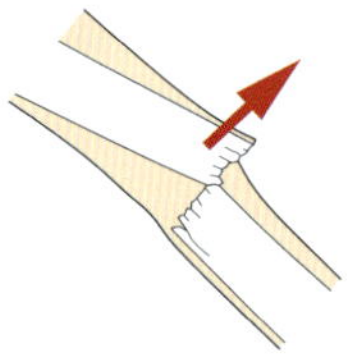

Displaced fracture

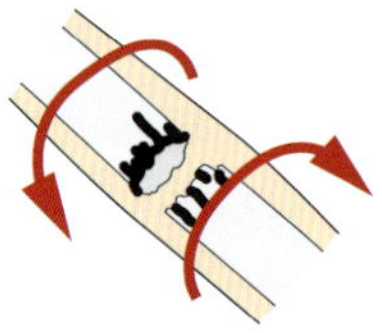

Rotated fracture

Bear these possible deformities in mind when you are trying to put the bones back to a normal-looking position.

Reducing a fracture or dislocation

- Aim to begin soon as possible and before the muscles go into spasm, which will tend to shorten the limb, making successful reduction more difficult.
- Find a stable position, and take usual precautions for setting up a procedure (pages 212–13).
- The casualty has to be relaxed and have plenty of analgesia because the procedure will be very painful:
  - Sedation: diazepam 5–10 mg orally
  - Analgesia: morphine 5 mg IM (repeat if necessary) or tramadol 100 mg IV or methoxyflurane inhaler (one only).
- Use gentle but firm traction. Reducing the fracture may take 10–30 minutes. Be patient and persist. Give more analgesia if required.
- Bones may return to the usual position with traction only.
- If they do not, try easing the fractured ends back together using direct pressure (see diagram).

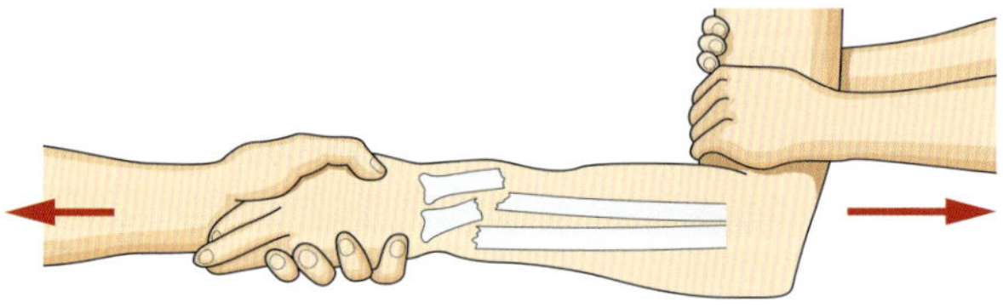

Gentle but firm traction for 5–10 minutes

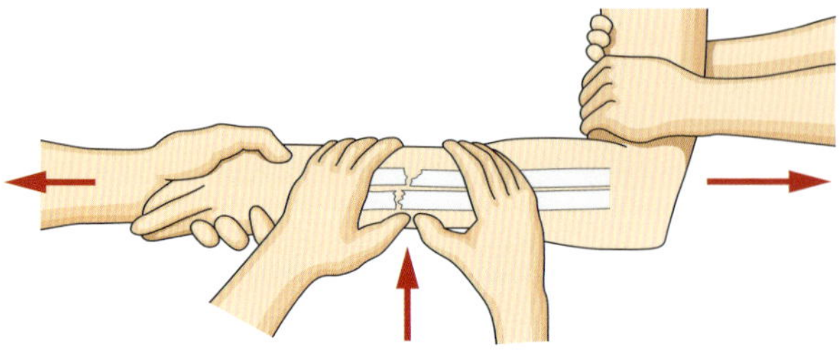

Press bones into normal position

- If any of the above manoeuvres increase the pain significantly, reconsider what you are doing. Check the blood and nerve supply (sensation) below the fracture. You may need to splint or support the limb as it is.
- Before releasing traction on a fracture, apply a splint to the limb (see below for splinting arrangements).
- Check pulses and blood supply to skin, and nerve supply (ability to feel soft touch) further down the limb after reducing a fracture or dislocation, and at frequent intervals until the casualty is evacuated.

Specific fractures and dislocations

Dislocated shoulder

You can use either of the following methods, but stop if bone grating is felt, and support the arm in a sling.

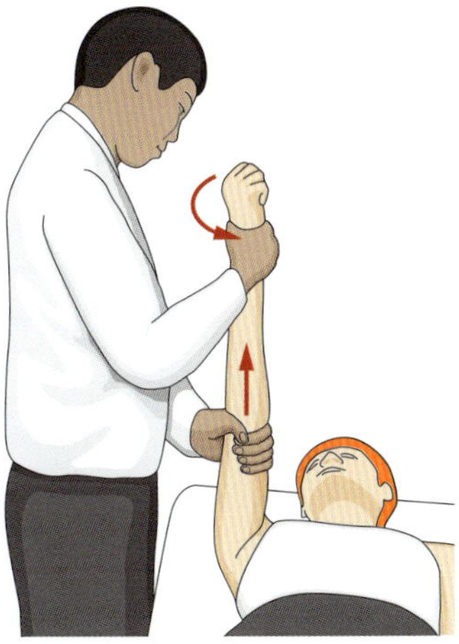

Method 1

- Lay the casualty on their back and grasp the dislocated arm around the wrist. Gently and slowly, lift it vertically.
- When in the vertical position, apply traction to the arm;
- While maintaining vertical traction, rotate the arm externally.
- If difficulty is experienced, feel the head of humerus in the armpit and gently push it in towards the socket to assist reduction, while maintaining traction with the other hand.

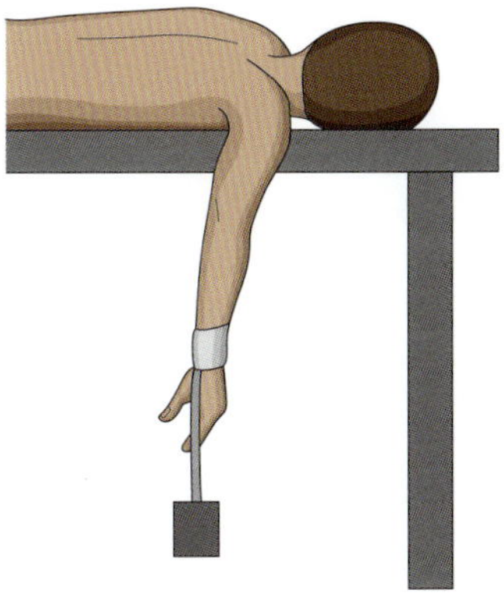

Method 2

- Lay the casualty face down on the galley table or bunk with the dislocated arm to the outside.
- Attach a 2–4 kg weight (depending on the size and musculature of the casualty) to the arm in the position shown in the diagram.
- Relaxation of the muscles, allowing traction and subsequent reduction of the dislocation, may take more than 30 minutes.
- After relocation, support the arm with a broad arm sling.

Fracture of the humerus

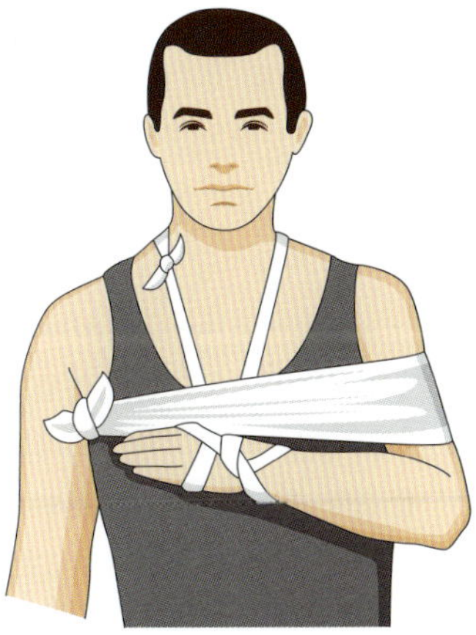

- Attempt manual realignment only if limb perfusion (pulses and skin blood supply) and nerve supply (sense of touch or ability to move fingers) are reduced when compared with the other side.
- Treat with a collar and cuff splint with the wrist brought up high, so the elbow hangs down with gravity and reduces the fracture (if sea conditions are rough add a bandage around the body and sling for extra support).

Elbow fractures and dislocations

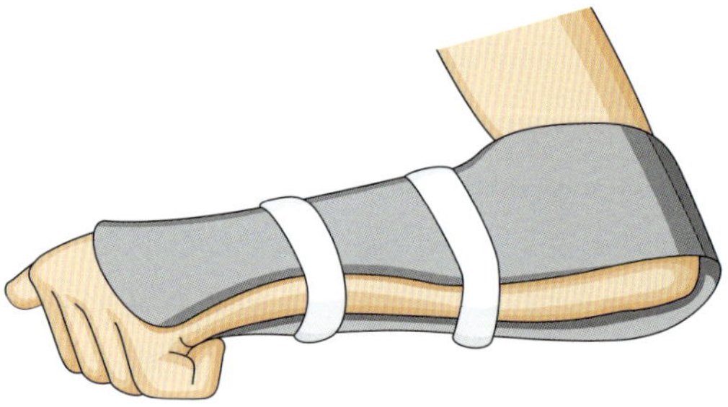

- The lower arm is nearly always pushed backwards through the elbow joint, and the bone may be just dislocated, or fractured as well. The elbow may be fixed slightly bent, but should straighten after reduction.
- Apply traction along the line of the arm, with an assistant holding the upper arm.
- As relaxation takes place, try gently bending the arm straight.
- You may hear a 'clunk' when the elbow has relocated.
- Support the arm with a splint (see diagram) and a broad arm sling.
- Check skin blood flow, nerve sensation and finger muscle movement in the hand as there is a significant risk to blood vessels and nerves from this injury.

Forearm and wrist fractures

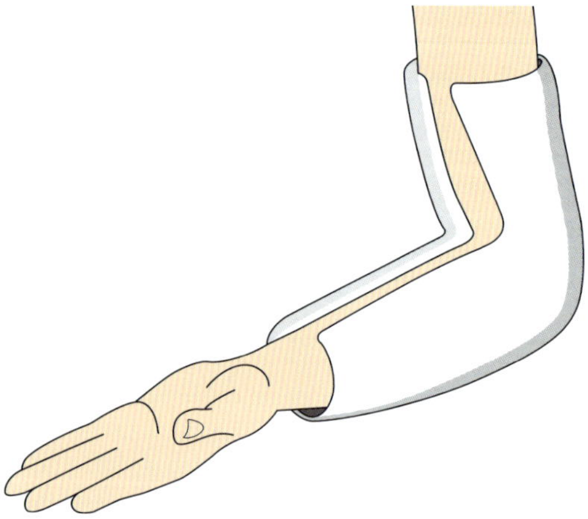

- Use the general approach described above. Immobilise the arm with a splint around the elbow and down to the hand (see diagram immediately above), curling the hand and fingers over something soft (e.g. rolled-up gauze).
- If time to evacuation will be several days, the splint could be replaced with a back-slab cast when time and conditions allow. The cast should run from above the elbow (held at 90°) to the hand (see diagram). Undertake this only under direct supervision of TMAS.
- Support the arm with a broad arm sling.

Finger and toe fractures and dislocations

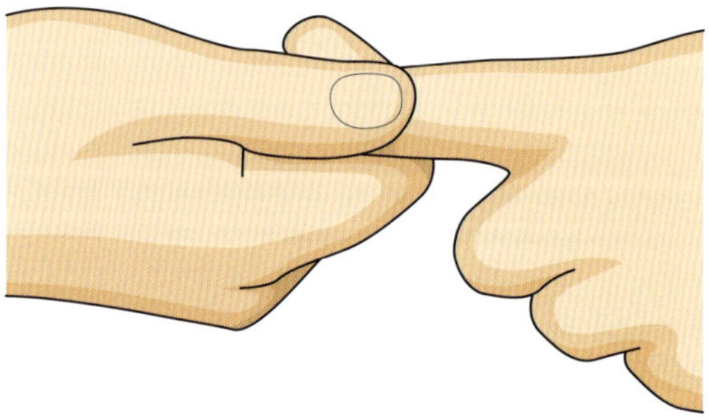

- Act quickly to realign any displacement after the injury before full sensation returns.
- If there is a delay, a ring block may be needed to ease the pain and allow realignment of any displacement (see page 244). Attempt this only under direct advice from TMAS.
- Pull the distal part of the finger (see diagram). There may be a pop when it relocates. The joint may require some pushing to get it back in line.
- Tape to an adjoining finger as a 'buddy splint' with a pad of gauze in between the fingers.
- If you think the injury was a dislocation, keep it immobilised for a week or so before mobilising. Keep fractures immobilised for at least several weeks.
- If an open wound prevents buddy splinting, use a piece of flexible splint moulded along the back of the hand (see diagram).

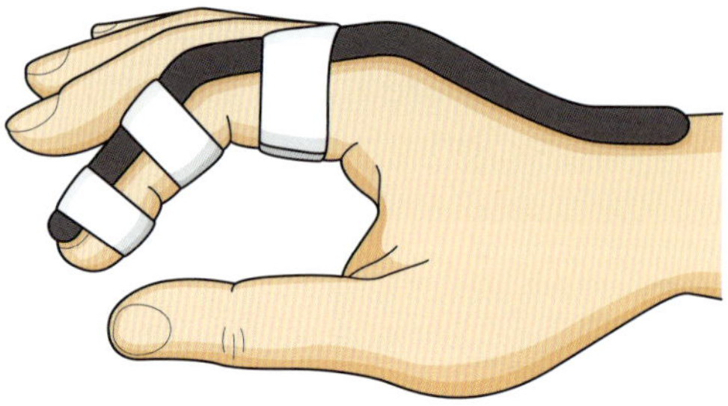

Hip dislocation

- The hip normally dislocates backwards, and leaves the leg rotated towards the midline (see page 98).
- Relocation should be attempted only if advised by TMAS. It requires very firm traction, and it will hurt.
- Use diazepam and morphine for sedation and pain relief, as explained above.
- Position the casualty on their back on the floor of the cabin.
- Bend the hip to 90° (this will hurt so do it slowly).
- Stand over them with their lower leg between your legs.

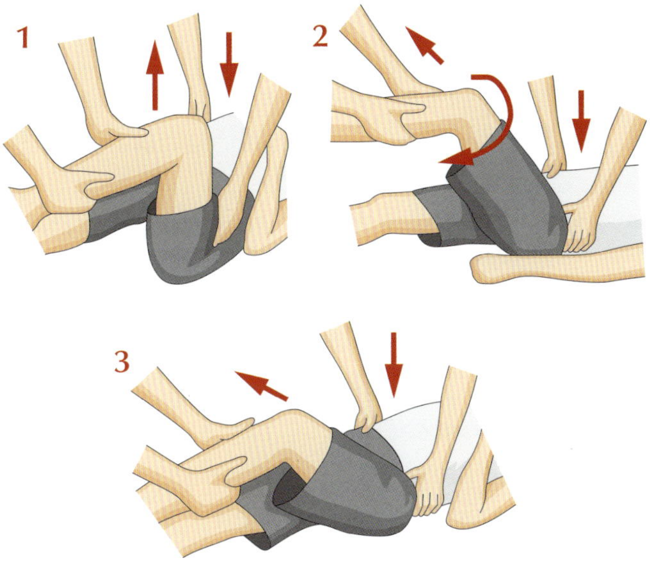

- Pull up on the lower leg behind the knee, while an assistant presses down on the casualty's pelvis to keep them from coming off the floor (see diagram 1).
- This will take some time (30 minutes or more), but as the hip relocates, rotate the thigh inwards (see diagram 2), and then carefully lay the leg down (see diagram 3) and strap it to the other leg, using padding between them.
- If there is a traction splint available, gentle traction may help keep the hip in place.
- Do not make more than three attempts to relocate the hip, and carefully check blood and nerve supply to the leg after each attempt.

Femoral and hip fracture

- Other injuries may be present, so treat the casualty in a systematic fashion (page 100).
- A traction splint (see diagram) is ideal for this major fracture. There are many types of traction splints with different methods of application (see page 240), but in general:
  - Provide as much pain relief as necessary.
  - Try fitting the traction splint to the uninjured leg, to get the size right, before moving the injured side.
  - Use only as much traction as necessary to reduce the deformity. Too much traction will cause further injury.
  - Check peripheral perfusion and nerve supply before and after applying the splint.

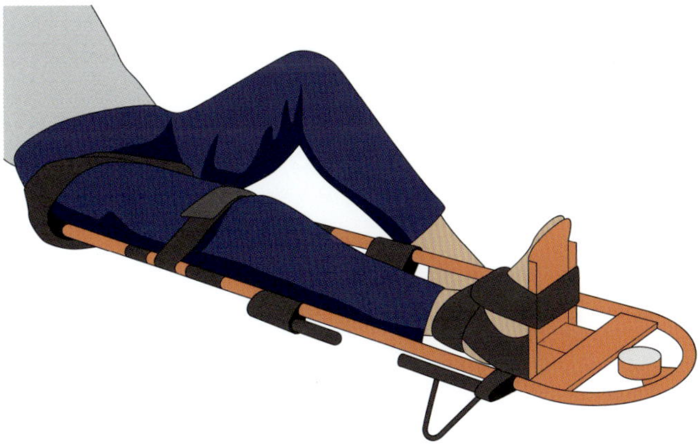

- If a traction splint is not available and cannot be improvised, use a simple immobilisation splint using any form of board, strapped down each side of the leg from armpit to below the feet (see diagram). Strap the legs together for extra support. Use plenty of padding between splints and leg, and between knees and ankles.

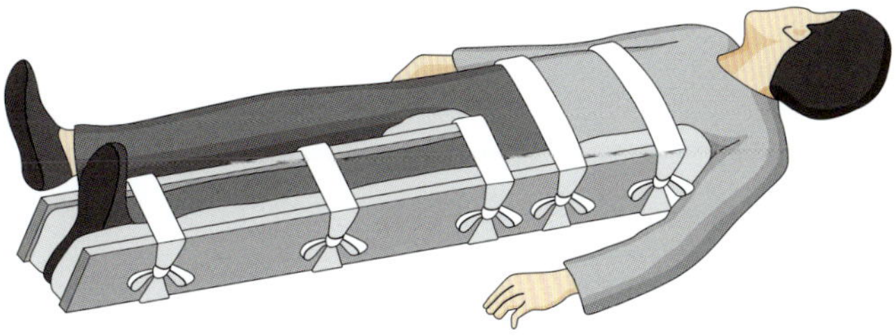

Lower leg fracture

- A lower leg fracture is reduced in a similar fashion to a fractured forearm.
- It is possible to use a traction splint to apply controlled, gentle traction to reduce deformity and apply a splint.
- A box splint (see diagram above) will adequately immobilise the leg, as will a malleable splint in a 'U' shape.
- It is very important to elevate the leg to reduce swelling, which can be very severe.

Ankle fracture and dislocation

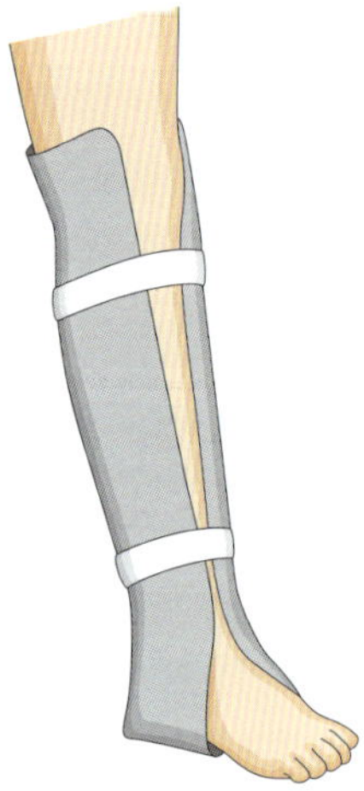

- The injury will commonly be a combined fracture and dislocation, and difficult to diagnose accurately on a vessel. Blood and nerve supply may be compromised.
- Reducing the fracture and/or dislocation requires reasonable force, and will be very painful. Use adequate pain relief and consult TMAS for advice on which medications to use and in what quantity.
- Apply traction to the foot, with an assistant holding the leg.
- Aim to get the ankle in line with the lower leg, with the foot in the normal position of 90° to the lower leg.
- Apply a 'U' shaped splint (see diagram) keeping the foot at 90°.
- Check perfusion and nerve supply. You may need to readjust if it is worse.

Part 5
Reference material

1 The body: structure and function

Introduction

The main purpose of this guide is to recommend how best to treat illness and injury at sea. An understanding of some aspects of the structure and functions of the human body is needed as it provides the rationale for many aspects of the management of medical emergencies.

Most of our conscious activities depend on the integration of information from sense organs (such as the eyes and ears) within the brain, leading to muscular movement. Many body systems, such as the heart and lungs, the digestive system and the kidneys, process and distribute the materials needed for our activities. Failure of any of these systems as a result of illness or injury can threaten the health and life of crew members.

Awareness, analysis, action

We are dependent on:

- Our senses (sight, hearing, touch, smell and taste) for information about our surroundings
- Our mind and brain, and what we have learnt during our lives, for the analysis and interpretation of this information
- Our muscles, bones and joints for taking action in response to such interpretations
- The network of nerves around our bodies that connect these processes.

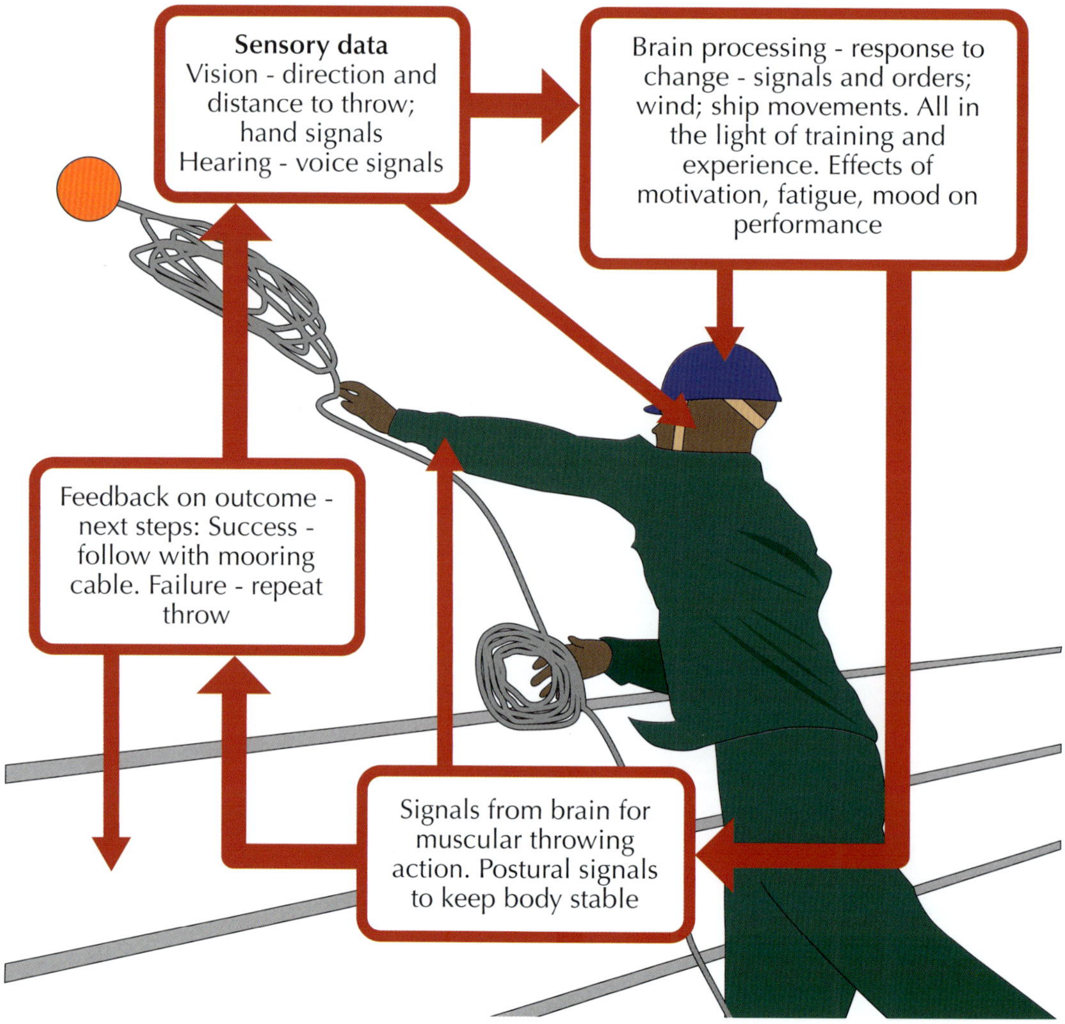

Awareness, analysis and action in a physical task

Failures to perceive, analyse and respond correctly to information about the surroundings of the individual and the vessel are the most frequent cause of maritime accidents and vessel disasters.

The ability to respond to emergency situations is often dependent on high levels of physical and psychological performance.

Vision and hearing performance vary, depending on distractions such as glare and background noise as well as on the effects of ageing on vision and hearing. Cold can reduce sensation in the hands (see page 44).

The brain's ability to prioritise and analyse information will increase with experience, but may be impaired by fatigue, alcohol, drugs and medication. Personality and mood also have effects on aspects of these processes (see page 182).

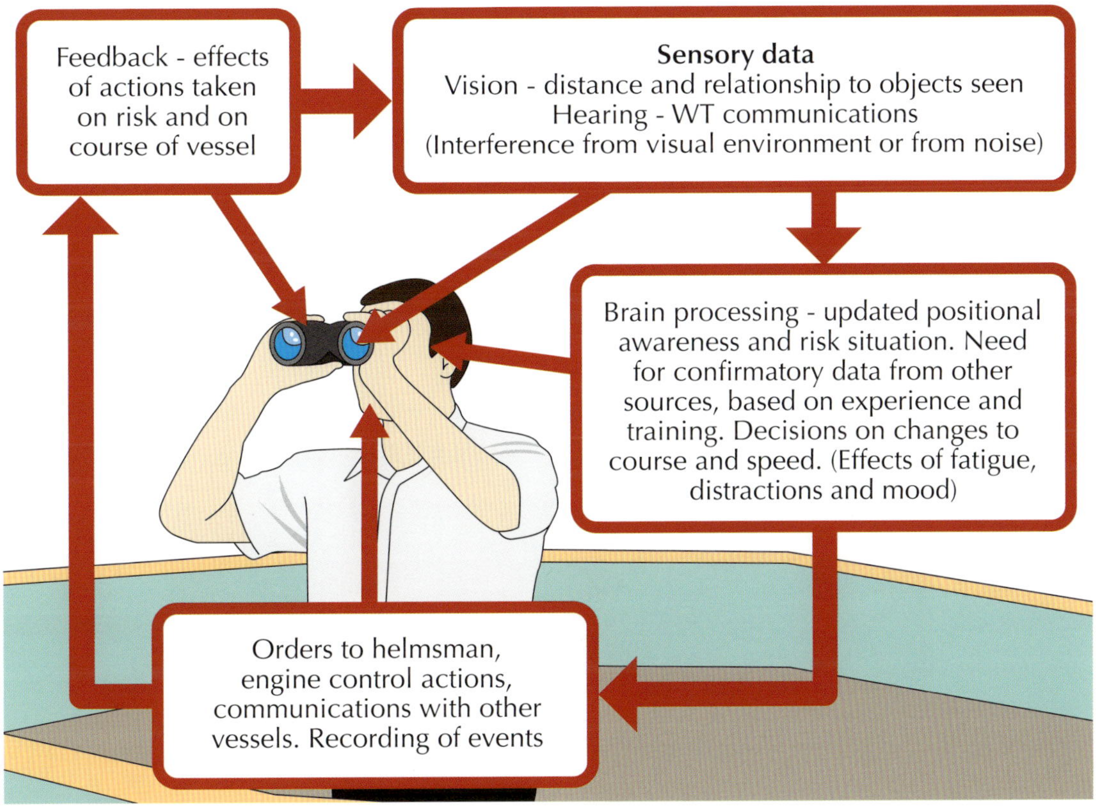

Awareness, analysis and action in safety-critical decision making

Effective muscular action requires full and pain-free movement of joints. Injury, overuse and forms of arthritis can impair this (see page 112).

Muscles move levers

Key points (see diagram):

- There are three parts to every muscle: origin, body and insertion (on the bone that moves)
- Tendons are at the end of muscles
- Muscles only contract (shorten) and relax
- Bones are levers that perform work
- Bones pivot at places called joints
- Bones are held together at joints by ligaments.

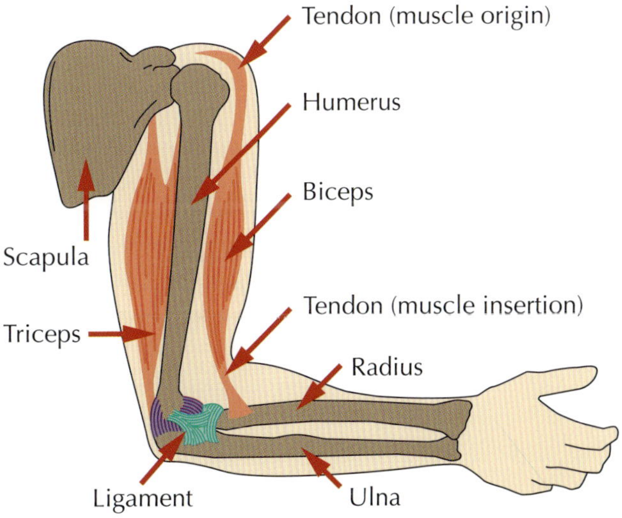

How muscles work

Tissue perfusion and energy supply

The key functions of our sense organs, brain, nerves and muscles, all of which define our individuality both at work and at leisure, require a constant supply of energy. An adequate flow of blood to and from all the tissues of the body (tissue perfusion) is essential to enable them to function effectively and remain viable. Within tissues transfer of substances to and from the capillaries to the cells takes place. Maintaining adequate tissue perfusion plays a key part in the management of medical emergencies. This is because perfusion:

- Supplies the nutrients and oxygen needed to generate energy
- Removes waste products and excess heat
- Conveys chemical messengers (hormones) that control aspects of cell function
- Provides the materials needed for continuing maintenance of cells and tissues.

The level of perfusion needed varies greatly between tissues. Some, such as the brain, require a constant high level while others, such as muscles, have demands that depend on the power and frequency of contractions.

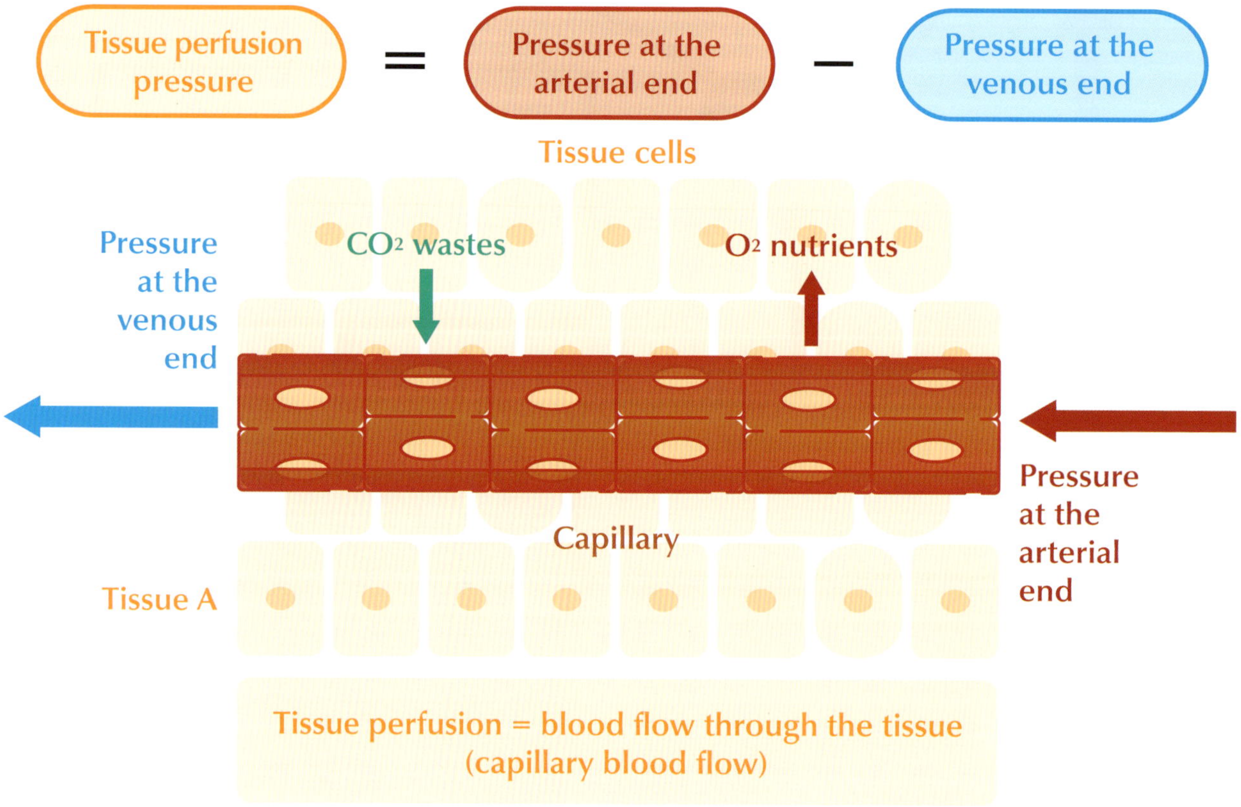

Blood flow through the tissues

What can go wrong?

Maintaining perfusion is a central part of emergency management. If blood or other fluids have been lost they need to be replaced. If they are not carrying essential materials such as oxygen and glucose then these must be provided urgently.

Inadequate function of any of the support systems described below will also adversely affect perfusion.

Support systems

Blood vessels and the heart

The high-pressure **blood vessels** (arteries) carry blood to all parts of the body. They split into ever-smaller vessels and eventually into the network of thin-walled capillaries that lie close to every cell, transfer nutrients to them and collect waste products. The blood returns in low-pressure vessels (veins).

The **heart** is a two-sided pump. The input to the left side is from the lungs and the output is to the aorta; this is the trunk artery off which all others branch. The input to the right side is blood returning from around the body and the output pumps blood through the lungs. The heart can massively increase its output when demands for oxygen and nutrients are high.

What can go wrong?

Blood vessels can become blocked: in particular clotted blood or other debris will, if it blocks an artery, lead to damage and then death of the tissues supplied by it. Blockages in the arteries of the heart (coronaries) lead to angina from oxygen shortage or to a heart attack if there is permanent muscle damage. Such damage may reduce the effectiveness of the heart as a pump or prevent it beating normally. Severe pain occurs.

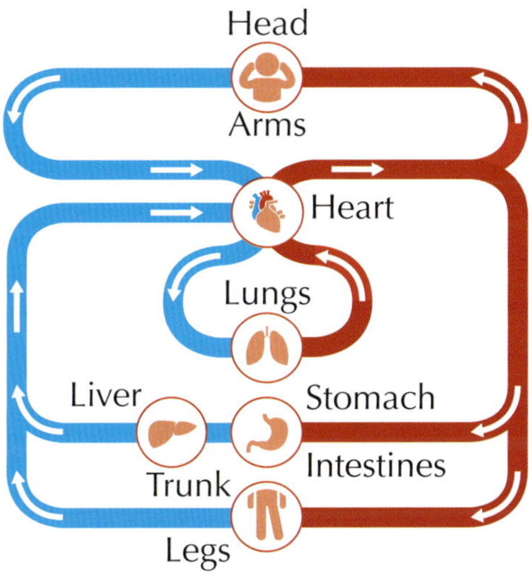

The heart and various circulations

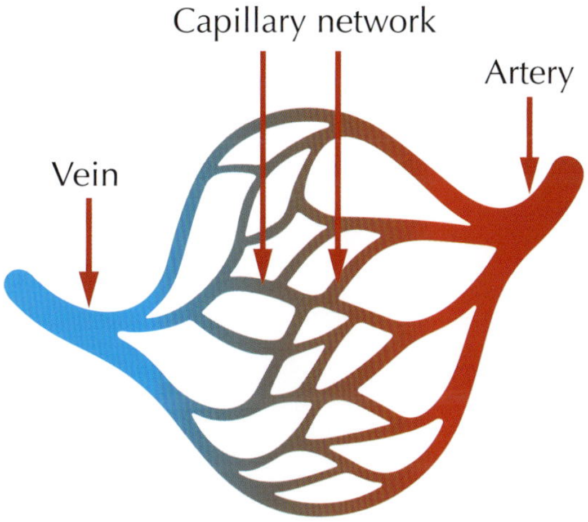

Capillaries

Strokes happen when arteries to the brain are blocked, and also when there is bleeding from them.

Pulmonary emboli occur when clots formed in the leg veins come centrally and lodge in the pulmonary arteries.

Internal bleeds from weak or damaged arteries can cause blood loss into the digestive system or body cavities.

Anaemia (haemoglobin shortage) reduces the ability of the blood to carry oxygen to the tissues of the body.

Unfitness from lack of regular exercise reduces the ability of the heart to support hard physical work of the sort that may be needed in an emergency.

The lungs and breathing

The **lungs** exchange gases with the air. This is breathed in by muscular actions of the diaphragm between the chest and the abdomen, with help from muscles between the ribs and in the neck when demands are high. Air is filtered in the nose and is distributed around the lungs by a branching tree of ducts (bronchi). The air comes into close contact with blood in the terminal air sacs of the lungs (alveoli) which have a very large surface area. The blood coming into the lungs has a high concentration of carbon dioxide carried in solution. This moves out from the blood into the alveoli and is then removed from the body by breathing out. At the same time the haemoglobin in the red cells of the blood takes up oxygen from the air, ready to transport it to all parts of the body.

What can go wrong?

Because of the large volume of air passing in and out of the lungs the respiratory system can become infected. Most commonly this takes the form of coughs and colds but more serious infections, such as bronchitis and pneumonia, can arise in the bronchi and lungs.

Infections, allergies and irritants can lead to narrowing of the airways, causing asthma and wheezing. This can occasionally be life-threatening.

Muscles of the diaphragm and chest wall are the force behind breathing. Their movements cause negative pressure in the chest cavity to draw air in. If there is any leakage of air (pneumothorax), blood or other fluid into the space between the chest wall then the lung will collapse and function will be impaired. Inflammation in this space causes severe pain with each breath.

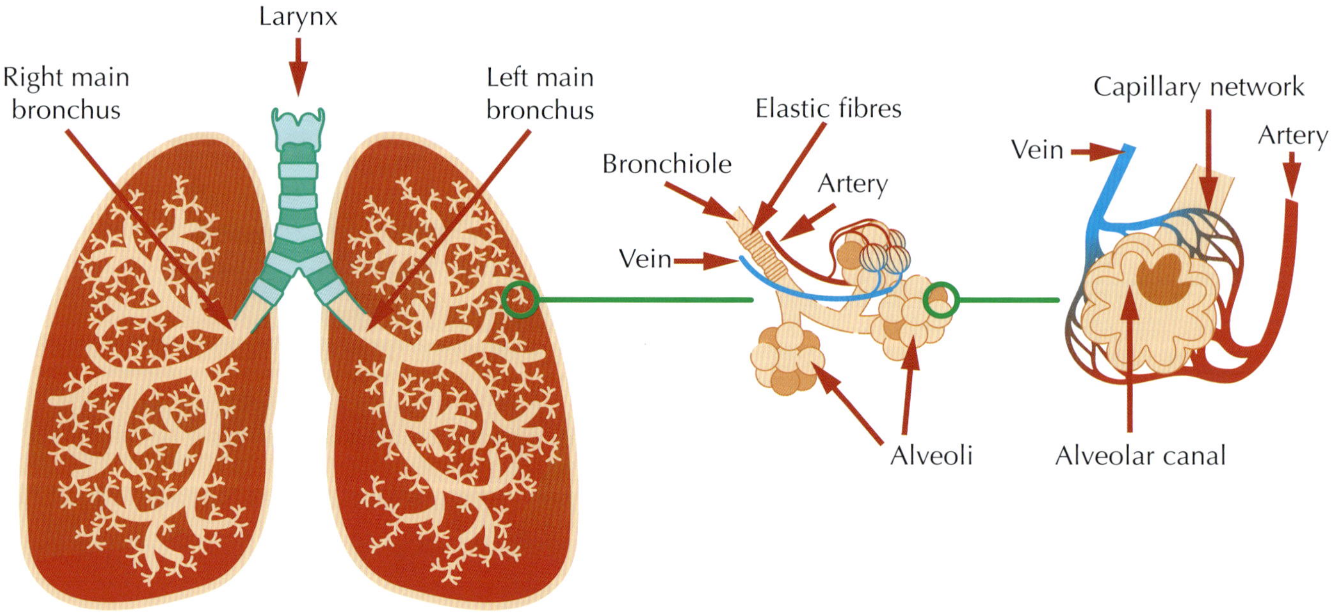

Lungs, bronchi and alveoli

The digestive system

Food is mechanically broken down in the mouth and then chemically processed as it moves through the stomach and small intestine, aided by enzymes and emulsifiers provided by glands in the wall of the gut and from the pancreas and gall bladder. Sugars, fats and proteins are absorbed in the small intestine and transported to the liver, where some are stored and processed. Some enter the bloodstream for circulation to user organs. The large intestine absorbs water from the gut contents leaving the residue ready for excretion as stool (see diagram on page 91).

What can go wrong?

Dental pain is a common cause of incapacity in crew members. The gullet and stomach can be harmed by irritation, usually from food or alcohol, or by infection, usually from contaminated food or water, leading to vomiting. Similarly the lower bowel can be affected with diarrhoea. Blockage, bleeding or leakage from any part of the digestive system can lead to a medical emergency. If this blockage is either from gallstones or within the liver then jaundice occurs. The pancreas also secretes insulin into the bloodstream; failed production or resistance to its effects causes diabetes. Imbalances in water intake cause dehydration, while over-consumption of food results in obesity with its many complications.

The kidneys and urinary system

The two **kidneys** filter the blood, removing water and water-soluble waste products from it. The kidneys are able to adjust the flow of urine depending on a person's state of hydration. Urine passes down tubes (ureters) from the kidneys into the bladder, where it is held until it is excreted through the urethra (see diagrams on page 157).

What can go wrong?

Infection of the bladder is common. If waste products are over-concentrated in the urine they can form stones, leading to severe pain and sometimes blockages (see page 158).

Control of support systems

We are aware of some controls, such as the effects of exercise on heart rate and breathing, but many take place without any conscious perception of their existence. There are a range of sensors in the body that detect levels of substances such as oxygen, carbon dioxide, glucose, salts and water. These trigger either nerve impulses, for instance to speed up the heart or respiratory rates, or the release of hormones, such as adrenaline, which prepares the body to respond to physically stressful situations. Other sensors initiate patterns of behaviour, such as relieving hunger and thirst or emptying a full bladder and bowels.

Defence mechanisms and the skin

The body needs to maintain a stable internal environment to function effectively. This can be threatened by external conditions. As the barrier between the body and its surroundings, the skin is central to many of these defence mechanisms (see diagram below).

The **skin** and its derivatives, nails and hair, have several functions:

- The durable surface protects underlying tissues from mechanical trauma and is thicker where this is most severe (e.g. palms and soles).
- Water is conserved as the skin prevents evaporation of tissue fluid.
- Skin pigment reduces damage from ultraviolet light.

- There are multiple nerve endings in the skin that detect touch, pain, heat and cold. It is therefore an important sense organ. These sensations are also essential for feedback when holding or manipulating objects with the hands.
- Body temperature control depends on the skin. When it is cold little blood flows through the upper layers and hairs are erect ('goose flesh'). When it is hot the blood flow increases greatly and sweating is initiated.
- The skin has a built-in mechanism for control of bleeding, wound healing and responding to infections.

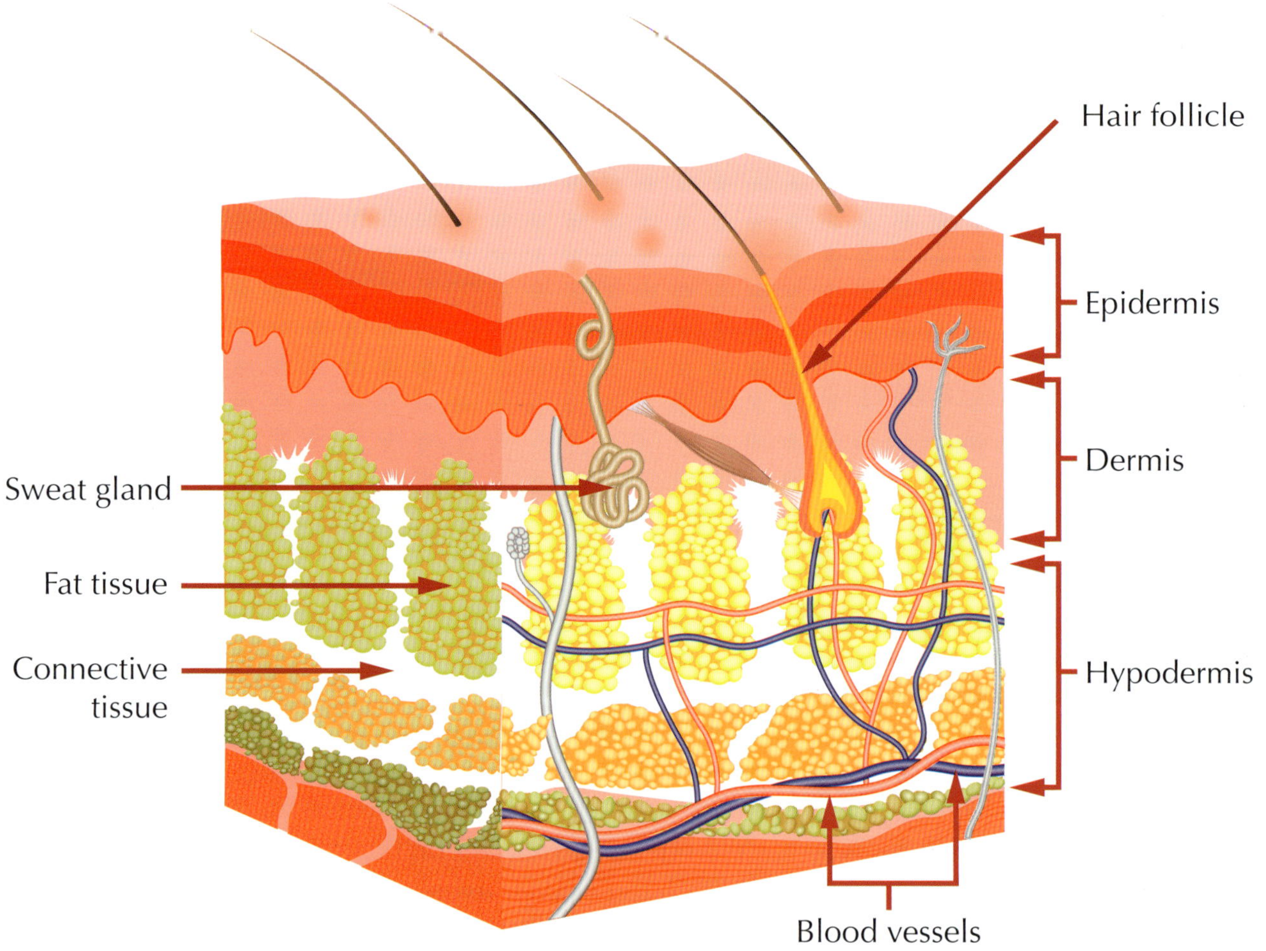

Cross-section of the skin

What can go wrong?

Acute trauma to the skin from cuts, grazes and burns is common. In the medium term exposure to friction, irritants or allergens can lead to soreness and dermatitis. Skin infections are frequent. They may complicate trauma or dermatitis, but they can also arise without this. Repeated exposure to strong sunlight causes skin pigmentation and can lead to skin cancers.

- **Blood clotting** Except when a major blood vessel is damaged, clotting controls wound bleeding. A series of chemical reactions take place that lead to the creation of a web of protein fibres that control the bleed. These form a scab which gives temporary protection while a wound heals and also keeps out infection.
- **Inflammation and wound healing** Any damage to tissues, both in the skin and elsewhere in the body, initiates the process of inflammation. Chemical messengers are released from the damaged cells and this leads to migration of specialised cells to the area. These can neutralise infection and replace blood clots with fibrous tissue to close the wound. Where specialised tissues such as bone are damaged bone-building cells move in.

- **Wound infection** Inflammation is the initial response to the presence of a source of infection. Some of the cells that arrive are capable of ingesting bacteria and other infectious agents, thus neutralising them. Others produce antibodies that neutralise them, or are triggered to do so by the presence of a novel infectious agent. These processes are accompanied by redness, swelling and soreness of the infected area and death of cells can lead to pus formation.
- **Bleeding** Cut surfaces will heal more quickly if the sides are held together. Bleeding may need to be controlled by pressure or haemostatic dressings. Infections may get out of control and need antibiotics to kill the infecting organisms.
- **Allergies** Sometimes non-infectious material can trigger the production of antibodies or the growth of immune cells. This can be the basis for allergic reactions to foods, medications and other substances. Common allergic illnesses include asthma and skin conditions such as eczema and some forms of dermatitis. Rarely, allergic responses can cause circulatory collapse in anaphylaxis (see page 42).

Lifecycle changes

Ageing

Increasing age brings greater experience, but some capabilities steadily decline with age; for instance the ability of the eye to focus from close-up to infinity and its ability to adapt to changes in light levels. Many illnesses increase in frequency with advancing age. These include diseases of the arteries such as heart attack and stroke, and cancers, where groups of cells escape from the control mechanisms that keep the body's tissues and organs functioning in a co-ordinated way. External factors such as diet and smoking also play a part in causing these illnesses and hence lifestyle changes can be an important aid to prevention.

Reproduction and childbearing

Gender has little effect on most aspects of working and living at sea. The differences in sex organs lead to some differences in the patterns of disease at sea (see diagrams on page 157). Reproduction can be effectively controlled by contraception, with different methods available to males and females. Bleeding from the vagina at the end of the female menstrual cycle may be associated with pain. Pregnant crew members can have specific care needs and there are some medical conditions related to pregnancy. Childbirth should not take place at sea, but if it is imminent contact TMAS for advice on its management.

What can go wrong?

Both genders can develop infections that are sexually transmitted, especially after unprotected casual sex (see page 159).

Males can develop infections of their testes and prostate gland; the prostate can also enlarge and block the flow of urine. Twisting of the testis can obstruct its blood supply (see page 158).

Females can have disabling bleeding and pain during their menstrual cycle. Inflammation of the reproductive organs in the pelvis can be the cause of fever and abdominal pain (see page 152).

Pregnancy may end prematurely in a miscarriage. There will be pain and vaginal bleeding. Occasionally the embryo may be implanted in the tubes leading from the ovaries rather than in the uterus. Such ectopic pregnancies end with rupture of the tube leading to severe abdominal pain and sometimes bleeding (see page 154).

2 Medical records

It is essential to keep reliable and comprehensive records of medical incidents occurring on board. Such records are to:

- Set down the history and examination findings from a casualty to help decide the appropriate action to take
- Follow the progress of a person with an illness or injury, in particular to record any changes in their vital signs
- Record all treatments given
- Hand over information between crew members when more than one cares for a casualty
- Provide the information needed when a casualty is discussed with TMAS
- Note the advice given by TMAS and the actions taken based on it
- Enable a full set of medical information to be sent ashore with any casualty who is evacuated or landed in port.

Certain other sets of health-related records also need to be kept. Many of these will form part of the vessel's safety management system (SMS) requirements:

- Information from statutory medical certificates of fitness for embarking crew on merchant vessels. Record any restrictions on their duties and the time before their next medical examination is due.
- Any additional medical information recorded on new crew members because of company policies on fitness criteria or company requirements to disclose medications. This may be collected so that medications are not considered contraband and do not risk problems with port state control officials.
- The master or medical officer may make enquiries about fitness to be at sea or obtain a medical report, where such information is not a statutory or company requirement, in leisure activities such as yachting or when non-crew members are carried on board (see page 268).
- Records of exposure to risk from work activities.
- Monitoring data on food and water hygiene.
- Information on incidents that lead to injuries or occupational illness.

All these record sets, in addition to assisting with immediate operational or treatment needs, are also needed if there are concerns about the adequacy of health protection measures or about the appropriateness of casualty management. Records of the use of medications and medical equipment are important for stock control, so that replacements can be ordered for items that are used or become out of date. There are additional recording requirements for controlled drugs such as morphine.

Confidentiality

Any record containing personal medical information on a crew member is a sensitive confidential document that must be held securely, with access limited to those who need the information in the interests of the clinical management of the casualty. In all but unconscious casualties, consent from the casualty must be obtained before passing information to others, even when they are providing care. Compliance with the UK Data Protection Act and the General Data Protection Regulations is required.

The nature of medical emergencies at sea is such that confidential medical information frequently has to be shared using unsecured methods of communication. This may include telecommunications, radio, and also internet-based media such as email, voice-over internet protocol (VOIP) and Skype/FaceTime etc.

It is essential that all those who have access to personal medical information recognise that it must not be shared with third parties, except when this is in the best interests of the casualty.

Record keeping

Medical records may be kept in paper or electronic format. Images and video are useful supplements to text, as well as providing a visual record for transmission to TMAS or other health care providers.

Access to clinical records should be restricted to those responsible for care of the casualty. Arrangements are needed for secure storage and for data back-up on board. Policies should be in place for the archiving of records that may need to be reviewed in the future.

The content of the record will depend on its type. All records of medical care need to include the name and date of birth of the casualty, the time at which the entry was made (this should be immediately after an observation was taken, a medication given or a procedure performed) and who made the record.

MCA form MSF 4155, which is compliant with the requirements of the MLC, provides a comprehensive means of recording information for an individual. This form can also be used when a casualty is evacuated or referred for medical care ashore when in port.

Forensic records

Detailed records, with validation from more than one witness where possible, are required in the event of allegations of assault, rape or other criminal activity as these may provide key evidence for any subsequent legal action. Contact TMAS immediately for advice on the clinical evidence that should be secured if there is any suspicion of violence. Photographic evidence of injuries should be recorded at the earliest opportunity and then repeated if there are any visible changes. The setting in which the alleged crime took place should also be fully recorded in photographs and sketches.

Where people are rescued from the sea and need treatment on board, detailed records, with the fullest possible identity and nationality information, should be taken.

It is essential to keep detailed records of any deaths on board as these may be required for statutory investigations (see Appendix IX, page 306).

3 Responsibility for healthcare at sea

The vessel's master is formally responsible for health and medical care at sea, but on larger vessels this responsibility is commonly delegated to a senior deck officer (known as the medical officer). In addition, many crew members have training in first aid and are expected to be able to act effectively in the early stages of an emergency (i.e. as a first responder) until the medical officer arrives. All crew members are also required to follow precautions designed to prevent injuries and work-related disease, and to take reasonable action to maintain their general health.

The medical officer, when acting in this role, must recognise that they have a duty of care to ensure that all practicable measures are taken to protect and preserve health, and that these responsibilities take precedence over other non-safety-related aspects of vessel operation.

The ethical responsibilities of the master and medical officer to the casualty are summarised in the *Medical Guide for Seafarers* (Seahealth Denmark):

- Be loyal.
- Be professional.
- Be informative.
- Observe confidentiality.

The medical officer's duties are as follows:

- Maintaining the sick bay in good order and immediately available for use. On smaller vessels, ensuring there is a designated area for treatment of ill or injured crew members, with arrangements for it to be dedicated to this use whenever needed.
- Maintaining the vessel's medical stores in good order. This includes ensuring:
  - all the items specified in the list of medical stores are present
  - medications are stored according to the makers' instructions
  - all out-of-date or used medications are replaced at the earliest opportunity
  - all out-of-date or spoiled medications are disposed of safely and legally
  - records are kept of all medications used, particularly the register of use of controlled drugs such as morphine
  - all medical equipment is kept tidy, is clean, is sterile when necessary and in working order (e.g. by replacing or charging batteries)
  - the contents of first aid bags and, where accessible, first aid equipment in lifeboats and rafts, are checked at regular intervals and replaced.
- Oversight of disease prevention measures on board, including:
  - food hygiene
  - water quality
  - crew vaccination status, taking into consideration the likely ports of call, both planned and possible
  - use of antimalarial medications if the vessel is visiting ports where malaria is a known risk
  - adequacy of screening to prevent flying insects that may carry diseases from entering internal vessel accommodation compartments
  - hygiene arrangements for shore-based workers coming aboard the vessel, taking into account the spectrum of disease present in the port
  - isolation and other precautions needed to control the spread of infectious diseases among crew members.

- Managing accidents and illness arising during a voyage using this guide as the basis for treatments, and consulting TMAS whenever there is serious injury or illness. TMAS should also be consulted whenever there is any uncertainty about the correct way to proceed.
- Making arrangements, with other relevant parties including TMAS and the appropriate coastguard, to evacuate casualties or divert the vessel to disembark casualties in need of urgent medical attention.
- Ensuring arrangements are in place so that crew members with medical or dental problems which require action in the next port of call are investigated or treated in an adequate and timely way.
- Maintaining full and confidential records of all cases of illness and injury on board, and ensuring these are archived for retention on a regular basis. You should only disclose medical information to other crew members or the employer with the permission of the casualty. This information should always be restricted to that which is required to ensure case management is appropriate (see page 258).
- Ensuring all crew members presenting with a medical condition are treated with respect and that they are aware that the medical officer is there to help them and will respect their wishes for confidentiality as far as this is possible.
- Recognising that health beliefs may differ between different ethnic groups on board and their knowledge of English for maritime usage may not be sufficient for adequate discussion of medical problems. Translation guides such as *Multilingual Questions for the Medical Assessment and Treatment of Seafarers* may be helpful (https://www.iswan.org.uk/resources/publications/multilingual-questions-for-the-medical-assessment-and-treatment-of-seafarers/).

Management of pandemic diseases such as COVID-19

In the event of an infectious disease causing a pandemic, close attention will be mandatory, to avoid spreading the infection through the crew, passengers and local population.

Detailed planning should include:

- Prior training of medical officers and other crew in the critical aspects of on-board management
- Identification of isolation regimes
- Treatment capability on board
- Monitoring of crew and passengers
- Provision of personal protective equipment
- Evacuation route pre-planning.

4 Continuing care

Once a casualty has had initial treatment for any illness or injury, decisions will need to be taken to guide subsequent management. For serious cases, management should be based on advice from TMAS.

The requirements for continuing care will depend on the nature of the initial illness or injury. This includes both subjective aspects, such as pain and malaise, and objective aspects, such as the presumed cause of the condition and possible complications.

The transition from initial response to continuing care will be highly dependent on the location of the vessel, the facilities and medical expertise on board, and the timescale of possible transfer to on-shore medical care.

Care planning: monitoring, treatment, dependency

Continuing care requirements may include:

- Monitoring of the casualty (e.g. appearance, conscious state, level of pain, vital signs) to assess response to treatment and detect onset of complications (see Appendix VI, page 294)
- Provision of active medical treatment
- Provision of normal requirements, such as fluids, nutrition, sanitation
- Stabilisation until evacuation is feasible
- Physical and psychological support
- Time for recovery or healing.

The level of care required will vary widely and will depend on the nature and severity of the illness or trauma; i.e. whether high- or low-dependency care is needed, and the answers to the following questions about the casualty and their duties on board.

Low dependency

The casualty has normal living arrangements. Care decisions are normally taken on board as they will be dependent on local patterns of duty:

- **Can the casualty immediately return to normal duties?**
  This will depend on a full range of relevant capabilities, lack of safety-critical impairment from the condition, and any consequences from it such as fatigue and side-effects from medications. The answer will relate to their duties; for example, a cook may be unfit to return for a period following a skin infection or diarrhoea while other crew members could be fit to do so.
- **Can the casualty perform restricted duties?**
  This will depend on the ways in which their normal duties can be adapted on board. Restricted duties will usually be better for both the casualty and their colleagues than a period of complete inactivity.
- **Is the casualty unfit for duties but able to care for themselves and remain in their usual cabin while joining other crew members for meals and leisure activities?**
  This will apply if they are able to care for themselves on board but their condition makes any form of duty impracticable or potentially dangerous.
- **Does the casualty have specific care needs?**
  These would include regular observations or medication.

High dependency

The casualty needs care in the vessel's sick bay or equivalent. Care decisions are normally based on TMAS recommendations:

- **Does the casualty need to be isolated from other crew members because of a risk of spreading infection?**
  This will usually be because of an infectious disease that can spread to the respiratory or gastrointestinal systems of other crew members (see page 162).
- **Is the casualty's level of care such that they need to be in the vessel's sick bay?**
  This may be because of severe limitation in mobility or self-care.
- **Is continuous observation of the casualty by the medical officer or an allocated crew member required?**
  This may be required to assess their response to treatment and to detect the onset of complications. Also, a casualty may require continual observation due to behavioural abnormalities caused by mental health problems, or altered states of consciousness caused by severe illness or trauma.

Careful planning is needed for transfers of high-dependency cases, whether around the vessel (e.g. from the location of an incident to the sick bay) or from either the location of the incident or the sick bay to the point of disembarkation by boat or helicopter (see Appendix III, page 282, Transport of a casualty).

Records and monitoring

The transition from immediate to continuing care provides an opportunity to ensure that full details of the original emergency and its circumstances are recorded. This record should also include the initial treatment given, TMAS advice and the use of medical stores (with a prompt for reordering).

It is essential to find out if the casualty has any pre-existing medical conditions and in particular if they are on any long-term medication. Advice will be needed on the management of such conditions and whether to continue medications, modify their dose or stop them completely.

Good record keeping thereafter is needed to monitor trends in vital signs, the state of fluid balance and the overall condition of the casualty. In more serious cases, a care plan should be devised, to provide prompts for care needs, timing of monitoring, the administration of medication or the changing of dressings.

Update records whenever an observation is taken or a treatment given. All crew members allocated to care duties must know what is required in terms of record keeping. Give the date and time of all entries and give the name of the person making them.

These records may need to be reviewed with TMAS if the casualty is to remain on board, and a copy will need to accompany the casualty if or when they are transferred to on-shore medical care.

You should keep standard documents for the recording of vital signs, for communication with TMAS, and with onshore care providers. Templates of these documents are provided in Appendices V and VI on pages 291, 294 and on the back flyleaf.

Caring for high-dependency casualties on board

Unless a high-dependency casualty can be rapidly evacuated, care will be either in the vessel's sick bay or in a cabin converted for this purpose. Ideally there should be sufficient space to access the bed from both sides. Dedicated washing and toilet facilities are essential for the use of both the casualty and their carers, as are good lighting and ventilation (preferably with a port or window) and peaceful and calm surroundings. Direct telephone and internet access in the medical facility will enable TMAS to communicate directly with both casualty and carers, and has the potential allow a video link and transmission of monitoring data.

The elements of continuing care for a high-dependency casualty are observation, treatment and general support:

Observation

- Vital signs (e.g. heart rate, blood pressure, respiratory rate, temperature, oxygen saturation, conscious state; see page 294)
- Complications such as infection or return of symptoms such as breathlessness, chest pain, vomiting or diarrhoea
- TMAS may advise on other specific observations that relate to the casualty's condition (e.g. urine dipstick testing, blood glucose)
- The nature of body fluids (e.g. vomit, urine, stool, sputum, nasal secretions)
- Skin problems on parts of the body in contact with the bedding (i.e. pressure sores).

Treatment

- Ensure an adequate fluid balance (see page 220).
- Administer the casualty's medications. This will, unless advised otherwise by TMAS, include long-term medications taken for pre-existing conditions (see page 266).
- Change their dressings and treat wounds (see page 58).
- Provide any other treatments indicated or recommended by TMAS; for instance, heat or cold packs or compresses for a musculoskeletal injury or cooling for fever or hyperthermia (see page 50).

General support

- There should be a bell or other means of communication from the sick bay to a continuously manned part of the vessel (such as the bridge) and responding to this must be a priority.
- Food and drink: respect the preferences of the casualty unless advised by TMAS that they need a restricted diet. Meals should be regular, with a good balance of nutrients and plenty of fibre from grains and vegetables, as this will reduce the risk of constipation. Fluid and non-alcoholic drinks should be freely available.
- Care of bed and hygiene: if the casualty is safely able, encourage them to wash or shower each day. This will provide an opportunity for carers to change bed clothes as necessary. If they are bed-bound, a daily wash from a bowl should be offered, with either the casualty or the carer performing it.
- If the person is safely mobile, encourage them to use the toilet. If not, a urinal or bed-pan should be used. This will often require assistance and in some cases they may need two carers. As much privacy as feasible should be allowed, but assistance with intimate tasks is preferable to loss of self-esteem from soiling the bed.
- Good care requires supportive human contact. Unless the casualty needs to be isolated, encourage other crew members to visit and chat, especially those with a common language, provided this is not too tiring for the casualty.
- Where a casualty is suffering from hallucinations, delirium or acute confusion, communication will be difficult and can, in some circumstances, worsen the condition. In such situations it is wise for two carers to work together, to provide support and a chaperone function.

5 Pre-existing medical conditions

Some crew members will be fit to work at sea but will have a continuing medical condition. They may be taking regular medication and may need repeat prescriptions or other forms of follow-up.

When a person becomes ill or is injured at sea they should be asked about their use of medications and any pre-existing medical condition. Contact TMAS early for advice.

Assessing existing or new medical conditions

- Crew members who hold a current statutory medical certificate of fitness will have had their health assessed within the last two years by an MCA Approved Doctor or by a doctor approved by another recognised maritime authority.
- An ongoing medical condition or disability may not be a bar to continued employment at sea, provided that it can be managed in a way that does not increase risks to the crew member, to others on board or to the vessel.
- Crew members must inform their approved doctor or issuing authority of any significant change in their medical condition, new or changed medication, or period of absence from work for medical reasons of over 30 days. The approved doctor will then decide whether their fitness category needs to be reassessed.
- The crew member is subsequently not obliged to disclose their condition on board. It will have been taken into account when the approved doctor either issued their medical certificate or reviewed their fitness in the light of a new condition or treatment.
- If a crew member declares, or is found to have, a new medical condition, it is important to enquire whether their fitness has been reviewed since it started. If not they should be referred to an approved doctor as soon as practicable.

Follow-up of existing medical conditions

- Regular follow-up on shore is needed for most ongoing medical conditions.
- Fitness to work at sea may sometimes be monitored and controlled by issuing a time-limited fitness certificate.
- Leave periods may also need to take account of the scheduling of follow-up appointments.

Existing medical conditions and new illnesses or injures

- If a crew member becomes ill or is injured, it is essential to ask whether they have any pre-existing condition or are taking any medications, as this may affect their response to such an illness or injury. Such an altered response may make it more difficult to assess them and may affect decisions regarding their immediate care.

Long-term medications

Common conditions for which long-term medication is prescribed include high blood pressure, raised cholesterol and diabetes:

- Any crew members on long-term medication should carry sufficient supplies for their whole period at sea, with additional stocks to cover over-runs of voyages.
- Crew members should continue to take the recommended dose, unless TMAS advises a change in dose.
- If crew members are unable to take their medication, for instance because of vomiting, ask TMAS for advice regarding further management.

Some long-term medications, such as anticoagulants, may severely limit work at sea because of their potential complications. Other medications, such as anti-epilepsy treatments, may indicate a medical condition that is usually incompatible with work at sea.

Prescribed medications, especially strong painkillers that can be abused, may be prohibited in certain countries. Where this is the case, the master will need to check whether any crew member is on such treatment so that it can be declared. It is good practice for any crew member who is prescribed a medication that could be subject to such prohibitions to carry a formal letter from the prescribing doctor indicating that it is being used to treat a medical condition.

Use of 'as required' medications

Sometimes medicines are prescribed for use in the event of a recurrence of a condition. These include treatments for asthma and known allergies. Contact TMAS if such a prescribed medicine fails to adequately treat the symptoms of the condition.

Aids to living and working at sea

- Glasses, contact lenses and hearing aids can be lost or damaged.
- It is essential for crew members to carry spares as well as sufficient consumables, such as hearing aid batteries, to cover the period at sea.
- Those who wear aids to vision and hearing must use them when performing safety-critical tasks that depend on these senses.
- Joint replacements, usually of the hip or knee, enable pain-free mobility. In the event of an injury to a joint that has previously been replaced, or should symptoms develop in its vicinity, you must consult TMAS urgently for advice.
- Heart pacemakers may be fitted to prevent disabling or life-threatening symptoms. Fitness to work at sea is conditional on a prescribed frequency of specialist follow-up.
- Chronic diseases of the bowels may be treated by removal of parts of the intestine and the use of a stoma and bag to collect stool. Users are trained in how to manage their stoma, but need cabin space with washing facilities to do so. They may have problems in the event of acute diarrhoea. If this arises, seek advice from TMAS.

6 Passenger health

The vessel's crew will be of working age and will have had their medical fitness to work at sea assessed prior to employment. Passengers may be from a wider age range and may have pre-existing medical conditions that would not normally be found in crew members.

Ferry passengers

Ferries carry large numbers of people of all ages, usually near to coasts and for short periods:

- Crew may be called upon to assist with illness and injuries in children, older people and those who have long-term illness or disabilities.
- Standard ship medical stores and the standard training of vessel medical officers may not meet the potential requirements for care in these groups.
- Some ferries on longer passages may carry a nurse or paramedic who will have such skills and who will have appropriate medical stores.
- There will often be passengers on board who have healthcare training and who respond to a request for assistance from a senior officer. For this reason some larger ferries are required to carry a 'doctor's bag' containing additional medications and equipment for use only by medically qualified individuals. It is the master's responsibility to decide whether to call upon health professionals among the passengers to assist with a particular medical situation. They are also responsible for briefing the health professional on the practicalities of care on board and, if requested by the health professional, to formally request them to use their skills to provide treatment. This will simplify the legal position of the health professional in the event of the quality of care being questioned.

In all other situations the vessel's medical officer will need to manage the situation:

- Make early contact with TMAS.
- Do not give medication to children without TMAS advice.
- As most ferries will be within helicopter range for most of the time and will reach their destination within a few hours, the preferred option will often be initial stabilisation of any serious health condition or injury, and early referral for ongoing care once on shore.

Cruise ship passengers

Most passengers will be on board for several days and are likely to be further from shore:

- Generally, all such ships are required to carry at least one ship's doctor.
- The doctor will work from an on-board medical centre and have range of medication and medical equipment that is far more extensive than that specified for other types of vessel.
- The ship's doctor will be responsible for the delivery of healthcare to both passengers and crew members, but officers with medical care training and other crew members may occasionally be called on to assist.
- Many cruise companies have their own arrangements for specialist telemedical support for their ships.
- The ship's doctor will advise the master on the need to call for helicopter evacuation or to divert to evacuate a seriously ill passenger or crew member. It is the master's responsibility to decide on the actions to be taken, based on this advice.

Adventure cruise passengers

Passengers are on board smaller ships visiting remote places, with activities ashore which may be inherently risky:

- A ship's doctor may be part of the crew.
- Arrangements are required to assess and minimise risk to passengers both on board and ashore. These may include a requirement or recommendation for medical insurance cover for the cruise and associated activities, medical screening of passengers and risk management for high-risk activities.

Evacuation or diversion to land of seriously ill or injured passengers or crew can be complex and costly. The cruise operator needs to make contingency plans for this.

Scientists, technicians, security contractors and embarked maintenance staff

Most of these passengers are likely to be working-age adults:

- They may not have been medically screened prior to embarkation and so may have medical conditions that could pose a risk at sea.
- Personnel such as divers or those in transit to offshore structures will have had some form of employment fitness assessment as a requirement for their other duties.
- Treat such personnel as recommended in this guide, but contact TMAS early if they have any pre-existing medical condition.

Family members of crew

The vessel's safety management system (SMS) should include procedures for the carriage of family members of crew if this is company practice. This may include requirements for a pre-embarkation medical or a medical certificate of fitness as well as suitable insurance to cover evacuation, diversion of the vessel and repatriation in the event of a medical emergency:

- As for all child passengers, dependants of crew members who are not adult should not be treated with adult medications.
- Contact TMAS early in the event of any illness in a child.

7 Port calls and crew health

Health clearance is required when a vessel enters port. Port calls provide an opportunity to arrange medical care for crew members (and passengers). Crew can be exposed to health risks while in port. If they go ashore they may be at risk of injuries.

Formalities

An International Declaration of Health may have to be completed and submitted to port health authorities prior to docking, in the format required by the port, either directly or through the vessel's port agent. This declaration is required to obtain advance information about any infectious diseases among crew members and to avoid unnecessary delays in docking. A completed declaration will enable *free pratique* to be issued (ie permission to enter the port in the absence of infectious disease on board). This will allow immediate berthing, provided there have been no deaths or illnesses on board which the authorities wish to investigate. The Standard World Health Organization form can be found on pages 56–57 of the International Health Regulations (2005), third edition, at https://www.who.int/publications/i/item/9789241580496

Port state control inspectors or health officials may come on board to review the vessel's healthcare arrangements and food hygiene as part of their inspections. They commonly investigate the state of the medical stores and the validity of the crew's medical certification. They may apply sanctions if these are deficient. Their priorities often include detecting out-of-date medications and record keeping for controlled drugs. They may also investigate crew members' personal medications; if the crew member has a letter from the prescribing doctor stating the medication is needed for their health it may reduce any potential problems.

Ill and injured crew members

Ill or injured crew members may need to be referred for medical or dental investigations and treatment. It is often difficult to arrange for this if the port visit is short. The ship manager or port agent may be able to arrange appointments in advance of berthing and thus expedite the process. The more information that is available to them about the nature of the patient's conditions the easier it will be to make appropriate and effective arrangements. Prior discussion with TMAS may also help by providing an assessment of the condition in medical terms, and sometimes by identifying the correct route for referral.

If it is not possible to complete the consultation before the vessel departs, it will be necessary to delay departure, repatriate the crew member (making sure that they have all their possessions and documents with them), or postpone investigation or treatment. Any such postponement should be done only with advice from the doctor who is managing the case, and with the agreement of the crew member.

Crew members may need to be repatriated directly, based on the recommendation of TMAS. Consultation with ship managers and insurers/repatriation service providers should occur prior to berthing.

Crew health risks in port

All crew members will need to be fully immunised against the risks present in the port area. They will need to be provided with, and strongly recommended to take, malaria prophylaxis appropriate to the local strains of malaria where there is a risk of infection. The vessel owner or operator should obtain information on the correct prophylaxis and ensure that it is available on board in advance of arrival. Those going ashore are likely to be at greater risk of infection than those remaining on board.

If there is epidemic disease in the port region it may be appropriate to prohibit all crew members from going ashore.

Depending on the risks present in the port and surrounding area, but especially if there are endemic diseases present, disinfection procedures may be required for on-board facilities used by port-based workers. If stevedores and other port staff are coming on board, sanitary provisions such as fresh water and separate lavatories may be required.

Embarking crew

New crew members should have a statutory medical certificate of fitness to work at sea valid for the flag state of the vessel. Such certificates should be reviewed on embarkation, and any restrictions or time limitations should be actioned.

Crew will often be embarking after lengthy journeys, sometimes involving changes of time zone. They should be given sufficient time (at least 24 hours) to recover from the journey and significant time zone changes before taking on safety-critical duties.

Medical stores

Ship medical stores must be checked, arrangements made to replace medicines that have been used up, and any out-of-date ones sent for disposal. The port agent or ship managers can make arrangements for this but formal ordering must be by means of a requisition from the vessel's master. It can be difficult to replenish supplies of controlled drugs such as morphine in some ports, so this needs to be planned in advance.

Outdated or spoiled medicines need to be disposed of in accordance with the statutory regulations of the port country. A maritime pharmacy supplying new medications will normally be able to arrange legal disposal of out-of-date medicines.

Food and water

Poor quality or contaminated food or water can harm the health of the crew. When resupplying the vessel's stores it is important to get confirmation that the food has been grown, manufactured and stored under good conditions. Water may need to be treated before use if the source is suspected to be of poor quality.

8 MCA regulatory requirements for medical care of crew members

The following Merchant Shipping Regulations and Merchant Shipping Notices issued by the Maritime and Coastguard Agency (MCA) are the basis for the provision of medical care at sea on UK flagged vessels:

- Merchant Shipping and Fishing Vessels (Medical Stores) Regulations 1995 (SI 1995/1802) and MSN 1905(M+F)
- Merchant Shipping (Maritime Labour Convention) (Minimum Requirements for Seafarers etc.) Regulations 2014 Part 9 MSN 1841(M) and MGN 482(M)
- Merchant Shipping (Work in Fishing Convention) Regulations 2018 Part 6
- Merchant Shipping (Standards of Training, Certification and Watchkeeping) Regulations 2022 and MSN 1865(M)
- The Fishing Vessels (Certification of Deck Officers and Engineer Officers) Regulations 1984 and MGN 411.

UK regulations are based on international conventions or regulations. Similar requirements are in place for most other maritime nations. Most requirements are specified in Title 4.1 of the International Labour Organisation (ILO) Maritime Labour Convention, 2006 (MLC) and Part 7 (Articles 29 and 30) of the ILO Work in Fishing Convention, 2007 (ILO 188). The full conventions can be downloaded from the ILO website. These requirements are ratified by nations that are members of ILO and form the basis for national regulations. The key requirements of these conventions are broadly similar, but with less detailed requirements for the fishing sector, in particular for vessels of less than 24 metres in length.

The MLC covers the following aspects of medical care for crew members on board and ashore:

- A duty on all countries that ratify the convention to provide health protection, medical and essential dental care, for crew members serving on vessels flying its flag. These include measures to protect occupational health, including any special preventive and treatment requirements relevant to duties on board.
- Health protection and medical care for crew members should be as comparable as possible to that available to workers ashore, including rapid access to treatment facilities. In particular crew members must have the right to visit a medical doctor or dentist when in port, wherever possible.
- Medical care and health protection service for crew members must be free of charge to crew members when on board or landed in a foreign port. Services need to include health promotion and education initiatives.
- A standard confidential report form should be used for medical communication between those providing medical care for crew members.
- Flag states are required to have laws or regulations that specify requirements for on-board medical care facilities. These need to include carriage of a medicine chest, medical equipment and a medical guide. Arrangements for regular inspection of these by a competent authority are needed. The details of their contents are to be determined according to the numbers of crew and the voyage pattern of the vessel.

- Vessels with 100 or more people on board on international voyages of over three days must carry a medical doctor. States are free to specify any other vessels that are also required to do so. Where no doctor is carried, one crew member must be designated as responsible for medical care or medical first aid, depending on the crew size and length and nature of voyage. They need to be trained according to the requirements of International Convention on Standards of Training, Certification and Watchkeeping for Seafarers, 1978, as amended (STCW).
- Flag states shall provide a telemedical advisory service (TMAS) to vessels. This should include access to specialist advice and must be available continuously. This should be available free of charge to all vessels.

These regulations provide a comprehensive framework for medical care. There is additional detail in other parts of the MLC and the Work in Fishing Convention; for instance on medical fitness certification.

The International Maritime Organisation (IMO) STCW convention covers the training requirements for medical care, while other conventions cover the provision of search and rescue services and precautions when carrying dangerous cargoes.

The requirements for a vessel's medical chest, medical equipment and medical guide are set by the flag state. There is no mandatory international list. The UK's requirements are currently in Merchant Shipping Notice 1905(M+F). The World Health Organization International Health Regulations give the requirements for the control of infectious diseases and for declarations when entering port.

The obligations under all the requirements derived from international conventions and incorporated in national regulations that apply on board are subject to inspection by flag and port state control inspectors, with sanctions applicable if the requirements are not met. These conventions also provide for crew members and those in the fishing sector to have access to complaints procedures if they consider that their healthcare does not meet the requirements of the relevant convention.

9 Work-related health risks

In addition to the high risk of injury among crew members, there is also a danger of ill-health caused by risks arising while crew are working at sea. Some diseases develop over many years; for example, deafness from exposure to excessive noise and chronic lung diseases caused by exposure to air pollutants. Others, especially some forms of poisoning, can develop rapidly and may require immediate treatment at sea. Mental health problems may also become apparent and the crew's living and working conditions can contribute to these.

Prevention of work-related diseases is the responsibility of vessel owners and operators. Precautions are specified in several publications including technical standards, the *MCA Code of Safe Working Practices for Merchant Seafarers* and in conventions, recommendations and guidelines issued by the ILO and IMO.

Some risks are common to most sectors of the shipping industry; these include exposure to heat, cold or chemical agents used in machinery spaces, galleys and in vessel maintenance. Others are limited to certain sectors, such as those arising from chemical and some other cargoes, or from activities such as the catching and processing of fish.

Work-related health risks

Examples include:

- Physical agents, such as vibration, noise, heat and cold (see pages 44 and 50).
- Chemicals which may cause poisoning, such as fuels, flue gases, solvents, detergents, acids and caustics, toxic cargoes or gases emitted from cargoes. These agents are most likely to enter the body via the lungs when breathing polluted air, or can contaminate the skin and eyes (entry by mouth from contaminated hands or food is rare as an occupational risk). However, accidental or intentional poisoning from swallowing medicines or other poisons can be a medical emergency (see page 178).
- Biological agents causing infections, such as hepatitis A in crew members working on sewage systems, or allergic reactions caused by organic cargoes.
- Repetitive movements, sustained awkward postures and inappropriate or ill-advised manual handling may lead to musculoskeletal pain.
- Excessive work demands and bullying contribute to mental stress and this may lead to more serious mental ill-health (see page 182).

Implications of identifying a work-related illness

- The crew member affected may need to cease the type of work that caused their illness, either permanently or until they have recovered.
- If one crew member is affected, others doing the same tasks may also be at risk and steps can be taken to identify them at an early stage.
- The illness may indicate that precautions are inadequate or are not being properly followed. It may be necessary to review the compliance with and efficacy of precautions to ensure that others are not put at risk.
- If the cause of a suspected work-related illness cannot be identified, further investigation will be needed to formulate new preventive measures. These may then be adopted across the industry to prevent similar cases.

Features of work-related illness

- A short time between a task with a risk of exposure and the development of an illness. For example, a crew member enters a confined space that may have a toxic atmosphere and subsequently develops breathing difficulties. A crew member's skin is contaminated with a solvent and it subsequently becomes itchy and sore.
- Indication of a risk to health on a material hazard data sheet or warning label on a product.
- The crew member affected suggests that their illness is linked to a recent task.
- More than one crew member is affected while doing a similar task.
- Certain symptoms appear (e.g. breathing difficulties, a feeling of dizziness and intoxication, skin irritation, soreness of muscles and joints, and mental distress). However, many forms of work-related disease share symptoms with non-occupational conditions; for example, wheezing and coughing or skin irritation. Crew members with a pre-existing non-occupational symptom are more likely to develop similar symptoms after a work-related exposure.

Responding to suspected work-related illness

- Treat casualties: follow instructions included in Part 1 (Emergency care), Part 2 (Trauma), and Part 3 (Medical disorders).
- Check if any other crew members are affected.
- If it is safe to do so, all crew members should cease performing the task thought to have caused the illness until the recommended precautions have been checked.
- Review the recommended precautions, including those given on any material safety data sheets. Take action to improve current precautions if these are inadequate or inaccurate.
- Contact TMAS with information on all crew members affected for advice on continuing treatment and prevention.
- Discuss proposed actions with company management and fully document all plans.
- Fully document all aspects of the incident and follow-up actions.
- Certain occupational illnesses on UK flagged vessels must be reported to the MCA (see MSN 1850 (M) or subsequent revision).

Part 6
Appendices

Appendix I: Medical evacuation by helicopter

Evacuation may become necessary for medical reasons. This may involve transfer by helicopter if no other possibility is available, or if medical urgency requires a rapid evacuation.

Such an operation involves risk to the casualty and crew of the vessel and helicopter. It is undertaken very rarely so up-to-date knowledge and experience among the crew may be limited.

Training exercises are invaluable so take advantage of any opportunity to do these.

The normal limit for helicopter rescue is within 200 nm of operational base.

Prior to any medical evacuation, a document should be completed describing all aspects of the incident and the casualty. This can be a confidential medical report form (MSF 4155), or an ATMIST AMPLE form. See Appendix III.

Evacuation methods

The normal methods for helicopter evacuation are:

- **Heaving-in line (Hi-line)** A line is lowered to the vessel and used to haul in the hoisting line, which is then used to retrieve the casualty, with the vessel's crew arranging the hoist on deck, under instruction from the helicopter crew.
- **Helicopter winching** A winch person is lowered to the vessel, and is then in full control of preparations for evacuation of the casualty, using a strop or stretcher. This is usually the preferred method as the rescue crew remain in full control of the rescue.
- **Helicopter landing** Rarely used as most vessels do not have helipad facilities. If it is used, full compliance with regulations covering helicopter ship operations must be maintained (e.g. IAMSAR Vol 3).

The *ICS Guide to Helicopter/Ship Operations* (a priced publication) covers this topic as it relates to merchant ships. It is available at https://www.ics-shipping.org/publications/guide-to-helicoptership-operations-fifth-edition/

Communicate

Good communication with shore and helicopter crew is essential to ensure coordination and to convey medical information regarding the casualty. The Aeronautical Rescue Coordination Centre and Maritime Rescue Coordination Centre will advise on the appropriateness of the evacuation. The helicopter usually carries a paramedic.

- Helicopter evacuation is requested through HM Coastguard when in UK waters. Local arrangements vary elsewhere.
- A good crew briefing is essential beforehand – it will be too noisy when the helicopter has arrived overhead.
- Communicate with the helicopter on VHF Ch 16. SATCOM and HF may be used at long range.

Prepare

- Refer to Appendix III for guidance on general preparation for evacuation of the casualty.
- Use gloves to minimise electrical shocks/rope burns. A static discharge (electrical earthing) lead hangs down from the winch person. This should not be touched.
- Clear the deck of loose objects. Clear the port stern quarter of obstructions.

- The casualty should be dressed and ready (with medical records, mobile phone, passport, other personal documents, money, credit card attached).
- All crew should wear lifejackets and other personal protective equipment if required.
- Use a bucket, into which the initial hi-line will be coiled.
- A flag or pennant should be displayed to indicate wind direction to the helicopter pilot.
- At night, any landing area to be used should be well lit, but avoid shining bright lights at the helicopter as that will temporarily blind the helicopter crew.

Position

The vessel should steer a steady, straight course (relative wind on the port bow or on port tack if a sailing vessel), with the helicopter hovering off the port quarter (the pilot normally sits in the right-hand seat; see diagram 1).

- The vessel should make enough speed to maintain steerage way.
- Rescue will take place from the starboard door of the helicopter and the port side of the boat (see diagram 2).

Method

- Do as the helicopter crew tell you – they are the experts.
- A weighted line (hi-line) may be lowered from the helicopter initially. Do not touch it until it has earthed in the water or on the vessel. Coil it into the bucket.
- Alternatively the winch person may descend straight away.
- In either case, **do not attach any line to the boat and do not let it get snagged**, particularly on any crew.
- Follow the directions from the helicopter crew, or the winch person when they arrive on deck.
- A double strop or stretcher may be used.
- In rough weather, recovery may be from a life raft trailed astern, from a vessel tender, or directly from the water.
- If necessary for indicating location, use a hand-held red flare or orange smoke as a signal. Do not fire parachute or mini-flares when the helicopter is close by.

1

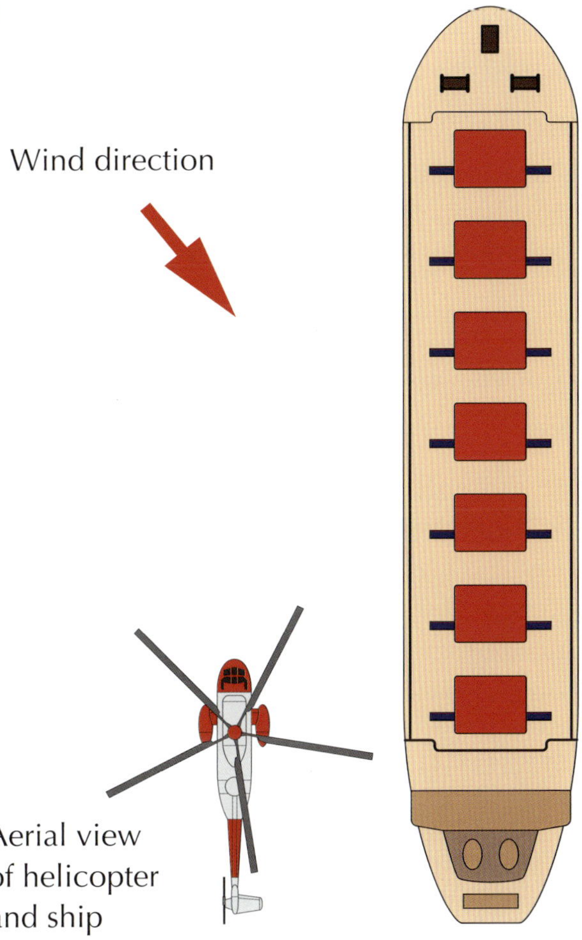

Aerial view of helicopter and ship

2

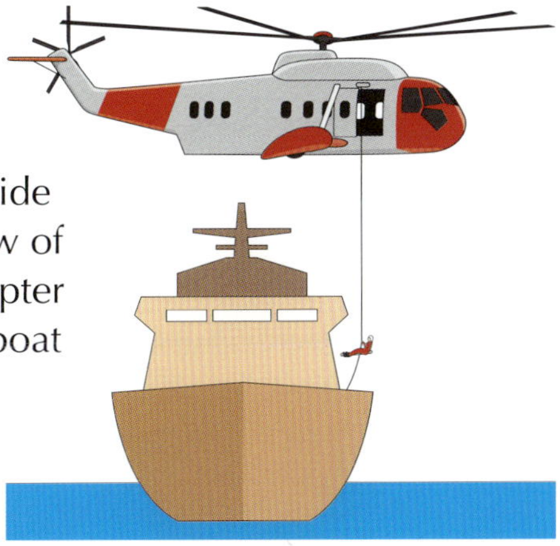

Side view of helicopter and boat

Appendix II: Medical evacuation by boat

Evacuation may become necessary for medical reasons. This may involve transfer to another vessel, which may be larger or smaller than the transferring vessel.

Such an operation involves risk to both of the vessels, the casualty and boat crews. It is undertaken very rarely, so up-to-date knowledge and experience among the crew may be limited.

Training exercises are invaluable; take advantage of any opportunity to do these.

Evacuation may be to a variety of other vessels:

- Commercial vessels, which may be larger or smaller, but with better facilities
- Naval vessels, which may have considerable medical facilities and personnel on board
- Fast boats from shore, which can rapidly transfer casualties. They may carry medical resources and personnel.

Evacuation methods

Vessel-to-vessel evacuation of a casualty may be achieved in a variety of ways:

- Direct transfer from one vessel to another, depending on the relative vessel sizes, sea state, weather conditions, access platforms and ladders
- Using a vessel tender or rigid inflatable boat, which may be deployed from either vessel
- Using a lifeboat or raft launched from the transferring vessel
- Transfer by placing the casualty in the water, suitably protected with dry suit, emergency position-indicating radio beacon (EPIRB) etc, to be retrieved by the evacuating vessel. There are obvious risks to this method, and it requires careful contingency planning by both vessels.

Communicate

Good communication with shore resources (such as Coastguard and Maritime Rescue Co-ordination Centre (MRCC) and the other vessel is essential to ensure coordination and to convey medical information regarding the casualty:

- Both vessels will need to coordinate their course and speed.
- An estimate of time to evacuation is essential. The casualty needs to be prepared and ready for transfer just in time, but not too early, as being placed on an evacuation stretcher is uncomfortable, and makes monitoring the casualty more difficult.
- A good crew briefing beforehand is essential. Consider what may go wrong, and what corrective actions may be required. All crew involved in the transfer should be involved in the briefing.
- The casualty should also be informed, if appropriate.

Prepare

- Refer to Appendix III for guidance on general preparation for evacuation of the casualty.
- Consider the time of day for the transfer. Daylight transfers are inherently safer, but the condition of the casualty will dictate whether delay for daylight hours is appropriate. This may require discussion between the vessel medical officer and TMAS if available.
- Choose an appropriate method for protecting the casualty for the transfer, such as an evacuation stretcher if the casualty is not capable of independent or assisted mobility.

- The casualty should be dressed and ready (with medical records, mobile phone, passport, other personal documents and money or credit card attached).
- Ensure that if the casualty requires oxygen, there is sufficient with them to cover the period of transfer to a suitably equipped facility.
- Ensure that any casualty monitoring system or other electric-powered devices have sufficient battery power to cover the period of transfer to a suitably equipped facility.
- Ensure that the casualty empties their bladder and/or bowels, or has a catheter or similar inserted, before evacuation.
- All crew should wear lifejackets and other personal protective equipment if required.

Method

Ensure the casualty is aware and informed of all movements before evacuation.

If the casualty is positioned on an evacuation stretcher, consider whether their arms should be secured within the restraining straps or allowed to be unsecured. In general the arms of an unconscious casualty should be restrained, whereas the arms of an alert and orientated casualty can be left unsecured. Unrestrained arms may maintain a feeling of reassurance in the casualty.

When the casualty has been secured on an evacuation stretcher, ensure that objects (e.g. lifting harnesses) do not fall on their face, which will be unprotected and susceptible to accidental injury during a transfer.

Ensure that the casualty, particularly if positioned on an evacuation stretcher, is under control at all times, with minimal risk of accidents and falls, particularly into water.

Once the casualty has been transferred to the other vessel, ensure that all information regarding the incident is passed to the other vessel or shore facility if they are already involved. Be prepared to provide further details if required.

Appendix III: Transport of a casualty

It requires careful planning and preparation to transport a casualty safely around a vessel, or off the vessel in the event of evacuation. This is for the following reasons:

- The casualty is at a significantly increased risk of direct and indirect harm for the duration of the move.
- It is more difficult to take effective observations of the casualty and monitoring of vital signs is often not possible.
- Any treatments that may be required are more difficult, if not impossible, to perform.

Therefore move a casualty only if absolutely necessary, and the casualty should be as medically stable as possible before commencing the move.

There are two main reasons for transporting a casualty:

- **Emergency move** Required to recover a casualty from the scene of accident (such as the engine room or an enclosed space) or the place of onset of illness (such as a cabin)
- **Planned move** Required when moving a casualty from one part of the vessel to another for a logistical reason or to the vessel's sick bay, or when evacuating a casualty from the vessel.

The casualty may be harmed during a move in two ways:

- **Direct harm** Such as by dropping the evacuation stretcher down stairs or into water
- **Indirect harm** Caused by actions such as inadequate observation or monitoring (failing to observe acute deterioration in the casualty), or deprivation of oxygen if the supply fails.

Risks to the rescuer may not be obvious, particularly in the case of an emergency move, and can be overlooked in the rush to rescue an injured casualty. It is critical for the rescuer not to become a casualty themselves as that will compound an already challenging situation. Therefore any emergency casualty move should involve a rapid risk assessment, considering the following potential problems:

- **Enclosed spaces** Presence of dangerous gases such as carbon monoxide, carbon dioxide, hot gases, and difficulties with restricted access
- **Exposed places** Open deck in heavy weather – extremes of temperature, danger of being swept down the deck, over vertical drops or overboard
- **Vertical elevations** Unguarded edges of cargo holds or deck, steep stairways (on deck or inside living quarters)
- **Overhead** Danger of falling objects, unsecured cargo in heavy weather, rigging
- **Underfoot** Icy or oily surfaces
- **Inflammable gases** Risk of explosion in the presence of a naked flame or even a small spark
- **Electricity** Exposed live cables or live metal surfaces.

Methods of moving a casualty

Manual methods

Manual movement of a casualty (i.e. by manual handling without any aids) may be a necessity in an emergency. For example, it may be necessary to remove an immobile or incapacitated casualty from a place of danger such as an enclosed space (e.g. cargo hold), or a very exposed site (an open deck in cold, rough weather). However, there are obvious risks to the rescuer, and the casualty should be approached cautiously, with the above risks in mind. In the rush to rescue a casualty, personal safety is easily overlooked.

The method of transport will depend on the situation of the casualty and the nature of the injury. Whatever method is used, try to gain the confidence of the person you are carrying by explaining what you are about to do and carrying out the manoeuvre efficiently.

Injured casualties in confined spaces can be difficult to extract. Everybody worries about keeping the neck still. It is always best if an injured casualty can extricate themselves from a situation as they are unlikely to do any further damage. If they are unable and need moving, then a pragmatic approach needs to be taken, while trying to ensure minimal movement of the neck. Use manual in-line stabilisation as much as possible.

Ordinary manual handling may be possible. This is where two helpers carry a casualty by each using an arm to support the casualty's back and shoulders and each using their spare hand to support the casualty under their thighs.

If the casualty is conscious they may help support themselves with their hands on the shoulders of the helpers, as shown in the diagram.

Four-handed seat

The four-handed seat can be used when a heavy person has to be carried. The disadvantage of this type of seat is that the casualty must be able to co-operate and to hold on with both arms around the shoulders of the two helpers carrying them (1). The four-handed seat cannot be safely used to negotiate ladders (2).

1

2

Three-handed seat

The three-handed seat has the advantage that one arm and hand of a helper is left free and can be used either to support an injured limb or as a back support for the casualty. According to the nature of the injury, it must be decided which of the two helpers has the free arm (see diagram).

Fireman's lift

The 'fireman's lift' should not be used unless the helper is a similar size to the casualty, but it is especially useful when you have to move a casualty by yourself and need the use of your right hand for holding onto a ladder. Roll the casualty so that they are lying face downwards. Lift them up so that when you stoop down you can put your head under their left arm (see diagram 1).
Then put your left arm between the casualty's legs and grasp their left hand, letting their body fall over your left shoulder (2).

Steady yourself and then stand upright, at the same time shifting the casualty's weight so that they are lying well-balanced across the back of your shoulders (3). Hold the casualty's arm above the wrist. In this position it is easy to carry the casualty up a ladder as one hand is free to grasp the rail (4).

1

2

3

4

Drag-carry method

As a last resort, the drag-carry method can be used in narrow spaces, particularly where there is wreckage following an explosion and where it may be possible for only one crew member to reach a trapped casualty and to rescue them. After initial rescue, two crew members may be able to undertake further movement through a narrow space. The method is demonstrated in diagrams 1 and 2 below. Ensure that the casualty's wrists, which are tied together, do not interfere with any breathing apparatus the rescuer may be wearing, and safeguard the casualty's head with a bump hat if possible.

1

2

Transport aids

Many aids are available to move a casualty safely and effectively, both around a vessel and off a vessel in the event of evacuation. These include sliding mats and scoop stretchers which fully immobilise the entire spine (some examples are shown in the diagrams below). Whatever equipment or system is on board, it is essential to undertake practical exercises beforehand. This will mean that if an emergency move is required the crew members will have the practical competencies to use it safely and effectively.

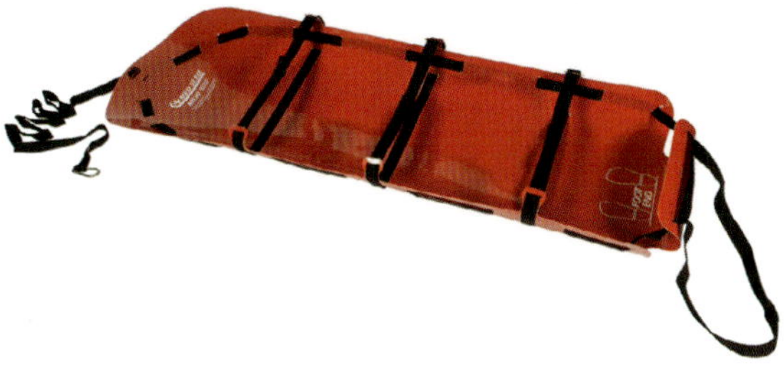

Example of a sliding mat

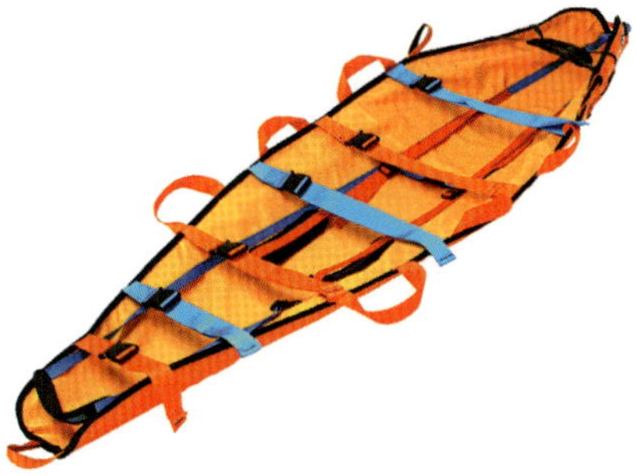

Example of a semi-flexible evacuation stretcher

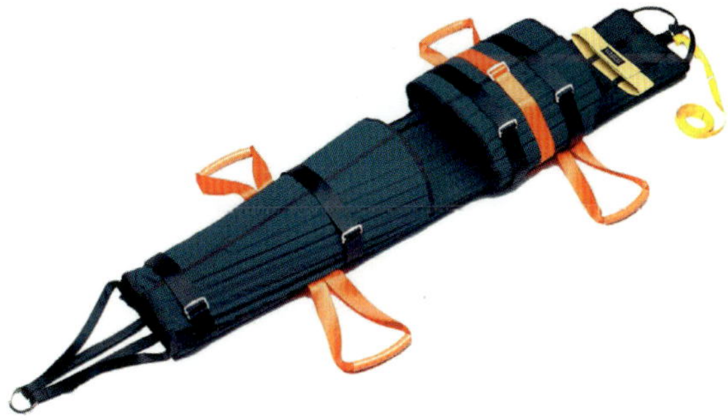

Example of a Neil Robertson stretcher

Example of a scoop stretcher

Communication

With the casualty

If the casualty is conscious and there is a possibility that they will understand, it is vital to keep them fully informed of the overall plan for moving them and every single action. When immobilised on an evacuation stretcher the casualty will feel exceedingly vulnerable and unable to help themselves. They will therefore need continual reassurance and information regarding actions that affect them. Casualties with altered states of consciousness may become very agitated during a move, and they may need sedation for their own safety and for that of the crew moving them. However, sedation under such circumstances must only be administered under the direct supervision of TMAS.

With the crew

The vessel's crew need to be fully informed of the impending move of a casualty so that other activities on board can be either replanned or rerouted. This will avoid inadvertent delays on the route along which the casualty will be moved. The route may need to be cleared of equipment or stores, to enable passage of a horizontal evacuation stretcher. In addition, extra help may be required for movement up or down stairways or out of confined spaces. On vessels these can be narrow and winding and a considerable challenge.

With rescue services (including TMAS)

In the event of serious trauma or illness, it is advisable to inform rescue services, and TMAS if available, of the movement of a casualty. They may give valuable advice on how to effect such a move more safely, particularly in the event of suspected spinal injury. Obviously in the event of an emergency move there may not be time to seek advice, and these are the circumstances where prior training becomes invaluable.

The rescue services and TMAS may have specific requirements for the preparation of the casualty before evacuation, and getting this advice in good time will ameliorate the evacuation process.

Preparing for a move

Thorough preparation is essential to effect a safe and efficient move of the casualty. Consider the following aspects before commencing the move:

- **Risk assessment** This should be brief but pertinent to the location of the casualty and the move to be undertaken. Consider all the risks noted above.
- **Safety** Is essential at all times. Prepare to halt a move if the casualty or crew members are exposed to undue risk.
- **Spinal protection** Consider spinal protection for all moves (depending on the mechanism of injury) and try to achieve as much protection as possible, given the circumstances of the move.
- **Eye protection** If the casualty is unconscious, or their arms are inside the restraining straps, their eyes have no protection from falling objects (e.g. as lifting harnesses), bright lights, salt or wind. Consider using eye patches or taping them shut if they are unconscious.
- **Arms in or out of restraining straps** If the casualty is unconscious or sedated keep their arms inside the restraining straps. If the casualty is conscious and cooperative, ask them what they would prefer. If the arms are out, take care not to harm them.

- **Sedation and other medications** Sedation may be required in rare circumstances, but must only be administered under the direct supervision of TMAS. Other medication required by the casualty (both to treat the acute medical condition, or existing medication) should be prepared and accompany the casualty.
- **IV lines and catheters** If IV lines or other indwelling devices (e.g. catheters) are in place, ensure that they are firmly secured to prevent accidental removal during the transfer.
- **Pain** Address all pain issues before commencing planned moves. Pain relief may not be possible with emergency moves but is a priority once the casualty is in a safer place. Anticipate that additional pain may be caused by the move so make sure there is the capability of giving more pain relief en-route.
- **Warmth** Ensure the casualty is provided with as much insulation as possible, particularly for exposed moves. Remember that injured casualties lose body heat easily, especially from the head. Also ensure all crew members involved in prolonged moves are properly clothed.
- **Oxygen** Enough oxygen must accompany the casualty to cover their needs for the period of evacuation until they reach definitive care. Incorporate a safety margin to cater for delays and also increased requirements by the casualty during the move.
- **Fluids** Ensure sufficient fluids (IV or oral, as required) accompany the casualty, incorporating a safety margin, to cater for delays and also increased requirements by the casualty during the move.
- **Electricity** In the event that the casualty is attached to any kind of electrical device (e.g. vital signs monitor or syringe driver) make sure batteries are fully charged, there are spare batteries, and also a means of plugging into fixed electricity supply if available en-route.
- **Toileting and hygiene** Ensure this is undertaken before a move if possible. Consider a catheter for longer moves. Take cleaning materials.
- **Life vests and flotation devices** Consider these for all personnel involved in the move, especially from exposed deck locations. Also consider if this is practicable for the casualty taking into account their injuries or mobility, especially for planned evacuations.
- **Communication methods (radios or phones)** The crew who are undertaking the move will need a way of communicating around the vessel, and so will need to take two-way radios with them. If the casualty is conscious and being evacuated they will need to take a mobile phone (that works in whichever country they are destined for further care) so that they can communicate, and so that next of kin, employers, insurance companies etc. can communicate with them.
- **Belongings (e.g. money, passport, credit card)** All these items should accompany the casualty in the event of evacuation, preferably in a secure pouch attached to the casualty so it cannot go missing. If someone is accompanying the casualty, they will need their documents as well.
- **Documentation** In the event of evacuation, the clinical team at the medical destination will require full details of the events on board, together with details of all treatments given (see page 291). Fill in a confidential medical report (form MSF 4155), which should accompany the seafarer who is being evacuated. As an alternative, an ATMIST AMPLE form should be completed and should accompany the casualty. A copy of all documentation should be kept on board. Details of the casualty's next of kin, employer and insurance company will also be required. Send a hard copy and also an email if possible.

Appendix IV: Medical assessment questionnaire

This medical assessment questionnaire is not a statutory document. It is for use as a template when passengers, or others who are not subject to a statutory medical examination, travel on board. It is not relevant to crew members who already hold a statutory medical certificate.

It is the responsibility of the vessel's owner or operator to formulate a policy regarding if, when and how this information should be gathered, who should screen the information disclosed (e.g. the company medical advisor) and how to subsequently give permission to travel.

Medical assessment questionnaire CONFIDENTIAL	
Section 1 To be completed by the person being assessed	
Name	
Date of birth (dd/mm/yyyy)	
Home address	
Contact telephone number	
Email address	
Personal doctor and contact details	
Past medical history Please record details of any medical conditions from which you suffer *(continue on the back of this sheet if necessary)*	

Specific conditions *(delete as appropriate)*	High blood pressure	Yes/No
	Angina	Yes/No
	Heart attacks (myocardial infarctions)	Yes/No
	Strokes (cerebrovascular accident)	Yes/No
	Jaundice	Yes/No
	Tuberculosis	Yes/No
	Rheumatic fever	Yes/No
	Diabetes	Yes/No
	Epilepsy	Yes/No
	Asthma	Yes/No
	Depression/other mental illness	Yes/No
	Blood infections (such as Hepatitis A, B or C, HIV or AIDS)	Yes/No
	Chronic back pain	Yes/No
	Kidney stones	Yes/No
	Cartilage/ligament injuries	Yes/No
	Musculoskeletal injuries	Yes/No
	Indigestion/reflux	Yes/No
If you answered Yes to any of the above, record details here		
Have you had any surgical operations? *Include details and dates*		
Are there any inherited medical conditions in your family? *Include details*		
Have you received medical advice or treatment during the previous 12 months relating to any illness, disability or condition whatsoever? *If yes, please detail*		
Please record any medications that you take, either regularly, occasionally or in the past *(include herbal or alternative medicines)*		
Are you allergic to anything? *Include details of circumstances and reactions*		

Do you smoke? *If so, number per day*	
Do you drink alcohol? *If so, units per week*	
Please detail all immunisations/ vaccinations you have had, with dates *Continue overleaf if necessary*	
What is your height (m)?	
What is your weight (kg)?	

I certify that, to the best of my knowledge, the above information is correct.

Signature .... Date (dd/mm/yyyy) ....

Section 2 Medical examination to be completed by the medical practitioner			
Overall appearance			
Pulse (bpm)		BMI	
Blood pressure (mmHg)		Pulse oximeter (air)	
Temperature (mouth/ear)			
Urinalysis result			
Cardiovascular system			
Respiratory system			
Abdominal system			
Musculoskeletal system			
Medical practitioner's name			
Address			

I certify that the information and particulars relating to

....

are true and correct to the best of my knowledge.

Signature of medical practitioner:

Signature .... Date (dd/mm/yyyy) ....

Appendix V: Medical reporting for evacuation

A detailed medical report should accompany the casualty when they are being evacuated, either to another ship, directly onto shore, or via a helicopter. An example of such a report is shown below. The purpose of the report is to inform the doctors on shore exactly what happened to the casualty, what treatment they have received and how they have progressed. It should give an indication as to possible diagnosis, and what treatments are required next.

A structured report is much easier to understand than a long rambling letter or verbal report, and may be read by doctors whose first language is not English. It is also an enduring record of what happened on the vessel. A copy should be retained on board.

The information that should be covered includes:

- Casualty's name, date of birth, home address and next of kin, together with contact details
- The main reason (illness or trauma) why the casualty is being evacuated, circumstances and timing of events
- The current vital signs observations, together with any observation charts already completed
- The treatments already given, and responses, including any information from doctors in previous ports
- All other details about the patient, including previous medical history, normal medications and allergies
- Details of the master of the vessel, and the crew member who was responsible for treating the casualty. These details may be important if the doctors onshore require further information.

If in doubt, include information rather than leave it out.

MCA Medical Form MSF 4155

This is the MCA model form accessible from the MCA website. It is more comprehensive than the form shown here, and may be used as an alternative.

Confidentiality

The medical report is confidential and should be used only for the purpose of treating the casualty. It should not be passed to any third party without the express consent of the casualty.

It is imperative that the storage and maintenance of medical records is undertaken correctly. The relevant principles and guidelines are included on page 258.

Medical report for evacuation
CONFIDENTIAL

Name	
Vessel name	Date of birth *(DD/MM/YYYY)*
Vessel owner/operator	Report date
Position of evacuation	Date of onset or incident
Main complaint	
History	
Examination	

Vital signs	Pulse		Resp rate		AVPU/ GCS		Pulse oximetry		
Time of observation	Blood pressure		Temp		Urine test		Blood sugar		

Treatment on board

Treatment on shore (This part to be completed by any on-shore doctor who sees the casualty before transfer back to the vessel)
Past medical history
High blood pressure/Angina/Heart attacks/Jaundice/Tuberculosis/Rheumatic fever/Diabetes/Epilepsy/Asthma *(Delete as appropriate)*
Normal medications (usually taken)
Allergies and reactions
Next of kin

Copies	Vessel's copy	Shore copy	**Signature** Role/Position
Vessel contact details			**Print name**

Appendix VI: Vital signs monitor chart

Temperature °C		40											
		39											
		38											
		37											
		36											
		35											
		34											
Pulse and blood pressure (mmHg)		190											
		180											
		170											
		160											
		150											
		140											
		130											
		120											
		110											
		100											
		90											
		80											
		70											
		60											
		50											
		40											
		Time	0:00	1:00	2:00	3:00	4:00	5:00	6:00	7:00	8:00	9:00	10:00
Glasgow coma scale	Eyes	4											
		3											
		2											
		1											
	Verbal	5											
		4											
		3											
		2											
		1											
	Motor	6											
		5											
		4											
		3											
		2											
		1											
	Total												
Respiratory rate													
Pulse oximetry %													
Urine output (ml)													
Blood sugar mmol													

Crew member name	Date
Vessel	Location

11:00	12:00	13:00	14:00	15:00	16:00	17:00	18:00	19:00	20:00	21:00	22:00	23:00

Appendix VII: Medicines guide

This is a list of the medicines referred to in this guide and reflects current best medical practice. It is not a comprehensive record of all indications, side effects, cautions and contraindications for every medicine. Consult the information leaflet with all medicines for full information.

Most medicines included here are also included in MSN 1905. However, some medicines are not in that notice but have been included here as their use reflects current best medical practice.

Abbreviations

Dose frequency

od	Once per day
bd	Twice daily
tds	Three times daily
qds	Four times daily
nocte	At night
prn	As necessary

Route of administration

IM	Intramuscular injection
IO	Intraosseous injection
IV	Intravenous injection
SC	Subcutaneous
PV	Vaginal route
PR	Rectal route
Oral	By mouth
Topical	External application to skin
Buccal	Applied to mucosa inside mouth, between teeth and cheek

Form of drug

amp	Ampoule
tab	Tablet
inj	Injection
supp	Suppository
inh	Inhaler
cap	Capsule

Medicine	Indication	Dose	Cautions
Aciclovir 5% cream	Cold sores (herpes)	5 times a day for 5–10 days	Start at first sign of attack. May cause stinging, dry skin. Avoid eye contact
Aciclovir	Herpes infections (cold sores, chicken pox, shingles)	400–800 mg 3–5 times daily	Gastrointestinal upset, dizziness, headache
Adrenaline (IM inj) (Epinephrine)	Anaphylaxis, resuscitation	See page 42 and page 2	Only for use in resuscitation and anaphylaxis
Amlodipine 5 mg tab	High blood pressure	5–10 mg od	Dizziness, drowsiness, headache, nausea
Amoxicillin	Ear/general infections	250–1000 mg tds	Avoid in penicillin allergy. May cause stomach upset
Aspirin	For cardiac problems, stroke (CVA), other thrombotic problems	300–900 mg qds	Avoid with indigestion, stomach ulcers, asthma
Atenolol	Antihypertensive	25–50 mg od	May cause low pulse rate, low blood pressure, wheeze, fatigue, cold hands/feet
Azithromycin	Chest infections	500 mg od for 3 days	May cause stomach upset, abdominal pain
Beclometasone	Asthma/wheeze	2 puffs bd	A few short-term side-effects
Bisacodyl	Constipation (stimulant)	5–10 mg at night	May cause abdominal cramps, griping
Ceftriaxone (IM or IV inj)	Severe chest/gut infections	1 g od IM or IV	May cause stomach upset, abdominal pain
Cetirizine	Anti-allergy (antihistamine)	10 mg od	Drowsiness, low risk of urinary retention, blurred vision
Chloramphenicol (0.5% drops, 1% ointment)	Ear/eye infections	2–3 applications every 8–12 hours	Transient stinging. Avoid prolonged use
Chlorphenamine IM IV inj	Anti-allergy (antihistamine)	10–20 mg Max 40 mg in 24 hours	Drowsiness, low risk of urinary retention, blurred vision
Chlorpromazine (IM inj)	Severe anxiety/ psychosis	25–50 mg IM every 6–8 hours	Drowsiness, low blood pressure, tremor, abnormal movements
Chlorpromazine (tab)	Severe anxiety/ psychosis	25–100 mg tds	Drowsiness, low blood pressure, tremor, abnormal movements

Medicine	Indication	Dose	Cautions
Cinnarizine	Seasickness	15 mg tds	May cause drowsiness, fatigue, blurred vision
Ciprofloxacin	Gut/urinary infections	250–500 mg bd	Caution in epilepsy. May cause tendonitis
Clopidogrel	For cardiac problems, stroke (CVA), other thrombotic problems	300 mg initially then 75 mg od	Diarrhoea; gastrointestinal discomfort, haemorrhage, skin reactions
Clotrimazole (pessary)	Vaginal fungal infection	500 mg pessary once only	A repeat dose may be required after a week
Co-amoxiclav (IV inj)	Severe chest/dental/gut infections	600–1200 mg IV tds	Avoid in penicillin allergy. May cause stomach upset
Co-amoxiclav (tab)	Chest/dental/gut infections	375–625 mg tds	Avoid in penicillin allergy. May cause stomach upset
Codeine	Moderate pain	30 mg qds	Avoid with respiratory depression, head injury
Codydramol	Moderate pain	2 tabs qds	Contains paracetamol
Cyclizine (IM inj)	Sickness caused by morphine	50 mg IM tds	May cause drowsiness. Painful injection
Dexamethasone 0.1% eye drops	Inflammation of the eye	3–4 drops every 4–6 hours	Contact TMAS before using in a 'red eye' or with signs of infection
Diazepam (IM/IV inj)	Fits (see page 16)	5 mg IM/IV prn	May cause drowsiness, confusion, respiratory depression
Diazepam (PR)	Fits (see page 16)	10 mg prn	May cause drowsiness, confusion, respiratory depression
Diazepam (tab)	Fits/anxiety/muscle spasm	5–10 mg every 2 hours prn	May cause drowsiness, confusion, respiratory depression
Diclofenac (supp) (NSAID)	Moderate pain	100 mg bd PR	Avoid with indigestion, stomach ulcers, asthma
Domperidone (tab)	Seasickness	10–20 mg qds	May occasionally cause stomach cramps
Doxycycline	Chest, gut, ear, skin, urine infections, malaria prophylaxis	200 mg initially then 100 mg od	May cause stomach upset, abdominal pain, skin sun sensitivity
Ergometrine/oxytocin (IM inj)	Anti-haemorrhage from uterus (miscarriage)	1 ml IM inj (5 units/1 ml) once	Nausea, vomiting, headache, dizziness

Medicine	Indication	Dose	Cautions
Erythromycin	Chest/gut/ear infections	250–500 mg tds	May cause stomach upset, abdominal pain
Eye and ear drops (Dexamethasone 0.05%, framycetin 0.5%, gramicidin 0.005%)	Inflammation/infection of the outer ear or eye	2–3 drops every 6–8 hours	Seek medical advice before using in a 'red eye' or with signs of infection
Famotidine	Indigestion, reflux, gastric/duodenal ulceration	20–40 mg bd	Gastrointestinal upset, dizziness, headache
Flucloxacillin	Skin infections	250–500 mg qds	Avoid in penicillin allergy. May cause stomach upset
Fluconazole	Fungal skin infections, candida (thrush)	150 mg single dose or 50 mg od	Gastrointestinal upset, headache
Fluorescein 2% eye drops	Staining for detection of foreign bodies and lesions of the eye	3–4 drops once only	Results in a yellow eye for several hours
Furosemide (IV inj)	Heart failure (diuretic)	20–40 mg IV od	May cause low blood pressure, dizziness
Furosemide	Heart failure (diuretic)	20–40 mg od	May cause low blood pressure, dizziness
Fusidic acid 2% ointment	Skin infections	Apply 3–4 times daily	Avoid eye contact
Glucagon IM	Low blood sugar in diabetics taking insulin	1 mg IM	Nausea, vomiting, abdominal pain
Glycerol suppository	Constipation	1 as needed	–
Glyceryl trinitrate (spray under tongue)	Angina, heart attack	1–2 sprays prn	May cause low blood pressure, flushing, headache, fast heart rate
Haloperidol (oral or IM)	Severe anxiety/ psychosis	5–10 mg daily oral. 1 mg by IM injection repeated 2–4 hourly, max 10 mg per day	Drowsiness, low blood pressure, dry mouth, tremor, abnormal movements
Hydrocortisone (IM or IV inj)	Anti-allergy	100 mg IM or IV every 8 hours as necessary	May cause indigestion, abdominal discomfort
Hydrocortisone 1% cream	Mild inflammatory skin disorders (eczema, allergic rashes, insect bites)	Apply thinly 1–2 times a day	May cause worsening of infection if present. Avoid prolonged use
Hyoscine butylbromide	Anti-bowel spasm/ colic	10–20 mg qds	May cause dry mouth, blurred vision, constipation

Medicine	Indication	Dose	Cautions
Hyoscine hydrobromide (patch)	Seasickness	1 patch behind ear. Replace every 72 hours	May cause drowsiness, blurred vision, urinary retention, confusion
Hyoscine hydrobromide (tab)	Seasickness	0.3 mg tds	May cause drowsiness, blurred vision, urinary retention
Ibuprofen (tab) (NSAID)	Mild to moderate pain	400 mg every 4–6 hours	Avoid with indigestion, stomach ulcers, asthma
Ibuprofen gel (NSAID)	Mild to moderate pain	Apply 3 times daily	Avoid with indigestion, stomach ulcers, asthma
Indigestion preparation containing sodium alginate, sodium bicarbonate and calcium carbonate	Indigestion	1–2 tabs prn after meals	–
Insulin	Treatment of diabetes (high blood sugar values)	As required	Always consult TMAS prior to treating
Lactulose	Constipation (softens stool)	15 ml bd	May cause flatulence, cramps, abdominal discomfort
Lansoprazole	Indigestion, acid reflux	15–30 mg od	Abdominal pain, diarrhoea, constipation, dizziness, nausea, headache, skin problems
Lidocaine (SC inj)	Local anaesthetic inj	See page 214	See page 214
Lidocaine topical	Local anaesthesia to skin, urethra, buccal mucosa	1–2 ml applied thinly to skin as required	Avoid prolonged usage. Use once for insertion of urinary catheter (see page 216)
Loperamide	Diarrhoea	4 mg and then 2 mg with each loose stool. Max 16 mg in 24 hours	May cause abdominal cramps, dizziness, drowsiness, bloating
Loratadine	Antihistamine	10 mg od	Low risk of drowsiness, urinary retention, blurred vision
Lorazepam (IV inj)	Fits (see page 16)	2–4 mg prn	May cause drowsiness, confusion, respiratory depression
Magnesium sulphate paste	Assist drainage of superficial skin abscesses	As required	If no improvement, or signs of spreading infection, consult TMAS

Medicine	Indication	Dose	Cautions
Malathion liquid	Head lice and scabies	Wash hair and body once a week for two weeks. Do not wash off for 24 hours	Hypersensitivity, eye swelling, angioedema, skin reactions. Hair may catch fire after treatment if close to naked flame. Do not use on broken skin. Avoid contact with eyes
Mebendazole	Gut worm infections	100 mg bd for 3 days	May cause abdominal pain, diarrhoea
Methoxyflurane inhaler (Penthrox®)	Moderate to severe pain associated with trauma	3–6 ml by inhaler. Avoid on consecutive days	Avoid in liver or renal disease, or diabetes. Use only under the direction of a doctor
Metoprolol	Antihypertensive	50–100 mg bd	May cause low pulse rate, low blood pressure, wheeze, fatigue, cold hands/feet
Metronidazole (supp)	Gut/dental infections	1 g tds PR	May cause nausea and vomiting (worse if taken with alcohol)
Metronidazole (tab)	Gut/dental infections	400 mg tds	May cause nausea and vomiting (worse if taken with alcohol)
Miconazole 2% cream	Fungal foot/groin infections	Apply 2 times daily for 10 days	Local irritation, itching
Midazolam buccal	Treatment of fits	10 mg buccal. Repeat after 10 minutes if still fitting. See page 16	Decreased conscious level, confusion, drowsiness, respiratory depression
Morphine (IM inj)	Severe pain	5–10 mg IM every 2–4 hours	Avoid with respiratory depression, head injury
Mupirocin 2% cream/ ointment	Skin infections	Apply 3 times daily for 5 days	Skin reactions
Naloxone (IV inj)	Reversal of opiates in overdose	100–200 mcg IV Repeat 100 mcg inj every 2 minutes depending on response	May cause low or high blood pressure, heart arrhythmias, collapse
Naproxen (NSAID)	Mild to moderate pain	250 mg every 8–12 hours	Avoid with indigestion, stomach ulcers, asthma
Ondansetron (tab under tongue)	Seasickness	4–8 mg tds	Occasionally causes constipation

Medicine	Indication	Dose	Cautions
Paracetamol	Mild pain	1 g qds	Avoid with liver disease. Do not take more than 4 g/day
Permethrin 1% cream rinse or 5% cream	Scabies and crab infestations	Apply cream to whole body, allow to dry and wash off after 12 hours	Avoid contact with eyes, broken, infected skin
Phytomenadione (Vitamin K) 2 mg/ 0.2 ml inj	Routine antihaemorrhage injection for newborn Reversal of anticoagulation with warfarin	For newborn babies, given after birth: 0.2 ml (2 mg) IM injection single dose For reversal of anticoagulants (blood thinners): 5–10 mg IV injection	Consult with TMAS prior to treating
Pilocarpine 1% or 2% eye drops	Treatment of glaucoma	Apply 1 drop to the eye qds	Diarrhoea, headache, nausea, skin reactions, blurred vision, vomiting
Prednisolone	Anti-allergy	10–60 mg od	May cause indigestion, abdominal discomfort
Prochlorperazine (IM inj)	Seasickness, other causes of sickness	12.5 mg IM, then oral therapy 6 hours later	May cause drowsiness, dry mouth, rarely tremor
Prochlorperazine (tab under tongue)	Seasickness	3 mg qds	May cause drowsiness, dry mouth, rarely tremor
Prochlorperazine (tab)	Seasickness	10 mg qds	May cause drowsiness, dry mouth, rarely tremor
Promethazine hydrochloride (IM inj)	Seasickness (antihistamine)	25–50 mg once only	Commonly causes drowsiness. May also cause urinary retention and dry mouth
Promethazine teoclate (tab)	Seasickness (antihistamine)	25 mg od for 3 days	Caution in asthma. Drowsiness, urinary retention, dry mouth
Pseudoephedrine (tab)	Nasal congestion	60 mg every 6–8 hours	Anxiety, fast heart rate, headache, insomnia
Ringer's lactate	Treatment of shock, flushing IV cannulas	As required	Consult TMAS before using
Salbutamol (inhaler)	Asthma/wheeze	2 puffs qds or as needed	May cause tremor, fast heart rate, headache with frequent use

Medicine	Indication	Dose	Cautions
Silver sulfadiazine 1% cream	Prophylaxis and treatment of infection in burn wounds	Apply to wound once daily or more frequently if discharging	Allergic reactions – itching, rashes, burning sensation. Apply in sterile manner
Terbinafine 1% cream	Fungal skin infections	Apply to affected area twice a day for 2 weeks	Skin reactions
Terbinafine (tab)	Fungal skin infections, fungal nail infections	250 mg od	Decreased appetite, arthralgia, diarrhoea, headache, myalgia, nausea
Tetanus vaccine IM	Prevention of tetanus	0.5 ml IM as part of treatment schedule	Allergic reactions, fever, local skin reaction
Tetanus immunoglobulin IM	Post-exposure prophylaxis and treatment	250–500 iu IM	Allergic reaction, low blood pressure. Always call TMAS if using
Tetracaine 0.5% or 1% eye drops	Anaesthesia for the eye	3–4 drops and wait several minutes	Stings the eye for a short time
Tramadol (oral, IV, IM)	Moderate to severe pain	100 mg every 4–6 hours oral or IM	Avoid with respiratory depression, head injury, epilepsy
Tranexamic acid 500 mg tab or 500 mg/ 5ml inj	Reduce bleeding e.g. in heavy periods, nosebleed, major haemorrhage	1.0–1.5 g tds oral 1 g IV/IO/IM over 10 minutes May repeat injection after 30 minutes if still bleeding	Always call TMAS if using

Appendix VIII: How to contact telemedical advice services

You can contact UK government telemedical advice (TMAS) services through the UK Maritime and Coastguard Agency (MCA). A medical emergency call to the UK Coastguard, either via radio or phone, will be answered by their dedicated call handlers who will collect basic details, including the casualty's illness or injury, type of vessel, next port of call or nearest port at which the casualty could be landed, and confirmation of the vessel's current position. The call will then be transferred to one of the UK TMAS providers:

- The call will be answered by a senior specialist doctor in emergency medicine.
- You will be talking directly to the doctor.
- This service is available 24 hours a day, 365 days a year.
- Calls are taken from anywhere in the world, but the majority originate from within UK waters.
- Calls will be taken for medical emergencies from ships of any flag.
- The Coastguard call handler will monitor the call between the vessel and the doctor, to ensure good communications and to facilitate the rapid dispatch of evacuation resources if required.
- Coastguard helicopters will be dispatched for a medical emergency only after consultation with TMAS.
- The UK TMAS providers keep a secure and confidential record of the consultation, in accordance with UK General Medical Council requirements.

How to make a TMAS call

Once you have decided to call UK TMAS, contact the UK Coastguard by the most convenient and reliable means you have and tell them you have a medical emergency on board. The Coastguard call handler will take details of the vessel and location while they are contacting the specialist medical centre.

Once they have the TMAS doctor on the line, the Coastguard call handler will connect you directly to them. The doctor will need to know:

- A brief outline of the problem
- The current state of the patient
- What you have already done
- What equipment and drugs are carried on the vessel
- What first aid training or clinical skills are available among those on board
- Past medical problems, regular medication and allergies of the casualty.

It is always easier if you are as close to the patient as possible when talking to the TMAS service, as you may be asked several follow-on questions.

The ATMIST and AMPLE form

A clear structure for transmission of information is needed. The headings for this have the initial letters A, T, M, I, S, T and A, M, P, L, E. The TMAS medical incident report form on the front flyleaf is the best format to follow when giving details in an emergency. It closely mirrors the emergency services' format and structures your thoughts and the important information.

The form structure is as follows, with descriptions of fields:

ATMIST

A **Age** Of casualty and name of casualty

T **Time** Of the incident or illness or when the casualty was discovered

M **Mechanism of injury** Brief description of circumstances (e.g. fall down ladder; hit on head by block)

Or:

Mechanism of illness Brief description of problem (e.g. shortness of breath, diarrhoea and vomiting)

I **Injuries** Give details of the obvious injuries (e.g. laceration to scalp and probable fracture of left forearm)

Or:

Illnesses Give a brief description of circumstances (e.g. chest pain; started last night, after dinner. Feels dizzy with it. Like previous heart attack)

S **Signs**

- **Respiratory rate** Watch their breathing for a minute
- **Respiratory effort** Can they count 1–10 out loud in one breath?
- **Pulse rate** The rate over a minute that you can feel at the wrist
- **Blood pressure** If not able to take, can you feel the pulse at the wrist?
- **Oxygen saturation** If you have a pulse oximeter
- **Pupils' diameter** In mm and note if unequal in size
- **Patient's colour** Pale, pink, blue, sweaty, grey?
- **Temperature** Under tongue (if unconscious, in the ear or under the armpit)
- **Blood sugar** If you have a glucometer
- **Conscious level** AVPU or GCS

T **Treatments** Give a brief outline of what you have already done for the casualty (e.g. put dressing on head wound, given them pain relief, laid them down and put a sling on their arm).

AMPLE

A **Allergies** and reaction if known

M List of normal **medications** if known

P **Previous** medical history (e.g. heart or lung problems)

L **Last** meal or oral intake

E **Events** leading to injury or illness

Appendix IX: Dealing with a death on board

Let me not pray to be sheltered from dangers but to be fearless in facing them

Rabindranath Tagore

Looking after the dying

Despite all efforts you may be unable to prevent a casualty from dying. This is traumatic for all concerned, especially if you know or are related to the person, or have been responsible for their treatment. Remember that even in an intensive care unit some patients die despite all possible treatments. Aboard a vessel in the ocean your treatment options are limited and you can only do your best.

However, even when you have accepted that the casualty will die, much can be done to ease the last few hours of their life. It is essential to get medical advice from TMAS if you are faced with someone who may be dying and to inform the next of kin.

Dignity

The casualty's dignity must be maintained. Replace any damaged or missing clothing to make sure the casualty is covered. Obey their requests if possible, and keep the casualty clean, as discreetly as possible.

Comfort

Comfort for the casualty is imperative, both physically and psychologically. Someone must stay with the dying person continuously and make sure they know they are being cared for. It is difficult to answer some questions such as, 'Am I dying?', but be truthful and compassionate. Physical comfort is just as important, so make sure the casualty is in a comfortable position, and is warm, clean and dry, as far as possible. You may need comfort as well, from your fellow crew members.

Relief of pain and distress

Aim to relieve all pain and suffering. If this cannot be achieved, seek medical advice from TMAS. Start with simple painkillers; if these are not enough, morphine or tramadol are beneficial to reduce pain and also to relieve mental anguish. They can both be given as an IM injection or IV if the casualty has vascular access. Give an anti-emetic (cyclizine) at the same time because both painkillers may cause vomiting, which will be upsetting at this time. If the casualty is agitated or distressed sedation can also be given (e.g. diazepam), but first seek advice from TMAS regarding dose and timing.

Communication

Communicate with the dying person. They may not be able to talk properly but they may wish to leave a message for loved ones. Make sure they know you understand and that you have made a written record of their dying wishes. Get a witness, who should sign and date any document.

Signs of death

Take your time when trying to establish if the casualty is dead, and preferably do it with someone else. It can be very difficult in poorly lit conditions and in bad weather. Make a written record of time and place of death, and both sign the declaration. There are several body functions to assess when determining death:

- **Breathing** has stopped. Listen, and feel with your cheek, very carefully over the mouth and nose. A mirror or glass held over the mouth and nose should not mist (a sign of breath being exhaled). There should be no sign of chest or abdominal movement. Watch for a few minutes.
- **Heart** has stopped. Feel for the pulse over the carotid (see page 192). Listen with your ear to the chest over the heart or use a stethoscope. There should be no noise of the heart pumping. Do these assessments for several minutes; longer if you are not sure.
- **Pupils** will be large and will not react to a bright light being shone into them. Use the brightest light you have, open the eyelids, watch the pupil carefully, and sweep the light across the eye.
- **Painful stimulus** provokes no reaction. Watch their face very carefully while firmly squeezing the nail bed of both hands, and rubbing firmly on the centre of the chest.

Mistakes when diagnosing death

Without monitoring systems used in hospitals it can be difficult to be sure whether a casualty is dead. Take your time – there is no rush to come to a decision. Some situations make it more difficult to diagnose death:

- **Hypothermia** may mimic death, especially if the casualty's body temperature is less than 31 °C. Take a rectal or oral temperature. If in any doubt, try to warm the casualty (see page 44) to above 31 °C and reassess. The pulse may be very slow and weak, and the breathing irregular and shallow.
- **Drugs** particularly sedative drugs such as benzodiazepines and opiates, may cause the casualty to have a very weak and slow pulse, with shallow breathing. Seek advice from TMAS if there is any suspicion of drugs being involved.

What to do after the death

Take some time after the death to look after yourself and your colleagues.

The body

The body should be handled as little as possible after death as it may be the focus of investigation by the authorities. This is especially important if there has been trauma or the death is suspicious. Do not wash the body or remove any medical interventions that have been attempted, such as IV access. Make sure the eyes are shut (tape might be needed), the hair neat and tidy, and the bladder empty (push on the lower abdomen). Bind the legs together at the ankles and interlock the fingers across the thighs. They should be left in the clothing in which they died, if this is in good condition.

Record keeping

Record all details of the following:

- the dead person's name, date of birth, address and next of kin
- circumstances leading up to the death (e.g. accident, illness and any suspicious circumstances)
- any distinguishing marks, injuries etc; take photographs of face and body
- clothing worn at the time of death (bag and keep it if it has been necessary to change it)
- all personal effects (bag these for handing over to the authorities)
- all medical record charts of vital signs etc
- time, place and position of death
- statements from each of the relevant crew regarding the circumstances of the death
- who assessed whether the person was dead
- any last wishes or messages from the dead person
- who provided medical advice.

What to do with the body

Ideally, the body should be kept, and transported to shore as quickly as possible, to be handed over to the authorities. This may not be possible if the vessel is weeks from port, in tropical climes. In colder oceans, the body should be placed in a body bag, if it is available, or wrapped tightly in whatever fabric is available and sewn up securely. The body should be stored in as cold a place as possible, within the vessel. The chiller compartment in bigger vessels can be cleared to take the body. Obtain advice from TMAS on safe and appropriate storage for the body if there is a delay of more than 3 days before next port. Do not use a freezer for storage without TMAS advice as this may make a possible subsequent post-mortem difficult.

Burial at sea

Burial at sea is no longer normally acceptable and every attempt should be made to transport the body to the nearest port. This facilitates proper investigation of the cause of death (by post-mortem), and also enables repatriation of the body.

If the body starts to decompose and it becomes unbearable to have on board, burial at sea may be the only option, but you must consult both TMAS and all relevant authorities ashore. If burial at sea is undertaken without prior permission from the relevant authorities, legal proceedings could be brought against the master and crew members.

If burial at sea is authorised, the body should be placed in a shroud made from robust fabric, and sewn in securely. A large weight should be placed in the shroud, and a hole made to ensure the escape of the gases of decomposition. An appropriate funeral service should be performed, followed by a dignified committal of the body to the sea.

Record the time and position of the committal in the vessel's log.

Glossary

ABCDE	Emergency checks on casualty: Airway, Breathing, Circulation, Disability, Exposure
AED	Automatic external defibrillator: a portable machine that reads heart rhythm and gives electric shock to restore rhythm automatically, if required
Adjunct (e.g. airway)	Piece of equipment to aid a procedure or recovery (e.g. to keep the airway open)
ALS	Advanced life support: advanced systematic approach to resuscitating a casualty who is not breathing or has no pulse
Anaphylaxis	Severe and potentially fatal allergic reaction affecting breathing and circulation
Anaemia	Abnormally low levels of red blood cells in the circulation
Aneurysm	Defect in artery wall causing artery to expand
Antacid	Drug to neutralise stomach acidity
Anticoagulant	Drug designed to slow the clotting of blood
Anti-emetic	Drug to combat sickness
Arrhythmia	Abnormal heart rhythm
Aspirate	To inhale fluids or solid substances into the lungs
Atrial fibrillation	Disturbance to heart rate giving an irregular pulse rate, sometimes with faintness
AVPU	Alert, Voice, Pain, Unresponsive: initial check on level of consciousness
Bends	Common term for decompression sickness after a diving incident
BLS	Basic life support: basic systematic approach to resuscitating casualty who is not breathing or has no pulse
Bolus	A defined amount of fluid, given rapidly intravenously or orally
bpm	Beats per minute
BSA	Body surface area: used when calculating area of burns
Bursitis	Swelling of bursa: fluid-filled pouch around knee or elbow
Cannula	Device with a needle and plastic tube placed into a vein to enable fluids or drugs to be given
Cardiomyopathy	Condition when part of the heart muscle stops pumping effectively
Carpal	Related to wrist, name of wrist bones
Cellulitis	Swelling and redness from infection of skin
Chaperone	A person, often of the same gender as the casualty, present to be a witness and to give support and reassurance
Clavicle	Collarbone
CPR	Cardio-pulmonary resuscitation: external support given to breathing and pumping action of heart

Crepitus	Feeling of grating when moving broken bones
CSF	Cerebrospinal fluid: a clear liquid that supports and protects the brain and spinal cord
C-spine	Cervical spine (bones in neck)
CVA	Cerebrovascular accident; a stroke
Cyanosis	Bluish tinge to skin when patient does not have enough oxygen
Decongestant	Drug to reduce swelling and fluid loss from nose or sinuses
Defibrillator	Portable machine to give electric shock to restart the heart
De-gloving	Injury that strips the skin from part of a limb
Diastolic	Blood pressure: lower level recorded
Distal	Part of limb furthest from the body
Diverticular disease	Condition with small pouches in intestinal wall that are liable to infection
Envenomate	Snake or other bite or sting that delivers poison
Epigastric	Region of central upper abdomen
EPIRB	Emergency position indicating radio beacon
Femur	Bone in the thigh
Fibula	Smaller bone in the lower leg
Foley catheter	Tube placed in the bladder to drain urine; it has an inflatable balloon at one end
Free pratique	Permission to enter the port in the absence of infectious disease on board an arriving vessel
GCS	Glasgow Coma Scale; formal assessment of person's conscious level
GI	Gastrointestinal: related to the organs for digesting and absorbing food
GTN	Glyceryl trinitrate: drug given under the tongue in heart problems
Haematoma	Collection of clotted blood, i.e. bruise
Haemostatic	Device (clamp, medication or dressing) used to stop uncontrolled bleeding
Humerus	Bone of the upper arm
Hydrostatic	Pressure exerted by fluid
Hypoxia	Low oxygen levels in the bloodstream
IAMSAR	International Aeronautical and Maritime Search and Rescue
ICS	International Chamber of Shipping
ILO	International Labour Organization. UN Agency concerned with working conditions
IM	Intramuscular: into the muscle
IMO	International Maritime Organization. UN Agency concerned with safety at sea
Inflammation/inflamed	Swelling, redness and pain around injury or infection

Intracranial	Contents within the skull
IO	Intraosseous: into the bone marrow
IV	Intravenous: into the vein
Jaundice	Yellow colouration of skin and eyes, usually from liver disease
Ketone	A compound that is produced in diabetes and gives a fruity smell on the breath
Lancing	Making a cut or incision to let pus out of a boil or abscess
LOC	Loss of consciousness
Lymphangitis	Inflammation of the lymph system, mostly seen in the legs
Malignant	Tendency of medical condition to become progressively worse
Metacarpal	Small bones of the hand
Metatarsal	Small bones of the foot
MILS	Manual in-line stablilisation. One person, usually kneeling at the casualty's head, places both hands, one each side of the head, at the sides just behind the ears. This keeps the head still and so prevents the cervical spine from moving. and prevents damage to the spinal cord
MLC	Maritime Labour Convention, 2005 (ILO). Internationally agreed requirements on conditions of work for seafarers
mm Hg	Pressure in millimetres of mercury. Used for blood pressure measurements
MSN	Merchant Shipping Notice. Document stating statutory requirements, from the UK Maritime and Coastguard Agency
Necrosis	Death and breakdown of tissue
NGT	Nasogastric tube. A tube that goes through the nose to the stomach
NSAID	Non-steroidal anti-inflammatory drug
Oedema	Swelling from fluid leak into tissues
Osteoporosis	Reduced mineralisation of bone: bone thinning
Palpitations	Feeling in the chest of heart beating irregularly or too fast
Patella	Knee cap
PE	Pulmonary embolism: a clot in the lung
Perfusion	Blood supply to the organs and skin
Photophobia	Pain in eyes when looking at light
Pleural space	Potential space in the chest between chest wall and lungs
PR	Medications given via the rectum
Prophylactic	Drug taken or intervention made to prevent illness
Proximal	Part of the limb nearest to the body
Radius	Bone in the forearm
Reduction	Realignment of a fracture or dislocation
RR	Respiratory rate

Shock	A sudden drop in blood flow through the body, threatening delivery of oxygen and nutrients to vital organs
Sinus	A space in the body with one opening; it may be normal (e.g. nasal sinuses), or arise from trauma or infection
Spacer	Device used to deliver an aerosol of medication to the lungs
Splenectomy	Removal of the spleen
SpO_2	Blood oxygen saturation level
Status epilepticus	Continued fitting for more than 20 minutes
Sterile	Free from contamination by bacteria or living organisms
Sternum	Breast bone
STI	Sexually transmitted infection
Stridor	Harsh noise heard when taking a breath in
Suture	Stitch to hold wound together
Systolic	Blood pressure: higher level recorded
Tarsal	Related to ankle; ankle bones
TB	Tuberculosis: long-term infection, commonly of lungs
Tendonitis	Inflammation of a tendon
Tetanus	Rare but serious wound infection; protection by immunisation
Tibia	Larger bone in the lower leg
Tissue	Part of a body organ, usually with several types of cell
TMAS	Telemedical Advice Service
Tone	State of a muscle; whether relaxed or contracted
Topical	Placed directly on the skin
Tourniquet	Strap placed around limb to restrict blood supply
Tumour	Abnormal growth of tissue in the body
Ulcer	An open sore on the skin or on an internal surface, such as the stomach lining
Ulna	Bone in the forearm
Universal precautions	Gloves, aprons and masks to protect the caregiver from bodily fluids. Includes the correct disposal of contaminated sharps and waste
Vertigo	Dizziness, especially with a sensation of rotation
Vial	Container for liquid drugs; either glass or plastic
Viscera	Internal organs, such as liver, intestines and kidneys
Wheeze	Whistling breath sound heard with stethoscope when patient takes a breath in or out

Index

Emergencies are indicated by **bold headings** and **page numbers**.
'FC' refers to flow chart.
'FF' refers to front flyleaf.
'BF' refers to back flyleaf.

Pain relief ladder

The severity of pain varies widely between individuals so you should assess the pain for each individual and treat it with the most appropriate pain relief. Stronger painkillers tend to have more severe side-effects so you must choose the most appropriate one to adequately control the pain while minimising any side-effects. Painkillers come in a variety of forms and strengths and work in different (often complementary) ways. Some can have adverse effects in certain situations or people, so check any contraindications before treating anyone with pain relief.

Combinations of differing types of pain relief are often effective in combating pain. For example, a person could take paracetamol and ibuprofen **or** diclofenac together, but not ibuprofen **and** diclofenac together.

The table shows the 'ladder' of pain relief according to the severity of pain. The same types of painkillers should not be taken together.

Note: NSAID stands for non-steroidal anti-inflammatory drug.

Name	Type	Severity of pain	Adult dose	Contraindications
Paracetamol	Paracetamol	Mild to moderate pain	1 g 6-hourly; oral	• Previous allergy • Not with codydramol
Aspirin	NSAID	Mild to moderate pain	Up to 900 mg 6-hourly; oral	• Previous allergy • Stomach ulcers • Asthma
Ibuprofen	NSAID	Mild to moderate pain	400 mg 4–6-hourly; oral	• Previous allergy • Stomach ulcers • Asthma
Naproxen	NSAID	Mild to moderate pain	250 mg 8–12 hourly	• Previous allergy • Stomach ulcers • Asthma
Codeine	Opioid	Mild to moderate pain	30–60 mg 4–6-hourly; oral	• Previous allergy • Respiratory depression • Head injury
Diclofenac	NSAID	Moderate pain	100 mg daily PR	• Previous allergy • Stomach ulcers • Asthma
Methoxyflurane (Penthrox®)	Halogenated ether	Moderate pain	Self-administered inhaler; 3-6 ml per day. Avoid using on consecutive days	• Renal or liver disease • Diabetes • Other nephrotoxic drugs
Tramadol	Opioid-like	Severe pain	50–100 mg 6-hourly; oral **or** 6-hourly IM inj If still in pain contact TMAS	• Previous allergy • Respiratory depression • Head injury
Morphine	Opioid	Severe pain	10 mg 2–4-hourly IM injection If still in pain contact TMAS	• Previous allergy • Respiratory depression • Head injury